I0138086

Le Football

Le Football

A History of American Football in France

RUSS CRAWFORD

University of Nebraska Press
Lincoln & London

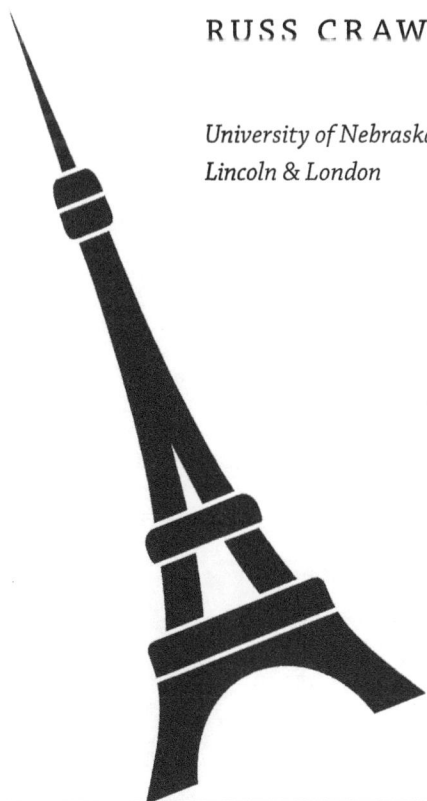

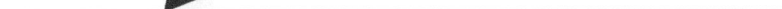

© 2016 by the Board of Regents of the University of Nebraska

All rights reserved
Manufactured in the United States of America

∞

Library of Congress Cataloging-in-Publication Data
Names: Crawford, Russ, author.
Title: Le football: a history of American football in France / Russ Crawford.
Description: Lincoln: University of Nebraska Press, [2016] | Includes bibliographical references and index.
Identifiers: LCCN 2015038288| ISBN 9780803278790 (cloth: alk. paper) | ISBN 9780803290280 (epub) | ISBN 9780803290297 (mobi) | ISBN 9780803290303 (pdf)
Subjects: LCSH: Football—France—History.
Classification: LCC GV959.54.F73 C73 2016 | DDC 796.3320944—dc23 LC record available at http://lccn.loc.gov/2015038288

Set in Chaparral Pro by M. Scheer.

CONTENTS

PREFACE

May 5, 2012. Somewhere in France . . .

My initial experience with American football in France would make a good movie. À la *Caddyshack* (1980) or *Meatballs* (1979), it featured classic confrontations: rich versus poor, old-stock French versus immigrants, and white versus black. Moreover, the underdogs rallied from early adversity to win the big game.

My friend Jean-Marc Burtscher and I arrived early at the field on an overcast, cool day. Only one of the home-team players was there opening the Spartan locker rooms for the game, which pitted Jean-Marc's team, the Red Star of Noisy-le-Sec, against the Kiowas of Garches.

Noisy-le-Sec is a *banlieue* (suburb) on the eastern side of Paris, and part of the Seine-Saint-Denis Département, which contains the highest proportion of immigrants of any department in France. It is also one of the poorest *départements* in the country.

Garches, the home of the Kiowas, is an affluent suburb on the western side of the city. The Hauts-de-Seine Département, where it is located, is one of the wealthiest areas, not only in France but in all of Europe.

The Kiowas were founded in 1989 by a group of friends including Mario Mancuso, Cristophe Mortier, and Philippe Roger. According to their web page, the friends had played on first division football clubs, and after leaving those, began throwing the ball around in nearby parks.[1] They then formed a team and found a sponsor in the mayor of Garches, who provided the field located nearby at Vaucresson. They chose the name Kiowas because Mancuso and Mortier were fond of

Native American tribes but didn't want one of the commonly known names such as Apache or Sioux. They finally settled on the Kiowas, a tribe that they described as one of the "most aggressive Plains Indians."[2]

The Red Star is a more recent team, founded in 2008 by a group of young men with a passion for the game. During their first year, the junior team (nineteen and under) won the Regional Championship, and a senior team was created. The seniors also experienced success and had played in the Regional Championship semifinals in 2009 and the finals in 2010.[3] Along the way they began to pick up coaching and playing talent from the Anges Bleus (Blue Angels), one of the storied teams in French football history, including Jean-Marc and his brother Eric.

According to Jean-Marc, who joined the team in 2011, the founders chose their name because it was recognizable in their area, one that many teams in various sports had used to signal their location within *le ceinture rouge* (the red belt—referencing their communist local governments) that runs through many of the Paris *banlieues*.[4]

The Kiowas arrived slowly. They were often dropped off by their mothers, who drove late-model Peugeots or Renaults. They were largely white and seemed young and small. They looked like American high school athletes more than semiprofessional football players.

After a bit the older, more diverse, and more physically substantial Red Star players began arriving. The first pair to arrive exited an older-model car to the accompaniment of blaring hip hop music, tossed down their last pregame cigarettes, and moved toward the locker rooms. They looked dangerous.

As the teams moved to the field, which was a rugby pitch ninety yards long with sparse grass, the equipment and uniforms tended to blur the differences in the players. They would soon, however, become apparent enough. The home team scored the first points of the game by returning the opening kickoff for a touchdown. Having played and coached football, I knew that a big play like that could very well set the tone for the game, and not knowing much about the Red Star team, I feared that it might collapse.

But experience matters. The coaches and players of the visitors had been around the block a few times and did not panic. They demonstrated that age and guile often trumps youth and enthusiasm, and the Red Star methodically began to impose its will on its younger opponents. The final score of 48 to 12 in favor of the Red Star did not accurately reflect how decisively the team from the poor part of the city dominated its more affluent opponents. The Kiowas, though they were defeated, went down as hard as they could manage.

The hitting demonstrated by both teams was an impressive introduction to football in France. The pads cracked from start to finish. Perhaps harboring prejudices that French football players would be similar to soccer players, who flop at the first sign of contact, I was pleasantly surprised by the enthusiastic violence displayed there. The players may have not been as large as some high school teams in the states, and they arrived to the action more slowly than I was used to seeing, but when they arrived, they did so with gusto.

The Kiowas, despite their apparent youth and frailty, gave as good as they got in on-field ferocity. What they lacked was the discipline and focus that the Red Star demonstrated that day.

The crash of the pads was not muted by any crowd noise, as only a handful of friends and family members stood in small groups along the sidelines—there were no grandstands. There was only sparse applause after the various scoring plays, and considerably more noise was coming from a nearby combination basketball/soccer court (with goal nets situated under the baskets). However, none of that mattered to the players on the field or on the sidelines. They were there for their teammates and for the love of the game.

Before and after the game, both teams displayed good sportsmanship, born perhaps out of a shared identity as outsiders in a French sporting culture that paid little attention to their courage and athleticism. This spirit of sportsmanship was another feature of the game that seemed, if not odd, at least unusual. As one who has been immersed in the win-at-all-costs football mentality of the United States for a lifetime, the environment of camaraderie and fair play was curious.

At one point, as the Red Star was driving deep into enemy territory, a receiver dived for the end zone and came up inches short. Standing close to the play, I immediately threw my arms up to signal a touchdown, attempting to induce the officials, who were not very impressive, to give my new team the touchdown. To my surprise, one of the Red Star players standing near me shook his finger back and forth and told me that his teammate was just short.

This shocked me. American football players are trained from an early age to take any advantage possible. Once during a high school game, an official asked me if I had recovered a fumble, and although I was nowhere near the ball, I replied, without hesitation, that I had. We were awarded the recovery and went on to win the game. This was not golf, where every gentleman calls his own penalties, but the grim struggle for victory that is football.

This level of fair play was what I would have expected of an English public school athlete in the nineteenth century, or at least from a kinder, gentler time in American football history. Perhaps the best example of that spirit in the United States occurred in 1940, when Cornell was inadvertently given a fifth down against Dartmouth. Upon learning of the error from the game film, Cornell voluntarily forfeited the score, which cost it the game, and possibly the national championship.[5]

The sportsmanship display continued following the end of the game, when both teams gathered at midfield to congratulate each other and shake hands. They also gave a cheer, which was not really deserved, to the officiating crew. Outside the locker rooms the players mixed freely, and goodwill was the order of the day. This is likely not the case for soccer matches in France, where a postgame hooligan-led riot is not rare.[6]

The contrast between football and soccer is one that French football aficionados enjoy drawing. Good sportsmanship rules on the gridiron, unlike the anarchy that often reigns in soccer. Football fans stand and sing along with "La Marseillaise"; soccer fans hoot and jeer during the national anthem. A football game is a safe place to take a family. Attend a soccer game, and you may end up doused with tear gas.

The distinction between the sports, however, demonstrates the difficulty that football faces in France. The French have built a significant football subculture, with 21,650 licensed players on 204 teams playing full contact. However, the games are not commonly popular enough to draw sufficient fans to hold a respectable riot.[7]

So how had I wound up being one of the few fans at Garches that day? My interest in the history of French football began in 2004, when I traveled to the country for the first time to visit Sophie, the woman who would later become my wife. One evening, she took me to meet her high school friend Agnes Burtscher and her husband, Jean-Marc. While we were talking, he left the room and came back wearing a football helmet. I was stunned. I had never thought that, outside of NFL Europe, the American game was played on the continent.

Jean-Marc not only had his helmet but also many photographs, some of which will appear in the pages to follow. He told me about his days as a member of Les Anges Bleus and also began to relate some of the creation story of football there, which turned out to be a fascinating story.

I learned that football was brought to France in 1980 by Laurent Plegelatte, an avowed Trotskyite. As a historian of Cold War sports, I experienced considerable cognitive dissonance digesting this information. My dissertation explored the role that sports such as football played in strengthening the "American Way of Life" during that struggle, so the idea that a communist convinced the French to take up the game seemed wild.[8]

We spent most of the time debating the Iraq war, and I didn't give much more thought to football there. I mentioned it from time to time, mainly to use the story to amaze my friends back home.

After we were married, Sophie and I continued to visit Agnes and Jean-Marc in France, and they came to our home in Ohio during their summer vacations. During their second trip we even attended an Arena League Cleveland Gladiators game, courtesy of tickets provided by Ron Selesky, their director of player personnel. Selesky, an old comrade of Jean-Marc's, had once played with him on the Anges Bleus.

We persisted in talking about football in France and continued to agree that this would make a good book. Finally, after the Gladiators game, the idea penetrated beyond the surface of our brains, and we began making plans to make it a reality. The result of this planning was my presence at the Red Star versus Kiowas game, and eventually, this book.

ACKNOWLEDGMENTS

First mention belongs to my wife, Sophie. Without her I would likely never have visited France. I also owe a huge *merci beaucoup* to Jean-Marc Burtscher. He introduced me to football in France and was an indispensable help in finding interview subjects, photos, and in general introducing me to the world of football *américain*. Without him this book would never have been written.

There are many others in France, including Eric Burtscher, who spent hours telling me stories about the early days of football there. A tremendous source of information came from the *Elitefoot* blog created by Olivier Rival, and the chapters on football after 1980 owe much to the information I found there. Julien Luneau of the Flash de La Courneuve welcomed me to practice, translated for me on RADIOSSA, and helped me with information about the early days of his team and the sport. Stephane Sardano and Yves Perelli assisted me with the history of the Anges Bleus. Mumu, Eclipso, Goldo, and the others at Radio Old School Spirit Association (RADIOSSA) also helped me tremendously. Thierry Soler and Olivier Moret at the Fédération Française de Football Américain offices took the time to give me the early history of the sport. The Red Star of Noisy-le-Sec welcomed me as a part of the team and offered stories about how they became interested in football. Thank you in particular to Axel Duez, Brice Beaudi, Dylen Cerna, Margaux Dewitte, François-Xavier Duqué, Yacine El Pendejo, Tym Ghex, Guillaume Griva, Jennifer Josset, Gary Mako, Evans So', and Julien Ozboyaci. Richard Tardits graciously took the time to remember his career at Georgia and in the National Football League (NFL).

The staff at the Bibliothèque nationale de France was very helpful and didn't laugh at my Nebraskan accent. Matthieu Chan Tsin, now living in the United States, enlightened me about the various reasons for playing the game in France. Finally, Chris and Vivette Mercadier, my French mother and father, housed and fed me on research trips and provided encouragement.

On the other side of the pond, I had the pleasure of interviewing a number of former players and coaches from United States Air Force Europe (USAFE) teams. First and foremost among them was Dave Madril. He told me of his days playing and about his participation in the 1961 tour. He also put me in touch with several other subjects, including Bernard A. "Barney Gill, an ex–lieutenant colonel in the United States Army and coach of the Supreme Headquarters Allied Powers Europe (SHAPE) Indians. Gill was without a doubt my favorite interview subject. To call him colorful does not do him justice. He led me to Russ Mericle, who played for Gill at West Point and in Paris. From the Laon Rangers I had the pleasure of talking with Jerry Curtright, the coach of the team, and with Chuck Bristol, who played for the Rangers and who provided me with some of his memorabilia. Ken Thrash also coached the Rangers and shared his memories of the early days at Laon with me. Dick Mullins, who ran an athletic program in Germany, helped me with the finances of the NATO-era athletic programs. Jose Nogueras, of Ohio Northern University, gave me the model for sports information divisions that I applied to the Argonautes. Ron Selesky, an American who played for the Anges Bleus, and Braxton Shaver, who played for the Flash de La Courneuve, told me about their lives as mercenary football players in France. Jim Foster and Stan Allspach regaled me with stories of their 1977 tour with the Newton Nite Hawks.

I also benefited from financial support that allowed me to visit France several times. Without the support of David Crago, provost of Ohio Northern University; Catherine Albrecht, dean of the College of Arts and Sciences, and Rob Alexander, the chair of the Department of History, Politics, and Justice, this project would have been much more difficult and costly. I also want to thank everyone at the University of Nebraska Press who helped make this book a reality; it was a pleasure to work with everyone there. Finally, special thanks go to the students in my Sport and Society class, who read over my manuscript and told me to shorten my sentences.

If I have forgotten anyone, I apologize. For those who helped in this process, I enjoyed every minute of our conversations, and thank you again.

INTRODUCTION

Playing pour l'amour du jeu

Despite Jean-Marc's assertions, the history of football in France did not begin in 1980. Following an exhibition of the sport at the 1900 L'Exposition Universelle in Paris, Americans played the first game there during the Great White Fleet's visit to southern France in 1909. The sport returned in 1918, when, along with rifles and bayonets, the American Expeditionary Force (AEF), aided by the Young Men's Christian Association (YMCA) and other organizations, also shipped footballs, helmets, and shoulder pads "over there" during World War I (1914–18). The games would continue through 1919 during the Inter-Allied Games, which were staged to celebrate the Allied victory.

Prior to Laurent Plegelatte's successful transplant of the game, the American military would be the force carrying the ball most frequently in France. Motivated by the same concerns that drove the athletic program in the First World War, American forces, beginning with their initial North African counterattack in late 1942, once again brought football back to French territory during the Second World War. They sponsored several "bowl games" there throughout the war, beginning with the Arab Bowl in Oran, Algeria, in 1943. Six of these spectacles were played on French territory during the war, although in the case of the Champagne Bowl, scheduled for Christmas Day 1944 in Riems, the Nazi's last-gasp Ardennes Offensive thoughtlessly caused a cancellation. After combat moved east toward Germany, support troops stationed in the rear areas of France created leagues in the various base sections of the country, playing full schedules and contending for regional championships.

After the war the gridirons went unused for a time. But from 1952 to 1966, when American bases were constructed in France during the Cold War, American soldiers, sailors, and airmen played more than a thousand games there. When French president Charles de Gaulle withdrew France from the North Atlantic Treaty Organization (NATO) and forced the closing of the American bases there, the military games finally stopped.

Even between wars and periods of international tension, there were sporadic attempts by Americans to generate interest in the game among the French population. College All-Stars, service teams, NFL players, college teams, and semiprofessionals all tried their hand at convincing the French that the American game was the wave of the future. Although not short on ambition, tours in 1938, 1961, 1972, 1976, 1977, and 1989 left little impression on the French.

These attempts to lure the French onto the gridiron, though they were unsuccessful, suggested that American cultural imperialism was at work here.[1] However, this seems to be a faulty theoretical construct to apply in the case of football in France, since the game only took off there when a Frenchman brought it home with him from a trip to Colorado. There was a moment that might fit the mold, when, in the late eighties, French television viewers were treated to NFL games on Canal +. But that came from a company owned by the French, hardly agents of American cultural imperialism.[2]

A more persuasive argument is that in the global marketplace of culture, only those products that find willing audiences in the target market are consumed. Football, despite numerous attempts to entice French consumers, never caught on until a Frenchman decided he had a purpose for which the sport would be useful.

Very little has been written about the history of football in France. A few articles have discussed pieces of the story, including "Football Tour de France," by Christian Joosten and Denis Crawford (no relation), published in the *Coffin Corner*, the journal of the Pro Football Researchers Association in 2011, which discusses the 1938 Crowley tour. "Demi Tough," a 1976 article in *Texas Monthly* by George Packard, reported on the 1976 exhibition in Paris between Texas A&I and Henderson State (HSU), two small college teams. There is also a chapter in George Golman Baker Jr.'s 2011 book, *When Lightning Struck the Outhouse: A Tribute to a Great Coach Ralph "Sporty" Carpenter,* that discusses the same tour. *Elitefoot,* a blog on American football in France, has a post that contains an interview with Dave Madril, an American who played during the Cold War era, and the blog is also a treasure trove of information on post-1980 French football.

There are a few monographs that briefly touch on the topic during the world wars. Among those are *Playing to Win: Sports and the American Military, 1898–1945,* by Wanda Ellen Wakefield, which discusses how sports such as football became staples for keeping soldiers in shape and were seen as inculcating values and skills that would create better soldiers. Her work, however, focuses more on the military's use of sport and only touches lightly on the games played in France as a part of that effort. *Football, Navy, War! How Military "Lend Lease" Players Saved the College Game and Helped Win World War II,* by Wilbur D. Jones, includes some information but little more than the names of various "bowl" games that the military played in France during the war, as its focus is on the game as it persisted on the home front. S. W. Pope also discusses football, along with other sports, played by the military in World War I in his book *Patriotic Games: Sporting Traditions in the American Imagination, 1876–1926.* There again, France, rather than being the book's focus, plays the role of the background for American efforts.

After completion of this manuscript, Eclispso, a French friend, informed me that a new book had appeared that covered some of the same information presented here. Massimo Foglio and Mark L. Ford have self-published *Touchdown in Europe: How American Football Came to the Old Continent* (2015). Although they focus on Europe in general, and on the game in England and Italy more specifically, they also include information about several of the events discussed here.

Other works, including *The Athletic Crusade: Sport and American Cultural Imperialism,* by Gerald Gems, and *Games and Empires: Modern Sports and Cultural Imperialism,* by Allen Guttmann, briefly mention the global spread of football as cultural imperialism. Few of these works, however, discuss French football in any substantive way.

There are works reportedly now in progress that also cover some of the information I discuss in *Le Football*. One is a book that Brian Powers is writing about the Newton Nite Hawks tour of Europe in 1977. Powers is a freelance writer whose father played on the Nite Hawks' team, which led to his interest in the event. Another is Michael Rindfleisch's book on USAFE football, which is reportedly in the final stages of preparation for publication.

The French have written even less than Americans about the sport in France. One of the most pertinent books that I have been able to find in French is *Le football américain* by Plegelatte, the father of French football himself. His work has only a short introduction to the history and evolution of the sport and is mostly a how-to book for new players. The same holds for *Le football américain: Les règles, la technique, la tactique*, a book for young players written by Olivier Moret, one of the FFFA officials I interviewed, and Nicolas Guillion.

Internet publishing and online documentaries have expanded the material available to explore the world of French football. In 2013 Quentin Dagbert created a web documentary titled *Le football americain a l'heure française*. Produced as part of his program of studies for a professional license in journalism and digital media at the University of Lorraine in Metz, the film is made up of four segments that explore the inception of football in France, a typical game day, the spread of football among women, and wheelchair football. The videos are embedded in a website that maps the spread of the sport in France, talks about the rules, and features interviews with Frenchmen who have played in the NFL.[3]

This then is the first attempt to construct a general history of gridiron football in France, from 1909 to 2013. The first chapter considers the initial games in France before, during, and in the wake of World War I. Chapter 2 tells the story of the Riess-Crowley Tour, the first real attempt to interest the French in football. The games played on French soil during and after World War II, including bowl extravaganzas and regional leagues, is the subject of chapter 3. Chapter 4 considers the establishment of teams and leagues in France during the first decade (1952–59) that France was a member of NATO during the Cold War. Chapter 5 continues the story of Cold War football to its end in 1966, when the French told the American military *au revoir*. Chapter

6 considers the various tours that sought to entice the French to play football from 1961 to 1976. Continued attempts to bring the French into the huddle from 1977 to 1989 are the focus of chapter 7. In chapter 8 football has finally arrived in France for keeps, imported by Plegelatte. The spread of football from the capital to the provinces is the subject of chapter 9. Chapter 10, the final chapter, considers the spread of women's football and the increasing presence of French football players in the United States. A brief afterword examines the state of the FFFA and football in France today, with a discussion of the 2013 Casque de Diamant and Junior Championship games, along with the French National Team's appearance in the World Football Championships held in Canton, Ohio, during the summer of 2015. It will also bring to a close the story of the Red Star in 2012.

In researching this work I have used several sources and methods, including some nontraditional means to learn as much as I can about the history of football in France. Among those sources has been archival research in *Stars and Stripes*, which has most of its issues since 1942 posted online, and other newspaper sources, both French and American. I have had access to a large collection of French football magazines thanks to Jean-Marc and his brother, Eric, and have conducted numerous interviews with current and former players and coaches. In addition to these more traditional sources, I have gleaned information from the FFFA web archives; the *Elitefoot* blog; *Amerfoot*, an online magazine; and other websites. I have also used Facebook to contact various interview subjects who provided information that will be included here. The use of social networks to do academic research is a new experience for me, but one that has proved useful.

Sport in France

"It was hard to discern more than a confused mass of players who seemed to want nothing more than to destroy each other; those at the edge of the scrum tearing at those in the centre; a huge shifting mass, a heap of bodies moving first to the right and then to the left."[4] Combative sports were not alien to France, as demonstrated by this passage written by an observer of the game of *la soule* in 1855. The rough-and-tumble sport that originated in Brittany in the twelfth century took the form of ad hoc contests between villages, primarily on religious holidays. The sport continued to be popular and was played despite sporadic royal efforts to suppress the violent and disorderly game.[5] A combination of secular and clerical forces was finally successful in stamping out the game by the mid-nineteenth century, as sentiment against violent sports grew. But the French loss in the Franco-Prussian War (1870–71) renewed French interest in team and combative sports.[6]

There is also a long history of the French importing games from abroad. With a physical culture modeled on the Germans and an educational system based on the English public schools, which had long valued games as a means to build more than strong bodies, the French began to import English sporting forms after their demoralizing loss to Prussia.[7] Rugby was imported to the Continent by English businessmen through the port of Le Havre not long after the sport originated in Britain. The Havre Athletic Club (HAC), formed in 1872, initially played a combination of what would later become the separate sports of rugby and soccer.[8]

The HAC was soon joined by the Union des Sociétés Françaises des Sports Athlétics (USFSA), created by the merger of two existing societies for the promotion of sport in 1887. The USFSA favored rugby over soccer because of the latter sport's association with the lower classes in England. It held its first rugby national championship in 1892, contested between the Racing Club de France and the Stade Français, two early clubs set up to play English sports. Pierre de Coubertin himself refereed the final match in front of an estimated 2,000 spectators.[9] Two years later the USFSA was forced to give up its resistance to soccer and held the first championship for that sport. By 1906 a poll of French boys found that 1,500 of 3,000 recipients favored soccer, while only 400 picked rugby.[10]

Following hard on the heels of rugby and soccer, basketball traveled across the Atlantic shortly after James Naismith created the game for the YMCA in 1891. Basketball missionaries began to spread across the globe, reaching France in 1895, when Emil Thiess first demonstrated the game to a group of Parisians. This initial demonstration did not create much enthusiasm, but when Naismith journeyed to France as an advisor to the AEF, he was convinced that the French would learn to love the game. After a game between American servicemen, a group of French spectators tried shooting the ball. Naismith recorded, "They were at first quite awkward in their attempts, but the rapidity with which they learned to pass and shoot was astonishing."[11] The French military created a team to play in the Inter-Allied Games of 1919, but lost both of their games against the Americans and the Italians.[12] By the 1930s, however, France and other European nations had begun to form national leagues as well as playing each other for international championships.

Baseball, the American national pastime, also made early efforts to gain a foothold in France. As *la soule* provided a precedent for later contact sports, the French also had a traditional bat-and-ball game called *thèque*. As the French newspaper *Le Temps* explained to the Americans who were in Paris to play a baseball game as part of Albert Spalding's heralded world tour of 1898–99, the game involved a player with a wooden bat hitting the "ball as far as one can with a swing of the bat, and while the ball is traveling . . . mak[ing] a tour of the 'bases' or angles of the figure . . . traced on the ground marked with posts."[13]

Spalding, a former player and team owner, as well as the owner of Spalding Sporting Goods, had conceived of the world tour as a way of spreading the national pastime around the world, while also increasing demand for his line of baseball equipment. The tour made stops in Australia, Egypt, and Italy, among other countries, before arriving in France.[14] The Chicago White Sox, owned by Spalding, and a chosen "All-America" team made up of star players from other teams in the National League, played their first and only game at the Aerostaique Park on March 8, 1899.[15]

Spalding had worked to get the press on his side, and that effort paid off in largely positive stories, but even the most admiring reporters confessed they had no idea what was happening on the field.[16] *Le Temps* comparison of baseball to the children's game of *thèque* likely did not aid baseball's attempt to create widespread support in the country.

However, the sport began to be played by teams such as the Athletic Club of Paris, which was created by American expats in 1908.[17] As would be the case with football a half century later, some Frenchmen also made it their mission to popularize the sport in their country. Emile Dubonnet, a famous ballooner, vowed that he would "introduce baseball to France," declaring that the sport would be bigger in France than in the United States. The number of teams increased during the next years, and the French Baseball Union promoted the sport.

Charles Comiskey, the new owner of the White Sox, also sponsored tours of France in 1913 and 1924.[18] The French formed leagues and continued to have small pockets of great enthusiasm for the game, but it never became widely popular. The native enthusiasts were augmented by *pieds noires*, the name for ethnic French living in Algeria, who were exposed to the game by GIs during World War II. When they were forced to flee from Algeria in the 1960s, many continued to practice the game.[19] The game is still played in France, but it has yet to progress much beyond being a novelty game there.

Despite France's tradition of violent games, and its willingness to import others' sporting forms, football would face an uphill battle when football missionaries made efforts to transplant the game to France. These difficulties were due to a combination of factors. Among them was the lack, until the 1930s, of a Spalding-like character, with his messianic belief that his game should globalize. The late arrival of the sport would also cause unfavorable comparisons between the static stop-and-start play of football with the fluid nature of rugby and soccer, which had already captured the public imagination.

Even when the stars did align and American missionaries combined with indigenous enthusiasts to attempt to entice the French to play, bad timing would prevent the development of any momentum for adopting the sport. And finally, in later decades, as football equipment became more specialized and expensive, the cost of the game would also be a hindrance, as would be the violence that necessitated the elaborate equipment.

Many of the same issues encountered by previous sporting imports such as soccer or baseball would be recapitulated with football in its attempts to establish a foothold across the Atlantic. There would be many games played by U.S. military personnel in France. There would also be attempts by both Americans and the French to popularize the sport. There would even be French converts to the sport who would begin to create pockets of interest in the game. Despite all of that, the sport would struggle unsuccessfully to gain traction in France, and even after it was finally transplanted there, it has continued to exist in the shadow of rugby and soccer in the minds of the most French people.

As mentioned earlier, if trying to introduce football to France was cultural imperialism, it was remarkably ineffective. That theory views the consumers of culture as passive receptors with no agency in deciding which foreign product will succeed in their country. Just wave a Coke bottle or a Big Mac in their direction, and the battle is over. The case of football in France provides an example that argues against this interpretation. Only when Laurent Plegelatte decided that football could be useful in furthering his personal and political goals did the sport finally arrive for keeps in France.

The successful importation of the game in the 1980s was a fascinating event, but it is not the whole story. A world cruise to show the flag, two world wars, a Cold War, and various missions to the wilderness would precede that great day when Plegelatte returned to France with the treasures he had found in Ali Baba's cavern.

ABBREVIATIONS

AAA	Anti-Aircraft Artillery
AADA	Advance Air Depot Area
AEF	American Expeditionary Force
AFB	air force base
AFN	Armed Forces Network
AFS	American Field Service
AP	Associated Press
ASA	Association sportive des arbitres
AUC	Aix University Club
BADA	Base Air Depot Area
Basec	Base Section
Com Z	Communication Zone
CRS	Compagnies républican des sécuritié
DBS	Delta Base Section
DOD	Department of Defense
EATS-ATC	European Air Transport Service-Air Transport Command
EC	European Command
EFAF	European Federation of American Football
EFI	European Football Investors
EFL	European Football League
ET	European theater
ETO	European Theater of Operations
ESTP	École spéciale des travaux publics, bâtiment et de l'industrie

FFFA	Fédération Française de Football Américain
HAC	Havre Athletic Club ETSP
HACom	Headquarters Area Command
HQ	headquarters
HQC	Headquarters Command
IFL	Intercontinental Football League
INSEP	Institut nationale du sport et de l'éducation physique
ISC	International Sports Connection
LFL	Legends Football League
MATS	Military Air Transport Command
MJC	Maison jeune et de la culture
MLB	Major League Baseball
MNEF	Mutuelle nationale des étudiants de France
MP	military police
MT	Mediterranean theater
MVP	most valuable player
NACom	Northern Area Command
NAIA	National Association of Intercollegiate Athletics
NATO	North Atlantic Treaty Organization
NCO	noncommissioned officer
NFL	National Football League
NFLE	National Football League Europe
NFLPA	National Football League Players Association
NSFL	Northern States Football League
OISFL	Oise Intermediate Section Football League
PA	public address
PDB	Paris Detention Barracks
PLU	Pacific Lutheran University
PTO	Pacific Theater of Operations
QM	quartermaster
SAFF	Swedish American Football Federation
SDSU	San Diego State University
SHAEF	Supreme Headquarters Allied Expeditionary Force
SHAPE	Supreme Headquarters Allied Powers Europe
SID	sports information director
SOS	Service of Supply

SSFL	Seine Section Football League
TACRECON	Tactical Reconnaissance
TDY	temporary duty
TSFET	Theater Service Forces—European Theater
TSFFL	Theater Service Forces Football League
USFSA	Union des Sociétés Françaises des Sports Athlétics
USAREUR	United States Army Europe
USAFE	United States Air Force Europe
VIP	very important person
WAC	Women's Army Corps
WBS	Western Base Section
YMCA	Young Men's Christian Association
ZI	Zone of the Interior (the United States, for those serving abroad during the immediate postwar period)

1. Football over There during the Great War

Given the combative nature of football, it is appropriate that much of the history of football in France revolves around conflict, in one form or another. The first widespread games there resulted from American presence in World War I (1914–18), the first great and terrible war of the twentieth century. When American doughboys went to France in 1917, football traveled along with them. The sport and its equipment were carried by earnest volunteers from a number of athletic and fraternal associations who answered the military's call to help maintain or improve morale, build unit cohesion, keep soldiers in fighting shape, and prevent those soldiers from partaking in various sorts of mischief.

The U.S. military had begun employing sports for those purposes in the Spanish-American War of 1898 and the Philippine insurrection (1899–1902) that followed. During the period following this first large-scale American military adventure abroad, and as new war concerns arose, the army formalized its somewhat haphazard sporting program by publishing the *Manual of Physical Training for Use in the United States Army* (1914).[1] The manual stated that the military encouraged sport to build "general health and bodily, vigor, muscular strength and endurance, self reliance and smartness, activity, and precision."[2] Maj. Gen. Leonard Wood, the chief of staff in the War Department, stated in the foreword that the purpose of the manual was to make "it possible to place this part of the soldiers' training upon a permanent and uniform basis."[3] In addition to the goals outlined in the manual, there were several other unstated reasons for

FIG. 1. Photo from the French magazine *La Vie au Grand Air* depicting the team captains and scenes from the 1909 match between the USS *Kansas* and the USS *Minnesota* at Nice. The teams from the ships of the Great White Fleet played the first football game in France. Photo located in the offices of the Fédération Française de Football Américain. Reproduction made by Russ Crawford with the permission of Thierry Soler, director of Technique Nationale.

the military enthusiasm for sports. Among these were building esprit des corps, creating an aggressive and independent spirit amongst soldiers and sailors, placing military affairs in a readily understandable common language, maintaining morale for homesick soldiers, and perhaps most importantly, keeping them away from the temptations that would lead to such calamities as moral ruin and, even worse, sexually transmitted disease.[4] Therefore, in 1917, when the AEF prepared its expedition to France, it would be bringing with it not only weapons and uniforms but also footballs, shoulder pads, helmets, and other sporting equipment. Its efforts would also be backed by an expansive philosophy of what sports could mean for the force's performance in battle.

Football was not completely foreign to France when the first soldiers arrived in 1917. The first game in France was a contest between teams drawn from the crews of two warships that were part of U.S. president Theodore Roosevelt's Great White Fleet. During the demonstration of American naval power from 1907 to 1909, the USS

Minnesota and the USS *Kansas* stopped at Villefranche-sur-Mer in 1909. While there, football teams drawn from the two ships played a demonstration game for dignitaries and the public who came out to look over American sea power. There had also been an exhibition of football during the Exposition Universelle in 1900, but the *Kansas* versus *Minnesota* match was the first actual game. *Kansas* defeated *Minnesota* 6–2, and according to John Fass Morton in *Mustin: A Naval Family of the Twentieth Century*, "The athletic contest so fascinated the French that the city of Nice presented his ship with a prize of $6,000."[5] Perhaps learning some of the aggressiveness that he would display later, among the players that demonstrated the American sport for the French was future fleet admiral William F. "Bull" Halsey.[6]

The game received some media attention that informed the larger population that football had reached France. A two-page collage of images from the game, along with photos of the two team captains and a punter in mid-kick were published in the sporting newspaper *La Vie au Grand Air* (Outdoor life). The photos of the captains served to demonstrate to readers the other-worldly equipment of the players, with leather helmets featuring nose and mouth guards attached to the front. The *Kansas* captain's uniform also featured external leather patches that served as shoulder pads. In the action sequences very few of the players sported such high-tech equipment, but the player pileups nonetheless appeared vigorous.[7]

There is also anecdotal evidence that France had already had the first of several influences on the American game. Sources disagree on the year that it occurred, but Lorin Deland, W. H. Lewis, or both, invented the formation known as the "flying wedge," reportedly by adapting the strategies of Napoleon Bonaparte to the gridiron.

Sports Academic, a website "for people who love sports and for people who love to hate them," maintains that Deland, who became the head coach of the Harvard football team in 1895, originated the formation after reading *Historie du consulat et de l'empire* (1845), by Adolphe Thiers. Though he was not yet an official coach, the advertising executive convinced the team to use his new idea in 1894. The idea inspired by the French emperor was to mass forces at the point of attack to break through the enemy line, and the flying wedge was the shape that this took on the gridiron.[8]

A reported witness with Deland that day was Pierre de Coubertin, who would go on to found the modern Olympic movement. Coubertin wrote in "Napoleon et le football," published in *Les Sports athletiques* in 1898, "Napoleon looked down on this event from heaven where he has been for only a short while, amnestied by the Lord. It warmed his warrior spirit and he prayed that Saint Peter would, when the day came, allow Mr. Deland, his prophet, to enter heaven straight away."[9]

An October 25, 1926, article in the *Harvard Crimson* credited Lewis with devising the formation when the then-coach of the team remembered a history lesson about Napoleon's tactics at the 1805 Battle of Austerlitz. Lewis substituted the "ends and tackles of a football team on the defensive for Napoleon's cavalry . . . and the centre could be reinforced by the backs, just as the French centre was strengthened by reserves." According to the article, this tactic was first used in a victory over the University of Pennsylvania in 1894.[10]

All sources seem to agree that Napoleon's tactics were the source of the formation, and Sports Academic goes so far as to give the emperor credit for transforming the American game, which had began as an evolution of rugby, into the game of "blocking and brutality" that it was when it was finally transported to France.[11]

Regardless of the claims for Deland, Lewis, or even Bonaparte, historians overwhelmingly credit Yale's Walter Camp with transforming football into a new American sport. Still, this is the first of several instances when France would have an important influence on the American game. However, advocates of the sport would still face enormous obstacles when they attempted to transfer the game to the country that had helped transform it in so many ways.

Coubertin, who also attended the Thanksgiving Harvard-Dartmouth game in 1889, would foreshadow some of those obstacles when he wrote, "Foot-ball transformed by the Americans has become a little more scientific maybe, but also more brutal and more dangerous."[12] The danger and brutality of the game would be what critics would focus on when discussing the game or dissecting the merits of competing sports.[13] However academic that debate is, the game that Napoleon may have influenced, and that was first played in France in 1909, was set to return to the country in a big way.

On April 6, 1917, when Congress declared war in response to President Woodrow Wilson's call, baseball was by far the United States' favorite sport, both in the nation and among the military. Football had spread to the West Coast but was still primarily the province of elite eastern and a few midwestern universities. As the country hurriedly geared up for combat in Europe, however, the sport would join the mix of pastimes encouraged by the AEF.

In an interview with the *New York Times* in August 1917, with the subheadline "Trained as for Football," Gen. John J. Pershing went so far as to maintain that soldiers should be prepared like a football team, "in which each man is trained to physical perfection under strict discipline, but is capable of brilliant individual action in a crisis."[14]

Football players took the general at his word and signed up for the military in large numbers. The entire 1916 Harvard football team joined some branch of the military, and the June 12, 1917, *New York Tribune* also reported that the same was true of "nearly all the big Eastern colleges."[15] By January of the next year, the *New York Times* reported that eighty-five athletes from Fordham University had enlisted and went on to tell readers, "As has been almost the universal case in American colleges the football players have made the best record."[16] Another *Times* article gave as an explanation for the high percentage of athletes signing up for military service an excerpt from the Harvard Alumni Association bulletin that stated, "The spirit that makes a man an athlete makes him at the very first call of his country a soldier." By the time the bulletin was published, "all but two of the seventy-nine men in the University football squad were in some form of national service or in training for it."[17]

Early in 1918, as Operation Michael, the all-out German spring offensive was beginning, former Yale University football player S. B. Thorne, of the College Committee on Recruiting Athletic Directors, was putting out the call for former athletes from his and twenty-eight other universities to volunteer for service as athletic directors. Volunteers would then work with the YMCA in setting up physical culture programs with the Allied Armies.[18] Football teams around the nation began to lose their coaches as they answered the call for physical instructors and among their number was Walter Camp, the "father of football" himself, whom the U.S. Navy placed in charge of all athletics at all their stations.[19]

Even before troops embarked for France, the War Department under Secretary of War Newton Baker impaneled the War Department Commission on Training Camp Activities in April 1917. The commission, commonly referred to as the Fosdick Commission after its chairman, Raymond Fosdick, sought to provide American soldiers with sporting activities to replicate those that the recent civilians had known at home.[20] The commission called on voluntary organizations such as the YMCA and the Knights of Columbus to carry out the actual work of setting up recreation programs and centers in the United States and France. Aside from easing the transition between civilian and military life, the games were to serve a multifold purpose for soldiers.

Athletics were to keep soldiers busy, provide them with a reminder of their former lives, prevent vice and corruption, and gird them physically for the rigors of war. According to the YMCA, athletic programs had at least five distinct major results that might "be set down as demonstrated beyond question," including "increasing the agility of the men to enable them to leap trenches, among other skills. Athletics also stimulated the fighting spirit, promoted teamwork, furnished recreation, and promoted morality."[21]

The purported benefits of athletics, widely publicized by the Fosdick Commission and other proponents of sport, are still those that are held up as examples of the positive outcomes generated by sports. These assertions were backed by academic sources that had been busy creating rationales for including sport within the American university.[22] These arguments, created by members of the academy and broadcast further by the exigencies of war, remain the controlling narrative when discussing the utility of sport in the United States.

As the doughboys began arriving in France in large numbers, they started their training in the peculiarities of trench warfare. They nevertheless continued to need outlets for the excess energies that might lead soldiers to the dangers of easily available alcohol and equally available women, another implicit goal of the Fosdick Commission.[23]

During a war in which the government struggled with monumental logistical problems that saw the AEF able to supply itself with uniforms and small arms but little else, these organizations somehow managed to deliver tons of athletic gear to the camps and rest areas set up across the French countryside.

In addition to calls for personnel to serve as athletic directors, American universities were also asked to supply sporting apparel and equipment in support of that effort. On February 16, 1918, before the AEF had seen its first major action, the *Chicago Eagle* and other newspapers contained a story about a donation of one thousand footballs by Harvard graduates to be sent to the troops serving in France. Due to the lack of the uniforms and pads necessary for the collegiate game, only one-fifth of the balls were for the U.S. version of the game with the remainder being for soccer, but that lack would be the cause for additional donation drives.[24]

By October, just after the AEF had commenced its first major offensive around Saint-Mihiel, newspapers were running an appeal from "Big Bill" Edwards, a former Princeton University football player and later referee who had received word from France that five hundred football suits were needed.[25] A few weeks later J. L. Anguish, the director of athletics for the Paris division of the YMCA, asked for only one pair of football pants that could be used as a pattern to allow French garment makers to begin sewing the first of what he hoped would be an ultimate twelve thousand pairs. The article went on to state, "Inasmuch as the great football stars of the past decade from the East, West, North, and South are with the American expeditionary force abroad, there should be some real all-American games staged behind the lines soon."[26]

From American entry into the war until the armistice, in addition to shipping tons of athletic equipment or having it made in France, the YMCA operated twenty-six rest and recreation centers in France, along with four thousand huts that offered athletic, recreational, and spiritual services to soldiers. While the YMCA handled around 90 percent of the welfare work for the AEF, other organizations such as the Knights of Columbus and the Jewish Welfare Board also added their efforts to serving soldiers in France.[27] The Knights of Columbus donated nearly $250,000 worth of sporting equipment to men on the front lines, including an additional five hundred footballs, which arrived in time for the traditional Thanksgiving game in 1918.[28]

During the war the War Department, aided by the various private organizations, provided soldiers with some 1,200 football suits. Interestingly, the forces received just 1,200 football shoes, footwear for only half of the soldiers who had uniforms.[29] Perhaps that was just another of the logistical problems that the AEF struggled with. Given the low priority that sporting equipment had, this was understandable. Perhaps the ship carrying those additional shoes was sunk by a U-boat. This was the case for the SS *Oransa*, which was sunk in 1918 while carrying $30,000 in baseball equipment.[30]

With the buildup of doughboys, which would reach nearly 1.5 million men by the end of 1918, and the construction of facilities to keep them occupied while not training or fighting, the games could and did begin. Soldiers had already begun playing football at training camps located in the United States, and they found more opportunities to play after their arrival behind the front lines.

Photographic evidence of this was provided by the *Tucumcari (NM) News* in its May 16, 1918, edition, just weeks before the first major offensive action at Cantigny. The image displays a gridiron team ready to snap the ball, while a mixed military and French audience watch. The story that accompanied the photo told readers, "Our troops have made baseball well known to the people of France by their constant playing of the game. Now they are doing the same service for the American style of football." The title of the article, "Football in France Keeps Liberty Lads Fit to Buck the German Line," dovetailed nicely with the narrative about the utility of sports promoted by the Fosdick Commission, the YMCA, and others.[31]

The games continued as the AEF became fully engaged in the fighting, coming to its allies' aid in blunting the German spring offensive at places such as Château-Thierry and Belleau Wood and then going on the offensive itself as an independent American army. The matches played were more than just exercise for the troops and to fulfill the high expectations of groups such as the YMCA; they were also staged as entertainment for the nonplaying soldiers. *Trench and*

Camp, a newspaper published by the YMCA War Work Council during the war, along with *Stars and Stripes*, a newspaper for soldiers
created at Pershing's direction, served to publicize the games and
made reading the sports page a habit for many soldiers who had not
included it in their reading before the war. *Trench and Camp* reported
in October that close to five thousand spectators had watched a football game between the Thirty-Second Infantry and the Sixty-Fourth
Field Artillery.[32]

According to YMCA records over 300,000 spectators watched athletic activities in September 1917. Spectatorship peaked in August 1918,
when over 5 million watched these activities. From September 1917
to December 1919, more than 50 million spectators watched over 44
million soldier-athletes perform in one sport or another.[33] For perspective, and to foreshadow the argument of how wartime football
affected the postwar sport scene, in 1925 estimates placed attendance
at college football games at 12 million.[34]

That so many soldiers watched athletic events in the midst of one
of the largest and most destructive wars in history is worthy of comment. It is also a tribute to the efforts of bodies such as the Fosdick
Commission to implant sports into military life, along with the YMCA,
the Knights of Columbus, and other organizations that made the commission's goals a reality.

As far back as the mid-1870s, Thanksgiving and football have gone
together like turkey and dressing. Despite the war raging all around,
and with the aid of the Knights of Columbus's five hundred footballs,
the American military continued the tradition. In the process of providing doughboys with a reminder of home, the military also introduced the annual spectacle to thousands of new fans. On November
27, 1918, the Associated Press (AP) reported that the army was pull-
ing out all stops to give as many soldiers as possible the traditional
Thanksgiving experience, which included turkey, cranberry sauce,
mince pie, and sweet potatoes, among other dishes. The feast would
be accompanied by "real American doings," including a football game
played by some "American stars" who were at the camp. The same experience reportedly would be provided in other towns where American
troops were quartered.[35]

For the most part the games played in France were for spectators, but mainly American soldiers. This was part of the effort to keep soldiers away from the temptations of women and alcohol and would set a precedent for future military sporting programs.[36] Some French people did manage to see the games, as evidenced by the photo mentioned earlier, and this often seemed to fill reporters with an irrational exuberance about the prospects of spreading the game worldwide.

A Texas reporter wrote of another 1918 Thanksgiving Day game between a team of engineers and another from the infantry. The game was watched by "thousands of American troops and a thousand French soldiers who were home from the front on leave." The crowd was reportedly enthusiastic, and "the shouts from the respective rooters were heard far afield." The writer asserted, "Towards the end of the game the French soldiers, getting the hang of it, became just as enthusiastic as the Americans and joined in the cheering."[37] The author did not record if perhaps the French soldiers had alcohol, and if their enthusiasm might have been due to that, rather than any enthusiasm for the game. Given the reaction of French crowds at other games that will be discussed later, one must consider that possibility.

Sometimes the weather conspired to keep French crowds from seeing the American sport, as happened in December 1917, when a "howling snowstorm rolled in from the mountains," and some of the scheduled football games were canceled. Fortunately "about one hundred small children" who were invited to the festivities had their day saved when an American corporal dressed as Santa Claus and bearing gifts arrived at a nearby field in an airplane. They were likely more impressed by the flying Santa than they would have been by a football game, had it taken place.[38]

Adding to the cornucopia of benefits that athletic programming provided to the AEF, Chairman Fosdick added yet another when he returned from a 1918 tour of camps in France. He told reporters, "Our soldiers in France are the finest sportsmen in the world. Their sportsmanship is manifested in everything they do. What is more, the sports our men are playing overseas such as baseball, football, soccer, boxing, and wrestling are making them better fighters." He went on to say, "Various sports are probably the most popular forms of diversion among our troops overseas. The men play at every opportunity and it seems that they instinctively turn to athletics for their amusement. I have seen soldiers return to their rest billets after a hard go in the trenches and immediately begin to play baseball, football, and soccer and engage in boxing and wrestling bouts tired though they were."[39]

Just as Pershing's order from Baker to create an independent American force would prove the fighting mettle of the doughboy, so to athletics were meant to show the superiority of our sporting men.[40] This would be a theme that American commentators would return to well into the future and also help feed the narrative on the utility of sport.

Among accounts describing the constant boredom of training and the occasional horrors of war that can be found in dairies of World War I doughboys, some also contain several mentions of football games in training camps in the United States, France, and in Germany after the war. The military, in addition to getting its soldiers in shape, was also introducing hundreds of thousands of young men to a sport they might have otherwise paid little attention to. A similar cross section of diaries kept by the run-of-the-mill American before the war would not likely have turned up so many mentions of the game, which was, at the time, mostly played by elite northeastern universities. This serves to illustrate that service football during and after the war had a larger impact in the United States than it would in France.

One diary, that of Nathaniel "Nat" Rouse, published online by his grandson Warren Rouse, contains three mentions of attending football games while training for frontline service and after recovering from his wounds. Rouse, who enlisted at age twenty-four two weeks after Congress declared war, served with the Sixty-Ninth Regiment of the Forty-Second (Rainbow) Division. The entries primarily deal with the weather and his daily activities, with some mention of combat leading up to the point where he was wounded. They continue through January 1919, when he was demobilized. One entry, dated February 2, 1918, provides the weather and brief mention of a game: "Foggy. We do nothing but sit around now, but wait until we get in. Went over to park and saw football match." More enthusiastically, perhaps because the war had ended a little over two weeks before the game, Rouse mentions a Thanksgiving Game on November 28, 1918:

"Rain. Had a great football game. Yelled myself hoarse. Had turkey. Went to church. Thanksgiving here." By December 8, 1918, Rouse was thinking more of home than of the game: "Went to football game between MTC and 116, score 0–0. Gee, I am homesick."[41]

In addition to his providing news of football, Rouse's general feelings may be read in the terse entries: anticipation of combat during the first game, jubilation at victory and survival during the second, and a wish for a return to normalcy during the last. From what can be gleaned from the diary, Rouse was promoted to acting corporal, the highest rank he attained. To judge from his low rank and the informal language he used in the entries, it was unlikely that he was college educated and therefore equally unlikely that he had been directly exposed to football before the war. He was twenty-four years old when he joined the army, so it is doubtful that he would have played after the war, but perhaps he, like many of his fellow doughboys, went home with an enthusiasm for a game that had not existed before the war.

Allen C. Huber, another enlisted man who was a barber by trade before the war and also in the army, likewise mentions football several times in his diary. Huber also enlisted in the 138th Infantry Regiment of the Thirty-Fifth Division shortly after declaration of war in 1917. He also attained the rank of acting corporal, though he did not keep the position. He served as the unit's barber in addition to his other duties. Just before the armistice, Huber mentions that he and a friend witnessed a "D-D [0–0 presumably] score football game between the convalescent camp and the hospital team from Vehy." A few weeks after the cessation of hostilities, Huber notes, "K & I Cp. Played football this afternoon and K Co. was victorious 6 to 0. Pretty stiff game boys!" On another occasion, on February 19, 1919, Huber writes of a less formal football experience when he mentions, "Company is at leisure this afternoon so they are enjoying themselves with a football outside the barracks." As part of the effort to keep soldiers occupied after the end of the war, Huber mentions that his unit will be taking part in "competitive drill in the morning and games in the afternoon, for the week, so the boys are out playing ball and soccer," and later writes, "The boys who were at Toulon pass, told us that the 7th Div. football team beat our divisional team 6–2 at a town near

Toul." In March the games were still going on, and he notes, "K Co's football team misplaying Regimental Headquarters this afternoon and were Beaten [sic] 13 to 0."[42]

Once again the tone of the entries and Huber's occupation argue that he had not been a college man before the war. He and Rouse were demonstrating in their diaries that they, and others like them in the AEF, were being acculturated to the sporting forms of the universities back home.

Football matches picked up their pace following closely on the heels of the armistice. According to the unit history of Thirty-Sixth Division, written by Lonnie J. White and posted on the Texas Military Forces Museum website, its football team "represented the division through two seasons of football, one before Pershing's order for a full program of athletics became reality and one after it." In its "first season," the team won the First Army championship played at Tonnerre in north-central France on New Year's Day 1919. The team then traveled to Paris for an unofficial match on January 20 against the SOS (Service of Supply) team from Saint-Nazaire. Though it was not a sanctioned match, it "was generally regarded as determinant of the best in the AEF." Unfortunately for the Thirty-Sixth, the SOS team would prove better that day and become the unofficial football champ.[43]

The frequency of the games would accelerate again, however, after Pershing, aided by the YMCA, set a course for a championship series that would determine the best football team in the AEF. The Texas-Oklahoma Thirty-Sixth Division would continue to dominate its side of the tournament in what it called its "second season." This time the championship game would be officially recognized, but once again the division would come up short.

While waiting for demobilization, the AEF Command and the various welfare agencies recognized that American soldiers needed organized activities as much as they had during the war, if not more so. In order to give focus to those athletic endeavors, the YMCA under the direction of Elwood S. Brown, the organization's director of the Paris Department of Athletics, proposed a "Military Olympics" that would be a contest between the soldiers of the victorious mil-

FIG. 2. Photo of American doughboys getting a better view of football games that were held as part of the Inter-Divisional Football Championship of the American Expeditionary Force in 1919. Photo used with permission of the National World War I Museum, Kansas City, Missouri, USA.

itary forces.[44] Brown, who previously had organized the Far Eastern Games held in Manila in 1913, began to work on what would be known as the Inter-Allied Games. As part of the effort, whose motto was "Every Man in the Game," the tournament featured "championships series . . . in the following sports: Football, basketball, boxing and wrestling, golf, shooting, soccer, tennis, track and field events, swimming and baseball, roughly in the order named."[45] The YMCA came to the aid of the AEF, which underwrote most of the cost for the games, by buying $2,785,196 worth of sporting equipment and shipping it to Europe.[46]

The football championship held between January and March was the first to be decided, and the elimination tournament to crown the best AEF team was one of the most popular in terms of numbers of participants and spectators. According the official report, compiled by Maj. George Wythe, 743,696 soldiers played in the championship series and 3,745,738 watched the games.[47] The report on the size of the overall crowds made no mention of how many of those were French people, although it was unlikely that many were, given the dearth of football knowledge in the country. The games did excite the troops waiting to go home, though, and the teams representing various units went to great lengths to make sure they were prepared. When the weather was inclement, soldiers used massive 400-by-150-yard airplane hangars to hold scrimmages and practices.[48]

The hard-fought nature of the games only added to the excitement. According to the YMCA's War Work Council, "for fighting spirit no football games in the history of the sport ever developed finer matched teams or more exciting contests than those for the supremacy of the Second Army."[49] The championship came down to a contest between four teams, which played five tie games before the Seventh Division defeated the Twenty-Eighth Division in a scoreless tie decided by a tiebreaker rule that was enacted specially for the games and gave victory to the team with the most total yards.

The lack of offensive output would put modern American football fans to sleep, but the War Work Council hailed these closely contested matches, reporting, "Such football games at Toul [where Huber's team lost], Bar-sur-Aube, Coblenz [Germany], Luxemburg, and Paris stirred not only the whole American Army, but a great part of the rapidly growing sporting population of France to an understanding of the true character of the American spirit."[50]

Matching the hyperbole of the YMCA report, according to the final report on the games, the games were "played before crowds so immense that the number of spectators could not have been increased except by the use of aeroplanes or observation balloons."[51] In one semifinal match between the teams of the First and Second Armies at Bar-sur-Aube, more than twenty-five thousand soldiers brought in by special train, along with John J. Pershing and the king of Belgium, watched the contest.

Other, intra-unit contests did not draw so many fans and sometimes confused the local population. During a match between Batteries A and C of the 101st Field Artillery, when the citizens of Varennes saw the doughboys playing the game in a muddy pasture, they "mur-

FIG. 3. Football players during the 1919 Inter-Divisional Football Championship. Photo used with permission of the National World War I Museum, Kansas City, Missouri, USA.

mured 'Quel horreur!'" The author of a history of Battery A imagined the French wondering "what punishment forced the Americans to so torment themselves."[52]

Americans learned of the games, not from the previously quoted after-action reports but thorough fairly intense press coverage. According to Steven Pope in *Patriotic Games*, the games were well covered by American newspapers, aided by the Committee on Public Information.[53] Many of these articles contained the same sort of breathless reporting evidenced in the YMCA and AEF reports. According to the *New York Times*, "In the history of American football, 1919 will always stand out as a memorable year, one of remarkable achievements, and of splendid promise for the future of a game that DAVENANT [*sic*] as long ago as 1634, pronounced heroic."[54] The article went on to tell readers that "the American Expeditionary Forces played football as they had fought. Every schedule was like a campaign, and each game was a battle of wit and brawn, into which the last ounce of strength was put, victory perching on the banner of the best captained and maneuvered team. Never was there such enthusiasm, such elation, such rapture as marked the changing tide of battle in these contests of American soldiers. It has been said by witnesses that the demonstrations at games played by Princeton, Yale, and Harvard had never been so extravagant."[55]

Not content with that impressive level of hyperbole, the uncredited author ratcheted up his rhetoric even more by stating, "There can't be a shadow of a doubt that some of the American football battles in France, waged by men at the top condition and aglow with victory over the world's enemy, were the hardest fought pigskin combats in which Americans had ever been pitted against one another. They were tremendous, Homeric, and the sport gained incalculably."[56]

The teams that played for the championship of the Second Army were peppered with former collegiate stars. Among the players representing the top teams was Harry Legore of Yale, captaining the Second Division; Hamilton Fish of Harvard, playing for the Fourth Division; and Eddie Hart of Princeton, Eddie Mahan of Harvard, and Johnny Beckett of Oregon, playing for the SOS team from Saint-Nazaire. That most of these luminaries were linemen might explain the lack of scoring during the series. Though stocked with prewar talent, the teams were not meant to be aggregations of All-Stars. Rules required that the original teams that began the series must continue to play together. This was done to foster esprit de corps among the units remaining in Europe. While that likely succeeded, All-Star teams might have provided more scoring.[57]

According to Harold Evans, writing in the *Kansas Historical Quarterly*, state pride was also an important element for the teams, particularly in the aftermath of the series when universities could trumpet the exploits of their former stars.

> On the 35th division team, which gave a good account of itself, were several Kansas collegians, including "Pinky" Beals of Washburn, George "Rook" Woodward of K. U., Hyndman of Pittsburg, and Kalama, giant Haskell center. When the 35th played the 7th division at Commercy one rainy afternoon in February, 1919, Beals looked across the field and saw

Lt. Sam Stewart, who was Washburn's 1916 captain. Stewart was in the backfield for the regular army team. This game resulted in a scoreless tie, but the 7th division won the play-off at Toul, 6 to 0. The 35th was thus eliminated from competition. The Kansas-Missouri guardsmen had previously defeated the 33d division, 3 to 0, thanks to a field goal from the toe of Kansas' Woodward.[58]

Diaries provided a somewhat more blasé view of the games, but in one case yet another benefit of football games in France is added to the already long list that has been discussed previously. Benjamin Edgar Cruzan, a bugler for the Eighty-Ninth Division, mentions in his diary that he and the other buglers in the unit were practicing their calls day and night to prepare for the semifinal game at Coblenz, and he also accompanied the team to Paris to play in the final game.[59] He and his fellow buglers no doubt provided some of the spectacle that accompanied the games in the attempt to replicate the college atmosphere of games at home.

More thoughtful and adding to the narrative of football's impact is a series of diary entries by Harry L. Smith, an ambulance company officer with the Fourth Division who was ordered to serve as the trainer and surgeon for the unit's football team. His team won its first game against Rouse's Forty-Second Division 7 to 0, which he especially enjoyed, noting, "Our division had gained nothing like the fame of the 42nd, although it probably had done fully as much at the front."[60] He also particularly enjoyed the team's triumph over the Second Division since it had a Marine Brigade attached. Smith reports:

> In the evening beer and wine flowed in luxurious profusion, and officers staggered about the bail shouting and bellowing at each other. One epithet that our men never tired of hurling at the Marines was: "Marines, Marines, the first to advertise!" This jibe alluded to the tremendous publicity given to the Marines in American newspapers after the battle of Belleau Wood, in which, as a matter of fact, as many infantrymen as Marines fought. The feeling among the soldiers was that the Marines had snatched all the credit for the victories in the early stage of America's part in the war. That evening the banners of the Marines must have drooped low, indeed, for the hall in which the riotous cele-

bration took place was well-nigh wrecked. It was never opened again while we were in Germany.[61]

Where he waxes more philosophic is in his consideration of the democracy demonstrated by his division's football team:

> The personnel of the 4th Division's football team reflected the democracy inherent in the United States Army, for the players were men whose ranks ranged from private to lieutenant-colonel. All of them had played football in college, and several of them had previously been All-Americans. Captain Hamilton Fish had played football for three years at Harvard University. He was an All America tackle on Walter Camp's team during the years of 1908 and 1909. Lieutenant-Colonel F. C. Sibert, Major R. M. Littlejohn, Major W. E. Coffin and Major F. P. Prickett all had played football at West Point. Captain P. G. Tenney had been an All America halfback at Brown University. Captain T. E. Henning had been a star player at Michigan State College. Lieutenant O. E. Smith had been a well-known halfback at Drake University. Lieutenant T. P. Moriarity had been a famous tackle at Georgetown University. The fastest man on the squad was an Indian who had played college football under Coach Glenn Warner at Carlisle Institute.[62]

Whether a team reportedly composed of many college-educated officers proved that football was a signal of the democracy inherent in the AEF is arguable, but it serves to add one more argument to the list of reasons why athletics were important to the army and the country. Smith's team eventually lost to the Eighty-Ninth Division team, which would go on to win the AEF title, despite the doctor doping Captain Fish with "a dose castor oil."[63]

The hard-fought championship finally came down to the Eighty-Ninth Division and the Thirty-Sixth Division, in a game played at the velodrome field of the Parc des Princes in Paris on March 29, 1919. The final was contested before an estimated fifteen thousand spectators that included AEF commanding general John J. Pershing.[64] The Eighty-Ninth "Midwest" Division, so called because its soldiers principally came from Kansas, Missouri, Nebraska, Colorado, and the Dakotas, along with solders from Arizona and New Mexico, could count on a number of players with college football experience.[65] Lt. George "Potsy" Clark, the left halfback and the star of the championship game, played for the University of Illinois and before the war had been the assistant head coach of the University of Kansas Jayhawks. Private Howard "Scrubby" Laslett, the left end, and Lt. Adrian Lindsey, the right halfback, had also played for the Jayhawks before the war, and later afterward. There were also players with high school football experience as well as former college players from the University of South Dakota, Springfield Teachers College, the University of St. Louis, Colorado College, Washington University of St. Louis, Penn State University, and Kansas State Agricultural College.[66] Seven of the twenty-one players on the team were enlisted men, and so gave some credence to Smith's contentions about the democratic nature of the football teams contending for the title, since at this time football was still very much a game of the American elite.

Despite official concern that the teams not be All-Star aggregations, that is essentially what ended up happening. While the goal was for teams to be originally formed "as low as the company level," in actual practice players were drawn from the division level, which numbered around twenty-eight thousand men during World War I.[67] In the Thirty-Sixth Division, for instance, games were played at the company level and then played against other companies until a division champion was determined. The division had a total of fifty-two football teams, and from these "the cream of the gridiron warriors played for the division team."[68]

This tension between allowing individual units to compete and drawing from larger formations would persist into the 1960s, when teams built around air force bases in France would contend with army teams drawn from the divisional level in Germany.[69] By that time the practice of drawing teams from larger formations would make economic as well as competitive sense. Only those in the small battalions seemed to mind, as the second war would replace the a-game-for-every-man ethos with a win-at-all-costs mentality.

According to the official unit history of the Eighty-Ninth Division, "athletics were extremely encouraged," and a series of inter-company and inter-regimental games were played in a variety of sports including football, but the "Division itself undertook the creation of a Divisional football team under the direction of Captain Paul Withington," a former Harvard player who had also been the head football coach at the University of Wisconsin–Madison before the war.[70] In military fashion the Eighty-Ninth set up a training headquarters at Malberg with "the best football talent in the Division." Unlike the Thirty-Sixth, the Eighty-Ninth rolled through its qualifying matches, scoring ninety-four points in seven games, while only giving up only thirteen, including a victory over Smith and Fish's Fourth Division by a score of 14 to 0.[71]

The Thirty-Sixth Division was built around the Texas National Guard and had a long history of successful football teams in prewar times. The Second Texas Infantry team, made up mainly of former college stars, was particularly successful, defeating the Seventy-Fourth New York Cavalry 102 to 0 in a game along the Texas border in early 1917 and also scoring a victory over a Twelfth Division team coached by Dwight D. Eisenhower.[72] In France the divisional team was primarily made up of former players from Texas and Oklahoma, coached and captained by Capt. Wilmot Whitney, formerly of Harvard.[73] The team also included former All-Americans from the University of Texas and Yale, among other stars. In fine Texas fashion the team had what would today be labeled its own training dorm, "a palatial chateau on a high hill surrounded by woods and iron fences" where "practices were conducted mornings and afternoons on a field in front of the mansion and a division work detail performed household duties and [players] were served double rations at meals."[74] Former University of Texas head coach Mack Brown could not have asked for better facilities.

The Thirty-Sixth earned its berth in the championship game by defeating the Seventy-Ninth and Eightieth Divisions, then the First Cavalry Troops. It defeated the Twenty-Ninth Division to win the first army championship and finally defeated the low-scoring Seventh Division team mentioned earlier to qualify for the championship game. While most of the games that the Eighty-Ninth Division played were with the forces occupying Germany, most of the games won by the Thirty-Sixth were played in France. During its "first season," the team played games at Tonnerre (about 200 km southeast of

Paris) and at Paris. During its "second season," the team defeated the Twenty-Ninth National Guard in a "natural amphitheater" outside Bar-sur-Aube, after which, in contradiction to expectations for one of the values of sports, the Thirty-Sixth's record for money orders sent home was broken the following week (i.e., soldiers cleaned up gambling on their unit, or in other words, engaging in immoral activities). The Thirty-Sixth also defeated the team from Le Mans at Auteuil, located to the west of Paris, and played again at Bar-sur-Aube in front of Pershing and King Albert and Queen Elizabeth of Belgium.

Confirming the democratic nature of the sport, the "towering bleachers" at the field were built "by and for the enlisted men." Several high high-ranking officers had to stand on the sidelines, and military police officers were banned.[75] Therefore, with its long record of experience playing in the United States and also in France during its "first season" before the final tournament was organized, and a possible advantage as the "home" team, the Thirty-Sixth would be a strong competitor in the final.

The first half seemed to bear that out as the game began with the Texans jumping out to an early lead. In contrast to the relative ease with which the Eighty-Ninth had won its preliminary games, and mainly due to an early error, the game was hotly contested. The Thirty-Sixth scored first, recovering an Eighty-Ninth fumble in the end zone in the first quarter, and the first half ended with the Thirty-Sixth leading 6 to o.

Indicative of the still-unfamiliar nature of the game for many of the soldiers in attendance, a significant number lacked a keen appreciation for the subtleties of football. When half was called, fans of the Thirty-Sixth Division, believing the game was done, charged onto the field for a snake dance in celebration.[76]

A common theme when the military played football in France and worldwide, was the importance, sometimes bordering on obsession, that commanding officers placed on victory as a means of instilling unit pride. In one sense this focus is no different from the spirit that motivates boosters of any team to urge their team to glory, but in another sense there is a fairly significant difference: commanding officers can give orders and expect them to be obeyed. This was illustrated during

FIG. 4. The championship game of the 1919 Inter-Divisional Football Championship in Paris. The Eighty-Ninth Division defeated the Thirty-Sixth Division by a score of 14–6. Photo used with permission of the National World War I Museum, Kansas City, Missouri, USA.

the halftime when the Eighty-Ninth players were despondent about their early error and seemed unmoved by their coach's halftime pep talk. However, as the soldiers were moving toward the field for the second half, they were stopped by Maj. Gen. Frank Winn, who told them, "When General [Leonard] Wood commanded the division, he never issued an order that was not carried out. I too have never issued an order that was not carried out. There is only one thing that I can do—order you to win the game."[77]

Apparently Maj. Gen. William Smith of the Thirty-Sixth forgot, or neglected, to give his players the same order. Perhaps he was used low-scoring games and was complacent with the lead. The Eighty-Ninth, though, obeyed Winn's orders and behind Clark's running and kicking, dominated the second half. Clark, who went on to be a head coach of the Detroit Lions, where he won the NFL championship in 1935, caught one touchdown pass from Lindsey and ran

FIG. 5. The championship game of the 1919 Inter-Divisional Football Championship in Paris. The Eighty-Ninth Division defeated the Thirty-Sixth Division by a score of 14–6. Photo used with permission of the National World War I Museum, Kansas City, Missouri, U.S.A.

for a 65-yard touchdown in the fourth quarter.[78] He also kicked both points after touchdown and so scored all the points for the midwesterners.[79]

According to a report in the *New York Herald*, following the game Pershing addressed the winning players, telling them, "I am glad of the opportunity to thank you for the splendid game you have played today, and for the wonderful spirit you have shown. You have carried out to the letter and spirit of the plan adopted to promote clean sports in the American Expeditionary Forces. You have gone at this athletic program and game today with the same dash and spirit you showed at the front and that is the spirit that makes America and Americans great."[80]

The newspaper added as one of its subheadings "French Quick to Understand Plays." Perhaps this was more wishful thinking than a statement for which it had actual proof. The *Herald* based its assertion on the amount of cheering that the French people in the crowd displayed, reporting, "The game at first was puzzling to the many French officials and civilians in the stands, but all, even the women, soon caught the Yankee spirit and cheered the plays." Belying its assertion the particular event that caused most excitement for the French was the premature victory snake dance that fans of the losers performed at halftime. The French in attendance were likely struggling with their own puzzlement over the length of the game and merely followed suit with the early celebration.[81]

The massive football series served to increase enthusiasm for the sport, at least among American soldiers, if not for the French, and was judged a great success. In contrast to the 1905 crisis that football had to weather, when eighteen high school and college football players died, Major Wythe proudly announced that "although more than 75,000 officers and men took active part, and despite the fact that some games were played on fields covered with snow or ice, there was not a single serious accident and only one broken bone was reported."[82] Before the war some critics had argued that football was too dangerous, pointing to the high number of deaths tied to the game each year. The furor over football's danger even led President Theodore Roosevelt to call a meeting of college leaders to discuss reforms that eventually led to the National Collegiate Athletic Association (NCAA). Compared to the danger that the doughboys faced during the war, however, the threat of playing a game, even one as violent as football, likely gave them no cause for concern.

Following the close of the Inter-Allied Games on July 6, demobilization continued to draw down the number of American troops in Europe. With the various souvenirs that soldiers invariably take home—an Eiffel Tower statue here, a spiked German helmet there—many also took a new appreciation for the game of football.

It is ironic given the difficulty that our game has had gaining a foothold in France, but that nation has in several instances played a role in boosting football in the United States. World War I, as we have seen, was arguably the second of these instances. Commentators at the time argued that World War I would likely have the same effect on the game as the Civil War had on baseball, namely, that the war would exponentially increase the popularity of the sport among the American people. Later historians have also largely confirmed that view.[83]

Only months after the nation entered the war, Louis A. Dougher of the *Washington Times* prognosticated that the war would spread the popularity of football, not in France but in the United States. Dougher mentioned the role that the American Civil War had played in spreading the popularity of baseball and argued that as more young men were exposed to the gridiron, they too would become fans. While football was increasing its visibility across the nation before the war, with high schools taking up the game and even professional teams forming in the Midwest, it was still particularly popular at the university level. Dougher argued that already, just six months after the United States had declared war, more than 64,000 soldiers on some 3,200 military-base teams were playing the game, which could not help but broaden its appeal. "Young men who never played the game are learning its fine points. Young men who could not play because of their hours of employment are now enjoying their favorite sport. Young men are going to return from Europe convinced of the physical value of football training and it will be most strange if they do not continue to play it."[84]

Earlier that year Walter Camp had told an audience of officials from the Intercollegiate Athletic Association that due to the football played at cantonments "there would be more football in this country than ever before." Fortunately the assembled delegates were able to defeat a proposal to modify and simplify the rules of the game by giving each side seven alternative downs, which might have confused the issue and wasted the effect on the game that the war eventually had.[85]

The unnamed and hyperbolic *New York Times* reporter who compared the AEF football series to Homeric epic joined the chorus. His article ended prophetically, asserting, "It cannot be said with too much emphasis that football owes more to the war in the way of the spread of the spirit of the game than it does to ten or twenty years of development in the period before the war."[86]

In spite of this heated rhetoric, historians have argued that predictions that the war would boost the popularity of the game at home proved to be correct. James Mennell, writing in the *Journal of Sport History* in 1989, was more judicious in his analysis of the effect of wartime football but concluded that the games at home and in Europe were significant. He admitted that when trying to pinpoint the primary cause of the increase in football's popularity after the war, it is difficult to separate the impact of wartime football from the effect of rules changes completed by 1912. Mennell, however, points out that since thirteen schools established football programs after the war, there is some credence to the war-agency argument. Although the evidence is difficult to locate and is somewhat spotty, attendance at college matches also seems to have increased dramatically after the war, which argues for the role played by the conflict. Mennell concludes that World War I military football had three important influences on the postwar football boom. First, service football increased the number of young men who experienced playing the game. Second, it familiarized even the nonplayer with the spectacle of college football. Finally, it drew in the friends and relatives of service players who rooted for their favorite's teams.[87]

In addition to the schools that added football teams, several programs, including Ohio State (1922), Nebraska (1923), and Texas (1924), constructed new cathedrals for the sport during the decade following the war.[88] Arguments for stadium construction were often met with skepticism that more than sixty thousand fans, in the case of Ohio State, would come out to see a mere football game. But the popularity of the game in postwar America proved the skeptics wrong.[89]

With the new interest in college football created by service football, and the recent excitement provided by the AEF Football Championship that culminated in France in March, football fans flocked to the games. Thousands of soldiers who either played or watched the games in France and Germany would return during the next year, and many would resume interrupted college careers or matriculate for the first time, now with an appreciation for football.

Grantland Rice, the Great Hyperbolist, prophesied, "Football is coming back with a greater rush than any other sport and it takes no prophet to forecast an unusual output of enthusiasm all along the line. Football players were plastered all over France during the late quarrel. The moleskin wearer rushed to war with a relish and those who still had time to serve in the collegiate halls will be rushing back to football with a greater relish still."[90]

So while the new American game had a negligible effect on French sensibilities, the hundreds of games played by teams stationed there did influence the preferences of the doughboys who took part as players or spectators. As mentioned earlier, this would be the second in a series of occasions when football played in France would have a disproportionate impact on the game at home. Later the German blitzkrieg attack on France would inspire a new offensive formation, and eventually a game played in Paris would help legitimize arena football.

While the opposing sides in the two world wars (1914–1945) paused to lick their wounds and go to the chalkboard to construct better tactics for the resumption of play twenty years later, football games in France halted not long after the guns had. Despite the often wildly optimistic and sometimes wishful-thinking pronouncements of writers who thought they saw enthusiasm for the American game in France, the war-weary population of that country had more weighty matters to deal with than importing new games.

Football in the United States, aided by the experiences that AEF soldiers had playing in France and elsewhere during the war, would flourish. As the halftime of the two world wars (1914–45) drew to a close, however, some in France would also begin to think that the country needed a new brutal game to prepare them for the new struggle that was becoming increasingly likely. A German writer for a Paris newspaper would decide that France should embrace football to compete with the Nazis, and so began the first great missionary effort to bring the French into the gridiron huddle.

2. The 1938 Riess and Crowley Tour

The games that AEF teams played in France during and after World War I left little impression on the French. Some French newspapers, including *Le Figaro* and *Le Petit Journal*, did carry brief announcements that the championship game between the Thirty-Sixth and Eighty-Ninth Divisions would take place.[1] Only *Le Petit Journal* followed up with a second story reporting the score and that "General Pershing and thousands of spectators" were on hand to view the championship. It noted, however, that very few civilians attended the game, and that the "impressive 'gallery' was nearly entirely composed of American or British soldiers."[2] Any mention of a bizarre sport played by foreigners was nevertheless noteworthy. This was particularly true at a time when the nation was struggling to recover from the loss of nearly two million soldiers.[3]

It was not indicative, however, of any French interest in the sport. As time passed and the scars of war began to heal, life slowly returned to normal. That meant that soccer and rugby leagues and games regained their former centrality in the nation. A typical Frenchman might read the occasional story of the American sport, or see a snippet of a game captured on screen. They might also have noticed that the strange sport, which some of his countrymen viewed as a bizarre punishment detail, was gaining great popularity across the Atlantic.

Pigskin missionaries lagged far behind promoters of other American sports in seeking to spread football worldwide. Albert Spalding's world baseball tour reached France in 1889, and the YMCA dribbled their basketballs in four years later. Football boosters eventually got around to it, but only after spotting the other major New World sports nearly half a century. Even then the Japanese began playing football in 1934, becoming the first nation outside North America to adopt the sport, four years before any attempt was made to interest the French.[4]

The motives for taking football on the road also differed from baseball and basketball, since initial efforts to introduce the gridiron game to France were prompted by a transplanted resident of that country, and not by Americans. However, through a combination of poor timing and native resistance, even local assistance was incapable of enabling apostles of the gridiron to gain many converts.

Attempts to plant the American game in France would continue to suffer from factors that limited the amount of attention and enthusiasm that the sport could receive. France after the Great War was not the same nation that at the turn of the century had sought to build a sporting culture to compete with the Germans. It also had more ominous matters to occupy its attention. By 1938, when the first tour took place, France had a mature sporting culture focused on soccer and rugby. The country and its citizens were also distracted by international tensions that would soon plunge the nation into a disastrous new war.

The 1938 tour could perhaps be seen as an effort in cultural imperialism, in that it was an attempt to convince the French that they should play football. However, if cultural imperialism could be seen at work here, it appeared in an odd form. The 1938 effort originated as the idea of a German expatriate, working for a French newspaper, to import Americans to promote football.

It was also a remarkably ineffective effort that gained few converts. Despite an initial wave of enthusiasm and grand plans for the future, no French teams or leagues sprang up as a result of the tour. Too few people managed to see one of the games, and those who merely read about them were informed that the players were unnatural freaks, and that the game was too complicated, too dangerous, or not fluid enough.

Baseball and basketball had fared better. However, those sports were designed to be played by relatively sedentary businessmen. Football, on the other hand, was a game that required a high degree of physical exertion, along with a willingness to hit and be hit. The rougher

game also required a great deal of mental preparation to learn formations, plays, and the like. Baseball and basketball required a great
deal of hand-to-eye coordination but demanded less mental preparation. Football also required coordination, but those athletic feats
had to be performed while carrying out complex group movements in
concert with teammates. Adding to the complexity, the players were
required to perform their individual roles as the opposition sought
to physically attack them.

The case of the 1938 tour and the subsequent tours considered in
later chapters serves to illustrate the central difficulty of the cultural
imperialism theory. If the indigenous population is not receptive to
the product being promoted, then no amount of urging can force it
to accept that product.

As we shall see in chapter 6, football would finally be planted in
France and take root there. However, that occurred only after a French
educator saw something attractive in the game and imported it for
his own purposes.

In the global marketplace of culture, a cultural product must be
useful to consumers. Coca Cola is popular, not because the United
States is a hegemonic power, but because it is a refreshing soft drink
that many locals find superior to their traditional brands. The same
is true of McDonalds, Wal-Mart, and Hollywood films. In the same
vein, if a sport does not satisfy a need felt by the indigenous population, it will not be adopted.

The Japanese used baseball to satisfy a need to appear "modern"
after the 1868 Meiji Restoration. Likewise Cubans found baseball to
be a useful tool to express resistance to Spanish imperial rule.[5] The
1938 effort discussed in this chapter was motivated by the same sort
of feeling—that the French needed football for purposes other than
exercise or amusement, but not enough Frenchmen would agree.

From 1938 to 1990 various and diverse individuals and groups
attempted to interest the French in the American game but had little success to show for their efforts. The initial tour took place in 1938
and involved two teams of college All-Stars, led by Jim Crowley. The
Fordham University head coach, who had also been a member of the
famed Notre Dame University backfield dubbed the Four Horsemen,

therefore had star power sufficient to draw considerable interest both at home and abroad. His collections played a series of five exhibition games from Paris to Marseilles and attracted some attention, especially for their initial games in the capital.

The excursion was instigated by Curt Riess, a writer for the French newspaper *Paris Soir*. Riess saw a use for the sport and felt that the French were ready to play the rough game. He convinced his paper to sponsor the tour, and the games received some positive press. French fans often displayed considerable interest in the novelty of the sport. However, despite optimistic reports that the French were taking to the game, no French teams were established as a result of this opening effort to build enthusiasm for football.

One factor that hindered the effort was certainly the lack of an expatriate community interested in playing football. Without that foundation the expensive and time-consuming sport faced nearly insurmountable difficulties in establishing a base of support. The expense and time commitment necessary to play would only increase over the decades as the equipment necessary to play became increasingly specialized. Still, many would later be willing to follow in Crowley and company's footsteps and give it the old college try.

Another limiting condition was that this tour, as well as later efforts, would seek to create an overarching league, then develop the game. The top-down idea that creating a league would create demand for a sport was a fallacious one. It flew in the face of the history of football in the United States, where the sport had grown out of informal campus contests that often pitted freshmen against sophomores, or seniors against juniors.[6] The first leagues would evolve only after several years of intercollegiate play.[7] As chapter 8 will demonstrate, the eventual adoption of French football would follow the traditional pattern, with the creation of a single team that then helped build others. Only after several teams existed would a league be created.

Riess, a Jewish journalist who left Germany before that nation's descent into madness, became a sports and entertainment writer for *Paris Soir*, a prominent newspaper during the 1930s.[8] Riess spent much of his time in the United States covering a variety of sporting events and personalities for his paper and while there became familiar with collegiate football. He recruited Crowley, then the head football coach of Fordham University in New York City. Crowley organized two All-Star teams made up of twenty-four players from eastern universities, including four of his Rams.[9]

According to Crowley, Riess originated the idea, and there were "a considerable number of influential people in France who are apparently hopeful of making that country more sports minded and feel that new sports are needed." He further stated that during the time that Riess had been in the United States, "he ha[d] seen our game and . . . liked it, but, more than this, he ha[d] been impressed with the great popularity it obtained with the American people as a whole—with the huge enthusiasm it created and his newspaper settled on the idea of having some American players go over and demonstrate the game to see whether it might catch on with the French."[10]

On the face of it, that explanation makes sense, but in an article Riess wrote for the *Nation* on March 1, 1941, he offered an additional purpose for his interest in football. The article began with Riess writing about the common view that the approaching war would be a technological struggle, and that machines of war would determine success or failure. However, he went on to argue that machines were not enough. He paraphrased the apocryphal statement attributed to the Duke of Wellington that the Battle of Waterloo was won on the playing fields of Eton to make his point: that machines needed human help. Riess also discussed the athletic programs, considered in chapter 1, that Americans had constructed in World War I to produce and maintain fit soldiers. He mentioned the preliminary steps that the War Department was taking to rebuild those programs in the wake of the Draft Act of 1940. He then compared those efforts to the national athletic programs set up by Adolf Hitler in Germany and Joseph Stalin in the Soviet Union that used sports as a means of enhancing their national defense. He argued, using unknown formulas and numbers, that a comparison of athletes using a "hypothetical field of a given size" in various nations would see 100 athletes using that field in America and Germany, 160 athletes in England, 30 in Russia, and 410 in France.[11]

By the time he wrote the article for the *Nation*, France had already fallen to the Nazis, and England was under pressure. The moral of his story, and likely his motivation for the 1938 tour, was that nations successful at emphasizing sports would fare better in war. Sports, he maintained, provided more than fitness; they also built individual character that we "sometimes called 'guts'" in America.[12] It seems likely, therefore, that in addition to making France more sports minded in 1938, he also saw football as a means of building national strength that France could use against Germany, just as French planners had sought to accomplish with soccer and rugby before World War I.

With *Paris Soir* paying the cost of the tour, Crowley and his players, along with Judge Carberry, one of his assistants, boarded the United States liner *Manhattan* and set sail for France on November 30.[13] There was some concern that the coach might not make the trip, but at the last minute both the Sugar Bowl and the Cotton Bowl declined to invite Fordham to their games, which cleared the way for Crowley to begin his quest.[14]

Despite strikes and threats of strikes at the port of Le Havre, an Associated Press bulletin reprinted in the December 8 *New York Times* reported that the teams had arrived and took the chance to editorialize on the "missionaries" chances for success.[15] The uncredited author treated the tour as an amusement, reporting, "Without wishing to alarm any one it must be reported that France was invaded tonight by a number of large individuals of fierce appearance from a far-off land. They turned out to be members of the first American expeditionary force of football players ever to come to Europe, but had they been Martians, they could scarcely have aroused any greater feeling of awe and trepidation."[16]

Though he suffered from an ignorance of the many football games already played by the AEF in France during and after the war, the author maintained that the gridiron giants would be demonstrating their game for "apprehensive" Frenchmen. He also declared that those Frenchmen "care nothing about the line-up or the score. What they want to see is the spectacle."[17] A narrative that the tour would add up to little more than an exotic sideshow had already been created before the first game, and would prove to be prophetic.

The writer might have been reacting to accounts in the French press that sought to publicize the game in preparation for the contests. He described press reports that had included "numerous photographs showing helmeted youths howling savagely and apparently tearing one another limb from limb" to illustrate why the aforementioned Frenchmen perhaps should have been apprehensive.[18]

The Associated Press did not specify the newspapers where those alarming images were displayed, but *Le Petit Parisien* did publish two articles to prepare the field for the barbarian hordes about to invade their shore. A preparatory article in *Le Petit Parisien* warned that "25 Frankensteins" with "astonishing flexibility and precision" were on their way to France. G. L Ancel, the paper's New York correspondent, was dispatched to watch a November 30 afternoon practice of the New York University football team coached by Dr. "Martin" Stevens.[19] The author was very impressed by the athletic abilities of this "team of Frankensteins" who could throw the ball "with one hand only, and with astonishing precision, fifty meters." The skilled players also could leave the line of scrimmage rapidly, unexpectedly zigzagging their way around the large men who wanted to tackle them.[20]

One player in particular, Howard Dunney, was singled out as an example of a "True Frankenstein." Dunney was described as standing one meter ninety-two (six feet four), weighing 97 kilos (214 pounds), and being able to run one hundred meters in under eleven seconds.

Ancel was also impressed by the coaching staff, who yelled at the players through cardboard speaking horns, stopping the scrimmage to give short instructions on what players were doing wrong and then starting play again immediately. The author took pains to warn his readers that football in this case was to be understood as an evolution of rugby, and not soccer. Marvin Stevens told Ancel that the players bound for France, including two (George Savarese and Dunney) from NYU, would travel under the authority of the Amateur Athletic Union and would be leaving later that night. Stevens declined to specify which other players would go, for he told Ancel that "most of his 'boys' would like to go," and those not chosen "would be too discouraged for a good finish to their season." Ancel then provided the dates and locations of the games in France and stated that after the final game in Bordeaux on Christmas Day, the players would return home

UN SOIR SUR LE N. Y. STADIUM
LES RUGBYMEN S'ENTRAINAIENT

25 *"Frankenstein"*
d'une souplesse et d'une précision étonnantes

Par notre correspondant particulier de New-York
G. L. ANCEL

...ET NOUS LES VERRONS BIENTOT EN FRANCE CAR ILS SE SONT EMBARQUÉS SUR LE " MANHATTAN "

Le rugbyman américain Howard Dunnay, de la célèbre N. Y. U. (New York University). Un vrai « Frankenstein », comme écrit notre correspondant : taille, 1 m. 92; poids, 97 kilos; court le 100 mètres en moins de onze secondes ; lance le ballon, d'une seule main, à plus de cinquante mètres !

FIG. 6. Article from *Le Petite Parisien*, December 1, 1938. Used with permission of the Bibliothèque Nationale de France.

to await the formation of a French football team that could then be invited to play in the United States.[21]

In contrast to the AP writer, Ancel seemed to believe that his countrymen would enthusiastically embrace the sport. Perhaps he had been contaminated by living in the United States. More likely he was merely concerned with putting the best possible face on his report in the hopes that something positive would result from the unusual venture.

Retreating somewhat from his previous report, and echoing Coubertin's earlier appraisal, Ancel wrote a follow-up article for the next day's issue that labeled football "the most violent sport that exists." In a more positive vein, he also told readers that the game was nevertheless "the most spectacular." Most of the article consisted of a conversation between Ancel and Stevens on the differences between football and rugby. Stevens was not only the head football coach of Yale from 1928 to 1932 but had also earned his medical degree as an orthopedic surgeon. According to Stevens he took courses at the University of Paris in 1929, where he became aware of rugby as played in that country. The American coach held that the most obvious differences between the sports was that in football the forward pass was legal, there was no off-side (a player from the team with the ball being closer to the goal than the ball) and that players could "interfere, shove (block), and even tackle players who did not have the ball." To this Ancel added that he thought spectators would be "astonished at the way players obstinately kept the ball when being tackled, rather than passing the ball laterally to a teammate." Having covered the basics, Ancel asked perhaps the key question, "Do you have the intention, through this tour, of winning us over to your point of view?" Stevens answered, "If the tour resulted in the French adopting the American game, [I] would be happy, but if not, we would simply be happy to show our French friends what we call football on this side of the Atlantic."[22]

An insert accompanying the story made the prospect of the French adopting our game a questionable proposition from an economic view. The insert featured Al Gurske, a Fordham running back, and one of the players headed for France. It marveled at the equipment that he modeled and told readers that in order to buy such protective gear, which was needed because of the violent nature of the game; one would have to spend $120, or more than €4,000! ($1,913 or €1,432 in 2013).[23]

In the midst of a worldwide depression, the only way football could have taken hold in France in 1938 would have been through the sponsorship of deep-pocketed patrons, such as governments or large corporations. Those potential backers, however, had more pressing matters that demanded their attention and their funding.

Adding to the difficulty of selling the expensive game, plans to find French athletes to take part in the game proved to be nearly impossible. According to Crowley the French had hoped to field a team composed of picked rugby players to take on the Americans. Riess cabled the coach to inform him that the difficulty of adapting to the unfamiliar rules had made that impossible.[24]

In what would form a general pattern for these tours, the French would react with some enthusiasm, if not a little confusion, to the games played there. Despite grandiose plans there would be few concrete efforts to exploit those enthusiastic moments, and any French athletes interested in playing the new sport would be disappointed. The absence of any sustained planning to take advantage of the momentary enthusiasms generated by the 1938 and later tours provided little opportunity for the game to take root among the native population.

As was only fitting, since the paper was paying the expenses for the tour, *Paris Soir* broke the news of the Americans' arrival in Paris on December 9. Unlike *Le Petit Parisien*, the sponsoring paper had not done much to advertise the tour prior to the teams' arrival at Le Havre. It did attempt to soften the monstrous image of the players in its headline that proclaimed: "New stars for Europe and rare athletes. Here are the American rugbymen: truly giant gentleman." The sponsor took pains to introduce several of the players and their backgrounds. It emphasized that all the players had finished their university studies, and Ed Franco, one of the players from Fordham, was even a history teacher. To emphasize that this was not a collection of semiliterate barbarians, they were further described as having been chosen from some of the largest American universities.[25]

The establishment of these giants and their first game in Paris was headline news in France across the political spectrum. The communist newspaper *L'Humanité* carried a picture of players in their uniforms in a narrow insert on its front page and announced the first game on December 10. It hyped the game by telling readers, "This afternoon at the Parc des Princes . . . padded and helmeted powerful athletes will show to Parisians the spectacular beauty and the virility of American rugby."[26] Inside the edition the paper told its readers the basics of the game—eleven players per side, a 100-yard field—and also described the basic positions. It also claimed that in this new game nearly everything, save for kicking and punching, was permitted. It described a typical play in which the defenders tried to knock down all the offensive players to keep them from aiding the ballcarrier.[27]

This was a somewhat overblown description of the controlled mayhem that occurred during a typical play and can probably be ascribed to an outsider's lack of understanding, or perhaps it represented a wish to sensationalize the upcoming spectacle. But it was also a portrayal that furthered the narrative that football was the world's most violent game. Such a depiction might have piqued the interest of sport enthusiasts or those interested in voyeuristic violence, but it was not likely to encourage the average soccer player to switch sports.

The conservative paper *Le Figaro* called the sport a "mixture of rugby, soccer, wrestling, track and field, and acrobatics." It also gave its readers a brief primer on the rules of the sport but warned them that these explanations were not detailed. Those who attended the first game, readers were warned, "must make an effort to understand" what they would see on the field. Even if they did not understand everything, they would doubtless be impressed by the "athletic and fast-paced game." In addition to its description of the rules, *Le Figaro* added that the "grand master" of the game was the coach, who, "after each play, or nearly so," gathered the players to tell them the next play.[28]

With hyperbole worthy of Grantland Rice, the story depicted the players merely as a collection of automatons that blindly carried out the play "exactly as their coach had indicated," regardless of what the other team did. *Le Figaro*, perhaps reflecting its more conservative orientation, which promoted authority, gave credit to the coaches (Crowley and Carberry) as being the "principal artisan of victory or defeat."[29] The players presumably were little more than living chess pieces that responded to the will of their leaders.

Le Petit Journal reminded readers that most potential spectators had at least seen the game played in films such as Harold Lloyd's *The Freshman* (1925). Many had also seen football games featured in newsreel reports on Harvard or Yale. Perhaps they had seen newsreel footage of important games such as those between Notre Dame and West Point or Army and Navy. From those examples they would remember the players wrapped in leather pads wildly chasing the oval ball while their fans, a "howling crowd," dressed as if for an immense parade, cheered their favorites and waved flags. Like reporters for the other newspapers, Jean Roux of *Le Petit Journal* provided his readers a brief description of the game but also offered his opinion that only twenty-four players, which included only two replacements, were not enough to perform a tour of France with six games in two weeks.[30]

Le Petit Parisien, continuing its extensive effort to familiarize readers with the game, stepped back a bit from its description of players as so many Frankenstein monsters. An article by Jean Monest the day before the first game on December 9 attempted to humanize the monsters through interviews with the players. Readers learned that the athletes were not focused solely on playing football, but that they wanted more from their visit to "Gay Paree." George Bell, a lineman from Purdue wanted to "drink your good wines." Warren King, a reserve from Dartmouth wanted to meet the beautiful young actress Simone Simon. Hubert Schultze, a lineman from Columbia, was obviously seeking to make a good impression with the locals when he claimed that he wanted "to be as gallant as the French!" John Killian, a lineman from Boston College, perhaps summed up what many of the young men were thinking when he asked, "When can we go dancing with French women?"[31]

Perhaps to relieve any fears that young French women or their parents might have at this pronouncement, the article described Schultze as a "perfect gentleman." Reportedly, the first things he asked upon arrival was "when walking down the street with a young woman, must the young man walk on the left or right side, and was it acceptable to help the woman up onto the sidewalk?" Monest editorialized that this was a "timid and delicious boy," possibly to allay fears that these monsters might run amok with the female population of Paris.[32]

His article also mentioned some of the player's other appetites, such as when one player, after having a breakfast of cheese, fruit, and coffee, surprised the waitress by asking for a rare beefsteak. Driving home the point that these Americans were unusually large, a photo that accompanied the article presented Tom Buckley of Boston College and Leo Shields of Holy Cross, two linemen weighing in at 92 and 94 kilos (203 and 207 pounds) respectively, posed precariously in full uniform on a small, but presumably standard, French bed. The caption, under the heading, "Aren't they cute?" reported that the two "*bébés*" were "relaxing before going to practice."[33]

Le Petit Parisien, on the day of the first exhibition, asked the key question in its' game-day preview. Monest wondered if "December 10 [would] become a historic date in French sport or a successful curiosity?" He also provided a brief history of the game's evolution from rugby-like matches played between Harvard and Yale. He overstated the relative popularity of the game, but jumped the gun only by some twenty years, claiming that football was more popular in the United States than baseball or heavyweight boxing championships.[34] Perhaps to spur French athletic officials into action, readers were also informed that, according to their "calculations," the number of spectators for football had reached "40 Million." Those fans paid an average of more than one dollar per ticket and had brought revenue on the order of "50 to 70 Million dollars, or more than 2 Billion Francs!" Given the popularity and the immense revenue of the sport in the United States, he held out some hope for transplanting the game to France. Monest ended on a semihopeful note, arguing, "It is quite possible [that French teams would be formed]," but warned that he would wait until he had seen the game.[35]

French readers, having been warned that a group of massive barbarians were descending upon the city, had been reassured that these monsters were really warm and cuddly, albeit large and hungry gentlemen, and they were now primed to enjoy the first spectacle. Those who read the papers also had a rudimentary understanding of the rules and an idea of how these behemoths trained for their grueling matches. They had further been enticed by visions of millions of fans bringing in billions of francs in revenue. What remained to be seen was how the actual game would go over with the French people.

The first game at the Parc des Princes on December 10 earned front-page photo coverage from most of the papers, along with more extensive coverage in the sports section. Along with the typical account of the game, in which the All-Stars defeated the New York team 25 to 14 in front of a crowd of twenty thousand spectators, various writers also gave their opinions of the novel sport. A caption accompanying *L'Humanité*'s front-page photo pictured large players seemingly flying in all directions and warned readers that this was not a game for "little girls." In the main article, after chronicling the course of the game, the author expressed doubt that the game would catch on in France. According to the author, "This rugby, which is more wrestling than soccer, needs constant timeouts to allow tactic choices for the players. We doubt this game can lead [succeed] in France."[36]

Le Figaro expressed no uncertainty in its article about the first game. This was, as a subheading boldly declared, "a game that had no chance in Europe." Like *L'Humanité*, *Le Figaro* stated the most often heard comments: "The game has no chance in France. It asks for a workout that is too severe, too meticulous, and is too driven to please our athletes. It is also too chopped with referee whistles to please our spectators." The author expressed admiration for the "players, their physical prowess, the courage and ardor that animated them, the running speed and execution," stating, "[These] are among the many beautiful things that we saw yesterday." The article went on to assert, "It is certain that football is a rough school for those who play it. It asks for decisiveness, will, and contempt for danger that few sports require." That contempt for danger, *Le Figaro* pointed out, led to the "25 to 30 deaths and 250 serious injuries per year." There, according to *Le Figaro*, was the rub. "The American people easily accommodate this danger, but our European people, and the French in particular, would they see a similar sport implemented? We very much doubt it."[37]

Monest of *Le Petit Parisien* also wrote about the toll that the violence of the game took on American athletes, claiming that there were "several thousand injuries during the last season." He stated that the game had not appeared so violent when he watched practice, but he now doubted that the twenty-four players would be enough to complete the entire tour. The author, or his editors, also solicited commentary from "specialists," chosen from among prominent French sportsmen. Mario Brun, a journalist and writer, declared mockingly, "Football? Gossip!" He agreed that the name of the game might be accurate since, from time to time, players kicked the ball, but that it was closer to rugby, and that it had nothing in common with soccer. Brun agreed that it was a virile and violent game, but after each play the teams held "small councils" that added a "comic note to the rough battle." Further, the preparation for the next play in the huddle robbed the game of initiative, inspiration, and spontaneity. Thus, in his opinion, he considered the name "football" to be mere gossip, and the game would be better described as a mix of rugby, track and field, and wrestling. Robert Marchand, a professional cyclist, also compared football to wrestling and mentioned the strange breaks in the action, which he interpreted as time for recuperation. The sole positive report in this section came from François Piétri, a politician from Corsica, who declared enthusiastically, "This game pleases me a lot." He was, in his words, "seduced by the agility and rapid reflexes of the players." Especially pleasing for him was the forward pass, which he held to be preferable to the backward passes of rugby. He went so far as to argue, "Fifteen of the players, given training in 'our rugby' would quickly be formidable adversaries for our teams."[38]

A larger section gave a point-counterpoint argument on the game. Roger Malher, an author, enjoyed the game watching the "twenty-two well-balanced 'boys' on the field dressed in fresh colors, who occasionally were taken by a frenzy of indescribable movement." Despite his enjoyment of the spectacle, Malher returned to the refrain that Brun and Marchand had identified, that the frenetic action was broken by too many stops, something that they "criticize[d] in European rugby." He argued that there were two camps in the stands, those who were conquered by the spectacle, and the skeptics. The former, whom he dubbed the "thrill seekers," were taken by the "passion and the violence" displayed on the field. However, in his opinion the latter camp was the largest and made up of those in the "press bleachers, along with conservatives who were critical of the childish nature of the game."[39] Given the importance that historians such as Michael Oriard have assigned to the weekly and daily press in helping grow the sport in the United States, this skepticism on the part of the press boded poorly for football's ability to catch on in France.[40]

Herman Gregoire, another writer, called the game "barbaric" and deplored the constant pauses, but argued that the careful planning for surprise, designed during the stoppages, gave the game a "superior aesthetic" that resulted from "flashes of genius." "Over there in America," according to Gregoire, "strength, accuracy, and technique are harnessed in the service of these concerted tactics." However, this careful planning robbed the players of "the personality and flexibility that [the French] ask for as part of the team spirit." That said, he went on to declare, "At first sight, I readily conclude that union rugby is a game of high civilization and football a barbaric game." He explained his statement by arguing that rugby's flash of genius was to simplify a complex game, and that the spirit of all the rules could be reduced to a single rule: "'the offside,' [which prohibits, among other things, the forward pass]. Football, on the other hand, allows the forward pass and lets players obstruct [hit] their opponents, even when they did not have the ball." Gregoire argued that, unlike the simplicity of rugby, these differences obliged Americans to create a "bunch of complicated and particular rules." While his logic that rules equal barbarism seems counterintuitive, he reaffirmed his point: "While stressing that this is a somewhat precipitate judgment, I say rugby américain is a barbaric game."[41]

Even Gaston Benac, a writer for *Paris Soir*, was disappointed in the game that featured "a few seconds of play, followed by minutes of interruption," and found the spectacle "chopped with halts and conferences." He also thought that the game was "quite complicated and quite subtle," even if its principles were simple. Benac had previously seen games in the United States and complained that the atmosphere of a college game there was absent in Paris. There were no bands, and thousands of students were not chanting the names of their schools, but he conceded that one couldn't have everything.[42]

A more positive view of the game was provided by *Le Petit Journal*, which ran a fairly short but laudatory article offering its view of the spectacle. According to its author, Jean Roux,

> Thirty thousand spectators had come to learn about its bitter contact, its multiple combinations [plays], and the special beauty as it unfurled. Fully informed by the explanations provided by the public announcer, the Parisian public turned from displaying a polite indifference to exhibiting more interest, and finally they unleashed, at certain times, an ambiance that matched the atmosphere of the United States: if they were only a few thousand, it must be recognized that the Americans cheering in the stands far outweighed their numerical inferiority by the ardor with which they hooted. It didn't matter that the [All-Stars] won. What matters is that in the two-hour match we could witness a demonstration of a very large number of combinations and amazing individual feats. These players are magicians such that not only the adversaries but [also] the public often wondered where the ball was; four or five men gave the impression of carrying it in their arms, running at full speed in opposite directions. The feints did not exceed the powerful kicking or the violence with which bodyguards [blockers] hustled everyone coming to attack the ballcarrier.[43]

In the article Roux did not consider the future of the game in France but simply celebrated the moment. And he argued that the majority of the crowd had done the same.

In addition to questions of whether football could succeed in France, some reporters also questioned the organization of the game and the tour. The *New York Times* article concerning the departure mentioned that Riess had intended the American athletes to play a picked team of rugby players, which might have increased the excitement of the French crowds.[44] Reportedly due to the inability of training enough players in the new sport, that plan never materialized and presaged some of the organizational difficulties that Riess and *Paris Soir* would have.

Le Figaro's account of the game complained that "the organizers failed, completely." It told readers, "The bottlenecks at the entries well before the start time of the game, the lack of police personnel and control in the stands have made this day one of the most disastrous in matters of sport organization." It rhetorically asked if the organizers "were surprised by the success of the exhibition."[45] The *New York Times* also mentioned the confusion at the gate in the subheadline of its December 11 article on the Paris game: "Traces of Many Sports Seen as Exhibition by Crowley's Teams Catches Fancy of 25,000 in Rain—2,000 Crash Gate."[46]

The lack of any agreement on the number of fans present, with each paper having a different number ranging from the twenty thousand reported by *L'Humanité* to the thirty thousand cited in *Le Petit Journal* gave some credence to complaints of a lack of organization. Whether the fans had to pay to get into the game was not specified, and if admission was free, there was likely no interest in keeping an accurate head count. Therefore, the general rule that supporters of an event estimate much larger crowds than opponents was allowed to operate.

Although the newspapers were unanimous in their appreciation for the speed and athleticism exhibited by the players, another critique that *Le Figaro* leveled against the tour was that the games were mere exhibitions and that there was no importance attached to any of them. Despite *Le Petit Journal*'s reports of enthusiasm growing during the game, *Le Figaro* blamed the lack of any stake for the failure to hold the interest of the fans and the lack of the ambiance that could be found in America. It also argued that various stoppages meant that in the ninety-minute game, there were perhaps ten minutes of action, which made it difficult for fans to become engaged in the game.[47]

Crowley himself referenced this factor when he told Robert Kelley of the *New York Times* upon his return, after a side vacation in Ireland, that he enjoyed the pressure-free environment of the tour: "It was great fun coaching, and I think playing, because the pressure was all off. They were good football players and the tackling and blocking were excellent. The backs were good too, but we tried things that would turn a coaches' hair gray if they were attempted in an American football game." He also laconically referenced some of the more prosaic problems, including rain in Paris, then snow and cold in Marseilles, that dogged the tour when he told Kelley, "I must admit we saw plenty of weather."[48]

After the extensive coverage of the first game in the capital, the following games in the *périphérie* drew fewer reports and fewer fans. The second game at Lyon scarcely received mention in the Paris papers, save for brief mentions in *Paris Soir, L'Humanité,* and *Le Petit Journal.* The *New York Times,* with reports from the AP, continued to publish news of the tour and reported that a crowd of six thousand fans saw the game. Reports of crowd reaction, which the New York paper had described as "catching the fancy" of the French in Paris, were now less enthusiastic. In reporting the outcome of the high-scoring game, in which New York beat the All-Stars by a score of 38–26, the AP stated, that "[despite] a barrage of razzle-dazzle plays today and many touchdowns . . . no one apparently cared—least of all the 6,000 amused French spectators."[49]

Paris Soir, although its article was more detailed, also mentioned that the crowd had no idea of what was transpiring on the field. "We looked in vain for the ballcarrier," the author reported. He also mentioned that the spectators would cheer at the end of the play without understanding what had happened, but noted, "Visibly, the tricks of this new game continued to amuse." The article also contained reaction from two spectators. M. Bergeret told the reporter that it was "truly unique." It seemed to be a chess match, but with a "solid physical quality." M. Bizet, on the other hand, was uncertain that French athletes could become accustomed to the huddles, where he felt the players were "talking shop."[50]

Le Petit Journal once again placed a more favorable spin on the game, reporting that "the two American university teams were happily introduced before some ten thousand spectators in the legendarily cold and difficult city. Many rounds of applause were given by spectators who did not understand any of the subtleties of the game, but who guessed at the possibilities it presented. To have found favor with the critics in the city of silk can be considered a real success."[51]

While coverage of the tour outside the métropole was scant, some newspapers did hold forth on the idea of transplanting the sport to France. Flushed with the success of the tour after the games in Paris and Lyon, Riess put the ball in play by reporting, "French athletes, this sport that is new to you, is not going to die after the Americans depart. You will go to the matches, some French players will play the most popular sport in the U.S.A., and better yet, we are going to create a league in France."[52]

He told readers, "There is only one conclusion to be drawn," and quoted an anonymous source who agreed. This "personality" was presumably Jean Galia, since Riess declared that his informer was a person that "would be recognized by all French sportsmen," and Crowley later reported that the rugby leader had plans to create teams. Riess's unnamed subject informed the German expatriate, "I have decided to create some American rugby clubs in France. After the players leave, I am going to tackle this project." He continued laying out his plans to find coaches from America or France and recruiting players in all the large cities. The plan was to form clubs and immediately create a league under whose auspices they would play. There was also mention that a French team might "traverse the Atlantic" for a game against an American team.[53]

This was a bold plan, and the top-down approach would also motivate later dreamers such as the French rugby club director Marcel Leclerc and the Yugoslavian American promoter Bob Kap, who would direct later tours that are discussed in the following chapters. It was a plan for an ambitious undertaking, and it was also perhaps premature. Galia, or whoever was behind it, might even have made the scheme work, had it not been for the outbreak of World War II. Whether he could have succeeded, absent other, more-pressing events, was still doubtful given the consternation and resistance that this announcement caused among Riess's fellow journalists.

Perhaps Riess's unnamed source was someone other than Galia, since shortly after the first game *Le Petit Journal* contained a story about Galia's intentions for promoting the new sport. The author of the article reported:

> [The rugby star,] who seems to ignore rugby union, intended, he told us, to implant the American football that fans in Paris and Lyon had seen demonstrations of, and that spectators in Marseilles, Narbonne, and Bordeaux would later see. We speak of the development of teams formed by French rugbymen currently playing and former American football players, and there are more than you think in France. We also

say that a French-American football league will be formed. Finally, as a bouquet, it seems that the Americans have already invited a team to come to the U.S. to play beyond the big pond. At least we are not going too fast.[54]

The sarcastic final line to the article suggests some skepticism that perhaps matters were progressing too fast or about the actual possibility of forming French football teams or leagues. Despite *Le Petit Journal*'s generally favorable reportage, the day after its story about teams and league formation, it ran an interview with Etienne Roland, the center of the French National Basketball Team, who argued that "basketball is a complete sport that the entire world can practice," as opposed to football, which required veritable Frankenstein monsters.[55] Though Roland did not mention football in his interview, the proximity of the stories in successive issues of the paper, which certainly may have been coincidental, nevertheless sent a message to readers that if Frenchmen were looking for a new sport, they might consider one that was healthful like basketball rather than the hyperviolent football.

Other papers such as *Le Petit Parisien* likewise were not in favor of the idea. Georges Briquet, in his Radio Reporter's Corner column, asked, "What are we going to do with this sport, in France, where we already have rugby fifteen and thirteen, and cycling? Furthermore, as radio reporter, I feel that few listeners would smile when listening to a broadcast of one of those games where there is no more than five minutes of actual play in a period that lasts a quarter of an hour. So without being asked my opinion, I give it: I condemn it, but . . . it can appeal."[56]

As in *Le Petit Journal*, Galia also was criticized by *Le Petit Parisien*. In an article by Jean Monest on the trials and tribulation of rugby in Bordeaux that was "at the crossroads," the man who wanted to create a football league in France was condemned for neglecting his previous creation. Part of the problem with French rugby, according to Monest, was the leadership of Galia and his lack of focus on rugby. Monest suggested that football was perhaps a threat to the established sport: "It is true that much time has been occupied lately by the football tour. And it is said that even the landing [of the Americans] would be an expression of resentment from certain members of the League who, without much to see in the new rugby football competitor tomorrow, are slightly annoyed at Galia's overflowing activity . . . and are very confused. Because, finally, there may be a threat from the new game that is so exciting."[57]

Alone among those reporting on the tour, Monest actually included some historical background that acknowledged this tour was not the first time football had been played in France. He also admitted that there was some enthusiasm building for the last game of the tour that would be played in Bordeaux.

> And what about the American rugby, the Bordelais, great lovers of the oval ball, were quite eager to know the impressions of those of us who had seen Saturday's match in Paris. Most rushed to *Le Petit Parisien* and are now waiting impatiently for Christmas day, when the last match of the tour will be played at home. But the old have already seen American rugby in Bordeaux, a great game itself, not to be laughed at: the famous U.S. Army-Navy game in 1918. . . . And I hope our correspondent from Bordeaux, Mr. Horsiangou, will soon tell us about his amusing personal memories on this subject.[58]

Other papers saw also the new game as a threat to the established order. *Le Figaro* worried that the Americans might have plans to transform French sports. It used the rumor that there were plans to establish a French professional football league, form teams, and send one to the United States to deplore the state of rugby in France. Under the headline "When the Boat Sinks," the author blamed the establishment of professional rugby in France for the possibility that the foreign sport might add yet another professional sport to the country that was engaged in a spirited debate over amateurism and professionalism when the tour arrived. *Le Figaro* lamented that if amateur rugby had held fast to the "sportsmanship of its birth and development, the mere announcement of a professional football league would raise unanimous laughter."[59] With the door already open to professionalism, *Le Figaro* apparently feared that this wild idea might become reality.

The concern over professionalism that roiled the rugby world in

1938 would also cause ripples of concern among the first Frenchmen to play football in their country. In chapter 8 we will see that, unlike rugby in the 1930s, the forces of amateurism would prevail in their 1995 struggle to keep the sportsmanship of football's founding alive. They would win, but it would perhaps be a Pyrrhic victory that consigned football to a minor role in the pantheon of French sports. But that is a story for another chapter.

The third game at Narbonne once again was hyped by *Le Petit Journal*, which reported, "In front of many of the public, who had invaded all the corners of the stadium, the New York team defeated the All-Stars by a score of 34 to 33."[60] Strangely, despite its otherwise blanket coverage of the tour, this game was one that the AP missed. The remainder of the French press, including *Paris Soir*, also failed to report on the match, so accurate numbers are not available.

The AP's coverage picked up again with the fourth game at Marseille, played before "a crowd of 15,000 puzzled but enthusiastic Frenchmen and sailors from United States ships in the harbor." This game, which received no mention in the French press surveyed, and a scant four paragraphs from the AP, was perhaps the key game of the tour from the perspective of spreading the game. The subheadline of the AP report declared "Rugby Players on Losing Side in 32–20 Game at Marseille." The article briefly reported that "Jimmy Crowley's all-star American football team beat a selected eleven of French rugby players and former United State stars 32–20 today."[61]

Christian Joosten, who, along with Denis Crawford, published an article on the tour for the *Coffin Corner*, theorized that rumors of rugby players being included were "probably legends."[62] However, in the *New York Times* article reporting on Crowley's return, the coach mentioned "Jean Galia, who [was] an outstanding rugby player in France and who was a prime mover in bringing the players to France."[63] The presence of Galia, one of the leaders in bringing rugby league (the thirteen-player version, as opposed to the fifteen-player rugby union) to France, and who stated his intention of implanting football there, indicated that perhaps the rugby players were more than mere legends, but this evidence is in itself inconclusive.[64]

Had Riess and Galia managed to find some rugby players to

try their hand at the new sport, perhaps they could have garnered more-positive press and laid the foundation for the establishment of the sport in France. Whether this was only a rumor or merely sloppy reporting, the lack of French players would bedevil efforts to establish the game there. Only after the French themselves began to participate in the game would the sport be successfully transplanted.

That would not occur until nearly another half century had passed, however. By the time the teams reached Marseille, even *Paris Soir* had seemingly grown bored with the tour. The paper's December 19 article mentioned that the New York team had defeated the All-Stars but declined to even mention the score. Instead it reported that southerners hadn't met the spectacle with any enthusiasm. The weather was cold and rainy, which no doubt dampened spirits, but the article focused on soccer and rugby players who complained that the American game had "too little action." One went so far as to lament, "What a shame that these beautiful athletes practice such a game. In fifteen-player or thirteen-player rugby they would be splendid."[65] This would be the last report in the paper on the tour that it sponsored, and it would be left to the AP, as published in the *New York Times*, to nail down the coffin on the tour.

The tour continued despite inclement weather, which was the subject of front-page headlines in the French press. Even Toulouse, where the teams played their fifth game, although located in the deep south of France, had snow that year. The AP reported that "five thousand shivering Frenchmen took time from their Christmas preparation to watch two teams of Americans demonstrate their game of football today. Although the field was snow-covered, the players used all the wide-open tactics of the previous games in a tour of France and the 'All Stars' won 26 to 19 over the 'New Yorkers.'"[66]

The final game in the tour was played on Christmas Day before six thousand spectators, who watched the All-Star team defeat the New York team 37–34 in Bordeaux. The AP writer labeled those fans "bewildered" and reported that the twenty-four players would leave the next day for Paris and would return to New York from there.[67] If the AP correspondent was to be believed, the enthusiasm that Monest saw in Bordeaux would fizzle into bewilderment when the rugby fans there finally had the chance to see the actual game.

AP coverage of the tour followed the narrative set by the *New York Times* before the teams left for France. Labeling the French fans "bewildered," "confused," "amused," and in general unimpressed by the games indicated that the reporter saw no future for the successful transplant of football in France. Perhaps the unknown scribe was French or had "gone native," but whatever the reason for the flippant tone of the reporting, it also turned out to be accurate.

With prominent newspapers declaring the game slow, boring, incomprehensible, too violent, or even worse, a threat to the established order, the prospect for transplanting football in the hostile soil was dismal. Viewing football mostly as a sideshow to amuse the crowds, the sporting fraternity in France, for the most part, seemed to be circling their wagons to reject the interlopers and keep their supposed professionalism out of France. Nor did fan reaction, described as confused, perplexed, or amused, bode well for creating a groundswell of popular support.

There were, however, some who thought that it could be accomplished, though bad timing would prevent their plans from succeeding. *Le Petit Parisien* told readers on December 20 that interest in the novel game was spilling over the French borders and that the Italians were interested in seeing a football game or two. Crowley and his team had been invited to play "one or two exhibitions in Milan and Turin." The coach thought that the "a visit to [Italy] would not displease the boys," but no definite financing had been settled on, and there was also the matter of finding time.[68] No further mention of an Italian detour appeared, so the plans must have come to nothing. But the mere possibility that other nations were interested in their sport must have been pleasing to Crowley and his players. That may account for some of the cautious optimism that the coach expressed on the subject of spreading football to France upon returning to the States.

Crowley echoed *Le Petit Journal* in the interview with the *New York Times* upon his return, saying that Galia was "considering the idea of taking an American coach to France early next Fall to teach a team of Frenchmen who might then repay the visit with a tour of this country." Adding credence to the idea that the inclusion of rugby players at Marseilles was a myth, the coach made no mention of their participation when he expressed disappointment that the original plan to have his players compete against French teams had been abandoned because "the French had not learned enough of the game." He went on to say that there were no plans to repeat the tour in 1939, adding, however, "The French liked it though, and I don't think it is not too far from possible that the game might be made to go over in that country."[69]

Perhaps *Le Petit Parisien*'s humorous photo of the large players trying to fit into the same bed may not have been too far from the truth, and the author asked Crowley about reports some of the returning players had given that "traveling and living conditions were not too good over there." The coach diplomatically had no comment on that but agreed that it was "great to be home." The food must have been good (*bien sur*), for he reported, "I am a little overweight."[70]

The aforementioned bad timing would make moot the question of whether football teams could be formed in France. Galia's plan to bring an American coach to the country "early next fall" would have meant that the chosen coach would likely have arrived in September 1939. By then the French, along with the rest of Europe, would have other, more-pressing matters on their minds.

The first football tour in 1938 generated some buzz but also encountered resistance from entrenched sporting forces determined to maintain the status quo. What might have happened, absent the global conflict that once again gripped Europe and the world, would have been interesting to see. But in all probability it would not have produced much French enthusiasm. With most of the press aligned against adding a new sport, or viewing it as nothing more than a sideshow amusement, the resistance of soccer and rugby officials would still have seen football facing a heavily stacked deck. A veritable Maginot Line of resistance had already formed after the first game and would likely have been more effective at keeping out our young Frankensteins than the actual line was at keeping out the Wehrmacht.

However, missionaries seldom allow minor setbacks to deter them from spreading their message. After the war new players, coaches, and promoters would renew attempts to convince the recalcitrant French that football was the game they needed. As was the case in World War I, the military would once again take the lead in trying to spread the American way of sport across the Atlantic.

Before that could take place, however, the French would have to endure the second half of the two world wars (1914–1945). On September 3, 1939, following the German invasion of Poland, France declared war on Germany, and the Second World War began.

During that conflict Americans would once again carry their footballs along with their rifles and machine guns as they invaded, fought over, and occupied French territory between 1942 and 1946. From North Africa to Paris, the military would stage a number of military "bowl games" during those years, and once actual combat had ended in the various areas of France, Americans would be busy forming leagues and playing their games across the nation.[71]

All these games, whether run-of-the-mill matches or extravaganzas, would ultimately have the same effect as all the games played in World War I, and the 1938 tour—few potential French athletes or fans would see the games, and they would create no groundswell of enthusiasm for the sport.

3. Football and the Crusade in Europe, 1943-1946

The first football game in France took place during the cruise of the Great White Fleet in 1909 and then continued during the Great War. Nearly two decades passed without any games, until the Riess-Crowley tour, which held some promise, even if wildly overstated, of creating French interest in the game. Any momentum that effort might have created was rendered moot, however, when Nazi Germany invaded Poland less than a year after the final game of the tour. When Americans became involved in the war, the gridiron game reappeared in France and its colonies as American soldiers once again crossed the Atlantic to fight on French soil.

This time, rather than depending on organizations such as the YMCA, the army tasked the Special Services Branch, its own organization, with providing athletic programs to keep the troops fit and entertained. Special Services would take over planning athletic competitions during the conflict, with a mission that was similar to that directed by the private charity organizations in World War I: keeping military personnel fit, entertained, and out of trouble. According to their manual, merely providing equipment would encourage soldiers to "engage in impromptu play and boredom [would] quickly follow."[1] Special Services officers were therefore directed to properly organize athletic events that focused on "universal participation and recreational sports and games."[2]

Despite concerns about avoiding overemphasis on catering to the athletically gifted, the football culture that sprang up on French soil provided numerous opportunities for the "first teams"

FIG. 7. American GIs using a jeep for a blocking sled during World War II. Capt. C. R. Goodwin, special projects officer of the Sixty-Sixth Division at Camp Joseph T. Robinson, Arkansas, is getting a "ride" while directing the training of a gridiron team that is part of the camp's athletic program. November 1943. National Archives and Record Administration 111-SC-180825.

to demonstrate their prowess. While combat was at it hottest on the Continent, games typically took the form of large spectacles, along the lines of American bowl games, which were designed to serve as diversions for as many men as possible. Therefore, the games that took place in France until the fighting moved further east were somewhat sporadic, and in one case, a scheduled Champagne Bowl had to be canceled due to the Germans' last-gasp Ardennes Offensive.[3]

By this time football was well established in the United States and in its armed forces. At training centers such as the Great Lakes Naval Training Center, sailors were required to play football in the belief that the sport would toughen them physically and mentally. Games would also be played wherever GIs found themselves, in all theaters of the war.[4] As soon as the fighting moved a safe distance away, leagues began to spring up to keep soldiers occupied during their off-duty hours.

The first of these military bowl games on French soil was the Arab Bowl, which pitted the army against the navy in Oran, Algeria, and saw Army win 10–7 before a crowd of 15,000 to 25,000 service personnel. Perhaps exceeding the scope of his duties as outlined in the field manuals, Cpl. Zeke Bonura, formerly of the Chicago White Sox, interpreted his responsibilities to include creating massive spectator events such as the New Year's Day game that featured as much of the spectacle of stateside bowl games as Bonura could arrange. To provide that spectacle, the former first baseman scheduled a guard of honor made up of Arabs in multicolored robes, a contest to choose the Arab Bowl queen, camel and burro races, as well as an exhibition of cowboy work by GIs using borrowed horses. Adding celebrity power, Hollywood star Rosalind Russell was named the honorary queen of the bowl. The contest between five women from the Women's Auxiliary Corps (WAC) and the Red Cross ended in a tie with Miss Army, Miss Navy, Miss Oran, Miss Casablanca, and Miss Stars and Stripes all sharing the honors. Halftime and between-game entertainment included WACs performing a drill and review exhibition, and music provided by the Mediterranean Base Section Army Band. Channeling his baseball background, Bonura described the event as "the first double-header football bowl game ever played." He could not do everything, however, and despite providing a taste of home for thousands of military personnel, along with a VIP box for generals and French and Arab officials, he could not scrounge actual uniforms. Not surprising, given that the initial Allied landings had taken place fewer than two months previously, and their strategic position was still extremely fluid.[5]

The teams provided a good show, despite the lack of equipment. In the opening game the Casablanca Rabchasers defeated the Oran Termites 7–6, with the winning point contributed by Sergeant John McDonald, who had played for Arkansas State Teachers' College (now the University of Central Arkansas). The second game saw Johnny DeMello, a Californian, kick the winning field goal with ten seconds left in the game to give Army the 10–7 victory.[6]

Despite the presence of a few French officials and possibly some of the local French population, the games were scheduled to entertain the troops, not to entice the indigenous population to take up the sport. However, after a five-year absence, football had finally returned to

French soil. Algeria would gain independence in 1962, but in 1943 the French considered the colony as much a part of France as Marseille.

Bowl-game extravaganzas such as the Arab Bowl would continue as American forces continued to push the Axis back toward Germany. The Ninth Air Force Thunderbolts and the First General Hospital Terrors finally brought football back to Paris on November 19, 1944, when they met in the Parc des Princes Bowl, a match named after its location. The air force team defeated the medics by a score of 6–0. The game, which drew an estimated crowd of twelve thousand, included a number of locals. *Stars and Stripes* reported that "approximately half" the crowd consisted of civilians. Perhaps some of those civilians had also witnessed a game in 1938, but it is impossible to tell from the sources available.[7]

In addition to the games given the "bowl" label, soldiers and sailors played other games with less fanfare. Following the Arab Bowl, Bonura moved on to Italy and then France, but football continued in Algeria.[8] On October 26, 1944, *Stars and Stripes* reported on games being played in the navy league there that included ten teams. The Navy Hospital Medics topped the league to that point, having won all three of their games so far. An outsider would have had difficulty deciphering some of the arcane names for the teams, such as the "N.S.D. collection" and the "513 CBMU," both of which lost on that day. The Port Pirates and the Dispensary Pharmacists might have been easier to discern, but despite names that confused the nonmilitary reader, football continued to entertain the troops and possibly some of the locals.[9]

With the fighting in Normandy finished, it did not take long for combat on the gridiron to replace combat in the *bocage*. *Stars and Stripes* put it in those terms, informing readers, "They're still mousetrapping the 'enemy' in Normandy, punching holes in the lines and daring him to come out in the open. The battles, however, are good-natured though rough; they're the weekly schedule of eight games in the Normandy Football League." The league, created by Lt. Sal Commisa, a former guard at Notre Dame, consisted of two eight-team conferences that "provide entertainment for thousands of G.I. fans and 500 players each week." Interest was high and plans ambitious. The winner of the league, which would be crowned at Cherbourg Stadium on New Year's Day, had been challenged by the Eighth Air Force "All Stars," who reportedly would fly in from England for the game. So the Germans' December offensive through the Ardennes canceled at least two games.[10]

In addition to turkey, Thanksgiving Day has traditionally been a day for football games, and the drive on Germany would not change that for soldiers and sailors in France. The 1944 schedule for the Delta Base Section in southern France included three games: two touch football games and a soccer game played between French teams. Organized by DBS Special Services, one gridiron game would pit the Army Engineers against the Prisoner of War Administration Company, followed by the soccer match, and then the day would wrap up with a game between the Delta Base team representing the army and a navy team. All games were played at the Stade Véledrome in Marseille, and the DBS Military Band provided touches of the spectacle surrounding the games that servicemen and servicewomen expected of such events. In the first game the Engineers and POW Company played to a scoreless tie, while the DBS team defeated the navy team by a score of 13–6. There was no report on crowd size or makeup, but presumably some French fans witnessed parts of the game surrounding the soccer match.[11]

Games were also played in the capital during the week around Thanksgiving. On the Sunday after, the Advanced Air Depot Area (AADA) Thunderbolts played the Engineer Raiders at the Stade de la Ligue Parisienne d'Athletisme. Both teams had played previously; the Thunderbolts had defeated the Ninth AF Headquarters (HQ) team a week before the scheduled match, and the Raiders had previously defeated the Engineers Maroon team on Thanksgiving Day.[12]

The matches continued into December, with games being played wherever American troops had penetrated. The Port Officers trounced Navy 31–0, and the Port Battalion defeated Port HQ 7–0 at Marseille.[13] In the Paris area a game between the Thunderbolts and the Fourth Service Group Blue Devils took place at Vincennes, with the AADA team winning its fourth straight by a score of 13–2. The Supreme Headquarters Allied Expeditionary Force (SHAEF) team defeated the Raiders 7–0 at Colombes, and the Ninth AF HQ team defeated the First General Hospital 13–0 at Chantilly.[14]

Christmas Day saw a battle of undefeated teams when the Thunderbolts and SHAEF played at the Parc des Princes, with proceeds from the gate going to the French Welfare Organization.[15] Meanwhile, in the south a game pitting the port officers against their enlisted counterparts topped the day's schedule, followed by a match between the 379th and the Tween Deckers. The southerners had not yet received equipment, so their games were still touch football. Festivities in Marseille included a parade that with military bands.[16]

Games in rear areas during fighting were nothing new. They had taken place in both world wars. What is somewhat surprising is that the games continued during such a critical time. In mid-December the Germans launched their attack through the Ardennes that would be known popularly as the Battle of the Bulge. Allied forces were fighting for their lives, and the American forces in the Belgian town of Bastogne were still surrounded on Christmas Day when several games took place. The scheduled Champagne Bowl between the Screaming Eagles of the 101st Division and the Skytrain team made up of the men who flew the paratroopers and maintained the C47s that carried them was called off. The same held for the challenge match that would have taken place in Britain between the winners of the Normandy Football League and the Eighth Air Force All-Stars. The 101st had been ordered to Bastogne, and American forces needed all their planes to drop supplies or attack German columns. That the AADA Thunderbolts were free is puzzling, if their name referred to units employing the fighter planes of the same name.

As an aside the same edition of *Stars and Stripes* that carried news of the games in Marseille also contained a story that indicated one reason why the effort to plant football in France that began in 1938 would not have legs. Jim Crowley, who had led the All-Star teams that visited France that year, was reported as focused on leading the All-American Football Conference, a new professional league that would challenge the National Football League after the war. The article mentioned Crowley's background as one of the Four Horsemen of Notre Dame and also his tenure at Fordham, but was silent on his experience as a football missionary. With Crowley occupied in new ventures, Jean Galia focused on resurrecting professional rugby in France after it had been banned by the Vichy government, and Curt Riess busy writing books about the Nazis, none of the leaders of the prewar tour were available to follow up on any momentum they had created in 1938.[17]

As the Allies regained momentum and began forcing the Germans to retreat, the New Year would see the resumption of military bowl games, with France hosting three games. A game between the Raiders and the Quartermaster Wildcats, set to be played in Stade Jean Bouin in Paris, was canceled on New Year's Eve.[18] Before the games *Stars and Stripes* estimated that four hundred thousand Americans would see bowl games in early January. That number included an estimate that one hundred thousand of those would be spectators at one of the games held in the European theater, which included the games in France and the Spaghetti Bowl in Italy.[19]

On January 1, 1945, two of the games, the Riviera Bowl in Marseille and the Mustard Bowl in Dijon, were played in front of a combined twenty thousand spectators. The Mud Bowl, scheduled to determine the championship of the Normandy Base Football League at Cherbourg, had to be postponed for a week, perhaps because of the necessity of keeping pressure on the retreating Germans.

At the Riviera Bowl crowd size did not meet the expected thirty thousand, despite the enticement, for French fans, of a rugby match between the Olympique de Marseille and an all-star team from the surrounding province. Military bands once again sought to provide the spectacle associated with bowl games, leading a parade through the streets of Marseille and performing precision marching at halftime.[20] The game itself was a runaway with the Railway Shop Battalion Railroaders defeated the Army All-Stars by a score of 37–0.[21]

At Dijon two thousand "GI's and civilians" watched another doubleheader bowl game. In the first match, the Army All-Stars defeated the Air Corps All-Stars by a score of 6–0. The Ordinance Grays followed by beating the Hospital Hypos 9–2. The article does not provide additional detail concerning the game, but one could wonder once again if any of the civilians present had been to the 1938 game.[22]

In both games "civilians," presumably locals, either were expected to attend or were reported to have attended. How many actually were there and what they thought of the American game was not reported.

The indigenous spectators present in Marseille were likely anxious for the Americans to finish so that they could enjoy the rugby matches that followed. The small crowd in Dijon was likely made up primarily of GIs, and any Frenchmen who attended might have been French civic officials who felt compelled to do so out of civic pride or the merely curious.

In the Mud Bowl, held at Cherbourg on January 5, the Mudcloggers, champions of the National Division, met the Peacemakers of the American Division for the championship of the Normandy Base Football League. In an evenly matched game, before an estimated five thousand fans, the Mudcloggers won by a score of 7–6. The prevalence of mud nomenclature provides a picture into what the GIs thought of the Normandy countryside, and they must have seen some of the weather that Crowley had mentioned.[23]

Another championship game was also held at Cherbourg on the fifth, but this one had received considerably less fanfare and was not given the title of a bowl game. The American military in World War II was strictly segregated, and the contest for the Port football championship (noncapitalization reflects the original) was contested by two "Negro teams." The Stevedores defeated the Mudslingers by a score of 2–0, with the only points coming when a Mudslinger was tackled in the end zone trying to run back the second-half kickoff.[24]

Even though the military and the Port championship game were segregated, there was some evidence that integrated games were played in the European Theater of Operations (ETO). In July 1945 the Stevedores contended for the Arles Staging Area Baseball Championship but lost 5–4 in eleven innings to the Engineers, a team that included a former Cincinnati Reds pitcher. Major League Baseball was segregated until Jackie Robinson joined the Brooklyn Dodgers in 1947, so this game was demonstrably integrated.

Even though *Stars and Stripes* carried stories leading up to the Spaghetti Bowl, which was to be held in Italy, it remained silent on the game itself. The *Daily Worker*, the official newspaper of the U.S. Communist Party, did carry the story, and it reported that the game was contested between the Fifth Army Doughboys and the Twelfth Air Force Blockbusters. In the game, which the Fifth Army won 20–0, the star was John Moody, whom the paper identified as a "former Negro All-American at Morris Brown College." Moody scored two touchdowns and "generally roamed the field at will." How he came to play for the otherwise, presumably, white Fifth Army team is unclear, but the Communist paper also mentioned that the twenty thousand in attendance cheered him on, signaling, not very subtly, that America was ready for integration, which was a particular point of emphasis for the paper.[25]

Full integration of the military would not occur until President Harry S. Truman issued an executive order in 1948, but the first signs of that process were evident in the initial steps taken by the European theater (ET) sports authorities, who allowed the integrated games to continue. The inclusion of African American players or teams in matches with or against all-white units might have been due to the actions of individual Special Services officers, but it at least required the acquiescence of those at higher command levels. As we shall see later, during the Cold War deployment to France, integrated teams were the rule, and by the 1950s the military had apparently made peace with the changes, well ahead of the rest of American society.

The January 6 edition of *Stars and Stripes* also reported that the game scheduled for Paris on New Year's Day and then canceled for "reasons of security" had been rescheduled. Now dubbed the Champagne Bowl, the game was scheduled to pit the Thunderbolts against the SHAEF Invaders at the Parc des Princes stadium.[26] The Champagne Bowl designation was originally set to be the match between the 101st Airborne and the Skytrain, but it had been called off because of the German offensive. The name continued to carry bad luck, however, and the game was called off once again on January 8 because of "the unplayable condition of the field."[27] The game finally took place on January 15, with a "slim crowd" and an ice-covered field. The Invaders managed only a safety to defeat the Mudcloggers 2–0. By the time the game was finally played, there was no mention of it being the Champagne or any other kind of bowl game.[28]

Though their win over the Mudcloggers was less than decisive, the Invaders still enjoyed an undefeated record, so they were scheduled for a final game to determine the best team in France. SHAEF's opponents were the likewise undefeated Thunderbolts, and after also having two games canceled for "security reasons," they finally met on January 21 to bring the football season to a close.[29] After four scoreless quarters the evenly matched, undefeated teams decided to play a "fifth quarter" for the championship. The Thunderbolt's Dick Tewksbury, formerly a fullback at Purdue, intercepted a pass and ran it back to the SHAEF 3-yard line, where a halfback pass from Jim Anderson to quarterback Rudy Petrina won the game for the Ninth AF. The game was the first overtime game ever in the European Command (EC) and was watched by some twelve thousand spectators at the Parc des Princes.[30]

Germany formally surrendered on May 8, 1945, and three days later the ETO announced what *Stars and Stripes* hailed as "the most ambitious athletic program in world history." As part of the plan, tournaments were to be held in "virtually every popular American sport" starting at the company level and progressing through the base section, theater, and inter-allied levels. The plan was temporarily put on hold until the German surrender since Supreme Allied Commander Dwight D. Eisenhower had ordered that no theater championships be held "while combat troops were unable to participate." The program was directed by Lt. Col. Frank G. McCormick, former athletic director of the University of Minnesota. Both touch and tackle football would be a part of the program, and sports would be used to keep soldiers in shape for occupation duty or while awaiting transfer to the Pacific Theater of Operations (PTO). Tons of equipment had been amassed, including sixty-seven thousand footballs and eighteen thousand football uniforms. Despite McCormick's concern that the program be accessible to all, he realized that theater championships would garner the most interest. His subordinates were securing venues for those games and to host visiting professional teams that "could accommodate more than 50,000 spectators." Included among the facilities considered was a spacious stadium near Nuremberg, previously used in the Nazi Party rallies in the 1930s, which would likely be the site of theater championship events. Though much of the attention focused on sites for the occupation of Germany, American troops and their football, would remain in France through the 1946 season.[31]

True to the plan, according to War Department statistics, by November 1945 there were 14,400 EC soldiers playing touch football on 1,200 teams, with 1,500 spectators. A further 5,600 played tackle football on 190 teams. The rougher variety of the sport was the more popular, with some 379,000 spectators watching games in the command.[32]

In France more than thirty teams played in three leagues. The largest league was the Oise Intermediate Section Football League (OISFL), which was made up of fourteen teams playing in two divisions located at bases in northeastern France. For the most part the team names, except for the Camp Washington Redskins, are lost to history, but teams represented various depots and specialized units such as the engineers, quartermaster, ordnance, and hospital units. The teams played a forty-eight-game league schedule, with other exhibitions against opponents from the other loops. At the end of the regular season, the division winners would meet to determine the league champion. Games were held at base locations that included Epernay, Riems, Compèigne, Metz, Langres, and Verdun.[33]

The Seine Section Football League (SSFL), operating in the Paris area, had eight teams, including the Engineer Atomites, the Signal Corps Green Hornets, and the Ordnance Red Devils, along with teams representing the Military Police (MP), Versailles, Villacoublay, the Medics, and the Air Training Command. Most games were played at Stade Buffalo, which had been built on the site of a velodrome named in honor of Buffalo Bill Cody, whose Wild West show had played there in 1889.[34] Some games also returned to the site of one of the first football games in Paris and later the site of the first training grounds for the Spartacus of Paris football team: Pershing Stadium.[35]

Six more teams, including the Seine Section Clowns, the Delta Base Bisons, the Chanor Base Maroon Raiders, the Bremen (Germany) Bears, the Normandy Lions, and the Oise Red Devils, played in the Theater Service Forces Football League (TSFFL). These teams, which were also located in the Paris area, shared space with the SSFL and used Stade Buffalo for their matches.[36]

As in the states, Thanksgiving Day could not pass without games, and teams from French bases helped the military provide a large slice of home to its personnel in 1945. The games also had an international flavor, with the Seine Medics traveling to Burton Wood, England, to take on the Base Air Depot Area (BADA) team, and the Red Raiders taking on the Lions in Brussels. Other games included the military version of intersectional contests as the Clowns played the Third Infantry Division in Paris, the Red Devils took on the Forty-Second Infantry Division in Reims, and Bremen battled the Twenty-Ninth Infantry Division at Marseille.[37]

Other, miscellaneous games were also played on French soil. In a reversal of its 1919 fortunes, the Eighty-Ninth Division lost in a runaway, 33–0, to the Seventy-Fifth Division Mules in a game played at Châlons-en-Champagne in northern France, on September 30.[38] Camp Twenty Grand at Rouen in northwestern France was the scene of a game between the 101st Airborne Division and the Eighty-Ninth Infantry Division. Making up for their canceled Champagne Bowl in 1944, the Screaming Eagles defeated the straight-legged soldiers by a score of 7–0.[39] Le Havre, the port through which many service personnel returned to the United States, also had a game when the 516th Port Battalion of Cherbourg defeated the Le Havre team 13–6 in a non-marquee game on Thanksgiving Day.[40]

At the end of the regular season, the Red Devils, the champions of the TSFFL, defeated the Redskins, who had won the OISFL, 36–9, at Reims. Tempting fate, the game was once again dubbed the Champagne Bowl, and the bad luck associated with that name continued. The game took place on time, but the Redskins were a last-minute replacement for the Devil's original opponent when the Forty-Second Division, based in Austria, couldn't make the game due to weather conditions that made flying hazardous.[41]

Before 7,500 fans at Buffalo Stadium, two French-based teams also contended for the championship of the Theater Service Forces–European Theater (TSFET) league. The Engineer Atomites, 8–1 for the season and winners of the Seine Section met the 761st Field Artillery Maroon Raiders of Chanor Base, which had a 7–2 record and were the champions of the TSFFL. The Maroon Raiders were able to scrape out a 12–6 win by scoring the winning touchdown with only minutes left.[42] Plans for the winner to go to Rome to play a team from the Mediterranean in the second Spaghetti Bowl apparently fell through, since the paper carried no mention that the game took place as scheduled on January 1, 1946.[43]

Following the 1945 regular season, the TSFET league chose an All-Star team, with the Delta Base Section Bisons placing six players on the first and second teams, followed by four apiece for the Seine Section clowns and the Chanor Base Maroon Raiders. *Stars and Stripes* proclaimed the Oise Red Devils the TSFFL champions, so how the Maroon Raiders ended up playing the Atomites for the TSFET championship is unclear. Perhaps there was some controversy with the team, since it also failed to place any players on the All-Star team, but that is merely conjecture. The discrepancy might also have been due to soldiers being rotated home, but no official explanation appeared in the press.[44]

Interest in football championships aside, American troops were impatient to leave France once the war was over. Their feeling was shared by Gen. Charles de Gaulle, who published a farewell and thank-you letter on November 12, 1945, in which he states, "Soldiers of free America! Having accomplished the victory, you are leaving the soil of Europe. . . . We will never forget you. Think of us sometimes." Given de Gaulle's often stormy relationship with the United States, one might conceivably read into this statement that the Free French leader felt that now the Germans were defeated, Americans should leave quickly and let the French get on with their lives. Demobilization went more slowly than either the GIs or de Gaulle hoped however, and the U.S. military would have time for one more football season before all troops had vacated the country.[45]

However slow demobilization seemed to the troops, it was proceeding, spurred on by "mass protests by soldiers urging the War Department to rescind its recent directive ordering a slowdown in demobilization and redeployment."[46] The reduced personnel caused changes in the organization of sporting leagues. In January the Oise Intermediate Section and Seine Sections merged into the Western Base Section (WBS). At the same time, the War Department also announced that the Chanor and Delta sections would be folded into the WBS later in the year.[47]

Demobilization also took away some of the ex-collegiate stars that ET teams had employed in 1945. However, Maj. John D. How, chief of the competitive athletic section, athletic branch, Theater Special

Services, and former teammate of Red Grange at the University of Illinois, reported, "There will still be plenty of keen, good caliber competition." How attempted to ensure that the quality of play would be up to standard by scheduling football clinics across the command.

Originally intended to be a ten-day program provided by the head coaches of Princeton, Tulane, and Pennsylvania, along with sessions by the commissioner of officials from the Southern Conference, difficulties in detaching officers and men from their duties made that too difficult. In place of the central conference, the coaches had to travel from post to post giving individual team sessions.

Competition would take place under the umbrella of the European Theater Football Conference, with the WBS and other subsidiary commands providing the teams. The season was scheduled to start on September 28 and last until December 7. Playoffs were to be held, in case they were needed, to crown champions, and plans included the possibility that postseason games might take place "in large cities outside the American Zone. Regular season games were to take place either at Stade Olympique Yves-du-Manoir at Colombes, a suburb of Paris, or at Orly Airfield."[48]

Postseason games would not decide the champions of the ET, however, as was announced when USFET disbanded the ET Football Conference in September. The move was reportedly due to the difficulties caused by "redeployment of key men and the inequality of strength of the commands."[49] This did not stop intersectional games from taking place, as when the 508th Parachute Infantry Regiment from Frankfurt defeated the WBS Headquarters Command (HQC) 33–12 on September 29.[50]

The scaled-down athletic program did not stop Bill Boni, sports editor for *Stars and Stripes*, from dreaming of the possibility of a theater championship between the top teams in the ET and Mediterranean theater (MT), with the winner traveling to the Zone of the Interior (ZI—the United States) for an ultimate championship game with the best team in the Japanese occupation force. As with the abortive Spaghetti Bowl of 1945, these big plans were never realized, perhaps because men like Zeke Bonura and Sal Commisa were now back home, leaving the ET with a lack of organizational and promotional skill.[51]

The WBS included nine teams, with the Paris Detention Barracks (PDB), the 3113th Signal Service Battalion, and the HQC deployed in Paris. The 55th Quartermaster Base Depot traveled from Rheims. Orly Airfield was home to the European Air Transport Service-Air Transport Command (EATS-ATC). The American Graves Registration Command and the 177th Quartermaster Battalion hailed from Fontainebleau. It is unclear where the 508th Engineers and the Thirteenth Traffic Control Group were stationed.[52]

While the HQC, the EATS-ATC, and the PDB made a run at the championship, in the end no team could keep up with the Fifty-Fifth QM Depot Rams stationed at Rheims. The Rams finished the season with a perfect 7–0 record. Their potent offense scored 330 points, and their impenetrable defense blanked all opponents.[53]

Unlike 1945 there were neither postseason championship games nor any resurrection of the Champagne Bowl. The season ended on Armistice Day, and the Rams' 50–0 victory over the 177th QM Depot would be the last football game on French soil for five years.[54]

General de Gaulle finally got his wish, and American personnel, save for those involved in NATO, left France for the ZI. They would not return in large enough numbers to field football teams until the expansion of NATO air bases in 1952.

The sporting program during and after Allied forces cleared French territory of occupying Germans demonstrated, however, that football had become a central feature of military life. The men who ran the American armed services had been indoctrinated in the culture of the sport as plebes and midshipmen. Many of them continued to play on scattered outposts during their years as junior officers, with some—Supreme Commander of Allied Forces in Europe Dwight Eisenhower, for instance—continuing in the game as coaches once their playing days were over. When these men became senior officers, they continued to encourage their Special Services arm to sponsor American sports, including football.

As we shall see in the next chapter, command interest often spelled the difference in a military installation having a winning or losing team. Whenever American servicemen in large numbers found themselves in France, therefore, football would travel along with them. For the most part this football enthusiasm was largely sealed off from the local population wherever games took place.

Hundreds, perhaps even thousands, of French men and women were able to see football games between 1943 and 1946. However, the military made no special efforts to entice the French population to adopt our game. Other than the occasional mention of an official party at a military bowl game or a reference to civilians in the crowd at a game, for the most part French notice of the games left no discernible lasting impression. There might have been Frenchmen who were taken with the game, but any records of what they thought of the gridiron have likely been lost to history.

Those French newspapers that continued during the Nazi occupation quickly ceased publication after the liberation. The new papers that took their place had more-immediate concerns and took no notice of the amusing and bizarre antics of the American soldiers in their midst. So for all the effect that these games had on the French, they might just as well have been played in Chicago, Annapolis, or West Point.

Once again, however, France would have an outsized effect on football in the United State. Watching world events with more than casual interest, Clark Shaughnessy, then the former head football coach for the University of Chicago and a current consultant for the Chicago Bears, began studying the blitzkrieg tactics employed by German general Heinz Guderian during the Polish campaign. Shaughnessy would adapt Guderian's tactics—aiming "the point of attack at a narrow hole to be punched in the thinned-out defensive line while simultaneously threatening an attack on the flank."[55]

Shaughnessy continued to watch with interest as the Nazi juggernaut rolled through France and was impressed by the way the Germans faked to the right through Belgium to draw the British and French forces away from the real main attack point of the Ardennes Forest. He incorporated this into his scheme by continually sending a man in motion to confuse the defense. His tactical innovation became known as the T Formation, which would speed up play on the field considerably, making for a more entertaining spectacle. He used the formation to defeat Nebraska in the 1940 Rose Bowl and also helped George Halas adopt the formation for his Bears, who went on to crush the

Washington Redskins 73–0 in the 1940 NFL championship. Shaughnessy, understandably, kept secret the source of his inspiration but finally told the story to a reporter in the 1960s.[56]

Regardless of the outsized influence that events in France had on the game in the United States, and the relentless American drive to play their game wherever war found them, life in France could now return to normal. The military's footballs were packed and returned home, along with the jeeps, trucks, and rifles that were part of the cargo transported across the Atlantic. Unlike in some Pacific islands, no cargo cults sprang up in France to worship abandoned footballs, shoulder pads, or helmets. Perhaps those few French citizens who had managed to see a game breathed a sigh of relief that now they could fully concentrate on soccer and rugby. Their peace was disturbed only by the occasional report of football coming in the films or in press reports depicting the antics of the Americans around Thanksgiving and New Year's Day.

The American military was not through with France, however. Between 1952 and 1966, football would return to the country under the auspices of the American military. Once again, thousands of soldiers, sailors, and airmen would chase the pigskin across the green fields of the nation. But, as with other American military excursions into the country, the French would take precious little notice of what silliness *les Américains* were up to on their bases.

4. Football in the Cold, 1952-1959

The second great conflict of the twentieth century was over, but almost immediately a new conflict emerged between the former wartime allies. The Cold War (1946–91) would keep American service personnel serving on far-flung bases around the world. They were the front line of defense against a possible Soviet invasion, and the forces in France were part of the effort to deter any Soviet thrust to take Western Europe. As defenders of the American Way of Life, those soldiers, sailors, and airmen, along with their dependents, were forced to live in unfamiliar surroundings, far from home.

With the end of the war, many of the athletes who had played during the conflict left the demobilization depots and headed off to college campuses with the help of the GI Bill. Coaches such as Paul "Bear" Bryant and Paul Brown, who had spent the war devising tactics to score points rather than capture territory, went on to become coaching legends.[1] Despite the draw-down of forces and the loss of considerable talent, the relationship between football and military life that began in the World War I would continue to be an integral part of the lives of many soldiers and sailors. Joining the ranks of the older services, airmen would now be added to this group when the United States Air Force became a separate branch of the service in 1947.

When military planners moved their airbases to the west side of the Rhine River to provide breathing space in case of a Soviet attack, it would be this new service branch that would bring football back to France in the postwar period.[2] From 1952 until 1967, when French president Charles de Gaulle removed his country from NATO, thousands of airmen, along with some soldiers, and even the odd British military policeman, played several hundred games as part of the various leagues that had sprung up in Europe to keep service personnel occupied and entertained.

In order to ease the separation from their lives as civilians, the services attempted to re-create the American way for those personnel and dependents at the strange locales where they found themselves. By the 1950s football was beginning to edge out baseball as the American national sporting obsession, so the game was an even more integral part of the military's efforts to remind servicemen and servicewomen of what they had left behind while serving their country.[3]

The same ideas that motivated the military's use of sport in the world wars would continue through the Cold War period. Sport was still important to keep personnel in shape and out of trouble. However, the Cold War policy of containment called for maintaining a long-term American presence around the globe. Therefore, the necessity of building and keeping morale high took on added importance. The aim was to accomplish this by re-creating a small slice of American life in places such as France, which was added to the multitudinous reasons for playing games while waiting for a possible third global conflict. For their part the teams became the focus of numerous activities such as pep rallies, booster clubs, and in general re-created the college atmosphere for many young men who had never attended.[4]

A majority of the games were played under the auspices of the United States Air Force Europe (USAFE) League, which included teams from France, Germany, England, and occasionally Spain. During the 1950s USAFE was divided into three districts that included the France, Germany, and the United Kingdom (UK) District. At the height of its popularity, ten French teams contended for the USAFE crown, including teams from Chambley, Châteauroux, Chaumont, Dreux, Etain, Evereux, Phalsbourg, Laon, SHAPE, and Toul.[5]

The United States Army Europe (USAREUR) league's Communication Zone (Com Z) Conference was also home for several French military installations that varied from six to nine teams. In 1954 nine USAREUR teams represented Metz, Toul-Nancy, Verdun, Croix Chapeau, Ingraindes, Bussac, and Fontainbleau.[6] During that year SHAPE also played in the USAREUR conference, and another team, an ordnance ammunition company (which one is unclear) played at a location that is likewise not specified but was probably Captieux.[7]

By 1961 only Châteauroux, Laon, SHAPE, and Toul still had football teams as leagues and conferences underwent realignment, with SHAPE in the USAREUR Continental Conference, and the others in the USAFE European Conference. The UK Conference had also decreased in size, going from eight teams in 1957 to only five in that year.[8] A similar contraction took place with the U.S. Army teams when they changed their organization from regimental to divisional level. All the French-based teams and their players that were originally in the USAREUR would be absorbed into larger units after realignment.[9]

In addition to the grown-up games that took place between USAFE teams, several high schools, filled with the dependents of servicemen and servicewomen, also played football in and around France. Play began in 1955 with four prep teams from Paris, Châteauroux, Orleans, and Rochefort fighting it out on the gridiron.[10] Even as some of the USAFE base teams fell by the wayside, the high school elevens continued to play, with teams in Châteauroux, Dreux, Orleans, Paris, Poitiers, and Verdun playing in the Com Z Conference in 1963. By 1967, when the end was approaching for NATO bases in France, only Châteauroux and Poitiers had dropped the sport.[11] Along with their peers in the ZI, occasionally the French high schools would also stage "Powder Puff" games, which allowed their female students to get into the action.[12]

These games, both at the base and the high school levels, were not contested as part of an extraordinary tournament such as the 1919 Inter-Allied games, nor were they one-time spectacles like the various bowl games played on French soil during World War II. Rather, like the Normandy Football League, the TSFFL, and TSFET, they were part of a highly organized effort that featured preseason coaching clinics, a regular season, playoffs, championships, All-Star teams, booster clubs, international travel, and the occasional interservice extravaganza. Both the USAFE and the USAEUR leagues crowned champions, and French teams won their share of titles during the late 1950s and early 1960s. During the 1963–64 season, one high school team, the Dreux Vikings, not only won the Com Z Championship by winning all six regular season games but were also allowed to play three additional games versus opponents from Lakenheath (UK), London, and Madrid.[13]

The Department of Defense (DOD) spent billions of dollars defending against any Soviet military move on Western Europe. A small but still significant portion of those funds were used to operate the various football leagues and their associated activities. Dick Mullins, the chief of sports and youth activities, remembered that his budget in the 1980s at Ramstein Air Force Base (AFB) was $1.5 million, which in 1957 dollars would be over $391,728, or more than $3.25 million in today's dollars.[14]

Using 1957 as a high point for service football and calculating that football, as traditionally the most expensive sport, would consume at least one-fifth of the annual athletic budget, the cost for the twenty-eight teams in the USAFE League would have been in the neighborhood of $11 million. This would be the equivalent of nearly $30 million in today's dollars. This was, and would still be, a relative bargain for running an entire league. According to USA Today, the U.S. Air Force Academy, hardly a football powerhouse, spent over $39 million on athletics during the period from 2006 to 2011, and big-time programs such as 2012 BCS Champion Alabama spent over $105 million during the same period.[15] Over the eighteen-year span of the U.S. Air Force presence in France, factoring in a relatively low inflation rate of 1.3 percent, the total possible expenditure might have been as much as $190 million in today's dollars.[16]

During the NATO era in France, the air force maintained an average of nearly seventy thousand personnel per year in Europe, along with their dependents.[17] The welfare of military personnel and their dependents was naturally a concern of the military since happy airmen and airwomen would perform their duties more efficiently. Therefore, the money was justified by asserting that military personnel already were serving far from home and needed a chance for recreational opportunities.

As seen in the cases of the world wars, sport teams could also be useful in building unit pride and in keeping airmen in top shape should the Cold War should turn hot. All the same arguments for maintaining a football program that were used during the previous world wars were continued during the Cold War, with the addition that football and other sports could provide a slice of the American way of life that military personnel stationed in France were defending far from home. The interview subjects that will be cited in this chapter uniformly posited this as a rationale when questioned about why the military spent so much money and effort on sport.

Negotiations between the French and NATO began in 1950, and some bases such as Châteauroux that used existing airfields began shipping in personnel. Others would need to build from the airstrip out, and construction also began on those bases during the same year.[18] USAFE football was also in its infancy in 1950 and 1951, with some already-existing bases in Germany and England engaged in blocking and tackling, but others played touch football only.[19]

By 1952 four teams, based at Châteauroux, Chaumont, Laon, and Toul-Rosières, fielded teams and played full ten-game schedules. They fared poorly against their more established opponents, winning only eight games, while losing thirty-three, with one tie. Likely this was due to the still-unfinished state of the bases themselves. With personnel living in tents and their base areas often engulfed in mud, commanders were hard-pressed to spare time, attention, or money for their football teams.

The 3–6 Toul-Rosières Tigers, on the strength of victories over the other teams from bases located in France, nevertheless won the right to play the 7–1 Burtonwood (UK) Bullets in the USAFE semifinals.[20] Despite the disparity in records and a mid-season Bullet lambasting of the Tigers by 46–0, the Toul-Rosières team acquitted itself well in the match. It was only a moral victory, but the French-base entry, playing at home in the first USAFE playoff game contested in France, held the powerful English invaders to only one touchdown in the first half. The Bullets, who had scored an average of 31.6 points per game while giving up only 39 points all season, scored two more in the final half, but the 21–0 final score was not a crushing defeat.[21]

With football in France still in its infancy in 1952, the USAFE championship was contested between Fürstenfeldbruck (Germany) and Burtonwood. The league nevertheless scored an important first by holding

1952 French Team Results

USAFE Conference	Wins	Losses	Ties
Laon (Rangers)	3	8	0
Chaumont (Mudhens)	0	10	2
Châteauroux (Sabres)	2	9	0
Toul-Rosières (Tigers)	3	6	1

Source: "1952 USAFE Football Record," *Stars and Stripes*, November 30, 1952, 11.

the championship match at London's Wembley Stadium, where the Minnesota Vikings and the St. Louis Cardinals, two NFL teams, played the first professional exhibition football game in Europe in 1983.[22] It was also the site where in 2007 the New York Giants and the Miami Dolphins played the first NFL regular-season game outside North America in the new Wembley Stadium.[23]

Stars and Stripes featured an article on the game that would mirror French reaction to the 1938 Crowley tour and foreshadow postwar attempts to interest the French in our game that will be considered in the following chapters. Sterling Slappey, the author of the article, noted that some British fans were impressed but quoted a disgruntled British fan, described as "a proper cricket type with mustache bristling," who felt the game was "deplorable." Another terse commenter added, "It's a shame, a complete shame." Again echoing 1938 French reports, some in the crowd of twenty-five thousand wondered how many fatalities teams suffered after viewing the mayhem on the field (eleven in 1953 and twelve in 1954).[24] Slappey concluded by asserting that even though the game had made a "general favorable impression" on the British, the chances for football taking off there were slim: "But don't think football will catch on in England. It hardly has a chance. England already has its cricket, rugby, and association football (practically no resemblance to the American kind), and those three are enough for any nation."[25] The *Stars and Stripes* writer was ultimately incorrect, and the British did begin playing football a few years after the French in 1984, but that is a story for another day.[26]

Oddly enough, the 1952 USAFE Championship in London provided the French with one of their rare opportunities to see the game played.

A newsreel report titled "Le Sport" provided footage of the game but focused mainly on the spectacle surrounding the play on the field. Cheerleaders were seen and heard going through their routines chanting, "Go team!" Other vignettes included male and female baton twirlers, a precision marching unit that entertained at halftime, and shots of the crowd. The action on the field was primarily provided as context to the celebration and mostly involved kickoffs and punts, presumably since this would give French soccer and rugby fans a point of reference. One humorous scene showed a stray dog that had wandered onto the field and began running along with the players.[27]

With teams forming on the NATO bases in France, command interest was a key factor in building a successful football program at any particular location. In a 2011 telephone interview, Lt. Col. (USA Ret.) Barney Gill, a captain and head coach of the SHAPE Indians between 1960 and 1963, remembered that Lt. Col. William Dodds, the commanding officer of the Headquarters Section at Paris was a "football freak." Dodds, whom we will meet again when discussing various postwar football tours of France, had groomed Gill as a coach when they were both members of the 504th Parachute Infantry Regiment in the States and was also instrumental in bringing the young officer to France. The colonel intended that his SHAPE team would dominate the USAFE ranks and reportedly used a contact in the Pentagon Office of Career Management to identify and procure top talent from young men doing their two-year national service requirement.[28] Stocked with talent gleaned from former college stars, SHAPE did indeed dominate USAFE football during the time that Dodds and Gill worked together, but more about that later.

Jerry Curtright, the head coach of the Laon (pronounced "lone" in the American patois) Rangers, also remembered, in another 2011 telephone interview, that Col. Chuck Hill, his commanding officer, was also very interested in the fate of his base team and told the coach, "If you ever needed or wanted anything [for the football program], let me know." Unfortunately for Hill and Curtright, during the 1961 district playoffs they ran into a general who was an even bigger football freak than they were. Curtright, in an article for the *Laon Ranger*, a newsletter for the Laon Air Police Association, asserted that they were robbed of a win by order of the commanding officer of Alconbury (UK) AFB. With the score tied at the end of regulation, the game went into sudden-death overtime for the first time in USAFE history. The Rangers scored what they thought was a winning touchdown only to have it called back on a penalty for too many men in the backfield. After another sudden-death period, Alconbury then scored a touchdown to win the game 12–6. Curtright added a postscript to the article mentioning that several years later he ran into the backfield judge from the game who told him that Alconbury's commanding general had briefed the officials before the game that his team WOULD "win the game, no matter what."[29]

While football could provide a slice of the American way for service personnel, perennial losing teams could damage a base's esprit de corps. The fortunes of individual teams would naturally fluctuate as officers and men rotated in or out of the theater, or football freak commanders arrived or departed. USAFE, however, was interested in providing coaches with the tools that would help them field competitive teams to avoid the morale-crushing consequences of constant losing. To ensure that teams had a serious chance at fielding a competitive team, the league scheduled annual coaches' clinics that brought in successful college and professional coaches to share the secrets of their success. They also sought to make sure that officiating was of high quality by hosting clinics for the zebras as well.

The 1952 European Command Coaches' Clinic headlined Charles "Bud" Wilkinson, the head coach of the University of Oklahoma Sooners, as its featured instructor. He also brought along three of his assistants, Gomer Jones, Bill Jennings, and Claude Ivy, to assist in the clinic. The Oklahoma coaches were also joined by Ossie Solem, the head coach of Springfield College, and Dudley "Dud" DeGroot, the headman at the University of New Mexico. A concurrent official's clinic featured E. C. Kreiger from the Big 10 Conference.[30]

How much these clinics cost is difficult to determine, but bringing over successful coaches would at least cost the price of tickets for the coaches, their room and board while in the country, and whatever fee they could command. Added to this would be the cost of transporting the attending coaches from England, France, Spain, and Germany to the clinic location, which was typically on a German base. Losses in productivity for the coaches being absent from their regular duties would also need to be factored into the total.

In a 2013 article in *Air and Space* magazine, Mariana Gosnell related that the U.S. Department of State paid $500 for her to travel to Oslo, Norway, in 1955. Her ticket was in first class and included a sleeper bed reminiscent of train accommodations, and she calculated that the equivalent in today's dollars would be $4,200.[31] Perhaps the coaches were transported using the Military Air Transport Command (MATS) flights, since many of the coaches such as Wilkinson had served in the military during the war.[32] More likely, given their fame, they would have been considered VIPs and would flown first class at military expense. Wilkinson and three of his assistants conducted the coaches' clinic for the EC at Garmisch, Germany in 1952, so at $494.40 per ticket, travel would have cost $1,977.60 in 1952. That would be the equivalent of $17,429.09 in today's dollars.[33]

Wilkinson's Sooners won the 1950 National Championship and had won forty-four of their last forty-eight games leading up to the clinic, so the coach would likely have commanded a top fee for his services. Currently, Nick Saban, head coach of the 2011 and 2012 National Champion University of Alabama Crimson Tide team, commands a speaker fee of between $20,000 and $30,000.[34] Saban would be a modern equivalent of a coach of Wilkinson's stature, and Saban's fee would have been $2,269.77 in 1952. The amount of money swirling around football has exploded in recent decades, so it is unlikely that Wilkinson would have asked for, or received a sum as high as that. Still, even a $500 fee ($4,400 today) per coach, plus room and board, would have cost the European Command nearly $5,000 dollars (more than $44,000 today).[35] Also, as previously mentioned Wilkinson and his assistants were not the only the headliners at the 1952 clinic. Other notable coaches also took part in the weeklong event, including DeGroot and Solem, and their presence would have also added to the cost of the program, adding perhaps $2,000 and making the total somewhere in the neighborhood of $7,000 ($61,680.30 in today's dollars).[36] With travel and fees the total cost might have been somewhere near $100,000 in today's dollars.

The numbers discussed here and on previous pages are highly speculative, and the cost of travel, per diem, and lost productivity for military personnel (approximately two hundred attended in 1952) would have added even more to the expense.[37] Despite the tentative nature of the amounts, discussion of possible expenditures is designed to demonstrate that USAFE invested considerable resources in its football program and therefore considered games to be important for its mission. To those who have read the fine works by Wanda Wakefield, Steven Riess, and S. W. Pope, among others, that have explored the role of athletics in the military, this is hardly breaking news. It is, however, useful to note here that the U.S. government spent perhaps $70 million on football.[38] Budgets are collections of priorities, and clearly football was something of a priority for the American military.

That said, it is astonishing that in the early 1950s, when football teams at French bases began, the defense department could justify spending such a great deal of money on sports. With a hostile Soviet Union still headed by Josef Stalin and a war under way in Korea, one might wonder whether critics questioned expenditure of funds on such activities. If those critics existed, they have left little evidence.

Leverett Saltonstall, a Republican United States senator from Massachusetts, did place a "stop order" on funding for any further construction of military bases in the United States and abroad in 1952, just as French bases were beginning to compete. He did so in the hopes that incoming president Dwight D. Eisenhower would find cost savings in the military budget, an issue that he had campaigned on during his election.[39]

Those savings apparently did not come from the athletic programs in Europe, or if they did, the cuts were insignificant. After fielding four teams in 1952, USAFE would expand its France Sports Conference to six teams the next year, and USAREUR would inaugurate play among eight French teams during that season. Perhaps Eisenhower, an all-around athlete in high school, a football player during his West Point years before injury cut his career short, and a sometimes coach at various army posts when he was a junior officer, could not bring himself to cut out a part of military life that had been so important to him.[40]

Fig. 8. The Châteauroux Sabres, ca. 1961. Photo courtesy of Dave Madril.

Congress likewise did not favor cuts in military sporting events. Senator Richard Russell, a Democrat from Georgia, made it clear at a 1954 Armed Services Committee meeting that he would not support even taking away radio broadcasts of football and baseball games as a part of the budget trimming for 1955. "I am willing to cut off a few guns," Russell said, "but I am not willing to curtail the overseas radios for men in the Armed Forces." He is also quoted as stating, "I think it [the broadcasts] is the most important morale factor we have."[41] The unwillingness to cut even radio telecasts for sports indicated that any moves against the actual sports programs in Europe, which were also justified as being important to maintaining morale, would gain little traction.

Evidence of cuts to the Special Services programs in Europe was also belied by a new facility being constructed in Leghorn, Italy. As part of the "multimillion dollar USFA project," construction included a "combination training building, gymnasium, and theater—with an eight lane bowling alley attached." The new base also included "two clay tennis courts" and a "turnabout baseball-football field."[42]

In France the ammunition depot at Captieux, located in an isolated spot in the southwest of the country near Bordeaux, saw considerable spending by the Special Services branch. The post boasted baseball and football fields, bowling allies, and other facilities that offered recreational opportunities to servicemen and servicewomen stationed there. Though the base dropped tackle football after 1954, it did play touch football, and played it well enough to reach the Com Z finals in 1955.[43]

Ken Thrash remembered that after the infrastructure of the base at Laon had been constructed, his engineering unit was tasked with building a football field. The commanding officer decided that the equipment and personnel were not being used at the moment, so they should have first-class athletic fields. Thrash asserted that they built one of the finest gridirons in the country, complete with a nice crown that allowed the constant rain of northern France to run off the field. Thus they avoided having to name their team the Mudcloggers or some such woebegone name as we saw in World War II.[44]

The clinics would be an annual affair and would bring in other well-known college coaches including Duffy Daugherty of Michigan State University and Bob Devaney of the University of Nebraska–Lincoln.[45] In 1964 college coaches were replaced by professional coaches and players from the NFL. That year the headliners of the clinic were head coach Don Shula of the Baltimore Colts and his star quarterback, Johnny Unitas.[46] The next year Bill McPeak, the head coach of the Washington Redskins, led the clinic and brought along two of his assistant coaches, including future NFL Hall of Famer Ernie Stautner. Also accompanying the coach were quarterback Christian "Sonny" Jurgensen and Bobby Mitchell, one of the team's top receivers and also the first African American to play for the Redskins.[47]

There were also concurrent clinics for officials that brought in instructors to help improve the quality of refereeing, although, in light of Curtright's story, there was no mention of sessions devoted to resisting pressure from base commanders. While veteran NFL referees such as Sam Cooperman at the 1965 clinic no doubt gave their students good advice on officiating, they proved to be poor fortune-tellers. *Stars and Stripes* writer George Eberl interviewed the instructor and also asked him for his thoughts on the recent draft of former Alabama star Joe Namath by the New York Jets. Namath had well-known knee problems, prompting Cooperman to reply, "I think it's largely a publicity thing. They've got their money's worth out of the signing already."[48]

1953 French Team Results

France Sports Conference (USAFE)	Wins	Losses	Ties
Laon (Rangers)	6	2	0
Bordeaux (Cardinals)	2	4	0
Châteauroux (Sabres)	6	2	1
Chaumont (Mudhens)	4	2	0
Fontainebleau (Foresters)	2	4	0
Orly (Comets)	2	8	0
Com Z Conference (USAEUR)			
ADSEC Metz-Moselle (Mustangs)	0	7	1
Orléans-Loire (Ramblers)	6	2	0
Toul-Lorraine (Dodgers)	2	3	1
Verdun-Meuse (Cardinals)	5	2	0
Basec-Bordeaux (?)	0	6	0
Bussac (Broncos)	4	3	0
La Rochelle-Croix Chapeau (Rams)	5	1	0
Poitiers-Ingrandes (Cardinals)	4	4	0

Source: "USAFE Conferences," *Stars and Stripes*, November 11, 1953, 14.

In the case of some French-based USAFE teams, the work put in during the summer learning the *X*s and *O*s of successful coaching began to pay off in 1953 with success on the field. That year ten French bases fielded teams spread over two leagues, and as a group they nearly reached the break-even level, winning forty-eight and losing forty-nine, with three ties. These games included exhibitions, which varied in number from none for the Toul-Lorraine team to five for Orly. Some of the exhibitions were games played against more-established teams from the USAEUR conferences, and some were against programs such as SHAPE that apparently were just beginning their football program, although *Stars and Stripes* provided no explanations of the criteria being used to differentiate regular from exhibition. The Laon Rangers and the Verdun-Meuse Cardinals led the way, contending for conference title in the France Sports Conference of USAFE and the Com Z Conference of USAEUR.

The Laon Rangers, playing in the France Sports Conference, earned a berth in the USAFE semifinals but were slaughtered. In an ironic rhetorical tip-of-the-hat to the French visitors, *Stars and Stripes* called the game the "goriest massacre since the Reign of Terror," as the Landstuhl (Germany) Raiders defeated the Rangers 76–0 behind the play of Jim Hook, the Missouri Tigers' leading rusher and scorer during the 1951 season.[49]

Clearly, even though they were beginning to have success, the USAFE teams from French bases were not ready to battle on an equal footing with their longer-established opponents based in Germany. Both of Laon's losses for the season were to teams from outside France. The Erding (Germany) Arrowheads topped them by a score of 28–9 in the Ranger's first exhibition game, and the London Area Rockets defeated them in an exhibition in their fourth game 18–6.

Meanwhile, in the Com Z, in the first USAREUR Com Z conference championship game on French soil, the Verdun-Meuse Cardinals defeated the La Rochelle Rams 46–18 on November 7, 1953. The Cardinals, who had won five and lost one during the regular season, overcame the previously undefeated Rams before what *Stars and Stripes* called a "Franco-American crowd of 3,000 spectators."[50]

This mention of French fans would be something of an anomaly for games played during the NATO years. Only Dave Madril, one of the interview subjects for this chapter, mentioned French fans at their games in an interview with the French blog *Elitefoot*.[51] All the others claimed that very few French people, if any, had seen games.

The French press, as far as can be determined, was silent unless a special event occurred, such as one of the tours that will be discussed in the following chapters. One of the few mentions of the French noticing these games was a single post on Facebook that featured the reminiscences of a man who remembered seeing a football game that preceded a rugby match in Paris when he was in short pants. Far from being impressed, the now-older man grumped that he was not happy that he had to wait for rugby to begin.[52]

Stars and Stripes, on the other hand, found hundreds of French men and women at the games. A few days after the story about the Verdun

Fig. 9. Dave Madril playing for the Châteauroux Sabres in 1961. Photo courtesy of Dave Madril.

victory, the paper ran an in-depth article on Willie Hall, one of the top running backs for the Cardinals. Along with the story about Hall and his fellow Redbirds, the paper ran a cartoon depicting a stereotypical Frenchman complete with beret and haughty expression. The caricature presumably represents a Verdun player since he is dressed in a football uniform, carrying a football, and walking with a knapsack over his shoulder in the direction of Germany (where the team would play next in Augsburg). A voice bubble proclaims, "*C'est si bon*" (It's so good).[53]

Another article, by Don Walter, on the same page claims: "The French have long been soccer fans and they are also followers of rugby, but Football, American style, however, was something new. But it seemed to click." Walter states, "A large percentage of the crowd at each Com Z game this season was French." And "In Bordeaux, during an exhibition game at the Municipal Stadium, 20,000 Frenchmen watched the Americans battle it out. League game attendance (with French support) sometimes topped 3,500." Referencing Shipley's 1952 article, he asserts, "Unlike the British, some of whom found an American exhibition game last year distasteful because they thought it was brutal, the French generally find it interesting." Walter also explained that the game programs were in both French and English, but that some terms, such as "touchdown," were difficult to translate, and therefore remained the same.[54] The actual article on the earlier exhibition between Bordeaux and La Rochelle only mentions that the game was witnessed by "an estimated 20,000 French and American fans, as La Rochelle won 33–0.[55]

It does appear that in 1953 the military was taking steps to interest the French in our version of football, or perhaps more generally in American culture. On December 17 two teams representing the Orly Comets and the Bordeaux Cardinals were given a trip to the resort town of Aix-les-Bains, where they put on an exhibition match for "6,000 French." Apparently, for the article was not explicit in stating the purpose for the excursion, the goal was to foster Franco-American friendship, which was toasted at a banquet held by the town's "leading citizens" represented by the deputy mayor, who presented "handmade emblems" to the head coaches. The football game preceded the banquet, and a French newspaper quoted in the article carried the headline "Six Tons of Players, Two Touchdowns, and Two Fractures in American Football Game." While the players were given passes to the famous hot baths, stayed in "one of the town's best hotels," and ate in an "elite restaurant," the headline of the paper likely sums up the feelings of the spectators, who witnessed the dangerous nature of the game.[56]

There purportedly was even a momentary burst of enthusiasm among Frenchmen for the game. According to Seymour Freidin and William Richardson, writing in the *Toledo Blade*, plans were afoot to organize "la ligue de combattants de football américain." The authors were Americans living in France and had been advising baseball leagues in the Bois de Boulogne, but with the visibility of football increased by the military outreach, they stated, "Like an inexorable flood, football finally washed over Paris." They repeated the story that thousands of French spectators were turning out for games in the provinces and added, "In cafes in Bordeaux, you can hear fierce arguments over 'le formation T and nos touchdowns.'" As Americans they were presumed to know football and were drafted to help at a practice. The workout turned out to be a farce, with the coach calling for a punt on first down and the punter, a martial arts practitioner, trying to kick an opposing player instead of the ball. Perhaps the entire article was written tongue-in-cheek, but no further evidence that the team continued to practice could be located.[57]

Whether the military officials were merely attempting to demonstrate features of American culture for their hosts or this was an opening salvo in a cultural imperialism offensive, the event and the year were outside the usual course of business for football in France. The reason for hosting French fans at regular season games and in special excursions was more likely the first possibility. The bases were still relatively new, and the European Command was no doubt anxious to build good relations with the French people. There may have been a few in the chain of command who wished to see our game transplanted to Europe, Colonel Dodds of SHAPE for one, as we will see in the following chapters. However, without any evidence to the contrary, building solid relationships with the local populace remains the most likely motive.

The aforementioned Hall of the Meuse Cardinals did his best, scoring two first-half touchdowns in the showdown against the Twenty-Eighth Division Special Troops Troopers. The score was tied 13–13 at halftime, but the Troopers dominated the second half, scoring thirty-nine unanswered points in the second half to win 52–13.[58] The pattern of teams from French bases being outclassed by their German counterparts would continue throughout the NATO period. They could hold their own with their British base rivals in USAFE, but USAUER in Germany topped them every time. According to one source, a problem that the newer loop faced against their more established foes was the "overemphasis" that Army teams placed on football.

Gill, the head coach of the SHAPE Indians between 1960 and 1963, claimed that the Army teams from Germany took football more seriously even than the football freaks in USAFE. He asserted that their programs were the equivalent of big-time Division I teams today. They, according to Gill, had changed the organization of their teams from being based on individual bases or regiments to encompassing entire divisions, allowing them to draw on as many as eighteen thousand men to stock, and stack, their football teams. He went on to claim that the army divisional teams excused their players from normal duties and collected them in special barracks with their own mess halls.[59]

Anyone familiar with contemporary Division I football programs knows that standard operating procedure calls for the use of widespread recruiting pools, athletic dorms, separate dining halls, and steering players into easy courses or majors. This is nothing new and predates the 1950s, so USAEUR was merely replicating the American way of football to a greater degree than its air force counterpart, much to the latter's disgust.[60]

Despite the relative importance that the various commands placed on football, another factor mitigating success for French teams was the still-fluid nature of the bases located there. Many of these bases did not have tackle football before 1953, and the history of the Verdun team that year highlighted the slapdash nature of their efforts. Lt. Donald Hemphill arrived at Verdun in mid-August and was ordered to build a football team. Hemphill, according to *Stars and Stripes*, had played for Louisiana State University (although an obituary found online with a picture and history that matches that found in the *Stars and Stripes* article states that he attended Fort Hayes State University).[61] The new coach reportedly had a difficult time building the team. Many of his players were stationed at "several widely scattered and relatively small units" that included "installations at Meuse, Trois Fontaines, Vassincourt, Sampigny, and Etain." According to the article, none of the players, other than Hemphill, had played at the college level, and while coaching the team, he also played end and guard, as well as calling the offensive signals in the huddle.[62] The Cardinals racked up five wins, all against Com Z conference foes that were likely as inexperienced as they were.

The Troopers from the Twenty-Eighth Division that defeated them were not inexperienced. Darrell "Shorty" Cochran, a running back who led their offensive attack was an all-around high school athlete and a member of the University of Minnesota's 1956 national champion baseball team.[63] Ken Tate, the center, played for Baylor, and Tom Dickerson, the quarterback, had played for the University of Tulsa. This competitive imbalance would be exacerbated by football-freak commanding officers who did more than order random lieutenants to build a football team.

1954 French Team Results

France Sports Conference (USAFE)	Wins	Losses	Ties
Laon (Rangers)	1	5	1
Bordeaux (Cardinals)	1	4	1
Châteauroux (Sabres)	6	3	0
Chaumont (Mudhens)	6	3	1
Orly (Comets)	0	5	0
Com Z Conference (USAEUR)			
Metz (Mustangs)	2	5	1
Orléans Area Command	3	7	0
Toul-Nancy (Dodgers)	4	4	2
Verdun (Cardinals)	7	1	1
SHAPE (Indians)	7	4	0
Bussac (Broncos)	4	4	0
Croix Chapeau (Rams)	7	2	0
Ingrandes (Cardinals)	0	7	0
Fontainebleau (Foresters)	2	6	0

Source: "Final Conference Standings," *Stars and Stripes*, December 2, 1954, 20.

With fifteen teams in two conferences, French teams continued their winning ways in 1954. Three teams, Chaumont, Châteauroux, and Toul, tied for the lead in the USAFE France Sports Conference with 6–3 records. With a better in-conference record (5–0), Chaumont played for the USAFE championship, due to a bye that sent the French winner directly to the finals.[64] There the Mudhens faced the London Area Rockets, who defeated them handily 21–0. The game was the first time that the Mudhens had been in the playoffs, while their opponents had played for the USAFE championship the previous year.[65]

Chaumont had the home-field advantage in the first USAFE championship contested in France, but that did it no good whatsoever; it lost to a team containing halfback Vic Bonfili, formerly of West Virginia, who had to put an NFL career on hold to serve in the air force. He was joined in the backfield by fullback Hank Williams, who had played at Toledo University, and Johnny Hill, the team's leading rusher, who had played for a year at Northwestern before being drafted. Bill

Farley, voted the game's Most Valuable Player, was a backup quarterback behind Babe Parilli at the University of Kentucky.[66] (Meanwhile, Parilli, who would go on to be an All-Star quarterback for the Boston Patriots of the NFL, was playing touch football for the Rabat, Morocco, AFB, leading the team to victory in the 1955 North African Touch Football Tournament.)[67]

The 6,500 fans who filled Stade Georges Dodin included Maj. Gen. Robert M. Lee the commanding general of the Twelfth Air Force. Lee presented the championship trophy to the wife of Rocket's coach Fred Russell, who was on emergency leave in the states attending the funeral of his mother and grandfather. The commander of the Twelfth was joined at the game by his counterpart of the Third Air Force, Roscoe C. Wilson.[68]

We have already seen how command influence affected the 1919 AEF Championship and read of how one general's orders to the referees could be decisive in championship games. One does not need much imagination to picture the banter that Lee and Wilson shared at command conferences during the following year. Command interest in football could be so conclusive in building programs to improve esprit des corps, but it could also aid in the esprit des les generals.

In the Com Z Conference, Croix-Chapeau, Verdun, and SHAPE all had seven wins, though Croix Chapeau had more wins in the conference. The Rams moved on to play the Eighteenth Regiment Vanguards at La Rochelle, France. The French USAEUR entry fared no better than its air force counterpart, losing to the Vanguards 12–0. The famous French weather, referenced by Crowley decades earlier, once again turned ugly. According to *Stars and Stripes*, "a shivering crowd of 3,000 watched the game," and the inclement weather, along with a "slightly muddy field, combined to make the game a sluggish one."[69]

None of the stories of the playoff games in France in 1954 mention any French fans being impressed by football. Perhaps the outreach to the locals was a one-year-only program, but the enthusiasm reported in the previous year seemed to fade quickly into oblivion. The possibility exists that some of the 9,500 fans who saw the games in France were indeed French, but *Stars and Stripes* did not take the same notice of them that it had the previous year.

1955 French Team Results

USAFE Conference	Wins	Losses	Ties
Evreux (Normans)	7	1	0
Chambley (Desert Rats)	4	1	2
Laon (Rangers)	5	2	0
CAMA [formerly Châteauroux] (Sabres)	3	4	2
Etain (Pioneers)	4	3	1
SHAPE (Indians)	3	4	1
Chaumont (Mudhens)	3	5	1
Bordeaux (Cardinals)	2	6	1
Toul (Tigers)	0	9	0
Com Z Conference (USAEUR)			
Meuse (Cardinals)	7	1	0
Bussac (Broncos)	6	2	0
Orléans (Orioles)	5	4	0
Chinon (Red Devils)	4	3	0
Fontainebleau (Foresters)	2	5	0
Lorraine (Dodgers)	2	6	0
La Rochelle (Rams)	1	6	0

Source: "1955 Conference Standings," Stars and Stripes November 12, 1955, 20.

For the 1955 season both USAFE and Com Z shuffled teams. In the France Conference, only Chaumont, Laon, and Bordeaux, and Châteauroux (now called CAMA) remained from the previous year. To make up their numbers, SHAPE and Toul were transferred in, and Evreux, Chambley, and Etain began play for the first time. In Com Z new teams from Orléans, Chinon, and Lorraine replaced the lost teams, and Verdun changed its name to Meuse.

Evreux, one of the newcomers, dominated the conference winning seven in a row before losing its final regular season game to Etain 7–6. It then faced the London Rockets, who were once again in the championship. The winner would go on to play the Landstuhl Raiders of the Germany Conference, which received the bye into the championship game. Once again the French entry fell to the British team. The game was played in France, this time at the SHAPE field near Paris, but that once more failed to be helpful, as the French team lost 34–7.[70]

The Normans, as a result of their being the loser in the semifinal match, were given a berth in the Ghibli Bowl. The game, named after the sandstorms that often plague North Africa, matched the Evreux team against the Wiesbaden Flyers, who finished in second place in the Germany Conference of USAREUR. Played at Wheelus Field in Tripoli, the game's result was largely the same for the Normans as their match against the Rockets, and the team from France lost 31–6.[71] The game was part of the Thanksgiving festivities for the soldiers, airmen, and dependents at the isolated installation. Officials made an attempt to replicate the pageantry of a typical Thanksgiving Day game, and the halftime festivities included cheerleaders from the local American high school, as well as the 591st Air Force Band.[72] Victoria Giraud, then a student at Wheelus High School, remembered that the local letterman's club raised money by selling hot dogs at the game to further the feeling that no matter how far from home, American culture could be celebrated in all its glory.[73]

Home-field advantage also did not do the Meuse Cardinals any good in their game against the Ninth Division Artillery. In the second play-off game at Verdun, the Cardinals hoped to repeat their unexpected victory over La Rochelle in 1953 but wound up on the short side of a 13–0 score. The French team could find no solution to the combination of the Redlegs' quarterback Harry Spears, who ran for 107 yards on twenty-seven carries and passed for another 51, including a key screen pass to former University of Indiana fullback Marv Clark.[74]

Some bases that had dropped from the tackle football league still maintained touch football teams, and the Croix-Chapeau Rams won the Basec (Base Section) touch title during a Veteran's Day tournament in 1955. The base's Medical Center 485th Preventative Medicine Company defeated the Quartermaster's Depot Headquarters' Service Company from Ingrandes by a score of 6–0 in a game played in Captieux, France.[75]

At least a few Frenchmen had the chance to see a football game that year. The Thirteenth Algerian Rifle Regimental Band was chosen to play during the halftime ceremonies of a game between the HACom (Headquarters Area Command) Lions and the NACom (Northern Area

Command) Black Knights. The game took place in Frankfurt in September and raised money for the Army Emergency Relief Fund. The 120-man French band marched through the streets to publicize the match and also performed at halftime, along with the NACom cheerleaders, all three of them.[76]

Special festivities such as these demonstrated that Americans were not only bringing their sports to Europe but also attempting to import the spectacle that went along with them. Around five thousand fans attended the game, which was won by NACom 13–0, but other than mentioning that the French band played, the story in *Stars and Stripes* was silent on what the musicians thought of the action taking place on the field.[77]

In 1956 French teams made forward strides, but the results were the same in playoff games. Beginning that season the EC had decided that leagues should be called conferences and conferences would now be known as districts. The USAFE France District also added the Dreux Plainsmen to bring the number of teams in the district to ten. The Orléans Orioles finished with the best record in the Com Z Conference but never mounted much of a threat, winning only five of the nine games they played.

In the France District the Toul Tigers ripped their way through the loop, winning all nine games in the regular season, during which they averaged over fifty points per game. They were led by player-coach Jim Hollingsworth, who previously had played and coached for Western Washington College. Assisting Hollingsworth was player-coach Keith Horn, who had played for Penn State and also had coached its freshman team. Bill Pappas, the second-string quarterback, threw for nine touchdowns and ran for five more and had played college ball for the University of New Hampshire. Gil Bettez, the starting quarterback, apparently had never played college football but became an All-Star during his long career in the service. During the 1956 season the Louisiana native threw twenty touchdown passes and ran for three more.[78] Its talent level had improved, but the French team once again fell in the final, losing to the Wiesbaden (Germany) Flyers 19–16 on the road.

Bettez must have been one of the longest-playing air force gridders of all time. His career in the air force and on the field began in

1956 French Team Results

USAFE France District	Wins	Losses	Ties
Toul (Tigers)	9	1	0
Etain (Pioneers)	7	1	1
SHAPE (Indians)	5	4	0
Evreux (Normans)	6	4	0
Dreux (Plainsmen)	6	4	0
Laon (Rangers)	6	4	0
Chaumont (Mudhens)	3	5	1
Chambley (Desert Rats)	3	7	0
Châteauroux (Sabres)	1	7	1
Bordeaux (Cardinals)	1	8	0
Com Z Conference (USAEUR)			
Orléans (Orioles)	5	4	0
Bussac (Broncos)	5	2	0
Toul-Nancy (Dodgers)	4	3	0
Meuse (Cardinals)	2	6	1
Chinon (Red Devils)	4	3	0
La Rochelle (Rams)	1	4	0

Source: "Conference Standings," *Stars and Stripes*, November 15, 1956, 20.

1955, when he played for the Hahn (Germany) Hawks football team. In 1958, while playing for Ramstein (Germany) AFB, the former state-championship high school player was voted the EC's MVP.[79] In 1959 he returned stateside and directed the Jets of McClellan AFB in Sacramento, California, taking them to the Shrimp Bowl.[80] Though the championship game for top service teams, played from 1955 to 1959 in Galveston, Texas, did not go well for Bettez—his team lost 90–0 to the Marines from Quantico, South Carolina—his career continued.[81] He returned to Europe in 1963 to play for Barney Gill and SHAPE and then switched countries again, playing in England at Chicksands AFB in 1966. He was still playing service football for the Rhein-Main Rockets in 1969 and helped teams from Ramstein (1958) and Rhein-Main (1967 and 1969) win USAFE championships.[82]

For the long-serving multisport athlete, military sports were the center of his career. Bloody wars make for quick promotion, but apparently guiding championship football, baseball, and racquetball teams do not; Bettez's rank in 1969 was topped out at technical sergeant. Officially assigned to security, he spent most of his time as a ranking noncommissioned officer (NCO) in charge of Special Services (read sports) sections on the various bases where he served. He argued that his main function was as an entertainer. He told *Stars and Stripes*, "I believe that the purpose of the Air Force sports program is to provide entertainment. . . . If our program didn't draw the fans and entertain them, there wouldn't be any reason for us to play. Winning is great, but our prime purpose is to entertain." The relatively diminutive football star (five feet seven, 170 pounds) went on to place the credit for the success of the teams on which he played to "command support." "I've never played at a base where our commander wasn't behind us 100 per cent. No sports program is better than what the commander makes it." The article also noted that the commanding officers of Rhein-Main, the powerhouse of USAFE football, were indeed football fans. The commanders at Darmstadt had favored baseball, with results that reflected their success in the sport.[83]

When asked about the money spent on sports programs, Bettez maintained that, while he "felt like something of a professional athlete" during his time in the service, "that was good, because it was good for people." He went on, insisting that "'top level team sports' served a worthwhile purpose in that soldiers and airmen, whether at base or divisional level, were able to identify with their teams." In another *Stars and Stripes* interview, he told the paper, "There's no question about it, this was very good for esprit des corps." He did feel that teams were more cost effective than individual sports, and thought that money spent on individuals generally only benefited them instead of the entire base. Even though he himself was a top golfer (he became a club pro after his retirement) and racquetball player, he thought that teams brought out the fans. As a star player, he was sometimes the target when fans from his opponent's base would vent their spleens, but he didn't mind. Bettez insisted, "It may cost more to run a sports program at that level (base and division), but that's missing the point. You have more spectators, and there's more identification with the team."[84]

Bettez's comments reflected the rationale that the interview subjects contacted for this chapter gave. While crowds were not huge during the regular season, providing a spectacle and a community building event for two thousand, three thousand, or five thousand people must have been seen as a successful campaign for the base commanders who spent so much time and energy building programs. Although American fans were ready to support their home team, Bettez failed to mention in any of his articles that any French (or Germans or British, for that matter) fans benefited from the display put on by the U.S. armed services.

While the 1956 Tigers demonstrated that French USAFE teams were beginning to catch up with the talent levels of the German and British teams, they were still unable to win the big game. That would change in 1957. The Toul Tigers once again coasted through the France District, winning all nine of their games while scoring 451 points and giving up only 13. The Tigers returned Watson, Pappas, and Ed White, a six-foot-four, 210-pound flanker, as their offensive leaders on a team that averaged 203 pounds across the front seven. Although paltry by contemporary standards, the 1958 NFL Champion Baltimore Colts averaged 243 pounds on their offensive line, and their opponents, the New York Giants, weighed in at an average of 244 pounds, so this must have been fairly large for a group that needed to be in good shape to stop any Soviet thrusts.[85]

Home cooking finally worked in their favor as the Toul Tigers defeated the Wiesbaden (Germany) Flyers 20–19. The rematch of the previous year's championship game proved to be an even closer game as the Tigers blocked two Flyer extra point attempts to provide the margin of victory. The Flyers dominated the second half, scoring all three of their touchdowns in the final stanza. They scored near the end of the game on a spectacular 81-yard pass play from Dave Sowell to Dick Murray to draw within a single point, but the Tigers gained possession when the Flyers' onside kick did not travel the necessary 10 yards. Pappas subsequently ran out the clock with three running plays, and France had its first champion.[86]

1957 French Team Results

USAFE France District	Wins	Losses	Ties
Toul (Tigers)	10	0	0
Etain (Pioneers)	7	2	0
SHAPE (Indians)	7	3	0
Laon (Rangers)	6	3	0
Chambley (Desert Rats)	5	4	0
Evreux (Normans)	4	6	1
Phalsbourg (Falcons)	3	6	0
Châteauroux (Sabres)	1	7	1
Chaumont (Mudhens)	3	5	1
Dreux (Plainsmen)	6	4	0
Com Z Conference (USAEUR)			
Orléans (Orioles)	10	1	0
Toul-Nancy (Dodgers)	6	1	0
Chinon (Red Devils)	4	3	0
Bussac (Broncos)	2	3	1
Verdun (Cardinals)	2	4	1
La Rochelle (Rams)	1	4	0
Fontenet (Saints)	1	6	0

Source: "Conference Standings," *Stars and Stripes*, November 11, 1957, 20.

Along with the championship game, USAFE added a "Runner Up Bowl" to its schedule. The SHAPE Indians of the France District traveled to Naples, Italy, to play the Sembach (Germany) Tigers in front of "approximately 2,000 football hungry Americans." A first-quarter safety gave the Tigers the margin of victory as they edged the Indians 16–14.[87] Stan Swift, who scored on a deflected pass with forty-four seconds remaining, remembered that the spectacle surrounding the game came close to the standards of bowl games at home, and mentioned that Charlotte Sheffield, Miss America 1957, was in attendance, along with the U. S. Navy Band.[88] In an odd twist of fate, the Tigers would continue their winning ways, but in 1958 they would be playing for Laon AFB in France.

The Orléans Orioles of Com Z improved in 1957, and they too won all their regular season games, finishing with a 10–0 record. They began their title chase playing at home against the Eighth AAA (Anti-Aircraft Artillery) Group Flaks. The Orléans squad started strong, after Mel Clanton, its "standout guard," recovered a fumble and looked to be on the verge of scoring in the first quarter when the Orioles' Jim "Lefty" Leftwich fumbled on the Flak 20-yard line. This took the wind out of the Orioles' sails, and the Flaks scored twenty unanswered points in the first half. In the second half the French entry, also playing at home, moved the ball seemingly at will between the 30-yard lines. The Orioles managed a late touchdown, but that was too little too late, and they lost 20–7.[89]

It is interesting to contrast the coverage in *Stars and Stripes* of the championships played in France with happenings back at home. The USAFE and Com Z playoffs took place in November 1957, a little more than two months after Arkansas governor Orval Faubus had called out his National Guard troops to block nine black students from entering Little Rock Central High School. It occurred around a month after U.S. president Dwight D. Eisenhower federalized those troops and sent in the 101st Airborne Division to enforce integration.[90] Conflicts centered on race relations were front-page news in the nation.

However, Carol Watson and Ed White of the Toul Tigers, along with Mel Clanton and Jim Leftwich of the Orléans Orioles, were African Americans playing on integrated teams. There were likely other black players among the athletes contending for the top spot in their leagues, but unless photos accompany the articles, it is impossible to tell.

U.S. president Harry S. Truman had issued Executive Order 9981, which integrated the armed services in 1948, and by 1952 administration officials maintained that integration had been accomplished "without any marked incident and without any-one even noticing it was being done."[91] As unlikely as that narrative was, the presence of integrated teams in championship games gave some indication that military sporting programs were successfully bringing the races together. The mere presence of integrated teams may not be enough to categorically demonstrate that integration had gone smoothly, but divided teams typically do not play for championships; therefore the argument can be made with some confidence that black and white players were working together harmoniously.

The argument is reinforced with the testimonials of some of the former players given in interviews during 2011–12. A 1961 team photo provided by Dave Madril shows that sixteen of the thirty players for the Châteauroux Sabres were black. Back in the states 1961 would see the final integration of the NFL when the Washington Redskins at last fielded a black player. Chuck Bristol, who played for the Laon Rangers from 1960 to 1963, recalled, "Black and white players worked together and played together. They were your friends. You could rely on them and they on you."[92] Ken Thrash, who coached the Rangers from 1958 to 1960 remembered that one of their black players named Smith married a Frenchwoman, and the coaching staff "chipped in to buy baby clothes" for the couple's baby girl; years later their daughter graduated first in her class from the Air Force Academy.[93] Both Bristol and Thrash are white, and I have found no black players to provide corroboration, so the case is fragile. Still, remembrances such as these, along with the color-blind reporting by *Stars and Stripes*, at a time when a person's race was routinely mentioned in other newspapers, along with the on-field success of integrated teams, point to some level of cooperative teamwork between the races during a time when that was largely absent outside the sports and military worlds.

When the Sixty-Sixth TACRECON (Tactical Reconnaissance) Wing rotated from Sembach, Germany, to Laon, France, Col. Robert Gideon cemented his spot in the football-freak column by arranging for the entire Tigers team to make the move intact.[94] There they became Laon Rangers and proceeded to dominate the France District, winning all nine regular-season games with a powerful offense, led by All Air Force Europe selection Bobby Klein and All USAFE guard Jim Bobbit, that had scored 250 points. The Rangers' stingy defense had given up only 22 points, and they seemed prepared to make it two in a row for France in the USAFE finals when they faced the Ramstein Rams, who were led by another transferee, Gil Bettez.[95]

The team from Germany enjoyed the home-field advantage, and Bettez, the EC MVP for 1958, passed for two touchdowns and ran for another as the Rams defeated the Rangers 30–8 in front of eight thou-

1958 French Team Results

USAFE France District	Wins	Losses	Ties
Laon (Rangers)	9	1	0
Toul (Tigers)	8	3	0
Evreux (Normans)	4	3	1
SHAPE (Indians)	4	3	1
Phalsbourg (Falcons)	2	5	1
Châteauroux (Sabres)	3	5	1
Chaumont (Mudhens)	1	6	1
Dreux (Plainsmen)*	0	7	0
Com Z Conference (USAEUR)			
Bussac (Broncos)	7	2	1
Toul-Nancy (Dodgers)	4	1	2
Verdun (Cardinals)	5	2	2
La Rochelle (Rams)	4	3	0
Fontenet (Saints)	2	2	3
Orléans (Orioles)	3	5	1
Ingrandes (Cardinals)	1	7	0
Chinon (Red Devils)	0	7	0

*Withdrew after fifth loss: remaining games forfeited.

Source: "Conference Standings," Stars and Stripes, November 27, 1958, 21.

sand spectators.[96] Even though the score was lopsided, Swift argued that the game was closer than the final tally indicated: "Ramstein had been winning games all year scoring about 60 points a game."[97] Holding the mighty Rams to only half their typical total therefore was something of a moral victory, and the Rangers scored in the third quarter to make the game 14–8. Early in the fourth quarter, they were driving for a possible tying touchdown, but on a key fourth down attempt, Laon Quarterback John Zin's pass was batted down. The Rams then scored fourteen unanswered points to put the game away.[98]

The USAFE title match was not only a match between two talented service teams, but also a clash between two base commanders who cared deeply about football. Sadly for the Rangers, they had the mis-

fortune to come up against an even bigger football freak than Colonel Gideon. The Rams were coached by Col. Herbert "Herb" Hartwig,
the Ramstein base commander himself, who had reportedly played
football for the New York Giants at one time.[99]

Although there is no record of any French fans watching the game,
football played in the nation would continue to influence the game
in the states. This would not be as momentous as previous examples
from the world wars but would affect individual players. When Michigan State University Spartans' head coach Duffy Daugherty headlined
the 1958 coach's clinic in Berchtesgaden, he demonstrated that money
and the chance for travel might not have been the only motivation
for a coach's attendance.[100] Ranger standout guard Bobbit must have
caught Daugherty's eye, or perhaps Phil Philpot, the Rangers' coach,
brought the young player to his future mentor's attention. Whatever
the circumstances, when his tour ended, Bobbit became a Spartan
and played well enough there to be drafted by the Cleveland Browns
of the NFL.[101] All USAFE back Bobby Klein also went on to play college football after his service was finished, starting as a halfback for
the Ohio State University Buckeyes from 1960 to 1962.

Also in 1958 the Bussac Broncos of the Com Z Conference appeared
for the first time in the quarterfinals of the USAREUR playoffs. The
Broncos' opponent in the game was the same Wiesbaden Flaks team
that had defeated Orléans in 1957. The Flaks were even bigger than
the previous year's Toul Tigers, averaging "more than 215 pounds
from end to end," and led their Western Conference in both offense
and defense. The Broncos, on the other hand, had only four players
with college experience and were smaller both physically ("just over
190 pounds on the line") and in player numbers. They had unsuccessfully sought the ability to augment their numbers by adding players
before the match, as was the standard operating procedure for baseball playoffs. According to Bob Wilcox, former Florida A&M player
and head coach, they relied on superior conditioning to outlast their
opponents. Wilcox had vowed at the USAREUR Coach's Clinic that
his team's goal was to make the playoffs and to "prove that 'Com Z
play[ed] a good brand of football, too.'"[102]

They might have demonstrated that by winning seven games and losing only one, but in the playoffs, God was on the side of the big battalions, and the Broncos went down to a 22–13 defeat. They did put up a good fight and outgained the Wiesbaden team on the ground. They scored the first touchdown of the game when fullback Bill Lee scored on a short run, which "set the overcoated crowd buzzing," and only trailed the Flaks 14–7 at half. The crowd of 5,500 at Wiesbaden, which included Lt. Gen. Francis W. Farrell, the commanding general of V Corps, saw the French team driving at the start of the second half, but a costly fumble gave the German team the ball. The Flaks scored eight plays later to put the game out of reach.[103]

The 1958 playoffs had demonstrated that both France District and Com Z teams were showing signs that they had begun to catch up with their counterparts from Germany and England. During the late 1950s and into the 1960s, teams based in France would be serious contenders for conference titles. The 1959 season would see the Laon Rangers once again contend for the USAFE finals but fall short, and the Orléans Orioles would rebound to top form after a disappointing 3–5 1958 season but likewise fall in the semifinals.

Laon advanced to the finals after racking up eight wins during the regular season and receiving the bye into the finals. The other Wiesbaden team, the Flyers, determined to revenge their 1957 defeat by Toul in the finals, were the Rangers' opponent in the semifinal match. The game, played in front of four thousand spectators at Laon in the local stadium nicknamed the "Beet Bowl," saw another defeat for the France District entry. Going into the final the Rangers were hampered by a difficulty that college teams did not have to contend with when the air force "unexpectedly" rotated Bobby Green, their top running back, out of the base. Given the level of command interest in football, one might speculate: did the Wiesbaden commanding officer have a friend in the personnel office? In any event the teams played a scoreless first half, but Flyers' quarterback Gerry Sullivan took over in the second half, passing for two touchdowns and kicking a field goal to lead Wiesbaden to a 17–0 victory.[104]

The USAREUR semifinals pitted the 7-0-1 Orioles against the 8-0-1 Gelnhausen (Germany) Braves in the game played in front of five thousand fans at Orléans's Patton Field.[105] The Com Z champions

1959 French Team Results

USAFE France District	Wins	Losses	Ties
Laon (Rangers)	8	2	1
SHAPE (Indians)	9	1	0
Toul (Tigers)	4	2	1
Châteauroux (Sabres)	3	4	0
Evreux (Normans)	3	5	0
Phalsbourg (Falcons)	3	5	0
Dreux (Plainsmen)	1	7	0
Com Z Conference (USAEUR)			
Orléans (Orioles)	7	1	1
Verdun (Cardinals)	5	2	1
La Rochelle (Rams)	4	2	0
Toul-Nancy (Dodgers)	3	5	2
Ingrandes (Cardinals)	2	4	0
Bussac (Broncos)	1	4	1
Fontenot (Saints)	1	5	0

Source: "Conference Standings," Stars and Stripes, November 26, 1959, 21.

were larger than the Braves, but the visitor's "Surly Seven" front line's hard tackling put running back George Coffey and quarterback Ralph Miller on the sidelines.[106] They also blocked two Orléans punts, and stuffed a key fourth down try by Coffey. The Braves ran up a 19–0 halftime lead on the running of former Ohio State University back Jim Roseboro, but Orléans came back in the third quarter and had drawn within one score. But when the Orioles' attempted an onside kick, the Braves recovered and added two late scores to win the game 33–14.[107]

The 1950s saw the beginning of USAFE and USAREUR play by teams from French bases. Although they had some success playing each other, the teams from France could not overcome their opponents from longer-established bases in Germany and England until 1957, when the Toul Tigers won it all. Although Stars and Stripes noted some level of popularity among the French population in 1953, evidence that the indigenous population continued to support football after that year was largely absent.

The first years of new decade of the 1960s would see French-base teams dominate USAFE but still fall to German teams as the EC added interservice championship games to its schedule. Two French USAFE teams would also mount an effort to excite the French about our game, with little success. Along with the base teams, high school competition would also reach a crescendo in the county. French bases would disappear after the 1966 season, however, as de Gaulle withdrew his nation from membership in NATO.

5. The Rise and Fall of French Teams, 1960-1966

With less than a decade of play under their belts, teams from bases located in France had gone from easy marks in championship games to contenders for the title, particularly in the USAFE Conference. The early 1960s would see teams from the France District dominate USAFE, while their counterparts in the USAREUR's Com Z Conference would continue to falter in the playoffs. Even the transfer of the mighty SHAPE Indians to Com Z would not enable entries from France to crack the top echelons dominated by powerful German teams.

By the middle of the decade, conference realignment, personnel transfers, and the de-emphasis of football on several of the bases would see teams from French bases back where they started. There was even a brief, and ineffectual, attempt by French and American entrepreneurs to interest the indigenous population in our sport, but that would come and go with little notice. However, for a few years, the SHAPE Indians and the Laon Rangers were contenders.

The France District of USAFE contracted a bit with the advent of the new decade, losing the Evreux and Phalsbourg teams, which had finished with lackluster 3–5 records in 1959. Likewise, the Com Z Conference of USAREUR had shed some of its deadwood when the 1–5 Fontenot Saints gave up the sport. USAFE, however, made up for the loss of the two teams by adding another district that was composed of teams from Spain and Morocco. The remaining France District teams would open a new chapter in USAFE football that would give the loop a pronounced French accent.

The Loan Rangers and the SHAPE Indians, who had finished at

1960 French Team Results

USAFE France District	Wins	Losses	Ties
SHAPE (Indians)	11	1	0
Laon (Rangers)	8	2	0
Châteauroux (Sabres)	4	6	0
Dreux (Plainsmen)	1	8	0
Toul (Tigers)	0	8	0
Com Z Conference (USAEUR)			
Orléans (Knights)	7	3	0
La Rochelle (Rams)	6	2	0
Verdun (Cardinals)	5	2	0
Toul-Nancy (Dodgers)	3	4	0
Ingrandes (Cardinals)	3	4	0
Bussac (Broncos)	3	5	0

Source: "Conference Standings," Stars and Stripes, November 29, 1960, 21.

the top of the district's standings in 1959, would continue to be the standard-bearers in USAFE, but their relative positions would switch. The work that Col. William Dodds had begun in 1959 would finally pay off in 1960 with the second USAFE championship for French teams, and his Indians would win three conference crowns in a row before transferring to the Com Z in 1963. The final ingredient that would cement the Indians' dynasty was the arrival in Paris of Bernard A. "Barney" Gill in 1959.

Gill had already fashioned a remarkable record of achievement in football before arriving in France. As a star halfback for the Granby High School team in Virginia Beach, Gill had led the state of Virginia in scoring during the 1945 and 1946 seasons, including scoring the first ever touchdown in the Oyster Bowl.[1]

As a freshman at the University of Virginia, he appeared for the first time in Stars and Stripes when it ran a photo of him tackling Chester Pierce, an African American playing for Harvard, in the first integrated game ever played by the Cavaliers.[2] Despite injuries, he played an integral role in the Cavalier backfield during his sophomore and junior years before "flunking out" in 1950.[3]

In the service Gill barely missed a step in his football career, starring for the Forty-Fifth Infantry Division. He led it to an undefeated season that brought the All Conference Southern Service title to Camp Polk (LA).[4] His play also earned him a place on the Service All-American Team.[5]

After graduation from boot camp, he joined the 504th Parachute Infantry Regiment of the Eighty-Second Airborne Division and completed Officer Candidate School. While at Fort Bragg, North Carolina, Gill fell under the command of Colonel Dodds, who would convince the young officer to hang up his cleats and pick up a coach's whistle.

Despite being drafted by the Baltimore Colts of the NFL, Gill decided to remain in the army. However, when Dodds transferred to the Pentagon, Gill was left in a tricky position with the command structure, and after spending a year on temporary duty (TDY) in Saudi Arabia, he returned to Fort Bragg, where he had been replaced as the unit's coach by a "former All-American at Mississippi."[6]

Dodds took care of his protégé and arranged for him to be placed on TDY as an assistant coach for the legendary United States Military Academy at West Point football coach Earl "Red" Blaik. While Gill served as a scout and junior varsity coach for Blaik, his duties also included representing the team at weekly press meetings held in Toots Shor's famous New York City bistro. It was at one of these meetings that Gill gave the name "Lonesome End" to the position played by wide receiver Bill Carpenter, who did not join the other players in the huddle.[7] After the press luncheons Gill would also be tasked with taking game films to the Waldorf Astoria, where he would screen them and discuss the game with retired general Douglas MacArthur.[8]

When Blaik finally retired from the academy after the 1959 season, Gill once again found himself "advised" that he needed to find a new home. Dodds once again provided a lifeline, bringing the now-captain to France to coach his prized SHAPE Indians.[9]

As mentioned in chapter 4, Dodds was, in Gill's words, a football freak, and with the help of a friend in the Pentagon, he had been building a team that could dominate the USAFE.[10] The enthusiastic colonel in charge of the Headquarters Section had done very well, building a team that included eighteen players with college experience, along with one who had even played a year of professional football.[11] Leading the way were the team's top offensive players such as Eddie West, a former honorable mention All-American, who had thrown for thirteen touchdowns in 1955 at the end of his career as the quarterback for the North Carolina State University Wolfpack.[12] Gill, who spent the remainder of the 1959 season as the top scout for the Indians, was in the sometimes enviable position of having several good signal callers. In addition to West, he could also call on the talents of Russ Mericle, the quarterback he had coached on the junior varsity team at West Point. Backing up those two was Harold McCurry, who saw enough playing time to lead the district in passing yards. Marion Rushing, a guard who had played at Southern Illinois University before playing during the 1959 season for the Chicago Cardinals, anchored a line that also included Bill Sims of Wiley College in Texas and Don Cogsville of Mount Union College in Ohio, two Little All-Americans at the ends. The Indians' cupboard full of talent allowed Gill to alternate Red and White teams and effectively overwhelm and wear down opponents. In addition to the surfeit of skill on the offense, the defense put together by Dodds and coached by Gill gave up only one touchdown during the entire season.

Mericle, the former West Pointer, was indicative of how far Dodds and Gill would go to secure top-level players. In a 2011 telephone interview, the ex-plebe remembered that after graduation, he had been assigned to the Third Armored Division stationed in Germany. While he and his wife, the daughter of an officer assigned to SHAPE, were visiting Paris, they attended an Ella Fitzgerald concert, where they ran into Gill. The captain set the wheels in motion, and Mericle found himself assigned as an aide to a general who already had one and did not need another. He mostly worked for Dodds in the Operation Section of Headquarters Command and remembered being a bit of a fish out of water there: "There were fifty-four general officers assigned to SHAPE, and one lieutenant from the Army—me."[13]

Nor was Gill a jingoist when it came to stocking his team. He remembered that at one point, he recruited a British MP sergeant who had experience playing rugby to join the team. Gill remembered that Brian Brandon, the British player, was very large and athletic, so he figured that "he could play our sport."[14]

Fittingly, the Indians' march to the 1960 USAFE crown began when they clenched the France District title by defeating the Laon Rangers 42–0 at their field located near the former royal palace of Versailles. The lopsided score increased the Indians' scoring disparity for the season to 419 points scored and 8 allowed. The Rangers had ended SHAPE's 1959 season with a 12–6 defeat, but the addition of Mericle and other offensive standouts had transformed the winners into an offensive juggernaut that Laon could not stop but only slow down by holding them to five points under their season average.[15]

The Suffolk Titans would be SHAPE's next opponent in the USAFE semifinals. No slouches either, the team from Britain had won the UK District for the past three seasons under head coach Bill Brigman. The ex–Georgia Tech quarterback was not hopeful for his team, whose players were mostly former high school gridders. After the runaway 56–0 game, Brigman told Stars and Stripes, "We figured that they could beat us by six touchdowns. They made eight."[16]

Despite the uneven score Gill was taking no chances. He took the unusual step of keeping Bill Brush and Tony Cillo, his assistants, on hand to help direct the game. For the regular season they had been on the road scouting upcoming opponents. The preparation included watching Laon three times, Suffolk once, and the Wiesbaden Flyers, whom the Indians would play in the USAFE finals once also.[17] The earlier scouting trip against the Flyers allowed Brush and Cillo to stay at home for the semifinal match. "We needed to win this one so we stayed here" Cillo told reporters.[18]

In an indication of how closely the personnel at SHAPE followed their football team, Stars and Stripes mentioned that even though the coaches missed watching their charges playing on Saturday, they could watch game films each week at the base's service club, where the films were screened for all interested.[19] Another pointer that indicated the football team was popular was that SHAPE had added additional bleacher seating to accommodate the crowd that would attend the Laon and Suffolk games.[20] The crowd for the Laon game was the largest, with 5,500 plus in attendance, and another 5,000 saw the semifinal win over the Titans.[21]

Wiesbaden of the Germany District defeated Torrejón (Spain) of the Spain-Morocco District in the other semifinal game to set up a match between the defending-champion Flyers and the insurgent Indians for the USAFE final. Wiesbaden had won its last twenty-five games, including its 17–0 drubbing of Laon the previous year in the finals.[22] Joe Romano, the Flyers' head coach, had no illusions about this being just one more in his team's march to perfection. "I haven't slept a wink in two weeks," he admitted. "All I see is Indians on the warpath." Romano was no doubt engaging in typical coaching habit of poor-mouthing his team and building up his opponent, but he was more correct than he hoped in his assessment of the Indians: "The best Air Force Team I've seen. Ever."[23]

Still, the Flyers gave the Indians their sternest test of the year in a match that was carried to thousands of fans in the EC by the Armed Forces Network (AFN) radio broadcast.[24] Playing at home before a crowd of some 8,500 spectators, they held the powerful SHAPE offense to only eleven points that included an 83-yard run for a touchdown by fullback Guy Hill. West added the two-point conversion and also kicked a 22-yard field goal, the first three-point attempt that the team had tried all season, to finish the scoring.[25] The Flyers were unable to score, but after recovering an Indian fumble, they were knocking on the door at the SHAPE 17-yard line. Faced with a fourth down, Romano decided to go for it rather than attempt a field goal, and the pass play was unsuccessful. Speaking to reporters, Romano took the blame for that decision and its role in their loss.[26] At the time the game was a scoreless tie, but when SHAPE took possession, the next play was Hill's back-breaking run that saw the diminutive back break several tackles on his way to the score.[27]

The SHAPE Indians, built by Dodds and directed by Gill, had won the second USAFE title for the France District, and Romano was likely correct in dubbing them the best USAFE team he had seen. In previous years that would have ended the football season for the victorious Tribe. However, in 1960, when, in a move designed to trim the defense budget, the military was in the process of drawing down the number of dependents who were allowed to travel overseas to join their spouses, they also had decided to add another layer to the playoff system.[28] In 1960 the Indians would play the USAREUR champion Mainz Troopers, who had defeated the Ulm Hawks 34–0 the week after the USAFE final.[29]

In a move designed to generate positive Cold War propaganda, the new game, dubbed the Freedom Bowl, was to be played between the winners of the USAFE and USAREUR champions. The proceeds from ticket sales for the game would be donated to the German Ministry for Expellees and Refugees.[30] No doubt the EC officials who created the game could argue that the game offered a chance to show their concern for the refugee problem that the Federal Republic of Germany (West Germany) was dealing with as more than twelve million had fled the Soviet-dominated Democratic Republic of Germany (East Germany) between 1946 and 1960. The publicity from the game would also serve to remind the world that millions of Germans were "voting with their feet" to flee Communism in the East. A little less than a year before the Berlin Wall went up as a visible symbol that Communists needed to build walls to keep their people from fleeing the dictatorial state created under Walter Ulbricht, the Freedom Bowl offered a chance for U.S. Cold Warriors to remind the world that the West was the focus of freedom.[31] In the larger picture they could thus argue that another football game deserved increasingly scarce dollars in a time of retrenchment.

There had been a previous match between the champions of the USAFE and the USAREUR in 1949 also held in Frankfurt, which was the location of the 1960 game. In the previous game the army's Fourteenth Constabulary Regiment Red Raiders defeated the air force's Rhein-Main Rockets 14–13. This time, instead of only the occasional championship, the EC planned to have an annual Freedom Bowl, played in 1960 at an air force site and at an army base in 1961.[32]

The hoopla surrounding the championship game that filled the pages of *Stars and Stripes* during the week between the USAREUR final game and the services championship game could have served as a model for the eventual media deluge surrounding the Super Bowl. Teams were dissected, bands were lined up for halftime entertainment, and the coaches had the chance to praise their opponents and downplay their chances in the title game. The extravaganza, which would be broadcast live by AFN and "filmed by service cameramen for the *Armed Forces Screen Magazine*, would be a contest between two evenly matched teams.[33] The Troopers, coached by Ralph Peterson, had never lost a game in the conference since joining it in 1959, and the Indians were 11–0 under Gill.[34] For the season the Indians had averaged 45.3 points a game and the Troopers 44.2. The Indians had given up only 8 points all year, and the Troopers were only slightly more generous, giving up 9. Both teams alternated units with the Indians, swapping Red for White, and the Troopers substituting Blue for Gold.

As mentioned in chapter 4, the teams differed, according to Gill, in the importance that they assigned to football. Though Gill and Dodds obviously ate, slept, lived, and died with football, the Germans took that emphasis to a higher level with separate barracks and the rest that is reflective of major Division I programs. Gill remembered that the Troopers were even more stacked with talent than his Indians, and that he had coached several of the Mainz players when he was at West Point.[35] The difference in emphasis between the German and the French bases also motivated ticket sales for the game, as players and fans from Com Z teams such as Orléans and Bussac, which competed in the USA-REUR, were reportedly rooting for the Paris entry to demonstrate that French-base teams could hold their own with the vaunted Germans.[36]

During the year the Indians had done something that no previous French team had accomplished; they knocked the USAREUR's coverage in *Stars and Stripes* to second place. In previous seasons the newspaper had typically discussed German teams on the earlier pages of the sports section and also devoted more space to those teams. The 1960 Indians' record of success had changed that, and no doubt Captain Gill also played a role in garnering more coverage for his team. A media savvy coach, Gill also displayed a knack for being noticed, with his 1947 photo in *Stars and Stripes* as a freshman at Virginia, for instance.

Gill's press duty during his service with Blaik had only sharpened his instincts, and he was often quoted in the *New York Times*, entering football history as the man who named the Lonesome End. During his first year in the EC, he had also garnered more press notice than his head coach at Paris and was interviewed by *Stars and Stripes* to handicap the 1959 USAFE championship match between Laon and Wiesbaden.[37] As was also evident in my conversations with the ex-coach, Gill was a great interview subject. When not engaging in coach-speak, he was a man who would call a spade a fucking shovel and therefore the type of colorful character that reporters love to cover.

During his days under Blaik, the head coach had called his assistant onto the carpet over reports that players were partying in Gill's quarters. Blaik demanded to know if there was "any fornicating going on" during the parties. Gill responded by telling the coach, "There might be fornicating, but there's no fucking going on."[38] So Gill, the successful coach and colorful character, had for perhaps the first time put French football ahead of the Germans in the press coverage race.

What he could not do was end German dominance on the field. The two teams were evenly matched, but in the first Freedom Bowl, the Indians learned how the Wiesbaden Flyers' Romano had felt after his team's loss. The game, played before over thirty-two thousand fans at Frankfurt's Wald Stadium who paid fifty cents or two Deutschmarks for a ticket (earning $7,895 for the German relief fund), put Gill in the Flyer coach's shoes when, behind 3–0 in the fourth quarter, the Indians attempted to convert a fourth-down-and-one from their own 49-yard line.[39] The Troopers stopped West cold and took over the ball. On the next play former University of Minnesota halfback Bob Blakey scored a touchdown from there that sealed the 10–0 Mainz victory. In a defensive-dominated game, the Troopers played better, stopping the Indians offense from gaining a single first down.[40]

Once again the game was interesting in the context of the times. Odle Canada, the African American player who kicked the first Trooper field goal, was pictured in the photo accompanying the *Stars and Stripes* article about the game. Though the paper routinely identified the race of subjects written about in other sections of the paper, no mention of Canada's race, other than the photo, appeared on the sports pages. This was the same year that Ruby Bridges had become the first black student at the William Frantz Elementary School in New Orleans.[41] Bridges, the subject of *The Problem We All Live With*, a famous painting and magazine image by Norman Rockwell that now hangs in a hallway outside the Oval Office, was excoriated by hecklers who hurled racial epithets at her as she walked to school escorted by four U.S. deputy marshalls.[42] There still might have been simmering racial tensions within the military, but after more than a decade of integration, the surface remained demonstrably calmer than it was in the ZI.

Blakey, the other player who scored a touchdown against SHAPE,

was also black, as were Ron Tracy and Leroy Ferguson, two other start-
ers on the Troopers' offense. The Indians' two Little All-Americans,
Cogsville and Sims, were also black.[43] That at least six African Americans played important roles in the EC championship game without that fact being explicitly pointed out by the military newspaper
is fascinating in the context of the times. It was likely editorial policy for the sports page not to include mention of a player's race when
mentioning his exploits, possibly done to send the implicit message
that race was no cause for notice but just the way the world was, and
should be.

An additional implicit message in such treatment of racial issues
was that an integrated military was the norm and that when people
of different races worked together, good things happened.[44] The model
for the United States therefore should be based on the EC championship example of racial harmony, not the discordant model of New
Orleans. The colorblind reporting of *Stars and Stripes* may have concealed many examples of overt and covert racism in the armed forces
and among fans of one team or the other, but one might also make the
case that integration of the armed forces was leading to less racism.

In the Com Z Conference in 1960, the Orléans Knights had rolled to
a 7–2 record during the regular season and were reportedly confident
going into their semifinal match in the USAREUR playoffs against the
Ulm Hawks. There was even talk of taking the conference championship by supporters of the team who echoed head coach Manny Gregg,
who told *Stars and Stripes*, "We have a good team, and we're ready to
prove it."[45] The Knights' headman, who was another longtime service
player and coach, having played at various posts in the United States
as well as coaching at an American base in Nara, Japan, felt that his
Knights were in better condition than the other teams he would face
in the playoffs. With forty players on his roster, he could afford to run
in fresh teams and eventually wear down opponents.[46]

In a sloppy game played in the mud at Ulm, a crowd of 4,500 fans
saw the theories of the Knights' mentor crash down as the football
gods continued to favor the big lines. Ulm's forward wall, with three
players weighing in at more than 220 pounds, kept the light but well-
conditioned Orléans team bottled up the entire game, save for a late

1960 French High School Results

High School Com Z Conference	Wins	Losses	Ties
Châteauroux (Sabres)	8	0	0
Paris (Pirates)	2	4	0
Orléans (Trojans)	2	4	0
Poitiers (Panthers)	3	3	0
Verdun (Falcons)	1	5	0

Source: "Conference Standings," Stars and Stripes, November 29, 1960, 21.

score by fullback Don Rose.[47] Even the presence of nine players with college experience, including quarterback Nelson Yarbrough, who had played the position for the University of Virginia, did not allow the Knights to overcome four turnovers, including two interceptions thrown by the former Cavalier.[48] Though the game was still close at 14–6 in the fourth quarter, the Hawks ran off a 73-yard drive for a touchdown that made the final score 21–6.

Although the 1960 season ultimately ended with losses for the USAFE and the USAREUR teams, one team playing in France completed an undefeated season with a championship and an undefeated season. The Châteauroux Sabres of the Com Z High School Conference ended the year with a victory over the champion of the Spain-Morocco District Torrejón Knights. Having won their conference championship, the Sabres invited the Knights to the first Châteauroux Invitational Bowl, which they promptly won. The Sabres finished their second straight undefeated season by smashing the Knights 35–0 behind the passing of senior quarterback Ron Fletcher, who passed for each of the five touchdowns scored by his team that day.[49]

Though undersized, standing only five feet nine and weighing in at only 159 pounds, Fletcher would leave Châteauroux to attend college at the University of Oklahoma in Norman. He tried out for football as a freshman but ended up selling hot dogs for the games. However, when he was a sophomore, the Sooner coaches, "liking his progress, gave him a full scholarship."[50] He would be most famous for throwing a 95-yard touchdown pass, still the longest in OU history, in a losing effort in the 1965 Gator Bowl.[51]

1961 French Team Results

USAFE European Conference	Wins	Losses	Ties
SHAPE (Indians)	11	1	0
USAFE Continental Conference			
Laon (Rangers)	5	2	2
Toul (Tigers)	1	9	0
Châteauroux (Sabres)	1	10	0

Source: "Final Conference Standings," Stars and Stripes, November 18, 1961, 20.

The decade had started well for the France District of USAFE, but in 1961 the teams playing for French bases were reshuffled throughout the European Command. To trim costs or, as Gill suspected, to increase dominance in football, the army eliminated or consolidated teams from the base level to the divisional level.[52] Instead of forty teams in five conferences, USAREUR would now be made up of nine teams in one conference.

The six teams that played for bases located in France would now be part of larger unit teams. USAFE would contract from twenty-two teams in four districts to seventeen teams in three conferences, plus two independents from Germany. SHAPE was now grouped together with Ramstein, Sembach, Wiesbaden, Rhine-Main, all from Germany, and Torrejón from Spain. The three remaining French bases, Laon, Châteauroux, and Toul, would now be grouped with Spangdahlem, Bitburg, and Hahn from Germany. Although Dreux lost its USAFE team, the base could still watch football as a team from there was added to the high school ranks.[53]

Despite the change from competing mainly against French bases, to the presumably more competitive German teams and Torrejón, the SHAPE Indians continued to dominate play in USAFE in 1961. They were defeated once in that season, but not on the field. After defeating the Rhine-Main Rockets 24–8, the Rockets complained that Gill had used ineligible players, and the league agreed, awarding the German team a 1–0 forfeit.[54] Gill had been warned by the USAFE athletic office that three of his players, who were stationed at a small Army installation a few miles from Paris, were ineligible, but he played them anyway. He argued that he faced an unfair disadvantage in that his team could only draw on "750 personnel in the SHAPE headquarters" while other teams had entire bases from which to recruit, but USAFE officials were not convinced.[55] The Rockets did not ultimately benefit from their complaints, however, and when both teams tied for the conference lead with 8-1 records, they met again in a playoff to determine which team would go forward in the USAFE title hunt.[56]

As a warmup for the rematch with the Rockets, SHAPE played an exhibition in Paris versus the Berlin Bears, one of the independent teams in USAFE. The Bears brought a 5-2 record that included victory over the Twenty-Fourth Infantry Division Lions, who were leading the USAREUR standings.[57] Three thousand fans watched the Indians defeat the Bears easily, 42–6, with Mericle passing for two scores, and West "electrified" the fans with a 63-yard run for another touchdown.[58] The Indians were clearly ready for another run for the title.

They began by avenging their only loss of the season, beating Rhine-Main 13–3 in front of four thousand fans on a cold and rainy afternoon. The Rockets played better than in their first encounter, and the game was only a one-score-affair until the final quarter, when West scored to put the game out of reach. Mericle again passed for a touchdown, and the defense allowed only one long run by the Rockets in the first quarter, which led to their only score.[59]

The Laon Rangers had also continued their winning ways and also had to go through an opponent that they had played in the regular season to win their Continental Conference. The Spangdahlem Pioneers and the Rangers had played to a scoreless tie in their first meeting and had tied for the conference lead with 4-0-1 records in the loop. The Rangers managed more offense in the final though and defeated the German invaders 11–0 in front of around two thousand fans. The shutout was their fifth for the season, and the team depended on its tight defense. Both teams were hampered by muddy conditions, and all the scoring took place in the first half as Devers Brannon kicked a 32-yard field goal, and halfback Steve Savage scored a second-quarter touchdown and added the two-point conversion.[60]

Laon's road to the championship lay through the Alconbury Spartans (UK), and that proved to be too much, but only as a result of alleged command interference. In the first sudden-death overtime game in the history of the USAFE playoffs, the Rangers fell to the Spartans 12–6 in front of a small crowd of only some 1,500 fans. Throughout the game and the overtime, the two teams were deadlocked in every category, and the score was tied 6–6 at the end of regulation.[61] As related in chapter 4, command influence was key in building teams, and in this case it turned out to be decisive, when the officials disallowed a touchdown by player-coach Jerry Curtright for illegal procedure. The score would have won the game for Laon, and years later he reportedly met one of the referees, who told him that the commanding general of the base had made it clear to the arbiters that they should do everything in their power to ensure an Alconbury win, so they were merely following orders when they called back Laon's potential winner.[62]

The Indians also had to travel to Britain for the USAFE final, but even direct orders from a base commander, if he gave them in this case, were powerless to divert the SHAPE team on its way to a 39–12 victory. The chance existed in the first half, with the Indians holding on to a precarious 16–12 lead going into halftime. However, West, whose fumble set up one of the Spartan scores, redeemed himself in the second half by running for two scores and passing for a third.[63]

Instead of playing a service championship game to determine the overall EC champion in 1961, the Freedom Bowl would bring together two All-Star teams from USAFE and USAREUR. The game would be still be called the Freedom Bowl, as it had been in 1960, and the hoopla surrounding the match mirrored coverage of a championship college bowl game in the States. *Stars and Stripes* coverage of the upcoming tilt eclipsed its notice of the annual bowl season back home. Readers were told about the opposing coaching staffs, and the top thirty-five players likely to make the respective teams were frequently reminded of the Cold War significance of the game.[64] As with the previous year's effort, the proceeds from the gate receipts would be donated to the relief fund to help settle Germans who had fled the Communist Democratic Republic of Germany.

While all interview subjects agreed that the military spent so much on sporting programs to raise the morale of service personnel and their dependents, the military found other uses for games as well.[65] The previous chapter mentioned 1953 football games that were attended by French spectators as one of those uses. American leadership no doubt felt that football, along with other offerings, would be a good introduction to our culture, which was being planted on small islands in their midst.

There were yet more uses for football, and the exigencies of the Cold War provided motivation for Cold Warriors to insert pro-American narratives into games such as the Freedom Bowl. The program for that game demonstrated how events such as this were framed into propaganda for the home team. It included welcoming messages from Heinrich Lübke, the president of the Federal Republic of Germany; Gen. Bruce C. Clarke, commander in Chief of the United States Army in Europe; and Gen. Truman H. Landon, Commander in chief of the United States Air Force in Europe. Printed in both English and German, their messages made no bones about the larger significance of the game.

Lübke's message thanked the players for helping to aid his people, and then the two generals cut to the chase. Clarke addressed the reason for the name of the match: "Naming this event the 'Freedom Bowl' was most appropriate. This game, featuring the friendly football rivalry between the Army and the Air Force, demonstrates America's military cooperation in support of the Free World. In giving the proceeds of this all-American contest to the Federal Republic of Germany to aid refugees from Communism, both Services are in a very real sense aiding the cause of free men everywhere."[66] Landon hammered the message home, telling readers,

This game provides our European friends and neighbors with a clear picture of American standards of competition, sportsmanship, and fair play. It demonstrates how Americans of differing economic and ethnic backgrounds can mold themselves into smoothly operating teams, as effective on the sports field as they have proved themselves in maintaining a strong deterrent power for peace.

Of particular interest to our German guests is the fact that the Freedom Bowl serves to show that Americans truly have 'heart,' the desire to help others in a time of need. For this game is being played to benefit those who have fled, with little or no personal property, to the freedom of the West from the tyranny of Communism.[67]

When Landon mentioned that soldiers and airmen from different economic and ethnic backgrounds combined to form "smoothly operating teams," he was perhaps doing his best to refute Soviet charges concerning the state of race relations in the United States, which were a constant thorny problem for American Cold Warriors.[68] On the field, however, Germans who had likely been exposed to ghastly accounts of how African Americans were abused in the United States, could see for themselves that the teams contending for the interservice title were nearly one-third African American (twenty of sixty-nine).

Events such as these helped Americans to at least attempt to refute Soviet propaganda, although images of police dogs attacking peaceful marchers in Birmingham, Alabama, only two years later would likely make those efforts moot. However, for one December afternoon, two groups of Americans would exemplify a world where young men were judged by their characters, or at least their ability to run, catch, block, or tackle, rather than the color of their skins.

When game day arrived, what demonstrably mattered was the players' background in football. Twenty-nine of the thirty-five USA-REUR players had attended college and presumably had played football while they were there. This reflected the change the conference had made, replacing base teams with squads organized on the divisional level. With around twenty thousand soldiers in the average division, coaches could be very selective about the players who made up their teams.

The USAFE All-Stars, on the other hand, were organized in the older manner, around bases, which housed far fewer airmen. As a result the USAFE All-Stars could only muster fourteen of thirty-four players who had previous college experience. That five of those came from SHAPE is a testament to the effectiveness of Dodds's recruiting pipeline to the Pentagon. All together eleven players from French bases would make the USAFE team for the Freedom Bowl. Eight played for SHAPE, and the other three came from Laon.

As was the case the year before, the contest went to the side with the big divisions, and the USAREUR team was able to dominate Gill's collection, winning by a score of 13–0. Not only were the soldiers drawn from larger aggregations, but they were also just larger. Elmer May, the head coach of the USAREUR team, who had played center and defensive tackle for the Iowa State Cyclones, sent out offensive and defensive platoons that averaged over 208 pounds across the line.[69] The USAFE unit was equal on the line, but Gill's backs averaged a little less than 196 pounds.[70] Since Gill stuck to his habitual ironman system, with athletes playing offense and defense, his team was outweighed, as well as less experienced.

The game was fairly even by the statistics, with the Air Force eleven slightly outgaining the Army on the ground. The army had a 30-yard advantage in the air, and both teams threw two interceptions.[71] Two USAFE fumbles, including one by Roy Ridley on the army 12-yard line, and another by Eddie West that set up the first USAREUR score, provided much of the difference. The stellar play of the USAREUR's star halfback Paul Flint, who gained 106 yards on the ground and added a key 43-yard pass reception made the loss particularly galling for Gill.

During his postgame interview he recalled how the speedy Flint had helped him win a divisional championship when he coached the Eighty-Second Airborne team. Flint had also helped the Mainz Troopers defeat the SHAPE Indians in the previous Freedom Bowl in 1960. Gill summed up his feelings about his former standout-turned-nemesis when he told reporters, "I'll be glad to see that [Paul] Flint rotate home."[72]

Although a loss for the USAFE team, the Freedom Bowl did succeed in raising money to help refugees. Over twenty thousand fans packed Südwest Stadium in Ludwigshafen, Germany to watch the match.[73] With tickets priced at fifty cents each, the military was able to donate thousands of dollars to the fund and to add a reminder that Germans from the East continued to vote with their feet against Communism.[74]

Meanwhile, back in France *Stars and Stripes* carried two stories on the front page that might have boded poorly for football, had anyone connected the dots. One story claimed that as many as 2,800 American service personnel in the country continued to live in tents, rather than barracks. It is not likely that anyone in the command structure gave any thought to staging a game to raise funds to help those soldiers and airmen. The article did, however, state that building facilities for those troops was a priority.[75]

The other story bore long-term implications and reported that France, under President Charles de Gaulle, was committed to building up defense forces independent of NATO. Americans and their other European allies were troubled by this development, and with good reason. De Gaulle would finally decide to leave NATO altogether in 1966. Aside from the strategic implications, it would mean the end of American bases and American football in the country.

That development would be years in the future, however, and Gill, along with his Indians, were not through with football in 1961. When Dodds, working with a French businessman and rugby club director, Maurice Tardy, began hatching larger plans than dominating the USAFE, his protégé would of course be involved in his machinations. Tardy hoped to popularize football in the south of France, where rugby enjoyed a large following. He and Dodds organized a two-game tour featuring games played by the Indians and their top rival, the Laon Rangers. This ultimately unsuccessful attempt will be discussed in detail in chapter 6, but this was not the only case of SHAPE going international that year.

The SHAPE basketball team hosted an international Christmas tournament that brought teams from France, Belgium, Italy, Canada, and England. Perhaps reflecting Dodds's desire to build winning programs, the basketball Indians were led by a six-foot-four center, Al Weir, and thought to easily win the tournament.[76] They might have been overconfident however, and the French team they had defeated 73–65 in the first game came back through the loser's bracket to hand the Indians their only loss in the tournament.[77] The French win forced a tie breaker, which the Indians won handily by a score of 79–66.[78]

That SHAPE, under Dodds's direction, was reaching out to the French in both sports was significant, since it was the first instance since 1953 that indicated the French were even aware of football. The games in Toulouse and Perpignan didn't cause much of a stir, and *Stars and Stripes* carried no reports on the game, but it likely demonstrated that Dodds's had grand ambitions, as we shall see in chapters 6 and 7.

An interesting character in his own right, Dodds had successfully commanded the Thirty-Second "Buccaneer" Regiment during the Korean War, initiating a sniper training program that may have been the impetus for the Army Sniper School instituted in 1955.[79] After leaving SHAPE and France, he continued to train indigenous populations in the American way, serving as a military adviser to the Moise Tshombe's Congolese government. During his tour there he was briefly listed as missing after an ambush that forced him and two other American officers to flee into the jungle for four days before they reached Leopoldville and safety.[80] After his retirement from the army, Dodds married a Frenchwoman and devoted some of his time to unsuccessfully attempting to interest the French in our game.[81]

Examples such as this were few and far between, however, and the military did not seem bent on making any sustained effort to interest the French in football or any other facet of American culture. Its sports program existed to entertain and occupy service personnel, and it reportedly did a very good job of this. Though the military occasionally used football as something of an artifact of American culture to amuse and entertain indigenous populations or to hammer home messages that contrasted the American way with Soviet tyranny, it generally kept its eye on the ball, and the ball most often remained safely within the boundaries of its bases.

1961 French High School Results

High School Com Z Conference	Wins	Losses	Ties
Orléans (Trojans)	6	0	0
Paris (Pirates)	4	2	0
Dreux (Plainsmen)	4	2	0
Verdun (Falcons)	3	3	0
Poitiers (Panthers)	1	6	0
Châteauroux (Sabres)	0	7	0

Source: "Final Conference Standings," Stars and Stripes, November 18, 1961, 20.

With the descent of Châteauroux from first to last place in the prep league, a new power rose. In 1961 the Orléans Trojans would begin a two-year run, winning twelve games and losing none. After the 1960 match between Châteauroux and Torrejón, high school teams tended to confine their seasons to playing only their conference opponents. Whether this was a cost-saving measure or designed to keep high schools from overemphasizing football remains an open question, but it is a bit unusual given the addition of interservice championship games such as the Freedom Bowl to the EC schedule.

1962 French Team Results

USAREUR Conference	Wins	Losses	Ties
SHAPE (Indians)	9	3	0
USAFE Continental Conference			
Laon (Rangers)	4	5	1
Toul (Tigers)	1	8	0
Châteauroux (Sabres)	0	9	0

Source: "Final Conference Standings," Stars and Stripes, November 9, 1962, 21.

A conference change finally managed to do what USAFE teams could not: keep the SHAPE Indians and Gill from winning their conference. During the 1962 season EC sports authorities transferred SHAPE to the USAREUR Conference, where the team that had dominated USAFE since 1959 would have to contend with the big divisions. Still, the Indians came close, and only the final loss resulting from a somewhat controversial, at least to Coach Gill, league decision kept them from being crowned co-champions. Despite uncharacteristically losing two games during the regular season, they finished tied with the Twenty-Fourth Infantry Division Lions.[82] Gill and his team had already defeated the Lions during the regular season and felt that the tie breaker should go to them, based on that win.

The USAREUR Athletic Office had planned to crown both teams co-champions in case of a tie. Likely this was part of a cost-saving effort to divert funds that might be better used to get servicemen and servicewomen out of their tents and into barracks. It may have also reflected the near nuclear confrontation over Cuba the previous October. By this time smaller French bases such as Verdun continued to field basketball and other, less expensive teams.[83] In football, however, the USAREUR Conference now contained only thirteen teams, and USAFE had fifteen.

However, according to *Stars and Stripes*, "as both the Lions and the Indians thundered down the homestretch, talk of a rematch between these two grid-iron juggernauts became louder and louder."[84] The Athletic Office listened to the talk and found the money to have the title decided on the field.

The upcoming "game of the year" was embraced enthusiastically by former Bud Wilkinson pupil and Lions' head coach Jack Shilling, who felt that his team was the better of the two despite its earlier loss to the Indians, which saw the Lions lose four fumbles.[85] Gill, on the other hand, felt that his team had "everything to lose and nothing to gain now." He feared that he might have trouble motivating his team for the game, which had been set up on the "spur of the moment." He also added, "We have a depth problem—they don't. If we have a good day we might win. If not, it could be 50–0 in their favor."[86]

Gill was likely following the instructions in the mythical coach's handbook that cautions one should never speak well of one's chances in the big game. But he also realized that beating the same team twice in one season was a difficult task, particularly when his two top rushers were either limited by injury or out for the season.

When the teams finally met on Woods Memorial Field in Kefertal, Germany, the Indians did not have a good day. Gills's prophecy of being blown out came true as the Lions romped over the Indians by a score of 34–12. Despite having the services of quarterback Jim Maxfield, who had played backup to Roger Staubach at the Naval Academy, the Indians were unable to move the ball, falling behind 34–0 before scoring two late, but meaningless, touchdowns. Paul Flint was not on the field, but Clarence Childs, formerly of Florida A&M, filled his role by rushing for 102 yards and three touchdowns in front of the capacity crowd of 7,500 spectators.[87]

In an interesting twist the coach of the Indians, who had typically been depicted in *Stars and Stripes* as a top-notch football mind, and who was always good for a quote, was now described by Bob Wicker of *Stars and Stripes* as the "controversial brain behind the SHAPE Indians." Perhaps after three years of dominating USAFE, Gill was finding the tougher USAREUR not altogether to his liking, so he had become controversial. Maybe Wicker had heard that Gill, possibly as a sign of his pique over having to play the Lions again, had decided that he would have "pressing duties elsewhere" that kept him from assisting Shilling, who would be the head coach in the EC's 1962 end-of-the-year All-Star game.[88]

Since the Berlin Wall had gone up in 1961, the flood of refugees into West Germany had dwindled to a trickle, obviating the need for donations from U.S. forces to support them. Also the military may have decided to shift resources to troop quarters construction. Whatever the reason, the EC decided not to stage a Freedom Bowl in 1962. The replacement USAREUR Scholarship Bowl would instead raise funds to give college aid to the children of USAREUR service personnel.[89] Since SHAPE was the only USAREUR team playing in France, only the four Indians, led by Eddie West, were there to represent football in that country.[90]

The fortunes of the other French-base teams had fallen even lower. Laon still had the best record of any of the French teams in the USAFE, but like SHAPE, it was now lumped together with the traditionally tougher German teams for the regular season. Perhaps Colonel Hill had rotated home and the new man at the top was not so concerned with football, but for whatever reason, neither the Rangers nor any of the other teams based in France could compete under those conditions. USAFE, with teams divided between Continental and UK divisions, continued to hold a championship game, but teams from France would not take part, and the heyday of French-base football had come to an abrupt end.

1962 French High School Results

High School Com Z Conference	Wins	Losses	Ties
Orléans (Trojans)	6	0	0
Paris (Pirates)	4	1	1
Verdun (Falcons)	3	2	1
Dreux (Plainsmen)	2	4	0
Poitiers (Panthers)	2	4	0
Châteauroux (Sabres)	0	6	0
Toul (Tigers) Class C Conference	2	3	0

Source: "Final Conference Standings," *Stars and Stripes*, November 9, 1962, 21.

The sole area where football expanded in France was among the high school ranks. Dreux had been added to the ranks of prep elevens the previous year, and 1962 saw a team from Toul begin playing in the Class C Conference. Altogether there were twenty-seven high school teams playing in five conferences across the EC. Presumably since UK schools used English, there was no reason to set up separate schools, so there were no prep football teams there. In France Orléans repeated as champions of the prep Com Z Conference, once again posting a perfect 6-0 mark. The Vikings capped their second undefeated season by defeating the Dreux Pioneers 13–6. Paris finished in second place, posting a 4-1-1 record.[91]

1963 French Team Results

USAREUR Conference	Wins	Losses	Ties
SHAPE (Indians)	7	3	0
USAFE Continental Conference			
Laon (Rangers)	0	7	1
Châteauroux (Sabres)	4	4	0

Source: "Final Conference Standings," *Stars and Stripes*, November 20, 1963, 21.

The glory days for French teams had ended through a combination of conference realignment and bases de-emphasizing their football programs. Gill and his Indians contended once again for the top spot

1963 French High School Results

High School Com Z Conference	Wins	Losses	Ties
Dreux (Plainsmen)	6	0	0
Paris (Pirates)	5	1	1
Châteauroux (Sabres)	3	2	1
Verdun (Falcons)	2	4	0
Orléans (Trojans)	2	3	1
Poitiers (Panthers)	0	6	0
Class C Conference			
Toul (Tigers)	0	6	0

Source: "Final Conference Standings," *Stars and Stripes*, November 20, 1963, 21.

in USAREUR but fell short, only managing a tie for third place. The 1963 season would be Gill's last at the helm of the SHAPE team, and from there he would rotate home before serving two tours of duty in Vietnam. The French entries in USAFE managed only four wins, all by Châteauroux.

High school teams would maintain their full schedules, and Orléans, which had won twelve games in a row, would fall hard as graduations decimated its ranks. The Dreux Plainsmen would take up the slack, defeating Orléans 31–0, and finish their season undefeated, while perennial second-place finisher Paris would once again occupy that spot.[92]

1964 French Team Results

USAREUR Conference	Wins	Losses	Ties
SHAPE (Indians)	5	5	0
USAFE Continental Conference			
Laon (Rangers)	3	6	1
Châteauroux (Sabres)	4	6	0

Source: "USAREUR, Prep Standings," *Stars and Stripes*, November 18, 1964, 21.

With Dodds and Gill laboring in far-flung jungles, SHAPE subsided into a second-division team during the 1964 season, posting a .500 record, but seemingly not much of a threat to anyone.[93] Laon

1964 French High School Results

High School Com Z Conference	Wins	Losses	Ties
Paris (Pirates)	5	1	0
Dreux (Plainsmen)	4	1	0
Châteauroux (Sabres)	3	3	0
Orléans (Trojans)	2	5	0
Verdun (Falcons)	0	6	0
Poitiers (Panthers)	0	7	0
Class C Conference			
Toul (Tigers)	2	1	0

Source: "USAREUR, Prep Standings," Stars and Stripes, November 18, 1964, 21.

and Châteauroux would also continue to play, but not well, posting equally futile records of 3-6-1, and 4-6, respectively.[94] The futility of maintaining an also-ran football program prompted SHAPE to drop the sport in 1965, and while Laon and Châteauroux continued to play, they also continued to struggle. They would not sponsor teams in 1966, and that year would be the last that French bases remained in country as France left NATO and expelled the Americans.

The last winning teams based in France would be high school elevens. Orléans returned to its former luster in 1965, winning its division by defeating Paris 18–8 for the title.[95] Paris would return the favor the next year, and by that time only Verdun, Dreux, Paris, and Orléans would continue to play.[96] By the next year they would be gone as well. Perhaps the final football game that would be played in France for ten years was that final match between the Paris Pirates and the Orléans Trojans for the final Com Z Conference championship in 1966.

Between 1952 and 1966 football played by teams of American servicemen had risen from nothing to dominate the USAFE Conference, featuring teams that perennially contended for the top spot. The Toul Tigers and the SHAPE Indians had won it all, and the Indians had nearly won the EC championship. As with empires of the past, they then they fell back to earth, succumbing to a combination of personnel changes, conference realignments, and cost-cutting measures in many locales. By the end, when Charles de Gaulle's decision to chart an independent course for France compelled Americans to evacuate their bases, the once-proud teams had once again become an easy win on the schedule.

Throughout their time in the country, the football teams from Evreux to Toul had succeeded in their primary mission: reminding service personnel and their dependents of what they had left behind at home. Hundreds of games, played by thousands of men, had transplanted a slice of the American way to France. For a time they had provided a great deal of entertainment for those stationed far from home.

What they did not do was make any meaningful impression on the French population. Despite spasms of outreach such as the 1953 effort and the 1961 tour, football existed in a sealed bubble. A few thousand French spectators might have managed to see a game, or perhaps more than one, if they tried hard, during the fifteen years that Americans maintained bases in France as a part of NATO. From all the notice that the indigenous population apparently took of the games though, the Americans might as well have been playing their games back home.

Cold War football was not, however, a project of cultural imperialism. It was an American game staged for the pleasure of a largely American audience. Whatever chances that the French had to witness our sport were largely incidental to the purposes of the European Command. When Americans left the country for good, so did football.

Ambitious men would decide in the next decade to bring the game back, and this time with the intent to convince the French that our game should be theirs as well. Their efforts, as we will see in the next two chapters, would end with exactly the same result: an apathetic *Alors là?* (So what?) from the French.

6. Postwar Tours, 1961–1976

Despite the failure of the 1938 tour to gain any converts to football, French promoters for the game were not through trying. The previous boosters of the sport had left the field, but a new generation would arise.

After the war Curt Riess had settled into a career of writing about a wide variety of topics, including espionage in occupied Berlin, but he seems to have left football behind.[1] Jean Galia was nearing the end of his life and was busy reestablishing rugby league after it had been banned in 1940 by the Vichy regime.[2] On the American side Jim Crowley had new duties as the first commissioner of the All-America Football Conference, which was mounting a challenge to the National Football League, while also helping integrate professional football. Even if he had any interest in returning to France, he would not have had the time to spare.[3] In any case, no attempts would be made to spread the game until the 1960s, so a new backfield would have to carry the ball.

By 1961 football had become the most popular sport in the United States, eclipsing baseball as our national obsession, if not as our titular national pastime.[4] As discussed in previous chapters, Americans were also busy crisscrossing France to play football games at the base and high school level. Those military sponsored games left little impact on a population that was, for the most part, unaware. However, the presence of American football teams did facilitate arranging one tour, since promoters would not have to find players or teams in America willing to travel.

As with Galia and the 1938 tour, rugby aficionados would provide renewed impetus for the attempt to interest the French in our version of football. The French promoter in the case seemed to have been Maurice Tardy, although the evidence for this is slim. Gill remembered, somewhat hazily, that the promoter's name was Tardy and that he was involved in rugby, but none of the other participants could recall his name.[5] There was also a passing mention that Tardy had influenced later French promoters such as Marcel Leclerc.[6] Tardy was a former player for and president of the Celtic de Paris team, as well as an associate of Jean Galia, one of the promoters of the 1938 tour. As further circumstantial evidence for Tardy's sponsorship, he had also been one of the promoters and organizers of a 1934 tour that pitted an English team against a hastily organized French selection. With Galia's death Tardy seemed to have picked up the ball from his former colleague and run with it.[7]

According to Gill, Tardy was interested in showing the American game to rugby supporters in the south of France, where enthusiasm for the rugby-league version of the sport was greatest. Perhaps he had some involvement in the 1938 tour and wanted to take another chance on once again taking up the cause of the gridiron sport. Whatever his motivations, the tour of two top military teams got under way in December 1961, between the end of the USAFE regular season and the Freedom Bowl. Presumably Tardy had high hopes for interesting his countrymen in the game, but those hopes would mount to little as lackluster crowds and a hostile press corps met the team at each stop. As with the previous Crowley tour, the teams' lack of stake in the game also dampened the enthusiasm of the spectators. Why should they care that two decent USAFE teams wanted to play football in their area? It was not a championship series by any stretch of the imagination. The games, which were planned to be competitive through the collusion between players and coaches, did not turn out that way.

The AP, however, in a story that ran in *L'Équipe*, the French national sporting newspaper, seemed to envision hope for the tour. It reported that the rugbymen of Toulouse were enthusiastic about seeing the sport "whose extreme virility, athletic and dramatic qualities ha[d] long retained their attention." This was clearly a test, according to the

AP, and several rugby officials planned to attend the game, "so that the amateur rugby player [did] not remain insensitive to a proposal allowing [him] to judge soundly [the sport] that brings him its share of strong emotions." This report seemed to justify Tardy's contention that interest in the game would be strong in the South, where rugby was also popular. The article concluded by arguing that Toulouse was a city that was open to sports novelties, and that its citizens might indeed take interest in this "bold move."[8]

Jean Lacour, a writer for *L'Équipe*, echoed the AP's sentiment on December 15. Lacour wrote, "The Toulousians are strongly intrigued by this 'football' from the other side of the Atlantic." They considered the game, which the reporter described as "the most spectacular, the manliest, and the most astonishing," as a member of the larger rugby family.[9]

Lacour also interestingly situated his report, at least in passing, in terms of cultural imperialism. When he wrote, "One more time, football, like Coca-Cola takes its chance in France," he was referring to the narrative of the popular soft drink being an agent of American global dominance.[10] The term Coca-Colonization for the spread of American culture was one that may well have originated in France and had been used there since 1950.[11]

To reiterate, if this was indeed cultural imperialism, it came in an odd form. The idea arguably originated with Tardy but also perhaps with Dodds. As we shall see, the interest that the AP and Lacour observed in the Toulousian rugbymen would be overstated, and this tour would accomplish little other than providing the participants with a nice vacation. Still it is also interesting, if not astonishing, to see a reporter seemingly exhibit a sense of history. When he indicated that this was not the first time that Americans had tried to interest the French in football, he may have been referring to some knowledge of the 1938 attempt.

Dodds attempted to put the best American foot forward and chose the two top teams based in France to take part. Predictably, he chose the SHAPE Indians, his own team, from USAREUR's European Conference. His handpicked coach Gill would also be in overall charge of the Americans during the tour. From USAFE's Continental Conference, the Laon Rangers, coached by Jerry Curtright, would oppose them. The teams were unbalanced in talent, so, without help, the games would not be even matches. SHAPE was loaded, according to Gill, so when Laon lost its quarterback during the tour due to a personal emergency, Gill offered the opposition headman one of his as a replacement.

Curtright remembered that he and Gill met before the games to settle on a script to keep the matches relatively close in an attempt to hold French interest.[12] Curtright said that Gill told him that the purpose of the tour was to "entertain the French," so they would "make things up" to provide a good spectacle. Besides, the French would not know that the games weren't real. The emphasis was on exciting plays, and often SHAPE would let Laon score on big plays.[13] As we shall see, these plans did not come together, and the French were sharper than they imagined.

In addition to the players and coaches, Châteauroux's Dave Madril and Jim Kelly traveled with the group as referees. Madril remembered that his inclusion in the tour was a consolation from his base commander for not being sent to an annual sports meeting. When he complained that only baseball people were being sent, he was thrown the chance to officiate the tour.[14] As it turned out, what should have been an easy job refereeing games between teams that had decided much of the action beforehand would become somewhat perilous.

After the arrival of the Rangers, who traveled from their northern base to Paris, the sixty players and officials of the tour left from Paris. They traveled from there through Châteauroux to pick up Madril and Kelly, then on to Toulouse for the first game. Madril remembers that they traveled by bus, along with a separate truck for equipment, and that sometimes the length of the trip and the lack of public restrooms forced the players to use wine bottles as impromptu urinals. He also remembered that there were "a lot of empty wine bottles." He remembered in particular that the large SHAPE players "could down wine," often drinking four bottles apiece with their meals. Madril also took the precaution of bringing Kleenex to use in place of the French version of toilet paper, which was "little better than wax paper."[15]

From Toulouse the teams went on to Perpignan for the second and concluding game. The entire trip took eight days and was seen by the players as "a great trip paid for by someone else." Madril said that he got "a nice trip and that the players got the chance to play two more games, so everyone was happy." As to the goal of teaching the French football, Madril was skeptical that they accomplished much and saw the trip as a personal "boondoggle."[16]

Tardy paid the expenses for the tour, and all those interviewees who took part remember that everything was first class. They stayed in good hotels and ate and drank well. Madril remembered one meal in particular with roast pork and truffles, along with the ever-present fine wine. Not all players looked forward to the culinary largesse of the French countryside, however, and the Laon quarterback reportedly brought along several cans of beans and weenies, along with bottled water and Coke (probably unaware of the connotations) because he did not trust the food. Tardy himself did not travel with the team, though Madril remembers that when they stopped, "a French guy in a fancy car would meet the team."[17]

The players also had some time for sightseeing, and they stopped along the road between Toulouse and Perpignan at the medieval fortress city of Carcassonne. While there the players gave the French occasion to mutter about "ugly Americans." According to Madril the players shoplifted everything they could. He remembers that one SHAPE player put on a pair of sunglasses from a store, then proceeded to buy a postcard and leave without paying for the eyewear. He said that the "French people were raising hell when they left." Following their departure from the city, motorcycle-borne gendarmes halted their buses to look for a chair that had been stolen from one of the shops. Though the search failed to locate the pilfered item, Madril recalls that the chair miraculously reappeared later.[18]

One can only guess what an airman wanted with a stolen piece of furniture. Likely the men were engaging in what they saw as a break, not only from their duties but also from the discipline they were expected to display daily during their time in the military. If the French knew of their purpose for traveling through their countryside, however, this could not have left a positive impression of football.

The games themselves were less than riveting affairs and did nothing to advance the cause. Given the disparity in talent between the teams, care had to be taken to keep the games close, but that did not prevent the powerful SHAPE team from winning both contests. Despite the actual scores, interview subjects reported that neither game was a runaway, and Madril remembers that Gill "didn't want a slaughter when trying to teach the game." At Toulouse SHAPE won the game, though none of the players or coaches remember the score, just that it was not a blowout. Madril said that a crowd of maybe two thousand saw the game and appeared to be mostly drawn from the young working classes. They were very quiet, not knowing precisely when to cheer, and didn't interact much with the players. The spectacle surrounding college football was largely missing, and there were no cheerleaders to give cues to the crowd.[19]

Of the national press, only *L'Équipe*, as far as can be ascertained, carried any mention of the game. Along with its coverage, *La Depeche du Midi*, a regional newspaper, also carried a few stories. The December 12 edition of that Toulouse-based newspaper, an article titled "Toulouse et Perpignan à l'heure du rugby américain" announced the game and covered the rudiments of the unfamiliar rules for its readers.[20]

In a follow-up article on December 15, the paper remarked that the game featured frequent substitutions, "as much for strategy as for its brutality." Reminding readers that the sport was one of the most dangerous in the world, the paper mentioned that the "savagery" was such that in 1905 the deaths of eighteen players caused Theodore Roosevelt to threaten to ban the game.[21]

The paper did also try to promote the game by discussing the quality of the teams that would play. SHAPE and Laon were described as "two of the best teams," drawn from the bases that play the sport in France and Germany. It asserted that the teams would "give [French spectators] a brilliant spectacle." It also announced that civic authorities would attend the game, and the teams would have the chance to meet the public that evening.[22]

The news that the teams had requested that three stretchers be placed at key points around the field furthered the narrative, found in the title of the December 14 article, "American rugby is war." Readers were assured that the players were protected by "sophisticated" helmets that protected their faces, but that "a spectacle of this quality [did] not end without fractures." The unnamed reporter went on to compare players with military formations in a manner that would have no doubt pleased Harvard's Deland and Stanford's Shaughnessy. "The biggest players serve as bodyguards for the ballcarriers. Others, the wreckers, attempt to take out of combat dangerous adversaries." Perhaps with some shock, it was reported that in the United States this game was considered the sport to shape the character of young men. The coaches were praised as men who had the qualities of "tacticians," and it was for this skill that "the good coaches [were] hired for gold."[23]

The programs for the game, in Toulouse at least, also made an attempt to familiarize spectators with some of the finer points of referee calls. The Toulouse program, provided electronically by Chuck Bristol, one of the Laon players, therefore indicated some preparation for the tour. Sponsorship for the programs, and presumably the tour, was provided by Phillip Morris, and the programs included images of Marlboro cigarette packages. Perhaps this was arranged by Dodds, given the precedence of SHAPE Indians on the cover, as well as the long history of cooperation between cigarette makers and the American military, but that is only conjecture.[24] Along with pictures of the game officials making various calls, the program included the signals translated into French. Some were easier than others to translate. For instance, a touchdown or field goal was translated simply as a "*but.*" However, holding became "tenu d'une façon illégitime" (holding in an illegitimate way), and unsportsmanlike conduct was rendered as "action contre les lois du sport" (action against the laws of the sport), which sounds considerably more menacing.[25]

Despite efforts to keep the games close, *Depeche du Midi* reported that SHAPE won the first game at Toulouse by a score of 29–0. The match drew only 1,502 spectators, but while the crowd was small, the game was also covered by Television de France-Bulgarie, so others had the chance to see the "spectacular and virile" sport. According to the paper, the gate receipts totaled 782,550 old francs, or around $1,900 in today's dollars.[26]

Something seemed awry, as *L'Équipe* reported the final score as being 30–0 in favor of SHAPE. The two reports agreed on the number of spectators, however, and that it was a fast and athletic game, but declared that it was not very popular with the crowd. According to André Passamar, "The public withdrew not entirely convinced by the virtues of [the] sport." He, like many in 1938, deplored the numerous huddles, which he described as *temps morts* (dead time). Passamar agreed that the players were physically impressive but complained that the ball moved too fast for those without a "trained eye" to follow. He concluded, "In summary, this American football, which is far from devoid of interest, somewhat shocked the Cartesianism of French temperament."[27] By that Cartesianism he likely meant that the French were too logical, and that they lacked room for the fantasy that surrounded the spectacle of football.[28]

And so the road show moved, or limped, on to Perpignan. The *New York Times*, the only American newspaper that mentioned the games, missed the match in Toulouse, but a stringer caught up with the tour in Perpignan. The *Times* alerted its readers to the futility of attempting to interest the French in football with its headline "Football? Merci, Non." Robert Daley, the article's author, followed this editorialized headline with "U.S. Sport in Perpignan Brings Ennui—C'est pour les Américains."[29]

Daley, who went on to author twenty-eight books, did report that the reason for the tour being held in southern France, rather than Paris, was that the south of the country was a hotbed of rugby enthusiasm. As demonstrated by *L'Équipe*, that enthusiasm for the game as belonging to the rugby family was predicted to be a selling point. The article did not mention Tardy and his ties to the area, nor was there any mention of the first game in Toulouse. Perhaps Daley did not stay for the entire game, for he also did not mention the fight that the players remember.[30]

Presumably the only reason that the article appeared was that Daley happened to be in the area and sent in the report for a handy paycheck. When contacted by letter and email, Daley stated that he did not even remember the article, understandable, since the event occurred so long ago. He did write several works on sport in Europe, including *The Bizarre World of European Sport*, along with three books on grand prix racing, so the report from Perpignan was likely merely a happy little accident.[31]

Daley did reference some of the newspaper coverage in the local papers. He reported that one journalist went so far as to reassure his readers, after inventing the fiction that "according to legend, the winners are allowed to take home the arms and legs of the losers as trophies. However, this appears to be an exaggeration." Once again the huddle mystified both reporters and spectators alike. One French writer whom Daily quoted complained about the numerous "consultations" and called the game "dull, displeasing" and opined that it "would never catch on in France."[32]

The precise reports in the French press that Daily mentions have not been unearthed, but perhaps the *New York Times* reporter had read *L'Équipe*'s article on the game. Its devastating report on the exhibition, written by Paul Izern, found nothing to recommend the game. It referenced the *ennui* (boredom) that Daley referred to, mentioning that the spectators nearly dislocated their jaws in yawning. If this was Daily's source, however, he ignored accounts of the fight, which was mentioned by the French paper.[33]

Izern's report began with the assertion that "even in the opinion of the organizers, the American rugby demonstration angered the approximately 1,600 spectators who had wanted to satisfy their curiosity and braved the cold rain." Gill and Curtright's attempts to put on close matches, which failed at Toulouse, also backfired at Perpignan. Even to the presumably untrained eye of the French reporter, "interest in the game suffered from the huge superiority of the victorious team." The Indians, whose skillful plays "mystified at every blow the Rangers," were clearly superior. He deplored the huddles, or "endless confabulations," as he put it, and argued that they led to limited movement.[34]

Daley's assertion that "most of" the crowd of 1,600 spectators there "appeared to be bored stiff," was echoed by Bristol, who remembered that in the second half of the 30–14 SHAPE victory, the players noticed the lack of enthusiasm and attempted to do something about it.[35] In order to add some pizzazz to the game, the players, without the knowledge of the coaches or referees, decided to stage a fight. Bristol recalled that the players told each other, "You hit me, and then I'll hit you." Players pushed and shoved each other and took wild swings to attempt to get the crowd to wake up a little.[36] Madril remembered the fake fight but also grumbled that the players had not mentioned their plans to the referees, and one suffered bruised ribs while trying to break up what he thought was the real thing. Madril remembered the fight lasted only until Gill yelled at them to "knock it off!"[37] Dodds apparently, according to the French press, was also not pleased with the brawl.

Izern had not fallen for the obvious attempt to keep the game close, nor was he fooled by the staged fight, noting, "It all ended, of course, with a general brawl that caused the intervention of an athletic colonel! But this spectacular gag—that some thought preconceived—failed to thaw viewers (in either the literal or figurative sense)." Izern closed press coverage of the tour with the pronouncement: "No, really, rugby made in the USA will have no place in Catalan country."[38]

Gill also joined the rest in describing the French fans as being underwhelmed by the games, claiming that the only play the French fans liked was the kickoff, and that Europeans in general did not like the game.[39] So Daley, Izern, and the rest were accurate in dismissing the possibility of football catching on with the French, at least for the time being. The 1961 tour, like its 1938 predecessor, came and went without leaving much trace on the French psyche.

Oddly enough, even *Stars and Stripes* failed to mention the games in its otherwise comprehensive sports page. None of the players or coaches recall any efforts to follow up on the tour, and the continuing hostility of the French press toward football meant that efforts such as this were speculative at best.

When his goal of popularizing football for the French failed to gain any traction, Tardy turned to enticing American servicemen to become involved in rugby. Gill was also involved in that effort and remembered coaching that sport for a short time. Unlike the fake fracas in the Perpignan game, the real thing did break out in one of those games. On March 4, 1962, the *New York Times* reported that in a game between a French military team from Joinville and an American team from SHAPE, a large brawl broke out at midfield after a particularly hard tackle on an American player. In this instance real tempers were involved, and an American player threw a punch at an opponent, which set off a general melee. The players must have been truly angry, for the French officials were unable to restore order and the game was abandoned.[40]

While Tardy and Dodds may have thought that staging the 1961 USAFE tour in the south of France was a good idea, the southern French enthusiasm for rugby league was not transferable to gridiron football. Playing the games in the *périphérie* also meant that the national publications paid scant attention to the tour. When they did report on it, both *La Depeche du Midi* and *L'Équipe* were dismissive or downright hostile. Without positive publicity, interesting a large number of natives in the game was less likely.

Once again violence, the static nature of the game, and the mystery of the huddles were cultural differences that would bedevil football in France and persist until the French themselves brought the game across the Atlantic. The failure of the 1961 tour would not end attempts to transplant the game, however, and the next effort, played this time by professionals, would once again visit the City of Light.

In the 1970s some Americans and Europeans were finally ready to approach the problem of how to interest the French in football in a more organized way. The National Football League had begun looking abroad for opportunities to expand its public profile and tap into hitherto unexploited markets. One of the leaders of this effort was Tex Schramm, the president and general manager of the Dallas Cowboys, who was interested in finding new talent in Europe. He had already secured the services of place-kicker and former Austrian soccer star Toni Fritsch.

The ground had been prepared somewhat by the 1970 hit film *M*A*S*H*, which followed the adventures of a group of army doctors during the Korean War. The movie concluded with a football game between the hero's 4077th hospital and a headquarters unit commanded by a general who could have been based on Colonel Dodds or any the other football-crazy officers described in the previous chapters. What French fans might have made of the fictionalized game, with doctors drugging their opponents and scoring the winning touchdown on an illegal play, is hard to tell. But at least they, like their 1938 predecessors, had seen football on the screen.

The game that took place on screen turned out to be perhaps a better introduction to the exhibition than what the NFL provided in 1972. As part of Le Semaine Sportive Américain à Paris, as the event was called, Parisians were treated to demonstrations of sports played by Americans such as softball, golf, and football. The week also featured performances by Bob Hope and Benny Goodman, a fashion show, a horse race, and other entertainment.[41] This American Sport Week was largely the excuse to offer an upper-crust audience a chance to party. The sporting events, such as the demonstration by NFL players, were inexpensive, however, with tickets ranging from five to thirty-five francs (one to seven dollars). Others, such as the touch football and softball, were free to the public, and the game was also televised in Paris. Therefore, the proletariat had chances to take part in the week without getting in the way of their betters, who were busy attending cocktail parties, visiting the wine country, and taking boat tours on the Seine.

To support Sports Week, sponsored by the National Football League Players Association (NFLPA) and the Federation of People-to-People Programs, the NFLPA sent forty-one players to put on a football exhibition for the people of Paris. Proceeds from the exhibition benefited the American Hospital of Paris. Players were generally up-and-coming talents, as was the case with quarterback Dan Pastorini of the Houston Oilers and Roger Staubach of the Dallas Cowboys. They were joined by those nearing the end of their careers such as Merlin Olsen of the Los Angeles Rams and Dick Butkus of the Chicago Bears. So the NFLPA sent players who should have created buzz for the exhibition. The most popular player turned out to be Bob Hayes, a wide receiver for the Dallas Cowboys, who reported doing at least eighteen interviews during the week. His popularity was due not to his football prowess, however, but to leftover fame from his gold-medal-winning performance in the 1964 Tokyo Olympics and his reputation as the "fastest man alive."[42]

The exhibition, which may have done more to retard the acceptance of football in the country, was not a real game. The exhibitions began on May 26, when NFL players including Hayes, Bill Curry of the Packers, and John Mackey of the Colts demonstrated touch football at Bagatelle, a castle and park near the Bois de Boulogne on the western edge of the city. The next day, at Stade Sébastien Charlety, a stadium that held ten thousand spectators located on the Left Bank of the Seine, the players dressed in full pads and demonstrated the game more fully. Acting on orders from team owners and their insurance companies, the players had been told to "tone it down," or not give full effort.[43] The format of the game seemed purposely designed to confuse as well; with offensive players dressed in blue and defensive players in red, this was not an actual game contested between two teams. Rather, the players demonstrated various plays such as the sweep, reverses, and draws, while the defenders made half-speed attempts to stop them. The play that drew the largest applause was a touchdown scored by Hayes on a "bomb" pass from Pastorini.[44] The *Bleu* team "defeated" the *Rouge* team 16–6, but it was hardly a game.

Also included was a demonstration of the two kicking styles then current in the NFL. Jim Bakken of the St. Louis Cardinals demonstrated the traditional straight-ahead kicking style, and Jan Stenerud of the Kansas City Chiefs gave a preview of the current practice by using his soccer-style delivery. Some confusion naturally occurred when Stenerud, though playing for the red team, kicked a field goal for the blue team. The *Washington Post* stated that Stenerud kicked for the blue team because only one kicker made the trip, but Bakken also took part, so it is unclear why the native of Norway handled all the kicking duties. Perhaps he was given precedence as a European or for his soccer kicking style. Maybe Bakken was injured, but no record exists of that.

Claude Pappillon, the announcer, attempted to make sense of what was occurring on the field for the eight thousand or so spectators in the stands.[45] He warned them that this was only a simulation and that "the real thing ha[d] lots more contact, lots more violence." Some of that violence was displayed when two players went off script or played their parts too convincingly and scuffled with each other. It is unclear whether this fight was part of the plan, as in the Perpignan game, or if real passions took control. Since the fight involved linebacker Rich

"Tombstone" Jackson of the Denver Broncos, the latter is quite possible.[46] Jackson, much to the probable delight and relief of team owners, who Michael Katz of the Washington paper claimed "were wary of their valuable property taking part in this 'charity contest,'" was the only injury, suffering a scratch on his hand.[47]

The sponsors sought to provide some of the spectacle of a normal football game, and the crowd was treated to the VII Corps's Eighty-Second U.S. Army band, which played the American and French national anthems. One lacking ingredient was cheerleaders, which seems to be something that does encourage the French to pay attention to football. Katz indicated the French "couldn't understand why the 'Blue' team always had the ball, and why, contrary to glimpses of football they had seen in movies like M*A*S*H, there weren't any 'pretty girl's to stimulate the team.'"[48]

As had been the norm for these tours, the weather seemed determined to spoil the event. Crowley's mention that his group had "seen some weather" continued through the game at Perpignan, which Daley described as being "played under a cold rain," and the 1972 game continued the trend.[49] It was described by Katz as "unseasonable football weather, including some of the Paris rain that never goes out of season."[50]

Not only was the physical climate unfriendly, but the same was true of the political climate. During the week before the exhibition, terrorists exploded bombs at the American consulate and the Paris American Legion building. More homemade bombs were discovered at the Pan Am World Airways offices, one on Wednesday and another on Thursday, the same day as the explosions. Game day brought a telephone bomb threat claiming that explosives were planted in the locker rooms of the stadium. A search turned up nothing, and the game went on as scheduled. Added to the other issues was a bus strike in the city that made getting the players to the stadium more difficult.[51]

With nature turned against them, radicals threatening to blow them up, and owners and insurance companies hindering their ability to provide a good show, it was no wonder that the players' efforts were panned in the media. The French were the most critical, but not far ahead of the unfavorable reviews in the American press. Even the players themselves were uncertain if they had done more harm than good.

While Americans understood the slow nature of the play was due to conditions beyond the control of the players, many French spectators believed this was real, at least according to John Vincour of the Associated Press. The French sports daily *L'Équipe* opined, "To us, these American football players seemed static without reflexes or imagination, lacking in enterprise, and in precarious physical condition. The crowd was very disappointed, and robbed by a show that was not worth 85 francs [thirteen dollars] for box seats. We were very disappointed, even if it was a benefit game." According to the same AP article, "*L'Aurore*, the conservative morning newspaper, said the sport was a disappointment and claimed that a 50-yard touchdown pass to Hayes was a setup that fooled no one." The paper went on to declare, "They went too far in setting up a nice show without risk for the actors. . . . Rugby can sleep soundly in France, there's no risk that American football takes its place."[52]

André Boniface, France's most popular rugby star, was even more critical. Of football he said, "It's got no rhythm or speed. I criticize them for not running enough with the ball and I think they're in poor physical shape. Most of all, they confirmed what I thought of them—that is they don't have any imagination. They think too much about their size and look like big machines dressed up in uniforms." Boniface reportedly learned all that from watching ten minutes of the telecast, claiming that he turned it off after that because "he couldn't take it."[53]

The headlines that the American press used to shape its narrative told a similar story. The *New York Times* proclaimed, "French Confounded as N.F.L. Players Make Debut" and followed that with an inside headline for the continuation of the article that told readers, "To the French, It's All Confusion as U.S. Football Stars Perform." The AP rightly reported, "French Rip NFL Show," and the *Washington Post* lamented, "NFL Stars Fumble Ball Introducing No.1 Sport." Even smaller newspapers piled on, picking up the fumble analogy, as when Ron Martz, a sports columnist for the *Fort Pierce (FL) News Tribune*, somberly noted, "Football Fumbles in France." Martz did accuse the French of being "narrow minded" but admitted that Americans behaved in much the same way when confronted with soccer.[54]

Stars and Stripes headlines were more favorable, arguing, "Frenchmen Hail U.S. Sportsfest," and "Parisians Turn Out for U.S. Football." The latter article upped crowd estimates to a near-capacity ten thousand.[55] Photos taken by Walt Trott, the author of the stories, also emphasized the positive, showing Merlin Olsen drawing the winning ticket for a car that an American business leader won during halftime. Another depicted crowds of fans seeking autographs from John Wilbur of the Washington Redskins and American author James Jones. The captions that accompanied the photos asserted that the crowd enjoyed the events, despite rain, bombings, bus strikes, and the failure of celebrities such as Brigitte Bardot to appear. Commenting on the strange nature of the exhibition, Trott argued that "fun was the theme."[56]

Despite attempts to put a brave face on the spectacle, even Americans players and Americans in the crowd were dubious of the effort the players gave. The *New York Times* article began with a supposed quote, "Hey, how about some football?" purportedly yelled in an American accent from the grandstands.[57]

Quoted in *Stars and Stripes*, John Mackey justified the exhibition by saying, "Our purpose is to show it, so that they can compare it to their rugby. . . . We're only trying to break it down and explain to them the concept of four downs to get ten yards," Olsen, always a deep thinker for a defensive lineman, was more concerned and interjected, "Yeah, but in a simulated activity like this, there's always the possibility that they might come away with an impression that all our games are like professional wrestling." Earlier in the article, the Rams player worried, "There's always the possibility that we'll just confuse them." Olsen did have a chance to explain the old bugaboo of the huddle to some French spectators. When they asked him about the constant pauses, he grinned and told the fan, "We have to stop and plan things out." He also tried to put a positive spin on the day's activity, saying, "There seems to be a general appreciation among all people for performance. . . . Even though we're larger than their rugby players, they can see we're still light on our feet." An American soldier who watched the game from the sideline summed things up pretty well: "It's better than I thought it would be, and they even tackled a few times. But I'm sure that they didn't manage to convince many Frenchmen of the severity of the game."[58]

In fairness to the players, this exhibition was conceived not as an effort to convince the French to play football but rather as a chance to raise money for a worthy cause while also seeing the sights of Paris. Others, however, would be looking at the market in France and in Europe in general as a fertile field for the expansion of our favorite game.

On June 5, 1974, a group of entrepreneurs represented by Bob Kap and Adalbert Wetzel gave a presentation to NFL owners encouraging them to back an effort to create the Intercontinental Football League (IFL), a professional football league in Europe. According to the bylaws of the league, "it is the purpose of the Intercontinental Football League to introduce and foster American style football as a sport and profitable industry in nations in which the game is not now played." The plan was to begin with six teams, blending American players and local soccer stars, who would handle the kicking and punting. Although they initially demonstrated some interest, the NFL owners eventually passed on Kap's brainchild. Again bad timing was partially responsible. Even though Wetzel made the argument that soccer's popularity was declining and interest in American football was on the rise, the financial and political situation both in the United States and in Europe was not conducive to the venture. The oil crisis that followed the Arab oil embargo of 1973 spurred inflationary pressures on both continents, and the bombings that greeted the 1972 exhibition were becoming institutionalized in Europe as Basque separatists, the Baader-Meinhoff gang in Germany, and the Red Brigades in Italy were beginning to explode bombs in many of the cities planned for the league. In any event the IFL had no immediate plans for a French team. Only after the initial offering with teams in West Berlin, Rome, Vienna, Munich, Barcelona, and Istanbul was successful would expansion to include new teams such as the Paris Lafayettes be considered.[59]

The IFL group did manage to stage an international match pitting the San Diego Chargers against the St. Louis Cardinals in Tokyo, Japan, in 1976, but lack of support from Pan Am Airways and the NFL doomed a professional league in Europe for the moment. Kap and his colleagues were not through, however. If they could not get NFL teams to play in Europe, they would find others who would. So the tours designed to convince Europeans that football was the wave of the future would continue.

The next effort would involve two of the top National Association of Intercollegiate Athletics (NAIA) college football teams. Texas A&I University (now Texas A&M University—Kingsville) dominated the NAIA championships during the 1970s, winning the title six times from 1969 to 1979. Its opponent in a game played in Paris in 1976 was Henderson State University, which it had defeated in the 1974 championship game. At the end of the 1975 season, the teams were ranked number one and two in the association.[60]

The NAIA sponsored the tour, along with the IFL, which continued to exist, at least on paper. The NAIA also secured additional support for the tour, which included an officiating crew from the Wisconsin State University Conference. It procured donations from companies such as Topps Gum Inc., Rawlings Sporting Goods, and the Spalding Company, which was again helping to spread American sports abroad.[61]

A mixture of old and new characters were behind bringing the A&I Javelinas to Paris to do battle against the Henderson State Reddies from neighboring Arkansas. Joining Kap and the now-retired Colonel Dodds was the French industrialist Marcel Leclerc. Leclerc, an industrialist from Marseilles, had considerable interest in sports. In 1955 he began *Télé-Magazine*, devoted to the new electronic medium, and in 1969, he added *But!* (Goal!), a soccer magazine, to his list of publications. From 1965 to 1972 Leclerc used revenue from his publishing ventures to rejuvenate the rugby team Olympique de Marseilles.[62] According to an interview in *L'Équipe*, Leclerc had been interested in football by Tardy. He then traveled to the United States, where he had seen for himself the commercial possibilities of a sport. He had seen a game between the Pittsburgh Steelers and the Dallas Cowboys. When he reflected that the ninety-thousand-seat stadium was full and that twenty-dollar tickets were scalped for one hundred dollars, his business senses must have tingled. He met with Kap and became one of the investors in the IFL.[63]

Kap and Leclerc, then, were continuing to drive the idea of the IFL, and that organization sponsored the tour, which also included stops in Berlin, Mannheim, Vienna, and Nuremberg. Dodds was presumably living in France in retirement. According to both Gill and Mericle, Dodds had divorced his American wife and married a Frenchwoman during his time there. Being a football freak, perhaps he thought that the only way he could easily find games to watch was to help form a league in Europe.[64]

Original plans for the tour, which sought to take advantage of the buzz around the American Bicentennial, included the presence of four teams, with the Tigers of Ouachita Baptist University (Arkadelphia, Arkansas) and the Salem (West Virginia) International University team, also named the Tigers.[65] The cost of sending four teams of seventy-five players, coaches, and others proved to be too expensive for the NAIA and IFL, however, and only the Javelinas and the Reddies made the final cut. The tour began in West Berlin and continued through Vienna, Nuremburg, and Mannheim before reaching Paris. Planned games in Rome, Genoa, and Florence had to be cancelled and the Nuremburg and Mannheim dates picked up due to the security concerns of the Italian government, which warned that the teams "might be too tempting a political target for political protesters since it was election time."[66]

This tour would not replicate the challenges that faced former efforts. Rather than pickup contests between All-Star teams as in 1938, the games would be hard-fought matches featuring two top teams. Instead of being played in the hinterland, as had been the case in 1961, the games would concentrate on capital cities, where media attention would be greatest. The mistakes and lackadaisical play of the 1972 effort would not be a problem with two competitive programs playing all out for pride. According to Gil Steinke, the coach of the Javelinas, Kap did attempt to impose certain conditions on the teams, mandating that passing plays from the drop-back formation make up at least 50 percent of the plays, and that defenses stick to basic schemes.[67]

The goal was to provide an exciting experience for the fans, but since both teams were committed to running the veer offense, which emphasized the option running game, this seemed to be an odd request. George Baker, the offensive coordinator for the Reddies, recalled, "We just ignored those bits of advice and went about waging the type of war that got us there."[68] The games would also be shortened to two twenty-minute halves, presumably to keep European spectators from getting bored by the length of a regular game.[69]

The games were competitive, though the Javelinas won all five. The NAIA only allowed players who would be eligible during the next season and who had already been on campus for eighteen weeks to take part, so the Reddies started two freshmen quarterbacks, which hampered their efficiency. The first game in West Berlin ended with a 17–8 A&I victory watched by between nine thousand and forty thousand. The AP was responsible for the former number, and Dick Nuesch, the A&I sports information director, who coincidently was also an alumnus of HSU, reported the second. According to the article in the *Arkadelphia (AR) Siftings Herald*, the number of fans was not the only error that the AP made. The AP also reported that the game was played between the Arkansas Razorbacks and the Texas Longhorns.[70]

Reinforcing stereotypical notions about Teutonic efficiency, Baker reported that the stands were nearly empty until the appointed start time, when twenty-five thousand fans quietly and efficiently entered the stadium en masse.[71] The remainder of the games leading up to Paris drew good crowds, how good depending on the source. The Javelinas continued to dominate, much to the disgust of the HSU coach, Ralph "Sporty" Carpenter, and his staff.[72] In Vienna the Javelinas won by a score of 21–7. The first two wins by the Javelinas were followed by 20–6 and 17–15 decisions in Mannheim and Nuremburg, the sites that replaced Italy on the tour. Due to the on-the-fly nature of those games, they were played in front of crowds that were largely made up of American servicemen.[73]

The tour apparently was meeting or exceeding the expectations of Kap and his confederates. The June 11 *Stars and Stripes* contained an article in which IFL public relations director Michael Kap, presumably the son of the promoter, told of plans for another tour the next year, which would feature an expanded roster of teams. Kap reported that negotiations were slated to begin in the next month with "several major NCAA football conferences in order to fill the slate" with "two to six college teams." Kap stated that the IFL now planned to bring college teams to Europe "over the next four years in order to establish the league in European cities and gain enthusiasm for the American brand of football among European fans."[74]

With the inclusion of more teams during the next year, the IFL hoped to create intercity rivalries and now had plans for inclusion of two French teams in Paris and Marseilles. Along with good contacts in the cities listed, which included German, Austrian, and Italian sites, the league hoped to also attract financial support from major European sporting goods companies.[75]

Bob Kap, in Paris, continued to argue that in Europe "the game of soccer [was] dying."[76] Michael Kap, in the *Stars and Stripes* interview, also added ammunition to that narrative by telling the reporter, without citation, that "only seventeen percent of fans at soccer games were under twenty-six." The younger Kap also provided more positive rhetorical evidence that all things American, such as blue jeans, Big Macs, and "aggressive and wild" behavior, were becoming the norm in Europe. He argued, "I think the young generations of Europe are looking for something else. A sport with macho. A sport that exhibits their masculinity. Something with contact and violence. American football has all of this and the Europeans are ready for it."[77]

No doubt about it, Kap could make a convincing argument. The Kaps were, however, underestimating the power that could be brought to bear by established sports federations and the press. As we have seen in past tours, this combination had so far been effective in protecting France from sporting invaders.

Christian Montaignac of *L'Équipe*, in an article that contained the Leclerc interview, gave some background for the Paris game. It quoted the French promoter as saying, "It is evident that we will not have Raquel Welch, three hundred cheerleaders, and the release of 50,000 balloons as in Miami [for Super Bowl X]." There would be, Leclerc asserted, some cheerleaders brought by the teams, a balloon would take flight, and a jazz band from Garches would perform, so some of the spectacle of big-time football would be present. Despite the differences Leclerc and Montaignac assured readers that the game would be competitive.[78] This would not be a lackluster exhibition that the French had seen in 1972 but rather a hard-fought battle between two top American university teams.

Despite those reassurances the article put this new venture in the context of Leclerc's seemingly mercurial nature and career. This had not been his first attempt to create a new league in France. His directorship of the Marseilles club had ended badly, with him being forced to resign from his position and also charged with embezzling team funds to help his media ventures.[79] He then tried his hand at creating a professional basketball league. Montaignac quipped, "After Marcel Leclerc and l'O.M., Marcel Leclerc and professional basketball, here is Marcel Leclerc and American football. Is this megalomania, a momentary enthusiasm, or a bluff?"[80]

Finally, the Javelinas and the Reddies arrived for their final date in Paris. The tour missed its original date for the game because of the imbroglio over the games in Italy, and *Stars and Stripes* also reported that money problems involving the IFL were also plaguing the progress toward Paris, which caused concern among the NAIA officials along for the trip.[81]

Problems with money would occur again during the next year's IFL-sponsored trip with more severe consequences, but this time they were quickly solved and the teams arrived in Paris only a few days late. For once the weather decided to cooperate, and clear skies greeted the game played on June 17.

The promoters, particularly Leclerc, had pulled out all the stops to make this game a true spectacle. As a part of the gala that surrounded the game was an appearance by Sheila, a French pop star, who had just released a number 1 hit song, "Les Femmes" (1976). To the delight of the crowd, she tried her foot at kicking a ball held by the elder Kap, while the two teams warmed up. Around them a group of acrobats tumbled across the field, the U.S. Marine Color Guard marched around the field, and a hot-air balloon was being readied for the half-time show. Leclerc and company seemed to have mastered the art of creating a spectacle around the game.[82]

There were even cheerleaders. HSU had eighteen from its squad, who had to pay their own way over, and this added to the reality of the show being put on by the teams. There was, however, some confusion about the role of the cheerleaders on the trip. According to Bee Harris, a member of the pep squad, the second half of

FIG. 10. French pop star Sheila with an unnamed Texas A&I player before the 1976 game in Paris. © Alain Keler/Sygma/Corbis.

the game in Vienna had been slow to start because the crowd had expected them to strip off their clothing.[83] Baker also had to put a guard on the girls to keep the rowdy and randy Javelina players away from them.[84]

Getting from the hotels where the teams stayed to the Stade Olympique Yves du Manoir, or more simply Columbes, was not a smooth process. The promoters assumed that the teams would ride to the game on the Paris Métro, the subway system. Carpenter, for one, would not hear of that, and he sent his assistant Baker to pass along the message that if buses weren't found, the team would not play. Once buses were found, the disgruntled driver of the Reddies' bus was going to leave some late-arriving players, so Baker took the keys and threw them out the door, which delayed the driver enough for the tardy players to arrive.[85]

Once the players were safely at the stadium, the game was once again dominated by A&I, which finished its sweep of HSU by winning 21–13. Leclerc had used his *But!* to do the usual fan preparation for the game, and he tried to improve the translation of football terms so that the French would find understanding the game easier.

He finally settled on *conseil* for the huddle. The word means coun-
sel, advice, resolution, determination, prudence, and wisdom, which
George Packard, a teacher at the American School in Paris, felt captured the essence of what was occurring. He also enjoyed the translation of the line of scrimmage into *ligne de mêlée*. Less successful,
especially if the players took notice, was *brassiere avec epaulettes* for
shoulder pads. The ground crew of the stadium, unaccustomed to setting up for football, had set the goalposts in the wrong place, and the
field was ten yards too wide, which the referees figured would make
passing more effective.[86]

With an enthusiastic crowd of eighteen thousand (twenty-five thousand according to Baker) watching, the teams put on a good show.[87]
Packard wondered what the crowd would think when the special teams,
which "wanted to make an impression in Paris," collided during the
first kickoff. He reported graphically: "When they came together it
was like a side of beef falling off a building, and I knew it was a sound
the French had never heard. The crowd let out a long, low moan when
they heard them hit, and American football had come to Paris." The
game, which of course was not the first time the French had heard
such collisions, was apparently interesting for children, and the author
reported that he had trouble moving about the stadium because "there
were little French kids everywhere, running, falling, trying to block
each other. They had come over the wall in a wave and were trying on
helmets, getting autographs, and running away from the police." Even
though there were "enough *gendarmes* to handle an average communist *manifestation* [strike] . . . they couldn't handle the kids."[88]

Despite the enthusiasm of the young fans and the excitement generated by pop singers, balloons and the like, the Parisians still had
their problems with understanding the finer points of the game. Packard, who walked around talking to spectators and offering explanations during the game, held that one of the most difficult features to
explain was "why a team kicked on fourth down when they still had
a chance for the first. I don't think the French will ever understand
that." He also reported that pass interference and illegal motion were
perplexing to the spectators. Packard humorously wondered when he
saw the white Citroën ambulance, what the attendants would ask a

player with a possible concussion, and what the player would make of being asked, "Quel jour es-il?" (What day is it?), or "Comptez au rebours de dix" (Count backward from ten).[89]

The tour had been a qualified success, drawing large crowds (eighty thousand by one estimate) but also experiencing financial, political, and meteorological problems.[90] HSU coach Carpenter was quoted as saying that it took the teams almost an hour to leave the field in Vienna because of the enthusiastic crowds mingling with players on the field. Aside from the more lightly attended games played on the army bases, crowds were large and enthusiastic.[91]

Carpenter also grumbled, "I don't know if it would have been possible to come up with a worse organization than we had."[92] He and the other participants of the tour, though, felt that the tour was the trip of a lifetime, and many singled out Paris as their favorite stop. The Reddies, according to Baker, particularly enjoyed trying out their French/Arkansas accents, saying things like "When will zee meel be served?" Purportedly, some thought that this actually made them fluent.[93] The Texans enjoyed themselves as well, particularly since they dominated the play. Larry Hirt, a defensive tackle for the Javelinas, declared that he "found Paris and the Louve [sic] the highlights of the trip," an opinion echoed by defensive end Christi Miller, who told the *Brownsville Herald*, "The monuments and palaces in Paris impressed me most."[94]

There were cultural difficulties, of course, and when Carpenter was given a large slice of French cheese after dinner, he spit it out and said, "Damn, that tastes like a bear's fart!"[95] "Brother Bob" Trieschmann, the HSU trainer and "spiritual leader," had his billfold taken by pickpockets on the Paris Métro, despite constant warnings about that danger.[96] One unnamed Reddies player wrote, "I predicate this last observation with the fact that I like classic rock and not classic symphonies, but the smile on Mona Lisa never tweaked an inquisitive bone in my body. She looks the same in your history books as she does in the Louvre."[97]

There was also the issue of the lower drinking age. After one particular long night on the town, several Reddies were nursing hangovers, and Carpenter told them, "Hell, I figured y'all would go out and have a few beers, but I never thought you'd try to soak up the whole damn town."[98] Despite a few mishaps Baker remembered that the Reddies players were good representatives of their country and "were determined to refute the 'ugly American' image and they did so in a convincing manner."[99]

This time after-action analysis of the tour was largely positive in the American press. Javelina sports information director Fred Nuesch gave this analysis: "Really one would have thought the game was played before American fans until they began to talk. They knew when to cheer and they picked up the tempo pretty quickly." He went on to tell about how "there would be a short practice the day before the game and as many as a thousand fans would show up and watch." Each game also featured demonstrations à la the NFL tour before the game to familiarize spectators with the game, and Nuesch asserted, "The players would take time to show them what football looked like and how to throw a pass." He was a bit disappointed that the spectacle that accompanies football was not well replicated. He told a reporter, "Football can offer the fans a lot more than soccer can, halftime shows, and controlled violence on the field. We were told they were going to have great halftime shows to prove this point, but they didn't. Oh, once or twice a band played and there was [sic] hot air balloons, but nothing spectacular." He also reported that "a couple soccer players came out to one practice to try their luck at kicking the football," but he was unsure if there was any follow-up.[100]

The NAIA, in its fall 1976 Newsletter & Alerts, used pictures and the accompanying captions to send the message to their readers that the tour had been a success and that Europeans were ready for some football. Under a picture showing enthusiastic adult fans shaking hands with players the caption reads: "Fans Greet Players . . . European fans were anxious to meet the players from Texas A&I and Henderson State ARK after watching the American players in action." Another depicts the stands of an unnamed stadium that was filled with spectators and reads: "As you can see by the stands, the football tour by Texas A&I and Henderson State ARK was a success as the two teams played five exhibition games." A third photo shows players interacting with adolescent boys with a caption that reads, "BREAK TIME . . .

Not only were the players busy on the field, but after the games the autograph seekers kept the players busy."[101]

The good press was also partially due to reporters depending on Bob Kap for quotes, and the ever-optimistic promoter worked hard to sell his idea. He told the AP, "The fans were very receptive to the game. We had 12,000 in West Berlin, despite a rain storm, 20,000 in Paris, and 25,000 in Vienna. That is pretty good when you consider that the average soccer crowd in those cities is 2,000." He went on to outline plans for selling franchises, locating talent for them from "soccer and rugby players, wrestlers and any other athletes from European sports." Kap asserted that he didn't think it would be a problem to fill rosters or stadiums and returned to the common theme: "I think European fans are ready for new sports. I'm sure they are ready for American football."[102]

The French press, on the other hand, was not so sure. Montaignac had already given his readers this assurance: "Let us add simply that Leclerc does not wish that we see this as a new challenge on his part any more than it signals the creation of a team of American football as being ready to disembark."[103] *L'Équipe* barely covered the game but ran a follow-up article that briefly referenced it. Most of the article then explained the allure of the professional sport in America. After reciting the statistics on number of fans and television revenue, the article's author, Henri Garcia, who had visited the Washington Redskins facility, detailed the rigorous physical training and mental preparation that players and coaches put into the sport. Through his description of the astonishing effort put into preparation, as well as the fantastic results, the game became not only the product of the new world but of another world altogether. Clearly this was nothing that the French could replicate.[104]

When confronted with Kap's enthusiasm in Paris, Packard reacted to the football missionary's assertions that soccer was dying by musing to himself, "The only thing that might die is a soccer official here and there, and then the profession of soccer officiating. Soccer can be like ice hockey, only with 100,000 people in the stands." When Kap asked Packard if he liked to "sit and watch men run up and down in short pants kicking a ball to make one point?" Packard, asserted, internally once again, "I didn't know what I liked, because I couldn't get a ticket to any soccer game I wanted to see, but I was pretty sure some people liked to watch them run up and down. The other night when Marseilles was in town the traffic of the Champs-Élysées got so bad that the gendarmes said to hell with it and went into the cafés." Packard was loathe to vocalize his doubts to Kap because, while he described the man as "shorter than Orson Welles," although he added, "He has the same kind of eyes—the kind that look right through you and then down the street and then off to some place you might have never been."[105] Even after the successful game in Paris, with so much enthusiasm demonstrated by the Parisian kids, the author reported that as he left the now mostly empty stadium, "far below [him] on the nearly dark field, the French kids were running up and down kicking a soccer ball around."[106]

The 1976 tour of the Javelinas and the Reddies had avoided many of the pitfalls of earlier tours. It also had some success at drawing fans in some of the locations, including Paris. The Kaps would ride that wave of success and return to France again in the next year. However, the lack of organization and money problems that briefly flared up in their first attempt would be even more severe during the following effort.

7. Postwar Tours, 1977-1989

There could be no doubt that Bob Kap was a true believer. He arguably was able to translate his vision into a reality of sorts. The 1976 tour had been relatively successful. Curious spectators had turned out in fair to good numbers, depending on whose report you believe. He was not, therefore, completely a wild-eyed visionary. His dream of planting football in Europe had evolved after the NFL rejected his initial plan. It would have to evolve further after he was unable to convince other college teams to take part in the next year's tour.

In 1976 two semiprofessional teams would pick up the loose ball and carry it toward the goal of a European football league. Kap's focus would shift to creating semiprofessional teams made up of local talent, along with American players who were not good enough to play professionally.[1] This effort, like all those that came before it, would not succeed, but the model was sound. It is how football would eventually evolve organically in France.

Had Kap been a billionaire instead of a refugee from Communist Yugoslavia, he might well have succeeded.[2] His vision for the future would also become the reality of NFL Europe, but that also finally failed. But all that was far off in the future.

In 1976 Kap was riding high on the at least partial wave of success created by the Javelina and Reddies tour. However, his plans for an expanded tour of four to six college teams never became reality. Perhaps coaches at schools such as Notre Dame, UCLA, and the University of Texas that the IFL asked to join the crusade noticed that the staffs at Texas A&I and HSU had their recruiting season severely lim-

ited by the tour. They might have also noticed the three injuries suffered by Reddies in the games.[3]

For whatever reason the next year's tour would not feature college
teams. Kap was never one for half-measures though. If he could not
find major college teams, he would settle for two semiprofessional
teams from Iowa and Illinois. But they would play for what he promoted as the "European Pro Football Cup."[4]

The teams chosen to represent the sport this time were two top
teams in the Chicago Pro Football League, which would morph into
the Northern States Football League (NSFL) in 1977. The Chicago Lions
and the Newton Nite Hawks were the two teams that made the cut,
though the Quad City (IA) Mohawks and the Chicago Heights Broncos
were also considered. The larger plans to take four teams were dropped
due to unspecified "legal problems" and negotiations that began late.[5]
Late negotiations may have been due to the original plan to take college teams again. However, the financial and organizational problems
of the 1976 tour would be magnified in 1977. The impression that one
draws from the challenges that surrounded the Kap-led tours is that
these efforts were spit-and-bailing-wire productions.

Nevertheless, the two teams selected to participate in the tour were
among the best that the NSFL had to offer. During their ten seasons
as a team, the Lions had compiled a 60-25-3 record, while the Nite
Hawks were a newer team, with a record of 24-15-1 that also included
the 1975 championship.[6] Not coincidentally, they were also two teams
that could raise enough money to help pay for the trip.

The tour was announced in New York City's Waldorf Astoria. The
presence of reporters from *Sports Illustrated*, and the *Sporting News*,
along with daily newspapers from New York, Chicago, and Washington added credibility, so expectations for the project ran high.[7] Accompanying Kap to the press event were team officials and supporters
from Chicago and Newton.

In Jim Foster, a leader of the Nite Hawks' effort, Kap had found a kin-
dred spirit. The young Iowan was interested in the business possibilities
of expanding football to Europe, and he was also a man with the bound-
less enthusiasm to match the IFL's leader. Foster told the press at the
conference that reports from the 1976 tour were positive and that "the

reaction of both the European public and press was quite good with more than 20,000 persons attending each of the three games and a great deal of television and newspaper coverage." He also expressed optimism for the upcoming tour, asserting, "Crowds this year are expected to be much larger and there will be Europe-wide telecasts of the different games."[8]

Some articles mentioned that promoters expected forty thousand to fifty thousand fans at some of the games.[9] Along with European television coverage, the possibility that American radio and television networks might provide coverage was also mentioned in Foster's comments.[10] From the expectations expressed at the news conference, it seemed that Europe would be blanketed with coverage of the tour. Foster was either emphasizing the positive by not counting the sparsely attended games in Nuremberg and Mannheim in the total, or perhaps Kap had failed to mention those blemishes during negotiations.

Indeed, one recurring problem that hobbled efforts to transplant football abroad was historical tunnel vision. There had been only tenuous attempts to tie current tours to previous efforts. Kap and company's efforts were the first real sustained campaign aimed at building on previous attempts. Of course, the time gap between the 1938, 1961, and 1976 tours had worked against the creation of any continuity between the various efforts.

The inclusion of Kap and the IFL in both the 1976 and 1977 tours allowed for some institutional memory to be created. Foster mentioned at the initial press conference that the investors, including himself, would be protected from "political or military problems or acts of God such as earthquakes." If such problems occurred, the insurance policy being arranged by the IFL through Lloyds of London would refund their investments.

Several of the Nite Hawks players and coaches had put up $25,000, as had the backers of the Lions. Together they formed a corporation called the European Football Investors (EFI) to provide money for the tour. According to Nails Florio, a columnist for the Chicago-based *News Journal*, this ability to raise money, rather than on-field prowess, was what allowed the teams to make the final cut for the tour.[11] This inclusion of the highest bidders continues to reinforce the impression that the IFL was operating on a perilously thin margin.

This did not dampen Kap's optimism in the least, and one can imagine him at the Alamo in 1836 enthusing over the wide target selection available to the defenders. In this case reporters passed along news that if the 1977 tour was a success, as it was sure to be according to all concerned, a new European league would be created. The Nite Hawks and the Lions, along with the Mohawks and the Broncos, would have the chance to purchase an IFL franchise for the low price of only $100,000. Other teams, presumably from the reported one hundred semipro teams that expressed interest in the tour, would have to pay $250,000 for their franchise. The future was bright indeed.

Along with Kap's familiar refrain that soccer was dying in Europe, a claim that most writers rightly met with skepticism, the narrative that the 1976 tour was a smashing success was repeated by most newspapers. In contrast to current concerns over the violence of football, this was seen as a selling point for European fans. One article quoted Kap as saying that in Berlin it "took the two collegiate teams two hours to reach their dressing rooms" because of fan interest in examining the protective equipment the players wore.[12]

Foster also joined in the hyperbole, arguing that the tour "could change the semi-pro football picture in the United States."[13] In another interview he added, "This is probably the single greatest thing that has happened to minor league football. . . . It will take a long time to rival the NFL, but this is an opportunity for minor league teams to make money."[14] In Foster, Kap had found an able acolyte. Foster would later go on to create arena football and would also later return to Paris to help popularize the new variant of the game.

Both Kap and Foster dangled the possibility that the teams could form the nucleus of the IFL, aided by their lower franchise fee. Foster's rationale was that "if you can't start another major professional league in the United States, why not try it in Europe"?[15] Perhaps this was aimed mainly at giving extra motivation to the players, who lived with the dream of one day being spotted by an NFL scout. This was not merely a fantasy shared by has-beens and never-weres. One Lions player had been given a tryout as a punter by the Cleveland Browns, and three Nite Hawks had recently been signed as free agents by the Washington Redskins.[16] If some of their fellows could make it to the big league, then perhaps the idea of starting a semiprofessional league in Europe could also come true.

The tour was just as ambitious as those of the previous years and even included the possibility of playing behind the Iron Curtain in Bucharest, Romania. This game was set to happen, if the U.S. State Department could work out the details.[17] Foster compared this possibility to the Ping-Pong diplomacy that "opened" relations with Red China.[18] Romania and the State Department never reached an accord, and the confusion that marked the previous tour also seemed to be surfacing again.

The schedule was still up in the air, with the possibility of games in Brussels, Belgium, and Copenhagen, Denmark, still being considered in late April. With just over a month before the tour was to begin, perhaps the fluid nature of planning should have sounded alarm bells among investors and the teams. As it turned out, the two teams played a total of five games. The first two were in France at Versailles and Lille. The tour then proceeded on to Kaiserslautern in Germany, before finishing with the final two games in Austria at Graz and Vienna.[19]

In addition to Chicago and Iowa papers, the tour received considerable attention from the press nationwide. The Associated Press and United Press International followed the tour and reported on its planning and progress. Newspapers from California, Nevada, Texas, Utah, and Florida carried those reports, so readers from across the nation, if they were interested, could follow the exploits of our latest pigskin missionaries. The European *Stars and Stripes* also featured several stories of the games in their neighborhood.

Some of the reports simply reported the news, but some played it tongue-in-cheek, mocking players' dreams of being noticed by the NFL and Kap's dreams of European football. "North Munich Forty: Semi-Pro Nobodies to Get Identity in Europe," by John Parshall of the *Oak Park (IL) Oak Leaves* was one of the latter. Playing off the title of *North Dallas Forty* (1973), the popular book by Peter Gent, Parshall described the Chicago Lions players who would make the trip as truly small time. Dan and Steve Horvath, brothers who had played high school football for the local team, were workers at their father's auto repair shop. Steve only became the starting linebacker for the team when his brother dared him to tryout after the team's previous starter was unable to go to Europe because one of the three drivers from the meat route that he operated had quit. The author went on to disparage the idea of football in Europe, referencing Kap's discount rate for the four teams to become part of the league. He asserted that "there just MAY (his skeptical emphasis) be more in this for them than meets the eye . . . After all, who would want to be a first round draft choice of the Cleveland Browns when he could go first class as a place-kick holder for the Versailles Sun Kings?"[20]

An AP writer piled it on, calling the players "big, grizzled beer hoisters with broken noses and missing teeth, playing football on rundown fields on the outskirts of town or in the shadow of smoking blast furnaces." The article did then venture onto positive ground, asserting that four Lions players had made it to the NFL. Jim Arceo, a police officer, remembered his team being destroyed by Quad Cities, whose quarterback Ken Anderson went on to a stellar pro career with the Cincinnati Bengals. Larry Ball, a mailman with no illusions that he would join his former teammates, at least appreciated the recognition that the tour would give them. He asserted, "At this point, half the people in Chicago don't know we exist." Steve Licht, another Lion, referenced the difficulties of players in the minors. He told the reporter that he didn't go to college because he was making good money working construction, but then he was laid off and broke his wrist playing for another team with no insurance. He hoped the European tour would attract the notice of colleges, and he maintained that since he had never been paid, he would still be eligible.[21]

The "semipros," a description that Parshall derided as being akin to "calling an unemployed person unengaged," were not to be paid for their play on the trip. They were never paid in the first place, which Parshall put forward as a possible reason why semiprofessionals were chosen over collegiate players. This time the IFL would send seventy players and some of their boosters, who had raised the money themselves to pay for the trip. During the 1976 tour "103 players, coaches, and cheerleaders," along with assorted college and NAIA officials, had made the trip.[22]

While eventually semiprofessional football would be the model for

FIG. 11. Newton Nite Hawks team picture, 1977. Photo courtesy of Stan Allspach.

football in France, this might not have been the best way to attract the French. The lack of star power, not to mention athletic talent, might have made economic sense, but it was not likely to create legions of fans in Europe.

The talent level was boosted by the teams, particularly the Nite Hawks, who held tryouts to bolster their roster.[23] They were able to get several players with previous college experience from various universities in Iowa, including the University of Iowa and Iowa State University. They also recruited the cream of the crop from small colleges in the area.[24] The Lions were not so lucky. They were coached by Palmer Pyle, an ex-NFL player, but were unable to match the Iowans.[25] With their roster bolstered by their reinforcements, the Nite Hawks, who had finished 6-5 during the 1976 season, won every game during the tour.

Foster gained valuable experience that he would later put to use selling arena football. He spent two and a half weeks promoting the tour at various European sites, taking quarterback Stan Allspach with him. He organized press packets that included all the information writers would need and held a press workout in Newton, complete with Nite Hawk VIP hostesses who would distribute the material.[26] In this he was ahead of his time, anticipating what every university's sports information department would routinely provide in later years.[27]

Once again, sponsors hoped that interest in football would already exist. Dick Altmeier, the Nite Hawks coach said, "They have the satellite and see all our big football games, like the Rose Bowl and Super Bowl, but they've never seen one in person."[28] Altmeier did not specify which countries had access through their satellite providers to these games, but according to an official from the Fédération Française de Football Américain (FFFA), telecasts were first regularly shown on subscription cable in the mid-1980s. However, *M*A*S*H* should have also still been relatively fresh in some people's minds as well, and perhaps some had seen *The Longest Yard* (1974) with Bert Reynolds. The football exhibited in those two films, however, might have scared more people than it attracted.

Interestingly enough, no mention of the fans who had seen football in 1976 has been found. Stories referenced the enthusiasm and the fine reception that the college teams had received, but nobody argued that the 1976 tour had any impact. There was some discussion that past enthusiasm would likely translate into good results in 1977. That enthusiasm would be increased by the previous year's effort should have been mentioned, had the sponsors considered it important. Word-of-mouth marketing did not seem to be something that the tour promoters considered, and perhaps the abysmal reaction in the French press to the various earlier tours in part accounted for that lack of focus.

With the preparation work done, the teams departed for France on Monday, May 30. After arriving in France they traveled to Lille, where they would practice for their first game at the fifteen-thousand-seat Stade Montbauron near Versailles on June 2. Awaiting their arrival in Europe was the redoubtable duo of Bill Dodds and Barney Gill. Dodds was the associate promoter of the Paris event, and he had brought back Gill. After leaving the army the former Indians headman had served as a coach and general manager of the Norfolk Neptunes of the Atlantic Coast Football League and was then director of the United Drug Abuse Council of Southeastern Virginia.[29] In addition to his participation in the 1961 tour, Gill had also accompanied a tour of NFL players around Vietnam to visit bases during his 1966 tour of duty, so he was an old hand at this.[30] His involvement with semipro football also gave him an insight into that world and made him an ideal choice to help publicize the tour. Besides, as he mentioned in one of our telephone conversations, "They still remembered me over there."[31]

The EFI might have cringed if it had noted Dodds's comment in *Stars and Stripes*: "We don't expect to make any money, but we also hope we don't lose any either." Short-term gain might not have been the primary motive, and the EFI would have applauded the former colonel when he asserted that "the ultimate goal for this tour [was] to bring American football to Europe."[32]

Gill seemed to have a different audience in mind for making football a success on the Continent. He told *Stars and Stripes* reporter Dave Cowan that he wanted to get support from soldiers stationed there: "If we can get the GI to show interest in football over here . . . we might be interested in bringing some teams each year to Europe. First we must prove we have fan support here." He went on to recall that when he coached the SHAPE Indians in the early 1960s, "football was big then," adding, "There's no reason why it can't be big here now."[33]

The idea that American servicemen and servicewomen would be a major component of the fan base in Europe was a new wrinkle for the football missionaries. While Leclerc, Kap, and Dodds seemed focused on converting the natives to the one true sport, Gill might have added a new dimension. During the 1970s the American military presence in Europe, particularly in Germany, was in a relative trough between its peak in the early 1960s and the Reagan buildup of the 1980s. There were still more than two hundred thousand service personnel stationed there throughout the decade.[34] This did not include France, however, as the NATO bases had been removed after French president Charles de Gaulle withdrew the nation from the defensive alliance in 1966.

The first game at Versailles on June 2 was decently attended, with an estimated eight thousand French fans watching as the Nite Hawks defeated the Lions 26–6. For a game on a Thursday night, getting eight thousand spectators into the fifteen-thousand-capacity stadium was a decent showing. Foster asserted that those who attended were

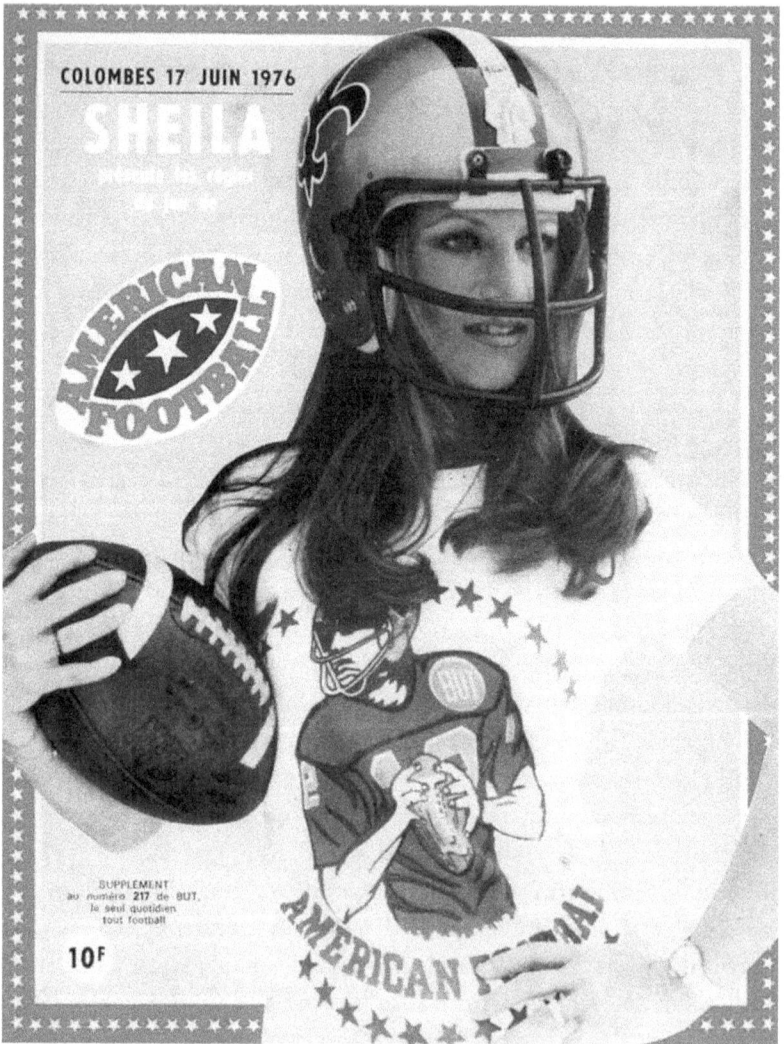

FIG. 12. The program for the Nite Hawks–Lions game at Stade Colombes in 1977. Pictured is Sheila, a French pop star who also took part in the publicity surrounding the 1976 Paris game between Texas A&I and Henderson State. Photo courtesy of Stan Allspach.

enthusiastic, and that after the game it took him a half hour to get into the locker room. "I must have signed 200 autographs," he told the UPI reporter who filed the story. According to the Nite Hawks manager and wide receiver, "Europeans do not completely understand American football, but they are fascinated by the passes and the helmets."[35] A highlight of the game was the 103-yard interception return that opened the scoring in the third quarter. When Iowan Bob Salter scored on the play, the *Stars and Stripes* reporter wrote, "Salter, whose brother, Brian, plays for the Miami Dolphins of the National Football League, had the nearly-packed audience (he estimated 12,000 spectators) frantic" with his exploit.[36] How many of the frantic fans were actually French is impossible to tell from available sources, but presumably the press tour that had preceded the contest generated some enthusiasm. That possibly included some who had seen the previous collegiate game in Paris and perhaps even a few who remembered the SHAPE Indians.

Once again promoters had reached out to French celebrities to increase crowd size. Popular comedian and celebrity impersonator Thierry Le Luron, who specialized in impressions of politicians, posed for a photo with some of the Nite Hawks players. In it former Iowa State Cyclone linebacker Ray King (six feet four, 225 pounds, No. 53) posed with Le Luron. Also pictured with the comedian was Karl Schueneman, a gargantuan offensive tackle (six feet eight, 270 pounds, No. 73). King and Schueneman, who resembled Dirk Keil's character Samson in *The Longest Yard,* bracketed the relatively diminutive Le Luron, who barely reached the top of Schueneman's jersey number. Also recycled from the previous tour was Sheila, whose image graced the program for the two French games.[37] The weather, however, continued to work against football, with windy and cold conditions and temperatures in the 40°F range.

The image, along with several others and many video clips of the tour games, can be found on a "Newton Nite Hawk" Facebook page that Nite Hawk QB Stan Allspach created for a 2012 reunion. The site also contains images of many of the press clippings from the tour, and a booklet made for the reunion.

Despite reports of a fair-to-good crowd at the first game, the sec-

FIG. 13. French comedian Thierry Le Luron flanked by Newton players Karl Schueneman (no. 73) and Ray King (no. 53) prior to the first game at Stade Colombes of the 1976 Nite Hawks–Lions tour. Photo courtesy of Stan Allspach.

ond game in Lille was hoped to be even more successful. The stadium there, which Foster compared to Iowa State's then-new Jack Trice Stadium, was larger. The teams had also been based there since their arrival in France and had made contacts among the locals. According to Foster the citizens displayed a great deal of interest. During one practice on a field next to the site where a track meet was being held, he reported that the schedule for the French event was suspended while the locals came over to watch the Americans train.[38] In a telephone interview with Foster, he recalled that the city was a more blue-collar setting, and that this had helped draw in fans who seemingly saw the unpaid players as their peers. In their off time many of the players had adopted a local bar and became regulars, if only for a week or so. One of the forty Nite Hawk supporters who came along for the trip also had ties to the area left over from World War II. The investor had been a soldier in the area during the war and had stayed briefly with a local family. Upon his return with the tour, he located the family for a joyous reunion.[39]

The capacity of Stade Nord in Lille is smaller than the promoters reported, and that points to odd discrepancies contained in accounts of the games on the tour. Crowd estimating is a difficult task, so the differences in numbers can often be brushed aside as meaningless anomalies that are likely a function of how the particular estimator feels about the game. The press of deadlines for filing a story might also prevent reporters from waiting for firm gate numbers, and promoters continually emphasize the positive. However, the stadium capacities are continually overestimated. Montbauron currently holds only 6,200 spectators, not the 15,000 reported. Stade Nord likewise holds a little over 18,000, rather than the 30,000 that *Stars and Stripes* reported.[40] These discrepancies can probably be explained away by reporters being dependent on promoters in the days before the Internet made information more readily available. Questions remain, however, about the accounting that went on during the tour and perhaps foreshadowed the problems that would occur later.

The second game, held at Lille on June 8, was the most competitive of the series, with the Nite Hawks eking out a 15–13 win on the strength of three field goals by their barefoot soccer-style kicker Kris Smith. Smith, who had played briefly for the New York Giants of the NFL and Birmingham of the World Football League, was emblematic of the personnel advantages that the Nite Hawks enjoyed over the Lions.[41]

The Iowa team was filled with college talent, and only five of its members had not played at that level. The Lions, on the other hand, had fourteen men who had only played high school ball or had played

175

FIG. 14. Newton Nite Hawks versus the Chicago Lions during their 1977 tour. As the tour progressed, and the Lions' losses mounted, tension between the teams led promoters to place them in different hotels. Photo courtesy of Stan Allspach.

in the military in various branches.[42] This advantage would help the Nite Hawks dominate the tour, and the Lions' lack of success on the field apparently led to friction between the teams. *Stars and Stripes* reported that the promoters had decided to house them at separate sites beginning with the German leg of the tour.[43]

According to *Stars and Stripes*, the American teams played before a near-capacity (or seemingly more-than-capacity) crowd of twenty-five thousand spectators (twenty-one thousand according to UPI).[44] The enthusiasm that the teams experienced in Lille would be the high point of the trip. Tensions mounted between the teams and also among promoter groups, and attendance began to precipitously decline.

The Versailles game did not receive coverage in the French press, but the second game at Lille was covered by the *La Voix du Nord*, a regional newspaper. A few days before the game, the paper had a brief article announcing the match and warning readers not to miss the parade of cheerleaders and the marching band that would precede the event.[45]

The day before the game, readers were given a primer on the basic rules and informed that a homecoming game in the United States often attracted one hundred thousand fans. The working-class denizens of Lille were also informed that the best players in the NFL could be paid one million francs per year.[46]

Reporter Jean Chantry counted twenty thousand spectators at the game and declared that this was the largest crowd ever to have seen an event there. He pronounced the match a "great experience" but also dwelled on the physical costs to the players. Chantry mentioned Jim Wingender, a former All Big 8 running back, who would finish the tour on crutches. Readers likewise learned that Howarth of Chicago had a twisted ankle. Lest one think those were the only injuries, the writer also noted, "Here and there, in the locker room, we see a blond guy make faces while moving his shoulder, a black one limping, another one putting a bandage on his injured eye." Animosity between the Nite Hawks and the Lions was reported with the comment, "Let's clarify something: those two Chicago [sic] teams, chosen for that tour, hate each other, refuse to stay at the same hotel or to drink together after the games. Only the blacks seemed to give a hint of a shy fraternization." Taking a bit of a swipe at American culture, the author theorized that the hard feeling might be purely commercial, adding, "With those Americans, who knows?"[47]

The focus on the violent toll that the game took on its players was nothing new for the French press. At least Chantry had not complained of the huddles. The game therefore had been a qualified success. The northern town had seemingly taken to the players and the sport in a way that few had before them. This would be the high point of the tour.

The sole game in Germany was not held in Berlin, as planned, but at Landstuhl, a small town near Ramstein Air Base. Perhaps this was in keeping with Gill's goal of demonstrating that American GIs would turn out to watch semipro games. That expectation did not materialize, nor was the hope that Germans would flock to the event fulfilled. The location was near the large base that served as USAFE headquarters, but the game was held "back in the woods" near the base hospital on a soccer field with no lights. Due to that restriction, the game lasted less than two hours. A sparse crowd, made up mostly of American service personnel, watched from the crude concrete, rock, and sand seats. Many took in the action from beyond the fence to avoid paying. Fans who paid for the game were irritated when the freeloaders beyond the fence were let in free at halftime, and comments collected by the *Stars and Stripes* reporter indicated that many were unhappy with the game. One group complained, "Hell, there is no hitting out there. Sembach and Ramstein put on a better show last [USAFE] season."[48] Perhaps the third straight win (26–6) for the Iowans was beginning to wear down their Chicago opponents, but the tour seemed to be running out of steam.

The Nite Hawks would clench the European Pro Football Championship with a 39–6 victory in Graz, Austria, in front of a crowd of 12,500. The crowd must have been a bit reserved because Foster mentioned that the "public address announcer didn't understand the game." He asserted, "European fans like to cheer the teams and it helps to have a good PA man." Apparently, due to the lack of decent mike work, the only spectators making any noise were the boosters who came along with the teams.[49]

The third and fourth games brought fewer spectators than promoters had hoped for. Instead of playing before the twenty thousand to fifty thousand spectators that were spoken of at the Waldorf Astoria in April, the games to that point had averaged only around ten thousand. The largest crowd of the tour had been in Lille. Even there the *Stars and Stripes* reporter Boo Odem wrote that one of the players' wives had told him that she had heard that "10,000 were let in free."[50]

The narrative contained in newspaper reports, which were somewhat positive, also concealed growing tensions swirling around the tour. Perhaps that development had begun to affect the play on the field as well. Those tensions would come to a head when the teams reached Vienna, a game that was anticipated as the event that would balance the books and justify investors' faith in the project.

The 1977 collegiate game had drawn between twenty-five thousand and thirty thousand in Vienna, and promoters expected to match or exceed that turnout. However, when the teams arrived in the Austrian capital, they found that little preparation had been accomplished, and only a tenth of the expected crowd filtered into the stadium. Foster told reporters later, "We knew something wrong that night [of

FIG. 15. Nite Hawks and Lions in Vienna. The empty stands spelled doom for the 1977 tour. Photo courtesy of Stan Allspach.

the game] when there were only 2,000 people in the stadium." The teams discovered the cause, and Foster reported, "There had been no promotion and since we got there on the day of the game, we didn't have any time to do any promoting on our own." Gill mentioned that the pregame publicity consisted of a sergeant posting all his promotional material on the same wall, and that caught up with the tour in Vienna.[51] With this financial disaster the tour was over. The final game in Linz, Austria, was canceled when the teams discovered that their hotel reservation and the rent for the stadium there had not been paid.[52]

Unbeknown to the players and the EFI group, a conflict had broken out among the other promoters. The conflict had caused the others, presumably Kap and his IFL backers, to depart the Continent for home. Although news reports did not specify who was to blame, this left the Nite Hawks, the Lions, and their boosters potentially stranded. Foster had to scramble to get the teams back home, though he reported, "There wasn't a sense of all out panic and we weren't thrown out on the street. It was just a matter of taking four or five hours and getting things worked out." Foster's midwestern understatement likely concealed some anger, bitterness, and confusion that must have been present before things were resolved. Fortunately, their return tickets had already been paid for, and the military provided housing in Munich for two days. In the meantime, the State Department arranged to cash a check that allowed the teams to pay for their hotel in Vienna, so the tourists were not actually thrown out into the streets.[53]

According to Nite Hawk QB Allspach, the promoters' problems had their roots in the 1976 tour. Allspach asserted that Kap had still owed money from the previous year's effort, and he had taken money out of the account set aside for the 1977 tour to pay for that. Conflict over robbing Peter to pay Paul led IFL president Carroll Catler to break with Kap, and according to the Nite Hawk quarterback, he "took off with the money" that was set aside to pay for the final part of the tour. Allspach also remembered that the Vienna crisis was a bit more tense than Foster mentioned to the press. Since the hotel was not paid for, the players were confined there until the money came through.[54]

A recap of the tour on the Nite Hawks' Facebook page adds some detail to the story of the Vienna snafu. According to the notes in the introduction, there had been several "minor problems" such as busing snags, mixed-up hotel rooms, insufficient meals prepared, and the like. Those inconsequential problems were overlooked because the tour was the chance-of-a-lifetime trip that the teams were enjoying. The fun was severely dampened, however, when the teams arrived in Vienna. There they found that the promoters, presumably Kap and Catler, had left Europe "almost a week prior to the game." The promoters still with the tour were discovered to have departed the evening after the game.[55] Allspach remembered that Michael Kap was along with them in Vienna with "25–40 posters that had not been put up."[56] That the elder Kap did not keep his co-investors informed of events is one thing but to leave his son gently twisting in the wind is shocking.

There was, it was reported, considerable fun packed into the trip before the final debacle. Allspach related some of the stories from the tour's stay in France. In one instance, while the team was touring all the usual spots in Paris, some Italian tourists at the Eiffel Tower mistook him for U.S. president Jimmy Carter. He and his teammates played the confusion for all it was worth, with his team-

Fig. 16. Nite Hawks quarterback Stan Allspach in action against the Chicago Lions in 1977. Photo courtesy of Stan Allspach.

mates pretending to be Secret Service agents guarding the president. As in the photos published during the 1938 tour, the American players also found that European accommodations were not designed with football-sized bodies in mind. This became clear at their hotel when eight of them crowded onto a small elevator built for three, and unable to move that much weight, it stalled between floors. The French technician who removed them "chewed them out" the entire time he was working to extricate them. He echoed some of the comments made by the previous year's tour when he mentioned that many of the players were suspicious of French food, particularly the meat, because they were afraid it was horse. Of their reception at Versailles, while he said that there was not a great deal of interaction with French fans, the players had been told to make sure they held on to their helmets by the chinstrap. They had not brought many extras, and they were told that "people [would] want souvenirs." Perhaps they were also trying to avoid what happened to Brother Bob on the Paris Métro. Since the officials marked the field at Versailles in the manner they were used to, as in 1977 the distance between sidelines was very wide. Former Iowa Hawkeye Bobby Lawson, who

Allspach claimed could run a 9.3 second 100-yard dash, ran many sweeps to take advantage and scored twice during the game. At Lille Allspach remembers the crowd being noisy, especially during punts, when the spectators could see skills that made sense to them. He described the field as having a moat and a chain-link fence around it, presumably to keep rioting soccer fans off the playing surface. Lille took to them because of their long stay there. Before they departed, the socialist mayor of the commune, Pierre Mauroy, who later served as prime minister under François Mitterrand, held a banquet for the teams and presented them with gold medals. The medals had a city scene and the logo of the city on one side and "Communaute Urbaine de Lille" on the reverse.[57]

Foster mentioned that the tour was the first time that most of the players and their families had been outside the United States, and Allspach confirmed that he had to get a passport for the first time to go on the trip. He also mentioned that one player was surprised to learn his real name when he filled out the paperwork for his passport. The importance of the tour in the lives of the Nite Hawks players at a time when European travel was not common for blue-collar football players was immense. Flying off to Europe was reserved, at least in the popular mind, for what George Jones and Tammy Wynette called the "jet set."[58] The centrality of the trip in the lives of many of the participants was demonstrated by the reaction that Allspach and the organizers had to their 2012 reunion. The gathering drew nineteen of the former world travelers, along with two wives of deceased coaches and players.[59]

Despite the chaos that marked the premature end of the tour, Foster and others were not discouraged from the idea of spreading football to the Continent. According to the UPI the "coaches and players who make the trip believe that the European continent is a fertile area for pro football and they are willing to try again."[60] Ron Maly of the *Des Moines Register* reported that the Nite Hawks were a "hit" in Europe and likened them to the Beatles, whose 1964 tour of the United States created a fever pitch of excitement. His subheadline, "Beatles-Type Fan Reaction for Football Team," set the narrative for the story. Foster told Maly that he "knew how the Beatles felt when they came to America," and that "the fan reaction was about the same." He went on to repeat his claim about the first game at Versailles and the fans who kept players on the field for half an hour after the game. "They kept wanting autographs," he told the reporter, adding, "That's quite a thrill for guys who aren't exactly National Football League players."[61]

Regardless of the obvious hyperbole of conflating the touring athletes with the mega-popular music group, Foster did admit that there had been problems getting the Europeans to understand the finer points of the game. Ever the optimist, he still held out hope. "Europeans like the contact—the bone jarring contact of the game. . . . Many of them had never seen football before, but they liked the same things Americans like. . . . They cheered for long runs and passes, but not a short run for a first down—unless some guy really got his bell rung." Again, that old bugaboo of trying to transplant our sport to France reared its ugly head. "They couldn't understand the huddle. . . . We tried to explain it as generals planning a war, as chess. . . . They just didn't get it."[62]

As mentioned in chapter 6, the IFL finally succumbed to a combination of factors, including inflation and the failure of a sponsorship deal with Pan Am Airlines that caused the cancellation of Kap's next big plan. He wanted to arrange an exhibition game in Italy between the Dallas Cowboys and the Miami Dolphins at Flavian Stadium in Rome.[63] With that failure Kap's run had reached its conclusion. He had tried college teams, semiprofessionals, and the NFL. Yet Europe still remained safely free of the American import.

Kap will be remembered for being the leading exponent of soccer-style kicking for American football with Toni Frisch of the Dallas Cowboys, not for exporting football to Europe.[64] A few years before his death in 2010, he hinted at a new crusade, integrating the NFL with female kickers, Mia Hamm, for instance, but that hasn't happened either.[65]

However, the football torch had been passed to a new generation. When Foster mentioned to the UPI reporter that he and others were "willing to try again" to bring our sport to Europe, he was serious. In 1979 Foster had moved on to the Moline and Rock Island area in eastern Iowa. While there he took the semipro Indianapolis Capitols and his team, the Quad City Black Hawks, on a European tour in 1979.[66] They skipped France, playing games in Brussels and Antwerp in Belgium and Rotterdam in the Netherlands, along with stops in Ludwigshafen and Frankfurt in Germany.[67] The final game scheduled to take place in Cologne between the two American teams was canceled and replaced with a contest between the Black Hawks and the Frankfurt Lions of the American Football Bund Deutschland (Football League of Germany). The Lions, who were in their first year of play, were a team composed of half American and half German players. If the 1938 news report was not mere fantasy, this was the first instance since then of involving the natives of the country where the game was played.[68] The tour, however, was not an economic success, with only two thousand spectators in Brussels and a few hundred more in Ludwigshafen. No other details of the tour have been found, and in the interview with Foster, he merely mentioned the tour without additional details.

The 1979 tour was significant, however, in that it demonstrated that football was beginning to catch on in Europe. Germany, with twelve more years of American military presence than France, led the way with the formation of the American Football Bund Deutschland. This was the first such league in Europe, and the game with the Black Hawks preceded the first official game of the Bundesliga between the Lions and the Düsseldorf Panthers on August 4, 1979. At first league rules required that at least three players on the team be German. By 1986, demonstrating the popularity of the sport among Germans, the ratio had reversed, and only two Americans were allowed on teams.[69]

Another ten years would pass before Foster once again tested European waters and brought another team to Paris. This time his teams would play indoors, thus avoiding the poor weather that always plagued games in the City of Light. By that time, however, football would have been successfully imbedded in France. The game had finally been brought to the country by Laurent Plegelatte, another missionary, but a Frenchman acting without American help this time. His story will be told in chapter 8.

By the time he was ready to make his third try at Europe, Foster had invented a hybrid of football. On February 11, 1981, while he was watching an indoor soccer game at Madison Square Garden, Foster drew the basic parameters of arena football on the back of a manila envelope. The new version featured a 50-yard field, an eight-player single platoon, and rebound nets off which the ball could be played. After testing the new version in Rockford and Chicago in 1986 and 1987, respectively, he was ready to launch the new league.[70] In its first three seasons, the "War on the Floor," as it marketed itself, had averaged nine thousand fans in its regular-season games.[71] Between twelve thousand and fifteen thousand had attended the first three ArenaBowls, the league's championship game.[72] Still more fans saw the game broadcast on *ESPN*. Then, in order to gain greater exposure and possibly expand the league to Europe, Foster scheduled two games between the Detroit Drive and the Chicago Bruisers in Paris and London. According to the founder, the 1989 games served their purpose and helped arena football over the hump. The international matches also reportedly aided in further expansion in the United States.[73] In 1989 France was still slowly building a football culture of its own but had once again aided the sport in the country where it originated.

Football in France still exists in the shadow of soccer and rugby, but the influence the country has had on the American game has been significant. Two of football's popular formations, the wedge and later the T, were influenced by the tactics of Napoleon and the 1940 invasion of France. The popularity of the game was spread by World War I, and finally, a game in Paris helped legitimize arena football. Americans may have had a difficult time convincing the French to play our game, but fans of the sport owe a big *merci* to the French.

In a fine echo of Bob Kap, Foster's plans were ambitious. In addition to the games in Paris and London, he envisioned a three-step process, with the 1989 contests forming the first step. They were to be followed by additional exhibitions in 1990, along with clinics for the natives. Finally, a league in Britain or on the Continent would be established. Foster believed that the presence of one hundred semi-pro teams in Britain, the simplicity of the hybrid game, and the popularity of the NFL on television would make the league a success in Europe.[74]

FIG. 17. French players from various teams make a television appearance prior to the 1989 Arena Football League game between the Chicago Bruisers and the Detroit Drive. From left, the players come from the Spartacus de Paris, Anges Bleus, Flash de La Courneuve, Spartacus, and Squales de Rueil Malmaison. Photo courtesy of Jean-Marc Burtscher.

The game took place in Paris on November 15, 1989, at the Paris Omnisport Arena and was fairly successful. The events surrounding the game demonstrated that Foster had learned from past experiences. As a "curtain raiser" for the spectacle, he used the modern technology available indoors and played a video demonstration of the rules of the game carried out by the Flash of La Courneuve and the Jets of Saint-Cloud, two of the top French teams of the time. For the master of ceremonies, Foster acquired George Eddy, the basketball and football expert from Canal +, the French television network. In Eddy, Foster had a PA announcer who could help explain the game to the audience. He also had plenty of glitz and glamour. The headliners were the Los Angeles Raiders' Raiderettes B Team cheerleaders. The article on the game in the football magazine *US Foot* told readers that if the "Pom Poms" were only the B team, it would be "better for [their] health not to think too much about the first team." The author admitted that the game lacked intensity, but added parenthetically that "it was really a demonstration," not an actual contest. Nevertheless, the writer was enthusiastic about the possibility of the hybrid sport and its unique rules. The crowd of around 8,000 (13,500 according to the AFL website) contained a large number of young people and included players from the Parisian football teams wearing their war paint (presumably team jerseys). These fans knew the rules and had already had played the game, so they were very excited to see professionals. Their insider knowledge gave them confidence, and they "strutted in" with their girlfriends on their arms. The old difficulty with huddles didn't raise its ugly head this time. Most of the crowd had spent time in one or could explain it to the uninitiated. The twenty-five-second play clock also encouraged teams not to linger between plays, and football games by this time were being carried on Canal + television. Therefore, an increasing number of French sports enthusiasts had now seen games and were familiar with its static nature. Jacques Accambray, the president of the FFFA, who had played football for Kent State in Ohio during the early 1970s, took center stage and welcomed "all football fans" to the event.[75]

Football had already gained a foothold on the previously hostile shores, and that gave Foster and company an edge that was not present in any of the earlier tours. For the first time American football missionaries were able to demonstrate their game before novices familiar with the strange rites of the sport. They were also able to draw on an already-established football culture to provide fans and support.

This did not, however, make the result any more successful. Arena football remains an exclusively American sport, played only in the continental United States. What the game did demonstrate was that football was no longer an exclusively American sport and that fans could be found worldwide. The twelve thousand fans, again according to the AFL website, who attended the London game were further proof.

However, all the tours and exhibitions by professionals had no demonstrative effect on the creation of this football culture. Cultural imperialism was not an effective tool in creating demand for football in France. Bringing amateur All-Star teams, collegiate teams, NFL players, and finally semiprofessionals had not struck a chord with the French.

Certainly, the tours were hampered by a lack of institutional memory, so that each succeeding effort had to figuratively reinvent the wheel. A hostile press also lessened the impact of the efforts that Americans put into popularizing the American game. Reporters accustomed to the free flow of rugby and soccer were not prepared to open their journalistic arms to a wildly different style of play. At best the Americans who demonstrated the sport in France were seen as curiosities, at worst as sideshow freaks. The entrenched British sports imported in the late nineteenth century were also jealous of their turf and made no efforts to allow in a competitor. Even the elements seemed to align themselves against football, from the weather that Crowley and his All-Stars saw to the rain and snow of later tours that suppressed spectator interest.

European "Yankee Go Home!" anti-Americanism that was evident during the latter stages of the Cold War did not make matters easier. Charles de Gaulle, in expelling NATO bases in 1967, fed into this attitude that Americans were trying to dominate the world. Football, as one of the most visible symbols of American culture, was seen as part of the process. Jean-Marc Burtscher faced such criticism when he began playing football in the 1980s and remembered colleagues asking him why he was a "Reagan American" because he played football.[76]

All these factors hindered the establishment of the game in France. Given the Manichean divides of the Cold War, it would be ironic that when the all-American game finally became established in France, it would be planted through the efforts of a man who described himself as a Trotskyite.

8. Lafayette, le football est voilà!

In the beginning (of the 1980s) there was Laurent Plegelatte.

The American military had played more than a thousand football games in France from 1914 to 1966. Entrepreneurial missionaries, including Curt Riess and Jim Crowley in 1938, William Dodds and Maurice Tardy in 1961, Bob Kap and Jim Foster in the 1970s, and finally Jim Foster alone did their best to convince the French that football was the future. After all that effort the autumn quiet remained unbroken by the crash of pads or the roar of the crowd.

As an exercise in cultural imperialism, if it could be called that, it was a miserable failure. That would change in 1980, when Laurent Plegelatte took a vacation to Colorado and was laughed at by an American football coach. His hero's journey would then see him visit the "Cavern of Ali Baba," where he would purchase enough equipment for one team. He would then return to Vail for a time to prove to the laughing coach that he was serious, and there he would gain advanced training in the sport. His preparation finished, he would finally return to France, where the Paris Spartacus team would be born.

So begins the creation story of football américain. The eighties would finally see the establishment of a football league of the French, played by the French, and for French purposes. Over the course of the first decade of French football, the number of teams would grow from Spartacus in 1980 to forty teams in 1989. The original teams would cluster around Paris and its surrounding suburbs, but by the 1990s teams would be playing across the breadth of the country. Founded on amateur ideals, the federation that grew to administer the new sport would struggle against forces that envisioned a different future for the game, but it would win in the end.

All this, according to legend, as a result of one high school football coach who saw only humor in the idea that Frenchmen could play football. Plus one Frenchman who was not amused.

In a 1991 interview for *US Foot*, Plegelatte retold the famous story of how he went to Vail, Colorado, on vacation in September 1980. While there he met the head coach of a local high school football team from nearby Eagle. "This is where I discovered football," he remembered. When Plegelatte told the coach that he wanted to introduce the game back home, the man "broke out laughing." Stung by this reaction, he decided to take matters into his own hands.[1]

Without telling anyone else who might laugh, he located a sporting-goods merchant in Denver who did not ridicule the idea but rather recognized the potential of the project. Perhaps this store owner, like Albert Spalding, saw the possibility of opening a new market for his equipment. Maybe he only wanted to unload some surplus stock. Whatever his motivation, the man led Plegelatte into what the budding football missionary described as "Ali Baba's Cave," where he was offered a deal: "ten dollars apiece for helmets and shoulder pads, and six dollars for pants." With enough equipment for twenty-five players, he went back to Eagle and convinced the coach of the Battle Mountain High School Huskies to teach him the game. Impressed by Plegelatte's seriousness, as evidenced by purchases that would have totaled nearly seven hundred dollars (F 2,800), the Huskies' coach wasted no time integrating the novice into his training camp.[2]

A bit of a Renaissance man, Plegelatte was a fine athlete, a musician, a painter, and a licensed pilot.[3] He was also no stranger to combative sports. In his job as a physical education instructor, he practiced and taught judo and boxing.[4] He was also a man of ideas, particularly in politics. Described by all as a Communist, and by most as a Trotsky-ite, part of his motivation was reportedly to bring football to France so that he could toughen up his "Red Guards."[5] Others, while acknowl-edging his political motivations, argue that the game became an end in itself for him.[6]

Upon returning to Paris, he arrived at around noon, and by 3:00

p.m., he had twenty-five players signed on to his project. Most of the new players were recruited from his students at the U.B.U. Judo Club. This core group, that would later take the name Spartacus, began practicing before the month had ended. Without a practice field to call its own, the group "squatted" on the grounds of Stade Pershing in the Bois de Vincennes.[7] Likely without knowing the significance of the site, they had symbolically closed the circle, training near the location where the Eighty-Ninth and Thirty-Sixth Divisions played the final game of the Divisional Championship in 1919.

The early days were as chaotic as one would expect, as a group of young men (Plegelatte was thirty-two at the time) struggled to start a new sport in a nation that had no infrastructure to support it. According to Plegelatte in a 1987 interview with *Quarterback Magazine* posted on the *Elitefoot* blog, after occupying the grounds of Stade Pershing for a time and using their car trunks as dressing rooms, the players found a center for young workers in the southeastern suburb of Charenton whose director allowed them to use his lawn for practice. Along with the field came a prefabricated eighteen-meter-by-fifteen-meter gymnasium to use as their locker room. They made themselves at home in the small building by bringing in old tires, roofing beams, and sandbags to build a "true obstacle course." However, when the director of the center paid them a surprise visit one day, she found the room in complete disarray, with the tiles and lighting fixtures broken, along with a spot where one of the enthusiastic novices had blocked his way through the wall. They kept their practice center but had to make repairs.[8]

Plegelatte and his new football players thought of a variety of possible names for their new organization, including the "Flying Camemberts" and the "Crocodile Tears." "We didn't want to copy the Americans, only [let them] inspire us, while keeping a sense of humor," he recalled. They sought a name that encapsulated "violence, aggressiveness, courage, and speed," and in the end they chose to name themselves after the Thracian slave and gladiator who had rebelled against the Romans between 73 and 71 BC. "We were sensible of the image of the helmet, the shoulder pad, and the arena of course, but especially that of the emancipator," Plegelatte explained.[9] The now-iconic Spartacus helmet featured a fist with the thumb pointing down. Plegelatte told a reporter in 1987, "[It is the] evocation of the defeat that we promise to our opponents, but also the awareness that the threat can turn at any time against us."[10]

In addition to his other enthusiasms, Plegelatte also enjoyed placing the effort in historical context. His 1988 book, *Le football américain*, primarily devoted to explanations of the techniques and tactics of the game, began by tracing the evolution of sport. He first declared, "Men are players. During all times they have practiced games with various forms and meanings." In fine Marxian form he presented the history of sport as being teleological. Sport began in earliest times with games that served as training for war, including games such as the rough-and-tumble *la soule* played in Brittany. It now had ended with the final evolution of sport being realized by the creation of gridiron football.[11]

Although likely unaware of the efforts of Riess, Leclerc, Kap, and their confederates, Plegelatte did not repeat their errors. Instead of building a league, he built teams. Once Spartacus had been created and the players were busy learning the basics of the sport, the one missing ingredient was an opponent. Plegelatte demonstrated his vision by requiring that his players learn all the offensive and defensive positions. His second requirement, that after they had learned the basics, they were to leave and form their own teams, demonstrated his bottom-up approach. It was this method that would finally succeed in firmly planting the sport in France.[12] By the next year there were four teams playing football in France. Three of the teams, Spartacus, Les Anges Bleus (Blue Angels) of Montreuil, and the Météores of Nogent-sur-Marne were arranged around the Bois de Vincennes, a forest located on the southeast fringe of Paris. They were joined by the Squales (Sharks) of Rueil Malmaison, which is a Parisian suburb to the west of the city center.[13]

Of those four original teams, the Météores were the second to form and the first opponent for Spartacus. They are the only one of the original clubs that still exists. They have relocated and now play from Fontenay-sous-Bois, which is still on the border of the Bois de Vincennes but a little further north and closer to the center of Paris.

The team was founded when two brothers named Dupuis de Mery sought to join Spartacus. Plegelatte agreed but only on the condition that they would stay long enough to learn the rules and tactics, then form their own team. The Dupuis brothers complied, and after three months there were two teams in France.[14] Spartacus later played the first all-French football game against the Météores in June 1981. Once again it was fitting that the game that signaled football had returned to France was contested at Stade Pershing.[15] The exact date and the final score have been forgotten, but Spartacus won the game, and competitive French football was born.[16]

During the first years of football in France, this "calving" of teams was the primary method through which the sport would grow from one team with twenty-five players in 1980 to four teams by 1982. Seemingly never content with the status quo, Plegelatte took football in France a step further. With enough teams to have a championship tournament, Plegelatte and his fellow travelers created the Casque d'Or (Golden Helmet), a trophy that would go to the best team in France. His Spartacus, as was only fitting, won the first Casque d'Or. The final was played at Stade de la Cipale, located within the Bois de Vincennes. Maintaining their proper place based on their birth order, the Météores finished a distant second, losing to the champions by a score of 44–0.[17]

With more teams coming aboard, in 1981 Plegelatte created the Comité français football américain, a national committee for the development of American football.[18] This was a legal association that allowed Plegelatte and others to open a bank account and negotiate for insurance to develop the sport.[19] In 1983 Plegelatte became the first president of the Fédération Française de Football Américain and began seeking recognition from the French Ministry of Youth and Sport. At that time there were nine teams and some six hundred players. Final recognition from the ministry came in 1985, under President Michel Gofman, and the FFFA thenceforth would be operated through that organization.[20] Chapter 9 will explore the evolution of the FFFA more extensively.

In addition to the Casque d'Or, French teams also contended for the Coupe de France, a game that was played only in 1984, 1985, and

1987. Though information on the games is scarce, other than the victors and the vanquished, this was likely an attempt to copy the popular tournaments that soccer and rugby staged each year. After three attempts that saw the Castors (Beavers), the Challengers of Paris, and then the Argonautes of Aix-en-Provence win, respectively, the tournament was called off. After that the Casque d'Or, later the Casque de Diamant, served as the only season-ending contest.[21]

Spartacus would appear in the first three Casque d'Or games, winning the first two before falling to the Anges Bleus in 1984. The 1985 championship was the first to be held without Spartacus, and a dispute over refereeing revealed another facet of Plegelatte's character: his fierce desire to win. According to Jerome Laval, a member of Spartacus, the founder had "a tendency to become angry and grumpy, and sometimes [he was] a sore loser."[22]

This was apparent in the controversy surrounding the 1985 Casque d'Or match. In the semifinals Spartacus faced the Paris Challengers, and a referee's decision sent the game into overtime, during which the Challengers emerged victorious. Spartacus appealed the decision to the FFFA, and Gofman decided that the two teams would play a rematch. As Barney Gill and the SHAPE Indians would have liked in 1962, the Challengers refused to appear for the game, and Spartacus was declared the winner by forfeit. After a series of negotiations, Gofman reversed his decision and declared that the final would pit the Challengers against the Paris Jets.[23]

On the day of the match, Plegelatte and Spartacus added a distinctly French touch to the game and took direct action in the form of a sit-in. They occupied the field at Stade Jean-Bouin and refused to move. Appeals to the strikers had no effect, and eventually the Compagnies républican des sécurité (CRS), the French riot-control police, arrived. As a cold rain soaked the field and the spectators, Spartacus continued to refuse orders to vacate until some thirty CRS officers compelled the team to vacate amid the booing of those spectators still in attendance. The Jets had also left, and the game had to be rescheduled for the next week. After all the hullaballoo, the Jets defeated the Challengers 6–0, in a game that must have been anticlimactic for everyone.[24]

During the 2013 NFL season, a blown call in the final weekend of the season in a game between the San Diego Chargers and the Kansas City Chiefs propelled the Chargers into the American Football Conference Wild Card round of the playoffs.[25] It is impossible to imagine the Pittsburgh Steelers, the victims of the call, occupying the field at Paul Brown Stadium in protest. However, sports take on something of the national character where they are played. This event, in a nation where strikes are part of the social fabric, helped the French place their unique stamp on the game. Indeed, Loic Brébant, a reporter for the then-extreme left-wing newspaper *Liberation*, was quick to declare, "At least this curious afternoon allowed French football to establish its originality compared to its American big brother."[26]

Acrimony surrounding the finals was not the only crisis that French football faced that year. In a more momentous challenge, Plegelatte's fundamental vision for football in France would also be disputed. He saw football as a game "accessible to all rather than to an elite of semi-professionals or professionals. [He favored] equality rather than elitism."[27] This dedication to the amateur ideal, likely inspired by his political leanings, continues to mark football in France.

However, in the early eighties, the Anges Bleus, a team formed to oppose Spartacus, both on the field and in the arena of ideas, would attempt to "professionalize" the sport.[28] This would be the first, and most serious, crisis of the eventful 1985 season, but it had its roots planted during the 1983 Casque d'Or final.

The primary casualty of the twin crises that season would be FFFA president Gofman, who would resign as a result. However, in the larger struggle the federation's dedication to strict amateurism would mostly survive, albeit with some modifications introduced by the Anges Bleus.

Stéphane Sardano and Olivier Passe, two friends who had discovered football and who had developed a passion for the game, were the founding fathers of the Anges Bleus. In October 1981 they formed the club in Montreuil, to the north and east of the Bois de Vincennes. After a few months they were joined by Yves and Jean-Luc Parelli, former players from Spartacus, and the team set about striving to supplant Plegelatte and Spartacus from their spot atop the new league.[29] They took their name from the 1930 Marlene Dietrich film *Blue Angel*.[30]

FIG. 18. Eric and Jean-Marc Burtscher as Anges Bleus. Photo courtesy of Jean-Marc Burtscher.

The rivalry between the two teams would become an epic struggle in the early history of football in France. Not only was their rivalry built around differing visions for what football should be, but there existed a political dimension as well. The Montreuil team was seen as representing more conservative interests as a counterbalance to the political radicalism of Plegelatte and Spartacus. So the rivalry pitted the amateur ideal against a professionalized model, and also right versus left.[31]

Jean-Marc Burtscher, who, along with his brother, Eric, played for

the Anges Bleus, argued that the reality was not quite so stark polit-
ically. He remembered that the front line of his version of the Anges
Bleus featured five players who each belonged to a different political
party that ranged from far right to far left. In his recollection "the
center and right tackle were supporters of Jean-Marie Le Pen, the
right guard was kind of a Marxist, but not a Communist, and the left
tackle did not vote." Jean-Marc also declared that he was apolitical.
He added that in 1992, the quarterback was Jewish and the running
back Muslim. Burtscher echoed the narrative that football in the
United States has often employed, when he declared, "There was no
black or white, only Blue!"[32]

Eric Burtscher acknowledged that according to legend the Spartacus players were "commies" and the Anges Bleus were "fascists," but
he also questioned that narrative. He suggested that the true gene-
sis of the rivalry might have had the more prosaic origin in competition over women.[33]

Julien Luneau, a player and later team president of the Flash of La
Courneuve, noted that the Anges Bleus were "more like bikers," and
"the Météores were the true right wing team."[34] Whatever the truth
behind the legend, the rivalry over the nature and purpose of football in France was quite real.

At the culmination of the 1983 season, the Anges Bleus and Spartacus faced each other in the final of the Casque d'Or; Spartacus won
by a score of 34–14. Spurred by the loss to a team he wanted badly to
defeat, Yves Perelli, who coached the Anges Bleus, decided he would
do what he could to "raise the level" of his team.[35] To add some zip
to practice, the Anges Bleus would train with the Météores on Sunday mornings, providing a change of pace from lining up against the
same player at each of the three weekly practice sessions that were
the norm. Sardano remembers that practices were so tough, as close
to the American model as they could manage, that the games were
"like a vacation."[36]

Like most of the first French teams, the Anges Bleus coaches and
players would also scrounge for any information they could find on the
game. Before the Internet eased the transfer of information, players
would ask friends in the United States or Canada to send game video-

tapes, books on formations, and whatever other information might prove useful. Still, information was often hard to come by, and players had to improvise. Jean-Marc Burtscher remembered that on his first team none of the players had ever seen a football game. Their first formation was a modification of the Roman legion's *testudo* formation, which would have resembled the flying wedge of early college football. Perhaps Napoleon Bonaparte even looked down with favor on their efforts.[37]

One of Parelli's steps that paid significant dividends was to take several players to the United States in 1984 to learn the game in its homeland. Apropos the Internet facilitating research, while I was writing about this event, Yves Parelli, via Jean-Marc Burtscher and Facebook, remembered how the trip came about. He stated that through one of his contacts in France he was able to get preliminary approval from San Diego State University (SDSU). An exchange of letters followed, and the group was off to the West Coast.[38] They traveled from Los Angeles to San Diego, where they watched the SDSU Aztecs practice. They absorbed not only offensive formations but also methods for conducting workouts. Parelli remembered that they did not take part in practice. In his words, "We could believe it on the plane, but not on the ground." They did receive "royal treatment," with access to practice sessions and meetings, and they were able to talk with coaches and players in the "canteen," which was presumably a local bar.[39]

Sardano remembered that fifteen players made the trip, and they rented a motor home, which also served as their sleeping quarters for most of the trip. This set the Anges Bleus apart from other French teams of the time in that they had learned the sport by doing something other than watching tapes or reading books.[40]

Sometimes, however, all their study and the information they sucked in led them to get ahead of themselves. They attempted to make their formations too complicated, and instead of just dominating play by bashing away at the opponent, they were too clever for their own good. Razzle-dazzle and misdirection plays sometimes fell flat when their opponents weren't proficient enough at the basics of the game to go for an obvious fake. Sometimes this was even a challenge for players on the Anges Bleus, as when coaches and experienced players would urge the team to "watch for fakes!" only to be asked, "What is a fake?!"[41] Their dedication produced immediate results on the field, however. They returned to the Casque d'Or and, rising to the top of a now eight-team field, avenged their loss in the previous season by defeating Spartacus 20–0. They also became well known, and in some cases feared, for their hard hitting and rough style of play. Sardano remembered that during one game with the Météores, their opponents complained that if the Anges Bleus continued to hit in the second half as they had in the first, the Météores would not play. The Anges Bleus agreed to take it easy, and the game continued.[42]

Though the Anges Bleus were taking steps to improve the level of proficiency, playing what amounted to a hybrid of amateur and semiprofessional football, they still had the moments of chaos that are inherent in such an atmosphere. The men who played still had to work their regular jobs, and getting everyone to practices and games was often a bit of a challenge. During one of the Anges Bleus international road trips, one V.R., whose nickname was an inversion of RV, as in "recreational vehicle, but on the wrong side," decided to fly to the game and meet his teammates on the field. Instead of renting a car when he arrived, which in the early 1980s might not have even been an option, he stole a car to drive to the game. His teammates were flabbergasted, but the late arrival told them it was not a problem. He would put some gas in the car and leave it where he found it. In another international match one of their players did not have valid identity papers, even for France, so he had to ride in a car trunk during the border crossing in the days before the European Union opened travel between member states.[43]

While the men were mostly playing for the love of the game, some players did receive a sinecure of sorts to play. The Anges Bleus, in their pursuit of quality play, were the first team to import players from North America. During the 1985 season they brought in Paul Troth, a quarterback/running back, and Bob Bopp, a wide receiver, both from William Jewell College in Missouri. One of the issues that Troth had to help the Anges Bleus with was their offensive line play. Sardano, who played guard, remembered that Troth told the line:

"Don't block like that!" when he saw that his protectors were using the old high school–style pass-blocking techniques that required linemen to keep their hands tucked against their chest instead of reaching out to deliver a hit on defenders.[44]

These mercenaries were paid but not a great deal. Ron Selesky, who played with the Anges Bleus in the early 1990s, remembered that he received "enough francs to get fed and to get to practice." He roomed with a player named Antoine Zerbato, who spoke good English. And to round out his compensation package, he was given a Métro pass so that he could get around the city.[45] Since some of the Anges Bleus held down jobs as bouncers, he also was given fee access to various nightclubs.[46]

Braxton Shaver, who played for the Flash de La Courneuve, remembered being paid €1,000 per month along with room, board, and transportation on the Métro.[47] The situation, therefore, was similar to baseball in the nineteenth century, when players such as Jim Creighton received money, often under the table, or as a salary for a fictional job, to play for the local nine.[48]

In addition to importing ringers to improve their performance, the Anges Bleus also sought coaching help from abroad. Troth and Bopp, while playing, also served as part of the coaching staff for the team, but the significant addition came in 1984, when Jacques Dussault came aboard. Initially, while Dussault was also coaching the Montreal Concordes of the Canadian Football League, the francophone coach spent three weeks giving the team an intensive clinic. Later he came back and served as head coach in the early 1990s. Dussault continued to sharpen the Anges Bleus' edge. Jean-Marc Burtscher remembered that the coach introduced the concept of *chasse touriste*, or tourist hunting. This was the idea that if, during a play, any of the Anges Bleus saw an opponent not paying attention, they should "knock him on his ass!"[49]

The team was also aided by the addition of a Frenchman who had played college football in the United States, and who also had important connections in the French sporting world. Jacques Accambray, a world-class hammer thrower, had also played one season as a defensive tackle at Kent State in Ohio. Accambray was a well-known sports figure in France, and his connections helped gain the Anges Bleus access to practice facilities operated by the National Institute of Sport. The facility included a weight room and an indoor practice field for use during inclement weather. These facilities put the team ahead in an "arms race" that at that time had only one participant.[50] Accambray would also share management of the team with the Parelli brothers and later would serve as the president of the federation from 1985 to 1996.[51]

The addition of North American players and coaches helped the Anges Bleus further along the road to professionalism. Having achieved their first goal of conquering France by winning the 1984 Casque d'Or, the team set its sights on Europe and beyond. After meeting Bertrand Lecuyer, an entrepreneur in the mold of Bob Kap, Parelli and company joined his new Amerfoot International.[52] This Switzerland-based organization was designed to promote gridiron football in Europe, taking advantage of the traction the game was beginning to gain in several Western European nations in addition to France, including Germany, England, Finland, and Italy.

The Anges Bleus' first international game, played concurrently with their successful march to the French championship, was a 19–8 loss against the Cologne (Germany) Crocodiles. They began getting their footing in international competition that year and later defeated the Milan (Italy) Rhinos, the Amsterdam (Holland) Rams, and the Helsinki (Finland) Colts. They continued their international success in 1985 by defeating the Düsseldorf (Germany) Bengals, the Dortmund (Germany) Giants, and the London (England) Black-Hawks.[53]

Their success playing for Amerfoot International did not, however, go unnoticed and led to the second crisis that the FFFA faced in 1985. The path that the Anges Bleus had chosen and the steps they had taken to realize their goal flew in the face of the ideals that Plegelatte had built into his Spartacus and the federation.

Amerfoot's restriction of membership to only the elite teams in each nation was akin to the evolution of baseball from an amateur game played by all to a professionalized sport played by the "first nines" in the early days of the sport in the United States.[54] The federation, bearing the stamp that Plegelatte had placed on it from the start, saw that development as threat to the amateur foundation it had built.

FIG. 19. Laurent Plegelatte of Spartacus (*left*) throws a pass against the Anges Bleus in the Casque d'Or game in 1986. The Anges Bleus won the championship by a score of 20–2. Photo courtesy of Jean-Marc Burtscher.

The rivalry that existed on and off the field was also a factor in the dispute. Sardano remembered that the Anges Bleus had grudges against the Spartacus-dominated federation for what they regarded as that organization siphoning off the best prospective players for Spartacus. They also had problems with officiating. Sardano again recalled that in one particular game against Spartacus, the officials, mostly supplied by Plegelatte's team, called back three consecutive seventy-one-yard touchdown plays for holding.[55]

In the end Plegelatte and the federation gave the Anges Bleus a choice: "Pick one federation or the other!" The offending team argued that they were not members of a rival federation, but that Amerfoot was simply another sponsor. They then went off to play in the game against the Finnish champion. The FFFA saw that as a decision in favor of Amerfoot and expelled the Anges Bleus from the federation, making them ineligible for the Casque d'Or.[56]

In the short term this did not slow the rebellious team down. It instead went hunting for even bigger game. Having been crowned the nominal champion of Europe by defeating the Finns, the Anges Bleus felt they were ready to take on the Americans, or as most sources phrased it, "the undisputed masters of football." The first game that they played against an American team was a match in Paris on June 30, 1985. Their opponent was an All-Star team made up of players from the Heart of America Conference. Likely this match, which was part of a ten-day tour by the All-Stars, was arranged through the efforts of Troth and Bopp, whose William Jewell College played in the conference.

Demonstrating that their training and commitment to excellence were beginning to bear fruit, the French team lost to the Americans, but they were not humiliated. The final score was 29–13 in favor of the All-Stars, and while Troth and Bopp accounted for most of the offense, the two Anges Bleus touchdowns were scored by French receivers Hervé Nicole and Francky Baudry.[57] The team had also lost its first international game against the Cologne team, but the setback did not deter it from trying again. The same would be the case for its loss against the Americans.

The next test against a team from the United States took place only a few days later and was more successful for the French. The opponent for the game was the U.S. Navy's Sixth Fleet All-Stars, and to add insult to injury, the French defeated the sailors 26–12 on July 4. The game, played in front of a reported forty thousand fans at Toulon, was a signal victory for the club.[58] The match was arranged by one of the executives of Amerfoot who had contacts in the United States, and many of the sailors came from the USS *Puget Sound*.[59] The crowd size was a major improvement over the estimated five hundred who had watched the game in Paris and must have been seen as a sign that the Anges Bleus had arrived in the big time. It also lent credence to Barney Gill's theory, described in chapter 7, that the way to establish commercially successful football in Europe was to draw American service personnel as fans.

The Anges Bleus had precious little time to gloat over their victory, however, as they faced their third American opponent in ten days. This time they would play a three-game series against the Lutes of

FIG. 20. Anges Bleus versus Sixth Fleet All-Stars in Toulon on July 4, 1985. The Anges Bleus defeated the American team 26–12. Photo courtesy of Jean-Marc Burtscher.

Pacific Lutheran University (PLU) from Tacoma, Washington. The games were part of the French Riviera Football Classic, which was to pit PLU in three games against the Anges Bleus, a French All-Star team chosen by the FFFA, and an Italian All-Star team. The Italian and French selections dropped out of the series as a consequence of the dispute between the FFFA and Amerfoot, so the Anges Bleus were left alone to face the mighty Lutes, who were at the time one of the top teams in the NAIA.[60]

The French representatives, cocky after their victory over the Sixth Fleet, consented to be the Lutes' opponent in all three games. Unfortunately for the Anges Bleus, the July 4 victory would be their only success against the Americans, and they proceeded to drop the games against PLU by scores of 40–12 in Draguingan, 38–0 in Nice, and 36–13 in Cannes.[61] Though it is not likely that anybody was aware of it, the Anges Bleus were also recapitulating the history of football in France by playing in Nice, the site of the first ever game in 1909.

The dispute between two teams and two models for the game—

FIG. 21. Jacques Accambray (*right*) during the celebrations following the Riviera Football Classic. The Anges Bleus lost three games to Pacific Lutheran University. Photo courtesy of Jean-Marc Burtscher.

Spartacus promoting an amateur game for the benefit of the players versus the Anges Bleus favoring a professionalized spectacle that would appeal to mass spectators—was resolved only when Minister of Sport Alain Calmat stepped in to demand that only one federation be put forth for approval. If both remained in contention, then neither would receive official recognition. Faced with that choice, the Anges Bleus severed their connection with Lecuyer and Amerfoot and were reinstated by the FFFA.[62]

With the "Fédération War" over, the principle of amateurism was firmly established in French football.[63] This was arguably a turning point in the development of the sport there. An equivalent moment in the history of the game in the United States would be the 1952 Ivy Agreement, which banned member institutions from playing in bowl games and likewise did away with spring practice. These steps effectively de-emphasized football on the campuses of what would become the Ivy League in 1954.[64] The same could be said of the FFFA's victory over Amerfoot. Its decision to favor the strict amateur model over the more professionalized and commercialized model put forth by

Amerfoot consigned football to a marginal existence in the French sporting world.

From that point it would continue to exist as a minor game, passionately embraced by its devotees, but one that would be unable to emerge from the shadow cast by soccer and rugby. Ivy League football is largely invisible in the contemporary world of American sport, and the same is true of football américain.

Contra-factual history is always a dicey tool. One can never be sure that other events and factors might have intervened to change the arc of history. However, the Anges Bleus' model had achieved success in both national and international competition. Had it and Amerfoot been allowed to continue their evolution, they might have promised a brighter and more internationally significant future for French football. Despite the uncertainty inherent in the argument, it is at least plausible. Therefore, the Fédération War of 1985 could be said to have consigned football in France to a future as a consuming passion for a few but an irrelevancy for most.

For many that future was precisely what they sought to create: a game for the players, not a commercial spectacle that American college or professional football has become.[65] However, a significant number of those who belong to the culture surrounding football in France chafe at the attention given to soccer or rugby and wonder what can be done to raise the visibility of their sport. They make a strong case that unlike soccer, football offers a family-friendly environment, without the fear of riots or hooligans. Several sources also mentioned that during the playing of "La Marseillaise," the French national anthem, soccer fans will boo and jeer.[66] During the 2013 Casque de Diamante game, which replaced the Casque d'Or in 1995, fans behaved much like Americans during "The Star Spangled Banner." For the most part they stood respectfully, and many sang along.[67]

Still, when talk turns to the win-at-all-costs mentality surrounding football in the United States, which the Anges Bleus and Amerfoot seemed bent on replicating, they hesitate to embrace it.[68] Nicolas Robert, a player for the Castors, gave a 2012 interview to the electronic magazine *Amerfoot Mag* in which he expressed the unease with which many French players regard the "American" model. He told the reporter:

All the North American coaches I have worked with in France carried with them a tactical, technical and human model that they attempted to somehow impose as the only possible way. . . . I think most do not understand the French mentality and the organization of amateur sport in France. For them college sport is a preparation for professionalism. Formatting and results go before the notion of human adventure. In France, the players are from very different social and intellectual backgrounds, have different levels, with a motivation based primarily on "playing" and focused on the technical aspect. Without the fun, they get bored very quickly. I have not seen any of these human characteristics taken into account by these coaches.[69]

Without a doubt Robert was correct, although he exempted Tom Bass, his American coach, from his indictment of the American way. Coaches brought up in the culture of American football are certainly immersed in a win-at-all-costs environment from Pop Warner football to the NFL. They may choose to opt out, but that is a decision fraught with career peril, beginning at the high school level, if not before. This focus on winning, however, along with the violence of the game, is precisely what has made football the premier sport in the United States. Therefore, many French football devotees are caught up in a catch-22 where they cannot gain visibility for their sport without transforming it into something with which they would not be comfortable.

Following what was perhaps their biggest challenge, and also perhaps their biggest loss in the Fédération War, the Anges Bleus had been brought back into the mainstream of French football. They now played out of Joinville Le Pont, but the experience they gained playing internationally in the 1985 season paid off once they were back in the fold.[70] They again climbed to the top of the federation and won the Casque d'Or in 1986. They also experienced the satisfaction of defeating their arch-rival, Spartacus, in the final by a score of 20–2.[71]

However, as key personnel began to find other things to do with their time, the team started a slow decline. Paul Troth left the team for the Amsterdam Crusaders in 1987, and others finally succumbed to injuries or pressure from work or family.[72] They continued to challenge for the championship of the Elite Division and reached the semifinals in 1987 before losing to the Castors, who went on to win the championship. They also finished second in the Coupe de France, losing to the Argonautes 14–12.[73] In 1988 they fell again to the Castors, this time in the finals by a score of 7–0, and suffered the same fate at the hands of the new power in French football in the 1989 semifinals.[74] The 1990 season was the first in which the team failed to make the playoffs, but it rebounded in 1991, winning seven and losing one before bowing to the Flash de La Courneuve 22–29 in the quarterfinals.[75] The 1992 season would be the team's last, and the following year some of the remaining players from the Anges Bleus would ironically join their traditional enemies from Spartacus to form Team Paris.[76]

The Anges Bleus would have one last international fling in 1989, when they represented France in the third Eurobowl under new Canadian coach Gordon Cahill. They defeated the Grazer (Austria) Giants before losing to the Cologne Red Barons by a score of 37–0.[77] That they were chosen as their nation's representative was only due to federation sanction of the Castors, the dominant team of the time, who had been ruled ineligible for international competition for two years because of their "questionable attitude toward the Eurobowl."[78] One of the negative consequences of the team's participation in the Eurobowl was that it was ineligible to join the French National Team for its game in Holland as part of the European Championship of Nations, another tournament that featured international play.[79]

It must be emphasized that Plegelatte and the federation had never had a problem with international competition. Spartacus defeated the Trojans of Finland, while the Castors defeated an Austrian team in an international tournament held in Paris and dubbed the Rose Bowl in 1983.[80] They insisted, however, that teams play under their banner and that the competition had to be for the benefit of the teams, not paying fans. Even today fans get into the Casque de Diamante, which replaced the Casque d'Or as the name for the championship in 1995, free of charge.[81]

As Spartacus and the Anges Bleus focused primarily on each other and their disputes, other teams were forming in the Paris area that would replace them in the top spot. In 1986, when the Anges Bleus won their final championship, and Spartacus appeared in the final for the last time, the federation now contained eighteen teams in two divisions. The Elite Division featured ten teams, which in addition to the four original teams now included the Challengers, the Castors, the Jets, and the Hurricanes of Paris, along with the Cherokees of Antony and the Flash of La Courneuve, which played in Parisian suburbs. The eight teams of Division 2 were often junior teams that fed players into the older clubs but also included independent teams.[82] Division 2 also served as a developmental league, and teams that had success there could move up to the Elite Division. That was the route that had been taken by the Challengers, the Hurricanes, and the Flash.[83]

The Jets of Saint-Cloud, formed in 1983 in a wealthy western suburb of the capital, took advantage of the Anges Bleus being excommunicated in 1985 and survived the confusion of the sit-in strike by Spartacus well enough to defeat the Challengers. The team enjoyed a "flashy" and "flamboyant" reputation, much as their American namesakes had in the 1960s NFL, and the players were often considered to be "smart-asses" by the other teams. They were, however, one of the first to develop the passing game, using French quarterbacks, which surprised many of their opponents.[84] They did have several American players on their team, including Grant Noome, who was listed as a quarterback, but only Ben Hobbins, a running back who had played for the University of Wisconsin–Whitewater, was listed as having any experience playing beyond high school.[85]

As with many French teams, or early NFL teams for that matter, the Jets did not last long. They were eliminated in the 1986 semifinals by Spartacus and in 1987 were humiliated in the final when the Castors defeated them by a score of 75–0. Marc Juniat, one of the Jets, demonstrated some of the bravado that his team was noted for, commenting that the crushing loss "truly proved that we were a Parisian team by giving up 75 points" (Paris license plates carry the departmental code 75).[86] After that game the team never advanced past the quarter-final round, and in 1992 it ceased to exist as an independent team when it merged with the Sphinx of another suburb, Plessis-Robinson.[87]

The Castors team, which had embarrassed the Jets in the 1987 final, would become the dominant power in the federation for the next several years, winning five Casque d'Or titles in eight years between 1987 and 1994 and finishing second three more times in the 1990s.[88] After losing 7–13 to the Anges Bleus in the 1987 Coupe de France, the Castors did not lose again until the Argonautes defeated them in the 1990 Casque d'Or game.[89]

A group of students from the prestigious École spéciale des travaux publics, bâtiment et de l'industrie (ESTP), a grande école for engineers in Paris, created the Castors in 1982.[90] The moment of birth occurred after a circus show that was part of the Gala of the Grandes Écoles, when the ESTP students who were performing suddenly had the desire to form a football team.[91] What precisely caused that desire is not clear, but they acted upon it, and by 1983 they had begun playing. They made the semifinals for the first time in 1984 and reached the finals of the Coupe de France in 1985. The next two years they lost to the Anges Bleus in the 1986 semifinals and the 1987 Coupe de France. Despite the loss in the Coupe de France, the Castors broke out of the pack with their 75–0 shellacking of the Jets. In 1988 they avenged their previous losses to the Anges Bleus, winning 7–0 in the final. They followed that with a win in the final Casque d'Or of the 1980s by defeating the Argonautes, who were the next rising power of the federation. They would then lose to the Argos in the final the next two years before returning to the top in 1993. Despite their success the 1993 season would be their last as an independent team, and players from the Castors joined with the Sphinx during the next year. In the short run the combined team enjoyed continued success, winning the championship in 1994 and finishing second to the Argos in 1995 before leaving the top ranks.[92]

The Castors also followed the trail blazed by the Anges Bleus. Like their elder, by one year, they imported American and Canadian players. From 1986 to 1993 they brought in twelve players, including Matt Stashin of Willamette University in Oregon, who played running back and linebacker for two years. Stashin, whose maternal grandmother was a French speaker from Switzerland, played offensive line and fullback for Willamette while majoring in business and economics. During a 1986 study-abroad trip to Neuilly-sur-Seine, some French students noticed him in his school sweats from Oregon and asked him if he would like to meet some of their friends who played football. He did, and for the next two seasons, he played with and helped coach the Castors.[93]

They did not recruit only from North America, however; Miodrag "Mickey" Cipranic, who played for a number of teams in the 1980s, including the Castors, hailed from Yugoslavia. Cipanic played defensive end for the team and, as of 2012, was the oldest player still competing for the Paris Mousquetaires at age fifty-five.[94]

The Castors also visited the football motherland and met with Stashin to observe his Bearcats practice in Willamette. Perhaps while learning American football, Stashin's teammates neglected to study American geography. The former Castor told *Amerfoot Mag* that when his teammates arrived for their experience, they flew into Los Angeles, some two thousand kilometers to the south, where they had to be retrieved by their friend and taken to the correct location.[95]

They also imported coaching talent from the United States. Tom Bass, the head coach of the Castors from 1989 to 1991, had been an assistant coach for the Cincinnati Bengals, the Tampa Bay Buccaneers, and the San Diego Chargers of the NFL. He had also coached San Jose State and San Diego State universities and had written several books on football. When he took part of an NFL junket to London to work with teams in the 1988 Eurobowl, he met players and coaches from the Castors who asked him to come back and coach for the team. Bass was hesitant, but after his wife, Michele, who taught French near their home in Tampa, took one of the calls, he remembered that "the deal was done."[96]

Bass was one of the most experienced American coaches ever to have practiced his trade in France.[97] He was so prominent in football circles that *US Foot* magazine went so far as to announce that the Castors would be guided by the "Hand of God" in 1989.[98] Bass was not, however, the usual American coach, according to one-time Castor quarterback Robert. When he criticized the typical American coach who attempted to impose his vision of the game on French players who had not been acculturated in that world, he made sure to include an example of a coach who had been different. "The only exception to this American model came from Tom Bass, coincidently the greatest of all those who visited us," he recalled. According to Robert, after watching the team practice for a few days, Bass created a system that took into account the strengths and weaknesses, both physically and intellectually, of the team. This approach reportedly paid immediate dividends. Even though the team had been dominating the federation since 1987, Robert maintained, "We immediately made up a notch in the efficiency and the understanding of the sport."[99]

As previously mentioned, the Castors also ran afoul of the federation, as had the Anges Bleus. Although what constituted their "questionable attitude toward the Eurobowl" remains unclear, they nevertheless were sanctioned by the federation with a prohibition on international play for two years.[100] Although the particulars of the case are not clear, there seems to be a pattern whereby once a team had risen from the pack to dominate play at home and abroad, the federation would step in to cut them down to size.

One novel feature that the Castors brought to their team was the team song. Perhaps the students who had originated the team had a sense of humor akin to that of Spartacus and were attempting to add an additional American touch to their repertoire. The song references "I Feel Like I'm Fixin' to Die Rag," the 1970 protest song by Country Joe and the Fish. That song, which begins with the iconic "Give me an F," and so on, to elicit the word "fuck." The Castors song begins with "Give me a C" and spells the team name. The song was meant to be sung by the fans watching the match and calls the team "colossuses" and "mastiffs." It proceeds to declare, "We become ugly," "Castors come and vanquish," and "For us, there is a sport: American football. True, True, True." A recording of the song can be heard online, and the work seems to be professionally done, with a background track of a crowd cheering for its heroes.[101]

As was the case with Spartacus, the Anges Bleus, the Jets, and many other Parisian teams, the Castors would fade away after the founding generation acquired jobs, families, or began to notice that their bodies no longer recovered as quickly as they had in their youth. Robert became a novelist; Stashin returned to Oregon and is a branch manager for a mortgage firm.[102] Others, including Mickey Miodrag and Eddie Diop, who played several positions for the team, remained involved with football. Diop, who reportedly saw playing football as "a way to get a piece of the American Dream," now "gives a helping hand to the Toulouse Bears."[103]

The Castors merged with the Sphinx in 1993 and disappeared from the roster of French teams, but the name was resurrected in 2009. Another group of students at ESTP brought the team back, and it now plays in the Ligue Univerisitaire, which includes a team from the even more prestigious Paris Institute of Political Studies, or "Science Po." The university is the most prestigious of all French universities in that it prepares the vast majority of France's political leaders, which may bode well for the future of football in the nation.[104]

It is unclear whether the new Castors make use of the "old school" fight song, but another one of the old guard, the Flash, has developed its own model for football and its own unique "sound." The Flash de La Courneuve began play during the 1984–85 season as a Division 2 team. Since the 1985–86 season, when it joined the Elite Division, the team has won the title nine times including eight of the fourteen Casque de Diamant (formerly the Casque d'Or) titles in the twenty-first century. Of the remaining six championships of the current century, the Flash has finished second in every year with the exception of 2004.[105]

The team's dominance has been built on a program that starts with Minimes (age thirteen and fourteen) and provides those who wish to continue the possibility of progressing through the ranks. Those include a Cadet team, two under-eighteen Junior teams, and two senior division teams, one in Division 3, and the flagship team in the Elite Division.[106] The team website identifies twenty-seven coaches, three medical personnel, and an administrative staff made up of President François Leroy and seven additional personnel, including secretary Jean-Yves Carlton, treasurer Franck Lacuisse, and correspondent Bruno Lacam-Caron.[107] The team today has more than 3,000 participants, including 183 licensed players in the senior division. Added to these are nearly 3,000 flag football participants of both sexes.[108]

In 1983 Leroy, originally a Spartacus player close to Plegelatte, began the team by visiting La Courneuve, one of the most impov-

FIG. 22. Players from the Flash de La Courneuve in their first uniforms. Photo courtesy of Bruno Lacam-Caron.

erished *banlieues* that surround Paris. With the goal of developing a youth football program that had the potential to grow, Leroy met with the mayor of the suburb and secured five hundred francs to buy footballs. At the time it was unusual in France for municipalities to fund sport teams, but Leroy and François Nivet, the deputy mayor in charge of sports for the city, both belonged to the Parti communiste français (PCF), which no doubt helped smooth the way, as did Plegelatte's help and Leroy's mission to work with youth.[109] The linkage between football and the PCF is somewhat curious given the nature of the 1980s. Jean-Marc Burtscher remembered that when some of his teaching colleagues learned that he played football, they called him—perhaps in jest, perhaps not—a "Reagan American."[110] Both Leroy and Privet were traditional Communists, as opposed to Trotskyites such as Plegelatte, but the American president did not generally make fine distinctions between different sorts of Communists.[111] Those on the left equally did not approve of Reagan's ideology or American policy in general.

At first the club had no stadium and had to play in local parks.

F IG . 23. Flash players at Stade Géo André, or "the beach," as it was sometimes called because of the sandy field. Photo courtesy of Bruno Lacam-Caron.

Julien Luneau joined the team in 1989 and played linebacker and halfback before graduating to the coaching staff and administration. The first game he saw was Super Bowl XXI in 1987, won by the New York Giants over the Denver Broncos, and he credits that with hooking him on the game.[112] After working for nongovernmental organizations in Morocco and Bolivia, where he instituted sport programs for street children, he returned to France, where he was hired as a primary-school teacher in La Courneuve.[113] He remembered traveling through the rough neighborhoods of the suburb recruiting players. The equipment was the hook that interested potential recruits, and he also appealed to their machismo by asking them, "Do you want to fight?" After eliciting the typical positive response, he would add, "With rules."[114]

Those efforts paid off and by 1986, the team had reached the quarterfinals of a ten-team field.[115] It had also moved into Stade Géo André, its new home. In the early days the field was sand, and games were reported as spending "a weekend at the beach."[116] Along with the stadium, which features a solid concrete grandstand on the home side, the complex also contains a multipurpose field with field turf that is large enough to accommodate football and the other sports played in the suburb. The area remains one that shows the signs of the poverty that grips the *banlieue*, and the stadium is bordered by an eyesore scrap yard belonging to Paprec, a recycling firm that is one of the team's sponsors.[117]

During a visit to a practice session to speak with Luneau, I observed the junior squad going through its paces. The practice was highly organized, with position coaches working on the fine points of the game. The only difference between this session and an American college practice might have been the absence of filming technology. At one end of the large field, some young men were playing what looked to be a pickup game of soccer, but the dozen or so players were vastly outnumbered by perhaps sixty or seventy football players. In addition to an absence of technology, the coaches, including two American volunteers, were not observed berating those players who made mistakes—correcting certainly, but not with the same tone of voice and volume that a typical American coach uses.

It was there that Luneau laid out the underlying purpose for the football teams in La Courneuve. He was candid about the nature of the area, mentioning that only a few blocks over one could buy whatever drugs one wanted, and that unemployment was endemic in the *banlieue*, as was crime. Football for Leroy and later for Luneau is a means to an end, not an end in itself. The Flash seeks to provide an activity in the community that offers young men and women a chance to take part in a positive experience, and one that may offer an alternative to a wasted life. Thomas Deligny, a writer for *4th&Goal*, has asserted, "When these young people walk through the gates of Stade Géo André, they belong to the family."[118]

Providing a sense of family to young men who lack that at home is a way to offer them an alternative to joining a gang or withdrawing into a drug-hazed isolation. In addition to helping youth avoid the pitfalls so prevalent in the area, the team also sponsors informational sessions and workshops in prisons. That program has also had success, and according to Luneau in an interview with Rémi Dupré of *Le Monde*, "many ex-convicts from Villepinte prison took their licenses [issued by the FFFA, allowing them to play] with the club."[119]

Project High School, a new effort by the team, is building a relationship with the American Field Service (AFS) International Programs. This program seeks to send four of its young players to the United States for educational opportunities, not to mention for sharpening their football skills.[120] This will not be the first time that Flash players have gone to the States. As had the Anges Bleus and the Castors, in the early days eight Flash players took a trip to Baker University in Kansas to learn from the experts. Baker is also a part of the NAIA's Heart of America Conference, the same conference that provided the All-Stars who took on the Anges Bleus in Paris.

The team also began to use American and Canadian players and coaches when that became the fashion. Its first foreign coach was Daniel Saint-Pierre from Canada in 1987.[121] David Wright was the first American who played for the team, beginning in 1989.[122] Between then and 2005, the team has enjoyed the services of twenty-five foreign players including the aforementioned Braxton Shaver.[123] Its 2014 coaching staff included head coach Patrick "Bubba" Cark and defensive coordinator Michael Wood, both Americans, and offensive coordinator A. J. Tufford from Canada.[124] During the final game of the 2013 Casque de Diamant, the Flash employed two American players but fell to the Black Panthiers of Thonon les Bains, who had two of their own Americans, by a score of 14–0.

The Flash has also played internationally, representing France in the Eurobowl in 1998 and from 2006 to 2010. In 1998, 2006, and 2009, the team finished second, with its closest loss being a 30–19 loss to the Swarco Raiders Tirol of Austria. It vanquished its international opposition in 1997, when it defeated the Gladiatori of Rome in the final of the European Cup.[125] Interestingly, the Gladiatori were one of the few successful ventures realized by Bob Kap, who, along with Bruno Beneck, created the team in 1973.[126]

While they followed in the same steps as other Parisian teams, Flash players in the early days were subjected to challenges that the other teams were not. Coming from La Courneuve, the players were stereotyped as being "thugs who had little respect for the rules of the game." Rumors abounded that the team would "play with knives or brass knuckles."[127] Former American player David Wright wrote that during a 1989 game against the Jets, the team captain of the Flash motivated his teammates by telling them, "For those bastard rich boys, we're the lowly Flash. Communists! On the dole! Niggers and filthy Arabs!" Castano, the captain, was himself a native of Corsica, which was likely enough to put him somewhat on the outside of French culture at the time. Their opponents in that quarterfinal game were the "smart-ass" Jets of Saint-Cloud, which, as Wright mentioned, was a wealthy suburb of Paris. It was the place of residence at the time of Jean-Marie Le Pen, the founder of the right-wing National Front Party.[128] It was a grudge match, in other words, and not only a clash of good teams but also something of a class struggle.

Although the football culture seems to bring together different classes and races in France, as it does in the United States, there are still additional obstacles that the players from the Flash and other teams from blighted areas face. Jean-Marc Burtscher even opined that nowadays, instead of calling football players Reagan Americans, many of those outside the football culture in France view most teams, regardless of their location, as being primarily composed of "niggers and Arabs."[129]

Those negative images were renewed for all teams playing out of the Seine-Saint-Denis *banlieues*, in the wake of the 2005 riots that began in nearby Clichy-sous-Bois. Luneau decried the stereotypes "hitting the suburbs" and stated that his "kids were tired of the evening news sending them a negative image of themselves."[130]

Perhaps in some ways, though, the team might be viewed as embracing that image of "the other." During the 2013 Junior Championship game, which the Flash won 23–10 over the Canoniers of Toulon, the home-team fans used a call-and-response chant reminiscent of the Zulu war chant meant to intimidate the British defenders at Rorke's Drift dramatized in the 1964 film *Zulu*.[131] The same mantra was used, to less effect, in the Casque de Diamant game. Cheers such as that are likely nothing more than the Flash's version of the Hakka chant and dance used by New Zealand rugby players, or perhaps an attempt to create their own sound as the Castors had done. Regardless of its effect, the chant and their approach to football indicated that the Flash had created a powerful synthesis of American football culture that served its unique purposes.[132]

Although the Flash traveled the same road as the Anges Bleus and others who sought to elevate the game in France, it has nevertheless remained true to its founding ideals. The spirit of amateurism remains the motivating factor for the team. According to Dupré, "more than a talisman, amateurism remains the sacred symbol of Flash." Despite operating what amounts to a big-time football program with an annual budget of more than €1 million, Luneau said, "The associative framework saves us from the pitfalls of commercialization." The team bans paying players, except for Americans and Canadians, and even those players are not generously paid.[133] Braxton Shaver reported that he had been furnished with travel expenses, room and board, plus €1,000 per month, which is only a bit more than the €790 per month that an American could make teaching American English through the Teaching Assistant Program administered by the French Embassy.[134] Performance-enhancing drugs are also forbidden, and the games are staged primarily for the players instead of being designed to draw large crowds.[135]

Despite those limitations, or perhaps due to them, Leroy, Luneau, other team officials, and their players have built one of the most successful football programs in the federation. They have experienced enormous success on the field, but above and beyond that, they have created an island of positive energy in an environment that often has little to celebrate. They have also remained faithful to the vision that Plegelatte infused into football américain: football for football's sake.

Laurent Plegelatte demonstrably had the last laugh. During the 1980s the newly imported sport grew from one team squatting on the grounds of Stade Pershing to twenty teams playing in the Elite Division, some with fine facilities. Another twelve teams played in Division 2, and they were joined by eight more in Division 3. Altogether forty teams played in France as the decade closed.[136] The Ministry of Youth and Sports had recognized the federation, and the 1989 season also saw the addition of a championship in flag football.[137] French football had also left its mark on the international sport, with the Flash winning a European Cup, and the Anges Bleus even defeating a U.S. Navy team.

The federation, driven by concerns that Plegelatte and others saw as a rush to commercialization and professionalization, had also beaten back challenges to its amateur vision for the sport. The most serious test of that ideal had been mounted by the Anges Bleus, but though their attempt to play to the crowds had been thwarted, their model still shaped the game as it developed. The top French teams would import North American players and coaches, contend for international titles, and in general raise their level of play. Absent the evolution of the sport as a popular and profitable spectacle, however, football in France would continue its obscure existence in the heavy shadows of rugby and soccer.

Football would continue to grow as a subculture, though, spreading like a slow virus throughout the nation. The original teams started in Paris and its suburbs. As early as 1984 the game had escaped the environs of the capital and begun to expand to the provinces. The first team created outside the Métropole would spring up in Nantes, some 239 miles to the southwest in Brittany. The Panthers Jaunes (Yellow Panthers) would be the first of the provincial teams. This team, although it has gone through several name changes, including Drakkars and Firebirds, still exists and plays under the name Dockers de Nantes. Although the oldest remaining active team outside of Paris, the team had little success under any of its various names.[138]

That would not be the case for the Argonautes of Aix-en-Provence, located almost five hundred miles to the southeast of the capital near the Mediterranean. This provincial team would dominate the Elite Division during the mid-1990s much as the Castors had in the late 1980s and early 1990s, and as the Flash has done in the first decade and a half of the twenty-first century. Chapter 9 will consider the Argonautes and the spread of football to the *périphérie* and will also discuss the culture made up of publications, radio, and television that has grown around the sport.

Although cultural imperialism, in the form of tours and other efforts to spread the sport, made little headway in establishing football in France, the arrival of televised NFL games would do much to help spread the game throughout the Hexagone. The Internet would also become a powerful tool that would enable the denizens of football française to communicate with one another and to publicize their game in the almost total absence of such coverage by the national press.

9. Football Américain Goes National

Laurent Plegelatte had successfully carried football to France, and by the end of the 1980s, forty teams were playing in the country. Beginning only a few years after the establishment of teams in the Paris area, the game began to spread to the provinces. By the twenty-first century, most regions of the nation would have teams.

It was not a straight march to victory and the Fédération Française de Football Américain (FFFA) has faced significant challenges over the decades. Along with those discussed in chapter 8, there were also money problems, charges of favoritism, poor officiating, and other concerns that had to be addressed.

More positively, during the latter part of the first decade of football américain, a complementary culture that included equipment retailers, publications, and broadcasts of NFL games formed around the sport. Due to a dearth of coverage by the national media, football would continue to be relatively invisible to most of the French, but in the latter part of the twentieth century and beyond, the Internet would provide new channels for publicizing the sport through websites, blogs, online magazines, radio broadcasts, and streaming video.

According to the FFFA in 2014, there are 204 teams playing football in France.[1] As of 2011, however, nearly that many, 195 teams, have disappeared from the scene. Most left little mark of their passing, but some should be remembered for their exotic, interesting, and sometimes disturbing names. Teams such as the Bacchus of Blanc-Mesnil might have liked the wild life too much to last. The B-52's of Saint-Denis might have been just too American, the Pink Panthers of Caen too silly, and the Druides of Saint Méen too spiritual. Along with the typical fierce animal and human names designed to inspire fear in opponents, one of the best of the disappeared teams with a name that would inspire disquiet was the Crack Heads of Charleville-Méziéres.[2] Hopefully they are now recovering in rehab.

A great deal of the fluidity demonstrated by the rise and fall of teams can be attributed to the methods in which teams have been formed and players recruited. The Anges Bleus and the Castors, mentioned in chapter 8, began when a group of friends caught the football bug. They played at a high level for several years, but when the core group began to age and their fire for the game dimmed, the team faded away. In the case of the Castors, a new generation of ESTP students has resurrected the name, but the Anges Bleus now exist only on Facebook. When those Castor enthusiasts graduate, find work, and start families, the team may disappear again. Only teams such as the Flash de La Courneuve, which has built a multitiered organization that recruits and trains young players who are then fed into their Elite Division team, have managed to survive player turnover.

The Flash actively recruits players from La Courneuve, which also provides the benefit of building a sense of community. Players on other teams, at least in metropolitan areas, are able to play for whatever team strikes their fancy. Jean-Marc Burtscher began playing football after he and his brother, Eric, saw a bumper sticker advertising the Huskies de Villeparisis, a northwestern Parisian suburb. He later joined the Anges Bleus when Eric convinced him to switch teams. Dylen Cerna of the Red Star of Noisy-le-Sec also followed a bumper sticker to his team. Many players, including Red Star players François-Xavier Duqué, Gary Mako, Julien Ozboyaci, Axel Duez, Guillaume Griva, Brice Beaudi, Evans So', and Jennifer Josset, the first female Red Star, also followed a chain migration to the sport when their friends urged them to give it a try. Margaux Dewitte, another female Red Star, who officiates games, is a second second-generation football player. She reported that her father played for the Gaulois de Sannois, and that she grew up with football. She filmed Gaulois matches and watched games with her father in bars. A new route to the game was reported by Yacine El Pendejo (presumably a nom de football), another Red Star player, who discovered the game by play-ing John Madden NFL, then decided to try the real game. Tym Ghex of the Red Star, along with Olivier Moret of the FFFA and Julien Luneau of the Flash, remembered that they first saw the game on Canal + television and were hooked.[3] That sentiment was echoed by a young man whom I noticed carrying a football on the Paris Métro. When asked, he mentioned that he had seen a televised game between the New York Giants and the Philadelphia Eagles that sold him on the game.[4] Other players came to the game in less prosaic ways. Jean-Marc Burtscher remembered that one of the Anges Bleus joined the team when he stumbled on a game while running from the police, liked what he saw, and began practicing.[5]

Those recruitment methods are interesting, amusing, and in some cases, perhaps even alarming, but they are not sufficient to keep a team viable in the face of periodic player turnover. What is necessary for long-term stability is a good feeder program that will move talent up through the ranks. Only a few teams currently have such programs. The Flash is, of course, one of those teams, but there are others. One of those is the Black Panthers of Thonon-les-Bains, from near the Swiss border, and the team that defeated the Flash in the 2013 Casque de Diamant game. The Black Panthers have a Cadet team and two Junior teams. The Kangourous of Pessac, a suburb of Bordeaux in the south-west, sponsor a Cadet team and a team in Division 3. The Météores of Fontenay-sous-Bois, the oldest still-extant team in France, played in Division 2 in 2013 and finished second there with a 9-1 record. They are apparently building for the future though and also sponsor a Cadet and Junior team. The majority of the remaining teams only have an Elite team or a single team in one of the lower divisions.

Football began in Paris with the Plegelatte's Spartacus, but it did not take long for it to escape the capital. The Panthers Jaunes of Nantes were the first team created outside Paris, in 1983. Laurent Leloup, the first president of the club, was another football disciple of Laurent Ple-gelatte, who collaborated with Leloup to get the team started.[6] Dur-ing the first years, the team was only able to play "friendly" matches against Parisian clubs, and they did not appear in the regular rosters of the Elite Division teams until the 1986–87 season.[7] By then they were known as the Drakkars (presumably a Viking longship), and after two seasons in the top level, they were demoted to Division 2. They would alternate between the Elite and the second division until they were disqualified for an unknown reason from the top division during the 1991–92 season.[8] A Nantais team reappeared in Division 3 during the 1996–97 season, now under the name of Firebirds, but would disappear quickly. As more teams began to play in the region, enabling the Nantais more opportunities to improve, the Dockers, as the team was now known, stabilized and experienced some success. From 2000 to 2004 they won the Ouest Bowl, a regional championship for teams in the Pays Loire region of Brittany.[9] In 2003 the team saw it most significant victory, defeating the Montpelier Mustangs 19–14 to win the Casque d'Argent (Silver Helmet) championship of Division 3.[10] After a brief two-year promotion to Division 2, the team sank once again to Division 3. It made the playoffs between 2005 and 2008 but could not reenter the higher level. It was demoted again to the regional level until winning the Regional Ouest championship at the end of the 2008–9 season. Since then, the club has stabilized in Division 3 but has added Junior, Cadet, and Flag teams to perhaps climb back into the higher levels.

In 2013, on the thirtieth anniversary of football in Nantes, Philippe Charon, the president of the club, told Denis Bourdeau of the *Presse Océan* that after some Division 2 teams had ceased play, his team had applied to the federation for promotion to that level. The team has added more coaches to aid Jonathan Herrera, its head coach from Mexico, and has told the FFFA that it can provide a budget of €36,000.[11] James Springfield, a defensive lineman from the University of Memphis, has also been recruited to play for the Dockers this season.[12] In what is becoming more common in French football, the team is also recruiting women to play on an *équipe féminin*.[13] The Dockers seem to be on an upward trajectory, but they have never been a factor in the Elite Division. That would not be true for the Argonautes, another provincial team from Aix-en-Provence, which would dominate the federation during the 1990s.

Aix-en-Provence, a small city located just north of Marseilles in the southeast, is best known for being the home of the Postimpressionist painter Paul Cézanne. It is also a university town, and in 1985 Wilfred Yobe began his studies there to earn a degree in history and geography.[14] Yobe had played handball in high school but had lost his enthusiasm for the sport by the time he arrived in Aix.[15] There was not a great deal for young men to do in the city, and Yobe remembered that he was feeling bored when he contacted the Aix University Club (AUC).[16] He had seen on television that there was a new federation devoted to American football, and with the AUC's help, he traveled to Paris to meet with officials to discover how he could create a team. With the aid of Jean-Louis Maguet, the director of sports at the university, he was able to secure time at the stadium set aside for the institution's use.[17] After flyers were distributed, the first meeting, held in the parking lot of a local swimming pool, brought ten interested students together. That number grew when Yobe met Claude Miraval and his sons, Jean-Benoit, Christophe, and Vincent.[18]

The new club was sponsored by the AUC and brought together students and faculty. In particular, Chuck Weir, a teacher at the Franco-American Institute, came to the aid of the fledgling club. Weir, who resembled the famous American actor Steve McQueen, even going so far as driving a red convertible, had played seven years of high school and college football in Canada before a work injury ended his career. A charismatic figure, Yobe remembered that Argos players seldom missed practice, in part because of their dedication to the new sport but also because they hung on Weir's every word. Yobe described the new coach as a "fine psychologist of the human soul, who was the quintessential representation of the best in man, but who could also talk to the guys." Weir would become the "spiritual father" to Yobe and the rest of the Argos, teaching them the finer points of a game most had only read about.[19]

When it came time to find a name for the team, most of the players wanted to use Centaures, but that name had already been snatched up by a new team in Grenoble. The senior Miraval suggested they use Argonautes, which alluded to the band of heroes who accompanied Jason in his mythical quest to find the Golden Fleece. This appealed to the players in that the trophy for the champion of France was at that time awarded the Casque d'Or. It also served as a tribute to Weir, who was from Toronto, home of the Canadian Football League Argonauts.[20]

With a heroic name in place, the enthusiastic players quickly climbed the ladder from the Second Division to the Elite Division. They made their first run at the Casque d'Or in the 1986–87 season. After finishing the season with four wins and two losses, they advanced to the quarterfinals and managed to defeat Plegelatte's Spartacus 12–8, before falling to the Jets 18–12 in the semifinals.[21] Their rapid rise would receive a further boost when they came to the attention of a local financier named Bernard Bonnet.

Bonnet began to take interest in the team during the late 1980s, when football was experiencing something of a popularity boom in France, propelled by Canal + and La Cinq, television networks that carried the Super Bowl and other NFL games. This was also an era when American culture had begun catching increased popular attention in the country. "Big bikes and bodybuilding" were becoming the rage, and along with those supposed symbols of Americana, football was gaining a larger following.[22] When Bonnet, who was connected with the Miraval family, began to use the knowledge and connections he had built in the economic and political worlds, the team would launch its quest to dominate French football in a way that no other team had done before.[23] Between 1989 and 2004 the Argos would play in the Elite final a record seventeen times, winning the championship eight times. This success eclipsed the record of eight finals appearances that the Castors had managed in the 1990s and is only one shy of the nine championships that the Flash began to amass during the latter part of the last decade of the twentieth century.[24]

Bonnet, following in the footsteps of Maurice Tardy and Marcel Leclerc, saw the possibilities in football in a region that had already embraced rugby. Although the 1961 SHAPE and Laon tour had failed to generate much interest, Tardy's idea may have had some merit, given the success that the Argonautes had following Bonnet taking the team under his wing. The new promoter immediately launched plans to raise the visibility of the Argonautes in the region. He attracted the best players by treating them like their mythical namesakes; he staged parades through the city, positioning them prominently on the sidelines of Olympique Marseilles rugby games, provided air travel to matches, and placed the public relations staff of his Team SAFIR hold-

ing company at the disposal of the club. Those services included someone to respond quickly by telephone to media information requests,
an in-house newsletter suffused with information, an effective video
service, and high-quality publicity material advertising the team's
games.[25] In essence the Argonautes were the first French team to have
their own sports information director (SID) office.

Under Bonnet's tutelage, the Argos team was transformed from a
university club to a semiprofessional organization. Its annual budget
of F1,000,000 provided the Aixois with resources that surpassed any
other French gridiron collective, which made their opponents nearly
delirious with envy. This competitive advantage convinced many of
the best French players to defect to the new power in the south.[26]
One defector to the red and gold was Philippe Gardent, a ferocious
tackling linebacker, who would help the team win the 2001 and 2002
Casque de Diamant, before going on to play for the Berlin Thunder
of the NFL Europe (NFLE), and attending training camps with the
Washington Redskins and the Carolina Panthers.[27] Gardent began
with the Grenoble Centaures, and perhaps it was poetic justice that
the Argos gained his services after conceding their preferred name to
the Grenoblois. However, Bonnet's ability to poach talent was another
factor that enraged the other teams in the federation.

Bonnet and the Argos followed what was, by then, a well-worn
route to success. After Chuck Weir left Aix for other pursuits and
the team severed connections to the university, Bonnet imported
coaches and players from North America. Perhaps the most significant of those imports was Larry Legault, who became head coach of
the team in 1990. During the 1989 Casque d'Or the Argos were the
first provincial team to contend for the Elite title but lost to the Castors 14–13. In Legault's first year the Argos would become the first
team from the *périphérie* to win the championship and would go on
to complete their only three-peat by also winning the 1991 and 1992
Casque d'Or games.[28]

Legault remained with the team for five years, but in his last two
years the Argos lost close games to the Castors. After losing a 1993
regular season to the Paris team, Legault's answer to a reporter from
US Foot demonstrated that French reporters had reached parity with

their American cousins in posing irritating questions. The member of the Fourth Estate asked the Argos coach if this loss meant that his team was through contending for the top spot. Legault told his inquisitor, "The question to ask is not why the Argos have been beaten, but why the Castors have won. . . . All the excuses—the Argos were missing their 'Ricains' [Americans], during the game are good. But if the Castors play like that all season I do not see who can beat them."[29]

Between Weir and Legault, John Mugglebee, who had played for Dartmouth, served as the head coach, and it was he who brought the team to the brink of success. There were other North American assistants as well who helped coach the team, and from 1985 to 2004 the Argos enjoyed the services of more than forty mercenary players. Most came from North America, but Bonnet seemingly scoured the globe for talent and located Yoshinori Ayoama (1988) from Japan and Willis Theagene (1989), who hailed from Haiti.[30] How he found these atypical players is uncertain, but Theagene contributed so well as a running back, that, though his team lost, he was named the Most Valuable Player in the 1989 Casque d'Or game.[31]

The Argos also took their show on the road and in 1996 became the first French team to reach the finals of the Eurobowl before losing to the Hamburg Blue Devils 21–14.[32] They also played host to a most unusual international match in 1990, when the Moscow Bears traveled to France for a series of friendly contests. The Bears were the first football team in the Soviet Union, which was, by that time, only months away from dissolution.

The Soviet team had requested technical support from International Sports Connection (ISC), an organization led by Kent Dunston, another promoter cut from the same cloth as Riess, Leclerc, Foster, and Kap.[33] The ISC's goal was to spread the sport worldwide, but, as with other dreamers discussed in previous chapters, Dunston demonstrated the same historical tunnel vision as his predecessors. He was quoted in a story published in the *Spartanburg (SC) Herald-Journal* as asserting, "In 1982, there was no American football in Europe, except for United States Military teams and U.S. School teams."[34] As mentioned in the previous chapter, Spartacus and the Castors had already played international matches against Finnish and Austrian teams as early as 1983, which was also the first year that Team France contended for the European Championship.[35] Those teams, along with teams in Italy, England, and Germany, had not magically appeared in that year.[36] In response to the request, the ISC sent a group of current and former NFL coaches and players to give the Soviet "rookies" a crash course in the rules and tactics of the game before and after their French tour.[37]

Upon the Bears' arrival in France, it quickly became apparent that it would take some time before they would be competitive. Though the players were large and athletic, they lacked experience playing the game.[38] Their first match was against the Ours (Bears) of Toulouse Blagnac. The French Bears were no powerhouse, posting a 4-2 record for the season and advancing only as far as the quarterfinals of the Casque d'Or.[39] Still, the February 18, 1990, game was a huge success for French football as a record crowd of more that eleven thousand fans turned out to see the French Bears defeat their Russian namesakes 37–0. Many likely also turned out to observe the novelty of helmets made in the United States adorned with the Soviet hammer and sickle.[40]

Six days later, on February 24, the Bears would face the Argos, the top team in France, on their way to a perfect record of six wins and no losses. That season culminated with the team's first Casque d'Or. The Bears would rise to the occasion by performing better against superior competition. They still lost, but only by a score of 24–6. The novelty had worn off by then, and only two thousand spectators saw the second game as the Soviets went 0-2 for the tour.[41] Even the leader of the French Communist Party, who was coincidently scheduled to speak in nearby Marseilles on the day of the game against the Argos, when asked if he would attend, replied, "No, I am going to be doing more serious things!"[42]

Bonnet, who prior to the game against the Bears, had estimated that the Moscow team had spent perhaps F300,000 or F400,000 to start their organization, left the club in 1993 to assume duties as the prefect of Corsica.[43] But the professional culture he had created for the team remained. This included an infrastructure for obtaining grants, recruiting foreign players, and developing young talent at home.[44]

The organization that the Aixois businessman built would continue to roll along and in 1995 won the first Casque de Diamant championship after the federation changed the name of the final game.[45]

On a less positive note, Bonnet's legacy also included bringing the team under the shadow of scandal. As the Corsica prefect in 1999, Bonnet became embroiled in a scandal arising from the deliberate burning of beach huts that ended with his conviction for conspiracy to commit arson.[46] When Olivier Spithakis, the director of Mutuelle nationale des étudiants de France (MNEF), a nonprofit company that provided insurance for students, was arrested for financial malfeasance, the paper trail also led to the Argos. Spithakis had channeled funds designated for students into his associate and friend Bonnet's sports-management business, which sponsored the team.[47]

Bonnet and the Argos success also raised jealousy among the other teams, and the federation regarded the Argos' benefactor as "another Bernard Tapie."[48] From 1986 to 1994 Tapie was a president of the Olympique Marseille soccer club, which won the French League title four years in succession. In 1993 the politician and onetime owner of Adidas was accused of fixing a match, and in 1995 he spent about six months in prison for the offense.[49] Deprived of Bonnet's "Silver Cup," the Argos continued to win and could still count on the support of city hall, which regarded the team as a beacon that shone a positive light on the city.

That beacon provided a strong light until 2006, when the Argos appeared in their last Casque de Diamant final, but a new power was forming that would relocate the power center of French football back to Paris.[50] The Flash de La Courneuve, discussed in the last chapter, would replace the Argos as the hegemon in French football, but it would not be a friendly takeover. The games between the Argos and the Flash became storied affairs, and the 1997 Flash victory over the Argos convinced the players from suburban Paris that they belonged at the top of the Elite Division. The southern team would play in eight more Casque de Diamant matches, defeating the Flash in three and losing to the Parisians in another three.

The competition between the two teams bled over into international competitions between the French National Team and other

European contenders and hampered their efforts to form a collective front against outsiders. That division was closed in 1998, when, after a 42–0 defeat by the English team, players from the Flash and the Argos, including Julien Luneau and three other Flash players, along with two Argos, stole the helmet of one Karl Ballard. Ballard was an American who had played at Colorado State University, then tried his hand with the Arena Football League before joining the London Monarchs of the NFLE, while also playing for the Hamburg Blue Devils. Adding spice to their acquisition, both French teams had lost to the Hamburg team in the Eurobowl, the Argos in 1996, and the Flash in 1998. Following that successful theft the winner of the Argo and Flash game would carry home in triumph the artifact, and their games thereafter became known as the "Ballard Bowl."[51]

The Argos began to decline following their last trip to the finals in 2006. The slide would be caused not by competition from the Flash or other teams but by internal problems that bedeviled the team. As had been the case with many top-level French teams, once the first generations of players began to leave the team, they could not be replaced. Up to 2006 coaching had been a source of strength and stability for the team, with only six coaches in twenty-one years, and one of those had been a bad fit for the team and had left after only one year.[52] From 2001 to 2007 Darren Holmes, who had played linebacker for Kansas State University, left the team. Holmes had taken the club to four finals and had won two. However, like Louis XV, who reportedly said, "After me, the deluge," after Holmes left, the Argos went through a period of instability at the top. In addition to not finding a stable coaching staff, they have had four club presidents in the past eight years.[53]

After tying for the worst record in the Elite Division at one win and nine losses during the 2011–12 season, the Argos were demoted to Division 2.[54] Like the Dockers of Nantes, the Argos are now trying to climb back into the Elite Division, which will require that they win the Casque d'Or, which is now the name of the championship for Division 2. They finished 6-3-1 during the 2012–13 season but fell to the Nîmes Centurions 28–27 in the semifinals.[55]

Perhaps the Argos can find their stability and once again become contenders, but Victor Bahabege, the new president, has been described as a man working at the bedside of a sick child.[56] The difference in competition between levels is large, but the funding differentials are even larger. The Argos are also suffering from cutbacks at the municipal and regional level, resulting in an "80,000 € hole in the budget."[57]

In the meantime, other teams have risen to prominence and have challenged the Flash for dominance of the Elite Division. In 2004, 2010, and 2012, the Spartiates of Amiens, a northern cathedral town, won the Casque de Diamant. Their first championship came at the expense of the Argos, whom they defeated 41–31. After a five-year drought, they defeated the Flash 24–21 in 2010 and bested the Black Panthers of Thonon-les-Bains, a small city located near the Swiss border, 10–7 for their third championship.

Olivier Moret, the deputy national technical director for the federation until his resignation in 2014, brought football to Amiens in 1987. In a 2012 interview Moret recalled that he was spending the weekend at his parent's house, where he watched the San Francisco 49ers play the New York Jets on a Sunday morning, and he was hooked. He and a group of friends bought equipment and started training. As with Spartacus, they had to build the team from scratch in an area that had no history of the sport. Moret mentioned that the first time he practiced in pads, he put his shoulder pads on backward. Some of their players wore motorcycle helmets during the first games. They aimed high though, and their first playbook was filled with formations and plays copied from what they had seen the 49ers running on television.[58]

After five seasons in Division 2, they finally broke into the Elite Division in 1993, but remained there for only two years before being demoted. In 1998 they returned to the Elite level and advanced into the quarterfinals with a 6–4 record before losing to the Molosses (Mastiffs) of Asnières, a small town north of Paris. From 2000 to 2012 the Spartiates contended for the title, failing to make the playoffs only in 2008 and 2009.[59]

They began recruiting foreign players in 1991, when they brought in a fullback known only as Dennis Z. Between then and 2005, they imported twenty more mercenaries, which allowed them to compete in the arms race that exists at the Elite Level.[60]

They also acquired a fine stadium, complete with field turf and permanent concrete stands on the home side. Located on the outskirts of the city, the location, which former Spartiates call "one of the most beautiful stadiums in France," is located in a pastoral setting surrounded by open fields.[61] During a 2012 match between the Spartiates and the Flash, the stands were not full, but a decent crowd of perhaps two hundred or so spectators paid the five-euro entry fee to watch a close and exciting game that was won by the Flash, despite some poor officiating. Although the score was close and the action good, the spectators mostly seemed to be having a pleasant evening out, rather than watching a grim struggle between two of the best teams in the Elite Division. The merguez (lamb sausage) and baguette stadium food was a nice change from hot dogs, and the halftime entertainment featured the five Spartiate cheerleaders forming a truncated pyramid.[62]

In an unusual move the Spartiates played for two years, 2010–11, without a head coach. Though they won in the first year of that experiment, they could not replicate their "magical" championship run in 2011, falling to 6-4 and losing to the Flash in the semifinals. The next season they returned to an American coach who had been with the team before, and brought in Jim Criner, who led them to their 2012 championship.[63] Criner had a long history in coaching at various levels, including stints with Boise State University and Iowa State University, where he forged a 76-49 record. He also had experience coaching in Europe with the Scottish Claymores of the NFLE. The 2012 season would be his third coaching in France, including an unsuccessful stint with the Argos during their period of instability.[64]

Criner left the team after its 2012 championship season to concentrate on leading coaching clinics across Europe with the goal of helping European coaches develop their skills.[65] The team fell on hard times in 2013, finishing with a 1-9 record with a resulting demotion to Division 2.[66] The Spartiates have taken steps to turn this decline around and have imported Jeff Hand, another American coach, with experience coaching at the university level. They have also imported Luke Zahradka, a quarterback from Bentley (MA) University, and Jesse Kirstatter, a tight end and linebacker from Western State (CO) University.[67] As of the 2013–14 season, they were leading their pool in

Division 2, but they were contending with the Argos, who apparently have located resources and were also leading their pool.[68] Meanwhile, a new power has climbed to the top of the Elite Division.

The Spartiates 2012 championship was a 10–7 victory over the Black Panthers of Thonon-les-Bains, who were making their second unsuccessful appearance in the Elite finals. The Black Panthers were founded in 1987 with aid of the Maison jeune et de la culture (MJC) of the city. They reached the Elite Division in 2004 by winning the Casque d'Or. Their focus on building youth programs that would feed into the senior teams had already proven successful. In 2006 both of their junior teams won the European Championship, and their under-eighteen flag team was the French champion. Additional help for the senior team arrived in 2005, when Larry Legault became its head coach. This helped the senior team catch up to the juniors in 2007. It appeared in its first Elite final but lost 21–6 to the Flash. The team also played in its first international final in 2009, when it lost 35–12 to the Prague (Czech Republic) Panthers in the European Federation of American Football (EFAF) Cup. The team returned to the finals in 2012 but lost to the Spartiates. The Black Panthers proved that the third time was the charm, as they avenged their previous final defeat to the Flash and defeated the one-time French dynastic power 14–0. They followed up that victory by becoming the first French team to win the EFAF cup by defeating the L'Hospitalet (Austria) Pioneers 66–6.[69]

After five years football had broken out of the confines of Paris and was beginning to spread, first to Nantes, and then to the south in the next wave. It took more than two decades, but Maurice Tardy was finally justified in his contention that the south would be fertile ground for the spread of the sport. In 1985 both Toulouse and Perpignan, the two stops in the 1961 tour, had teams. The Centurions played in Toulouse, and the Gladiateurs called Perpignan their home. That same year the sport also migrated north to Rouen in Normandy, where the Iroquois played.[70]

Expansion continued the next year, and the historic province of Brittany saw its first team, called the Celtics, formed by a group of friends in Lanester. Christophe Saint-Cyr, one of the founders, related a story that illustrates once again the flexibility that pioneers must

exhibit. He remembered that Christophe Cailloce once arrived at practice with shoulder pads made of wall insulation.[71]

Eventually, a large majority of the sites where USAFE or Com Z
teams played games had football teams. Châteauroux had the Orcs,
La Rochelle had the Barracudas, Orléans had its Chevaliers, Dreux
the Monarchs, Verdun the Gardiens, Poitiers the Dragons, Chambly
the Jaguars, Bordeaux the Lions, Rochefort the Alligators, Fontainebleau the Kaisers, Metz the Artilleurs, and Toul-Nancy a team appropri-
ately named the Tigres. The Chateauroux Sabres, a new French team,
plans to begin play in 2015. The team explicitly chose its name from
the USAFE team, and maybe this will signal the start of a movement
to pay homage to football in France before 1980.[72]

The same held true for cities or villages that were sites in the various tours.[73] The 1938 Riess-Crowley tour visited Lyon, where the Gones
(kids) now play. Narbonne, the site of the third game, has two teams,
the Black Knights and the Cathares. Marseille currently has the Blue
Stars, as well as previously the Rebels and the Phocéens (Greek colo-
nists who founded the city), which have disappeared. Toulouse, the site
of the fifth match, currently has the Ours and the Phoenix, and earlier had the Tuniques Bleus and the Centurions, two teams that have
since disappeared. Bordeaux, where the New York and the All-Star
teams played their final game, is home to the Lions. The sites chosen
for the Tardy tour in1961 now are home to the Archanges of Perpignan
and the aforementioned Toulouse Ours. Carcassonne, another stop on
that tour where the soldiers behaved like so many rampaging Vikings,
now is home for the Black Hawks. Lille, the only other city aside from
Paris that served as a tour stop, now has a team called the Vikings.[74]

While most of the sites where service personnel played and where
tours stopped now have teams, that is most likely merely coincidental. Bases and tour locations were chosen because they were located
near population centers, which offered access to transportation for
the former and potential spectators for the latter. Those same factors
are also necessary when building a new sport in a nation that has no
tradition of including football as a part of the educational offerings
of the local school, as is the case in the United States.

The only club that might be construed as having a connection to the

NATO period would be the Nancy Tigres, which has the same name as the team of the Toul-Nancy area air base that existed there in the 1950s and 1960s. The official history of the French team makes no mention of the current incarnation has any sense that its name has historic connotations. Rather, its history began when Xavier Wagner, who had spent a year studying in the United States, decided to import the sport to his hometown in 1987.[75]

More teams meant more licenses paid to the federation, and more revenue meant the chance for more visibility, both within France and internationally. Success also brought new challenges for the FFFA. In the first years under Plegelatte and Gofman, the organization had managed to weather challenges posed by player strikes and the threat of professionalization. Under the leadership of Jacques Accambray, who served three terms as president from 1985 to 1996, French football would undertake an ambitious agenda of international competition and would also begin to dream of the Olympics.

Jacques Accambray was a world-class athlete who had experienced football in Ohio, the state where the NFL was born. As a marketing student at Kent State University, Accambray had also starred for the Golden Flash's track team as a weight man. The international student became a seven-time All-American during his years there, earning a spot on the honorary team four times in the hammer throw and three times in the indoor weight throw. In 1971 and 1973 he won the NCAA hammer-throw championships.[76] His 1973 indoor weight throw of seventy-one feet ten inches stood for forty years before it was broken in 2013.[77] While at Kent State he also played one year on the football team. Understandably, Accambray's track coach did not want him to suffer an injury while playing football, so the young man deferred satisfying his interest in football until his senior year. When head coach Don James, later the head coach of the University of Washington, asked the six-foot-four, 275-pound athlete to play with the team, the young man took his chance. During that year he practiced with Jack Lambert, who went on to be an All-Pro linebacker with the Pittsburgh Steelers, and had the chance to play in the Tangerine Bowl. Accambray also later mentioned that Nick Saban, now the head coach of the University of Alabama, was also part of the coaching staff at Kent State.[78]

After Accambray graduated, the Cincinnati Bengals showed some interest in him, and Marv Levy of the Montreal Alouettes invited him for a tryout. His technical skill was insufficient, however, to earn him a spot on any professional team. He was also concerned about training with the French Olympic team in preparation for the 1976 Montreal Olympics, so he went home. In the 1980s, while training at the Institut nationale du sport et de l'éducation physique (INSEP), Accambray noticed some people practicing football in the Bois de Vincennes. This led to a meeting with Plegelatte and some of his Spartacus players. Accambray's interest was piqued, and when Bertrand Lecuyer of the Anges Bleus approached him, he became a part of that team.[79]

In 1985 Accambray was elected to his first term as president of the federation, after his team had been expelled for professionalism. As president of the FFFA, he used his contacts at the highest level of the French sporting world to help secure legal and official recognition from the Ministry of Youth and Sports. In 1990 he also gained approval for the FFFA from the Comité national olympique du sport français. He continued his push to gain recognition for football, and in 1993 the federation received the designation Sport de haut niveau (high-level sport) from the ministry.[80]

Not surprisingly, given the history of his Anges Bleus team, during Accambray's tenure the French fully embraced international competition. The French National Team played nine friendly matches against international competition and took part in the Eurobowl and the EFAF Cup.[81] He also led the effort in the federation to regularize the rules allowing the importation of foreign players, a motion that passed in 1989.[82]

With the goal of growing the sport in France, under his leadership the federation instituted both a flag championship and the Casque de Bronze, a championship for Division 3, which began in 1993. The flag division was designed to involve more players in the sport, but without the cost and violence of the original game. This would also be among the first efforts to interest females in playing football. In 1994, still under the former Olympian's direction, the Casque de Bronze championship was upgraded to the Casque d'Argent (Silver), when the Elite championship became the Casque de Diamant.

Accambray moved easily among the elite of the French sporting world, and while he used those contacts to the advantage of the federation, some felt that he had lost contact with the daily concerns of the teams that made up the sport. After he was elected to his second term, the building tension erupted at a contentious meeting of the General Assembly on October 28, 1989. The immediate cause for concern was the threatened expulsion of several teams, including the Flash, the Ours, the Spartiates, and others that had violated the organization's rules.

All teams had three requirements levied on them by the federation. They were required to help defray the expenses of the FFFA and the European Football League (EFL), and they had to furnish a letter from their city hall attesting that the team had a proper field on which to play. Finally, each team was required to furnish at least two game officials to the Association sportive des arbitres (ASA), the body that furnished referees for the games. Those persons could not also be players, and the difficulty of finding persons interested in interpreting the rules during a game opened space for women to officiate in the sport.[83] For instance, one of the referees at the Anges Bleus victory over the Sixth Fleet was Yves Parelli's mother.[84] The teams threatened with expulsion had failed to furnish officials, and many federation officials called for their expulsion, while many others urged clemency.[85]

The extraordinary session opened on Saturday, March 28, with a general meeting to hear the concerns of the "good people." Laurent Plegelatte spoke about the amateur spirit of the discipline, and the humane duty of the federation toward its teams. He reflected, "Today on the eve of the ninth anniversary of the arrival of football, things have changed. Tolerance is no longer the order of the day. Without scruples, the federation punishes. At the slightest discrepancy, the ax falls." He warned attendees that he was reminded that 1989 was the bicentennial of the French Revolution, which calamitously ended with the Reign of Terror. Joël Desserre, another Spartacus player, remarked, "Here is what happens when [decisions are made by] you elite people, who are far from the reality on the field, who know nothing of the daily problems of the teams, who do not know the difficulty of recruiting players, finding fields, and locating referees."[86]

This was likely a familiar refrain at such meetings, given the open political divides that existed among some of the teams. Vice President Philippe Cotin stated, "The federation cannot allow such administrative laxity," and the guilty teams then threatened to resign en bloc. Cotin later denied making the remarks, but the anger of those teams and others boiled over completely after Accambray's reelection was announced. The president of the Ours complained that the only communications he ever received from the federation were financial requests. He continued by protesting, "I do not want to be a banker for the FFFA!" Antoine Mannina, the president of the Bron Scorpions, one of the new Division 3 teams from near the Swiss border, grumbled that teams like his had to "beg the federation to obtain the schedule of their matches." Without those schedules, Mannina continued, they lose their "credibility at the regional level." The president of the Centaures pleaded, "Above all, it is important that the federation not be the enemy of the clubs. On the contrary, it should be their best ally." Yazid Mabrouki, the president of the Flash, leveled the following criticism: "Everyone is talking about money, sanctions, and creating a president's association. I don't believe that is the solution. The federation must help us. It should be the big brother of all the clubs. The counselor. And that is what is most lacking from the federation."[87]

The meeting was divided between the "les durs," or more colloquially, the hard-asses, who wanted tough sanctions, and those who felt clemency would be best for the sport in France. Eric Penot, the outgoing president of the Anges Bleus, did not want to be counted as a hard-ass, but he nevertheless felt that the Elite Division should be more exclusive. This was in keeping with the experience that the Anges Bleus had with *Elitefoot*, so he supported sanctions against the offending teams. Michèle Hayère, the secretary-general of the FFFA, argued that "the clubs should cease functioning on the basis of cronyism and adopt the business practices of small companies, which brought some humorous confusion. There were few smiles however, when the director of the Ours threatened that if the penalties were levied, he would be in a "great mess," and that if his club was dissolved, he would work to ensure that no other football team developed in his area.[88]

The word finally came down that the offending teams would be granted more time to provide letters from their city halls and would likewise be allowed more time to pay their back dues. Those offenders who had not furnished referees, however, would be excluded from the Elite championship and demoted to a lower division. Pandemonium erupted, with leaders immediately getting on their phones to avoid talking to any of the sanctioned parties. After pressure mounted on the president and his staff, they relented and allowed the offending teams to make good on all their deficits by November 25. If they did so, all would be forgiven. Accambray still came under fire for abstaining from taking a position on any question other than that of whether foreign players should be regularized. Luc Bouchard of *US Foot* editorialized that the president seemed to care more for the professionals than for the 2,500 French players in the federation.[89]

In a 2007 interview with Florian Thiery for *Elitefoot*, Accambray maintained that his actions as president were predicated on building support for football at the ministerial level, which was necessary for the sport to grow. At that he succeeded, but often at the cost of alienating rank-and-file French players. His focus on international competition likewise resulted in large deficits, which he justified by claiming that the FFFA was legally obligated to provide teams for those competitions under its agreement with the EFL.[90]

As a result of the Elite-centered policies, the growth in the number of teams slowed as the deficits rose. By the time Accambray stepped down, there were seventy-eight clubs with around four thousand licensed players. Despite the growth that had occurred in the first decade and a half, the numbers had begun to stagnate toward the end of his third term.

Frederick Paquet succeeded Accambray, and his first goal was to tackle the budget deficit. An immediate step was to suspend international competition for three years. By 1998 the federation had finally climbed into positive numbers financially and even reported a budget surplus that year.[91] It would take longer to retire the debt that the organization had acquired, but the new president was able to finally accomplish that goal as well.[92] In addition to his administrative reforms, Paquet created the regional leagues, which increased the number of teams. In 2003 he also introduced the new discipline of cheerleading. This discipline had its own competitions and provided some of the spectacle that is a typical part of the game in North America.[93]

Paquet was a change from the flamboyant, freewheeling style of previous presidents. He was seen as a "serious" administrator. He brought a businesslike atmosphere to the federation meetings and a professional management style to the organization. The number of teams, particularly with the addition of the regional divisions, grew during his twelve years in control, but the FFFA continued to lack the resources necessary to break out of the relative anonymity under which the sport labored.[94]

The longest serving president in the history of the FFFA, Paquet may have had little of the flamboyance of his predecessors, but he also avoided many of the crises that they had faced and at times precipitated. At the end of his leadership tenure, football occupied a solid place in France—solid but not very visible.

The three presidents who have followed him have suffered from the same inability to attract much national media attention. The failure of the NFLE to include a French team certainly did not help matters. Many commentators felt that soccer and rugby forces had conspired to keep the sport out of France, though Accambray argued that money was the real culprit. He argued that "even setting up a show match [at the Parc des Princes] would have cost more than a Pink Floyd concert, and that the French could not guarantee that they could attract enough fans to make it pay."[95]

Marc-Angelo Soumah, president until his resignation in late 2014, is well known in international football circles. Soumah began his career with the Météores, where he helped them win championships in Divisions 3 and then 2. He then transferred to the Flash, where he also played on Elite championship teams. A talented wide receiver, he played that position with the Frankfurt Galaxy of the NFLE from 2001 to 2004. He also played later for one of the top German semi-pro teams, the Hamburg Blue Devils. His skill allowed him to join the very exclusive group of French players who have had the chance to try out for an NFL team when he attended training camp with the Cleveland Browns. Only Soumah, Gardent, Accambray, Sebastien Sejean, and Richard Tardits have been able to scale that particular height. His background in the sport, along with a master's degree in sport law and economics, elevated him above most of the possible contenders for the presidency. In addition to that impressive résumé, Soumah is also the first Frenchman of African descent to head the federation. Despite his international renown, outside the football culture he remains little known in his own country.[96]

While unable to generate much national attention, French football has built its own subculture around the sport. Over the years this started with a sporting-goods store dedicated to the fledgling sport and has branched out to include print magazines that have come and gone. With the spread of the Internet, this subculture has grown to include several football blogs focusing on the sport both at home and abroad and a proliferation of Facebook and web pages devoted to individual teams. The World Wide Web has also made possible *RADIOSSA*, an Internet-based radio program, and even televised games that can be accessed on sites such as Dailymotion.com.

The first center of the nascent complementary culture that began to grow around football in the 1980s was Kick Off, a sporting-goods store that supplied French players and teams. Claude Pariente was working at his father's pizzeria in 1982, when, while stopped at a red light, he noticed a bumper sticker advertising the Anges Bleus. He began playing as a flanker with the team that year, and later, after meeting Plegelatte, he transferred to Spartacus as a running back.[97]

After taking a trip to the United States, where he attended an NFL game between the Green Bay Packers and the Oakland Raiders, he decided that instead of working in the restaurant industry, he would rather open a photography studio. After a series of conversations with a neighbor, where the topic continually focused on football, the friend suggested that Pariente put plans for a studio on hold and instead open his own store devoted to football.[98]

His first step led him to the U.S. Embassy's library, where he "searched like mad" for any publications on football. He stumbled on a magazine, a "veritable bible," in his words, filled with addresses of businesses that dealt in football equipment. Here he faced an internal moral struggle. "I am not a thief in my soul," he told *US Foot*, but, he told himself, "I cannot leave this magazine here!" He telexed several companies for catalogs, and fifteen days later, after it had mistakenly been sent to Perpignan instead of Paris, the first arrived from Riddell.[99]

Pariente found a location for his store. He described it as a "ruin" measuring 120 square meters at 16 Avenue Claude Velletaux (not far from the HQ of the French Communist Party).[100] On March 7, 1985, he launched his enterprise. The first day was a bit chaotic, and at one point a man entered the shop and asked for a "kick burger, s'il vous plait." Despite that, Kick Off became a central gathering spot for the growing football culture in France. Over the years several players had their first experience of football when they wandered into the store. In 1988 Pariente launched *Kick-Off News* to publicize new equipment, comparisons of various models, and information on clubs. He also franchised stores in Grenoble and Rennes.[101] It is unclear, but at some point he apparently sold his interest in the stores, or they may have failed. No record, other than historical, is available on Google.fr, and the only Claude Pariente on Facebook is now retired in Nice. While it lasted, though, Kick Off was an anchor for the new sport in France, where devotees could gather and later leave with the tools of their new trade.

Philippe Laville, who as a young man had originally seen his first football during after-midnight broadcasts of "unusual sports" on channel F1, would begin the publishing piece of the French football culture. After his initial exposure to the sport, he tried to start a university team in Le Mans, a small city best known for car racing, but had no luck. He finally was able to begin playing in 1985, when the Le Mans Caïmans (Alligators) debuted. Around the same time as *Kick-Off News*, and a few months after Luc Bouchard began publication of *Quarterback*, his *Football Américain* (FA) became the second magazine devoted to the sport, in 1987. Launched with the financial aid of *Maxi-Basketball*, an already-existing publication in Le Mans, FA had the services of Bruno Fablet, a professional photographer, who also worked for the basketball magazine. The technical and financial expertise of the older publication made FA the first "true mag" in France, according to Laville. The magazine sold well, and Laville reported that FA had sold 220,000 copies over the run of the publication and had thirteen thousand subscribers. After Laville ended his association with *Maxi-Basketball*, he ceased publication of *Football Américain* but went on to publish *Sports Action*, a multisport magazine that included football.[102]

Luc Bouchard, another pioneer of the French football press, arrived in France from Montreal. After a short run with *Quarterback*, which lasted only seven issues, Bouchard and François Leroy of the Flash joined together with other friends to publish the more successful *US Foot*. At the time Bouchard was coaching the Villepinte Red Devils, but when the president of that club "ended up in prison," he jumped to the Flash as a coach. François's father, George Leroy, the owner of the printing company Graphics 66, became the sponsor of the new magazine. The publication enjoyed some success and ran from February 1989 to 2000. In later years the magazine dropped some of its coverage of the game in France and focused more on the sport in the United States. Bouchard explained that shift was due to the lack of traction that French stories generated. "I can tell you," he later told Greg di Belette, "that, commercially speaking, French Football has never been a good deal for *US Foot*. Year after year, the biorhythm of our sales has always been the same: NFL Championship, sales increase. France championships, declining sales." The first issue of the magazine sold nearly 10,000 copies and averaged around 7,500 copies for following issues. The editors typically labored in an environment of limited resources, but one that existed as a spot for volunteers to contribute photos or to earn the occasional "byline." Bouchard returned to Canada in 1995 but kept his hand in the operation of the magazine until the end. He also attempted to launch a Canadian version of the magazine but reportedly lost $35,000 in the failed effort.[103]

Elitefoot, which now exists only as a website, also existed as *Elitefoot Mag*, a print magazine, from 2005 to 2007. Upon announcement of the new publication, "Pro-Bowler" from Saint-Germain-en-Laye made the following post on the NFL-NCAA Forum: "A football mag has little chance of success in France. There is little or no customer support likely to buy a mag, since more is available on the net. Conclusion: I welcome this courageous initiative and wish them luck, but I fear that this adventure will collapse quickly."[104] The blog *Elitefoot* (http://www.elitefoot .com/) remains an indispensable source for the history of football in France since 1980. *Elitefoot* is joined by other blogs such as *FootballAmericain* (http://www.footballamericain.com) that focus largely on the game in America but also contain information on French teams. *Sideline*, another blog, has recently ceased posting and can no longer be located.

Though traditional print publications are faced with declining sales worldwide, a challenge that is even more difficult for a football magazine in France, a new French football publication debuted in September 2012. *4th&Goal*, which is an appropriate name for a magazine beginning during what seems to be the twilight of the medium, is the latest attempt to succeed where Laville, Bouchard, and others have failed. Thomas Deligny, the director of publication, admitted that this was a risky undertaking in an editorial that began the first issue: "A paper magazine? That will never work! Are we masochists, naive, or both?" Despite the seeming insanity of launching such an effort, Deligny told readers, "We feel your desire to see your sport develop, feel your desire to live football. So here we are!"[105]

However, as Pro-Bowler asserted, while the Internet has made print publication more financially hazardous, it has also made it easier for French football players and fans to find information about their passion. In November 2011 *Amerfoot Mag*, a new online-only magazine, debuted. According to its opening message to readers, the free magazine seeks to focus on the game as played in France and more broadly around the world. It will include information on the NFL and the NCAA, but the editors have noted, "We remembered that when we played were always pissed off by the fact that there was almost no media coverage about what was happening on the local level."[106]

The online offering, now in its ninth issue, has 2,322 subscribers, according to the site. The Internet as a platform has also made it easier for researchers to use, as it is available both in French and English. Interview subjects have included Tommy Viking of the International Federation of American Football, along with former NFL stars Tony Mandarich and Anthony Munoz. French players such as Gardent, Sejean, and Tardits, who have played in the United States, have also been featured. Subject matter has also included the histories of some French teams such as the Jets, the Castors, and the Anges Bleus, as well as North Americans who have coached for FFFA teams. Other stories have explored the history of football's rise in Serbia, Argentina, and Turkey, among other exotic locales for the American sport.[107]

In 2003, when Renaud Cramaix and Gégé, two former Anges Bleus and current coaches, were bored driving home from a practice, and they began complaining that "it was not like that in [their] time." That rant led to the creation of the Old School Spirit Association and to caustic news posts online. The men quickly decided that they should put their news and views on web radio, and so RADIOSSA was born. During football season, which for France runs from November to June, RADIOSSA broadcasts a weekly radio program on Monday nights between 9:00 p.m. and midnight. A regular cast that includes Cramaix, who uses the nom de football Mumu; the similarly named Eclipso; and Goldo form the core of RADIOSSA. In addition to Cramaix's connection to the Red Star, Eclipso and Goldo also play for the team. They discuss the news of the week and interview coaches, players, and others—including, on three occasions, this author—who have something to say about football in France.[108] The broadcast emanates from a variety of locations. One site is a private apartment in the Fifteenth Arrondissement of Paris. The studio occupies a small room of the apartment and features a microphone-covered table, some chairs, and a wall covered with football memorabilia.[109]

Due to the lack of television coverage of the game, many teams have taken to the Internet to broadcast their games. Some effort was made in the early days to broadcast games on French channels, but the 75–0 shellacking that the Castors laid on the Jets in 1987 destroyed any credibility that the Elite Final had at the time.[110] The Flash regularly appears on Internet television through the site Dailymotion.com.[111] The Black Panthers also have their own dedicated Panthers TV site (http://www.les-black-panthers.org).[112] Other teams receive occasional airtime during the playoffs or for championship games. One fan in Ohio, therefore, was able to watch the transmission of the Noisy-le-Sec Red Star's regional championship game in 2012.[113]

The Internet has also created space for web-based documentaries such as Le Football Américain a la heure française and Elles osent le football américain, which will be described more fully in chapter 10. Works such as these have helped fill the void left by mainstream press indifference toward football.

As previously mentioned, while teams do receive coverage from local news sources, there is an almost complete lack of coverage for FFFA teams in the national press. Le Monde, the nation's largest newspaper, covers the sport in the United States, with an emphasis on the negative. The paper has kept close watch on the concussion issue that has been a focus of the NFL recently. With headlines such as "Football américain: Lésions fatale [fatal injuries]," "Au football américain, un siècle de dégáts [a century of damage]?," and "Le football américain, c'est pas bon pour les neurons" ["it's not good for the neurons," i.e. the ability to think], the coverage is not designed to make easier the task of recruiting players for FFFA teams.[114]

When *Le Monde* is not publicizing the health risks of the game, it is seemingly reminding its readers that Americans are religious zealots. During the period when he was with the Denver Broncos, the paper featured stories on Tim Tebow, who is more famous for his religion than his passing.[115]

L'Équipe, the top sporting daily in France, covers Ping-Pong and handball and advises readers on "how to bet on horse racing" in its "other sports" section online. However, it almost totally ignores a sport played by more than twenty thousand Frenchmen and a growing number of Frenchwomen.[116] During the Casque de Diamant weekend in 2013, *L'Équipe* carried one story on game day about how this was the third time the Black Panthers had been in the final. The day after the Casque de Diamant, the paper oddly contained no mention of the game's outcome. Since its thesis in the previous day's report had been the inability of the Thonon-les-Bains team to win the big game, that it failed to notice that that team had finally reached the top seems odd.[117] *L'Équipe*'s website did have a short paragraph about the Black Panthers' victory posted on the day of the game, but there was nothing in print.[118]

The inability to gain notice from the mainstream press is one of the significant challenges that football faces in France. Internet sites can help raise the visibility of the sport, but any advantages that might accrue are largely offset by reports focused on the negatives of the game. Several positive mentions in local papers can likely be wiped out by a single concussion story in *Le Monde*.

Football is well established in France, even if it is largely invisible to most. Early on the game escaped from the environs of Paris and now has spread to most regions of the country. It has not been a triumphal process; teams have come and gone in rapid procession. The federation has weathered financial and moral crises and has success-fully guarded the amateur spirit that Laurent Plegelatte envisioned for the game. Unfortunately, this nonprofessional status is also argu-ably the cause for the sport's relative anonymity.

French teams are once again active on the international scene, and in the summer of 2013, the French Junior team barely lost, 20–14, to an American team from Illinois's Augustana College. Thanks to the Black Panthers, the French won their first ever EFAF Cup in 2013. Magazines have come and gone, but in the twenty-first century, the Internet has allowed the sport to break out of the news blackout that exists in the mainstream media.

It has been over one hundred years now since the Great White Fleet first brought football to France. Despite more than a thousand football games played by service personnel from 1917 to 1967, along with the explicit efforts of promoters such as Riess, Leclerc, and Kap to entice the French to adopt our game, they remained steadfast in their refusal. Plegelatte changed that, and football is now in the midst of its fourth decade in the country. The pull factor of consumers in a global marketplace of culture choosing a product that meets their needs has demonstrably outweighed the push by cultural imperial-ists to impose the game.

However, new currents are roiling French football culture, causing new grumbles among the denizens of the culture. The French are also beginning to expand in new directions, breaking the long-standing gender barriers that have traditionally kept females on the sidelines. Increasing numbers of Frenchmen are traveling to North America to play the sport on the university level, and the experience they are gaining is helping improve the game when they return. Some French players have scaled the heights to have their shot at playing in the NFL, and if one of these expatriates should become a star, perhaps France will experience a Yao Ming effect.

10. Leveling the Playing Field

Present in all regions of France by the turn of the century, football in France is well established, and shows some indications of growth. In the past decade the Casque de Diamant has drawn an average of 5,500 fans, with the 2013 game drawing a slightly larger-than-average crowd of 6,000 to watch the Black Panthers of Thonon-les-Bains defeat the Flash de La Courneuve 14–0. While this is a smaller crowd than many Texas high school football teams attract on a weekly basis, it is decent support for a sport that exists on the fringes of the national consciousness.

With more than twenty thousand players, the federation may find chances for continued expansion difficult, but there are signs that some changes have already begun. Football has become increasingly popular with women since the creation of all-female teams in the past few years. Male French players have also found some success outside the borders of the Hexagon, and perhaps international accomplishment will lead to increased visibility for the sport.

Clumsy attempts at cultural imperialism had little impact on convincing the French to adopt the game until one of their own found a reason to play. Likewise, the possibilities for football's rapid growth have been deliberately and consciously limited by federation decisions. Whether the game can make any significant further expansion is dubious and perhaps provides a cautionary tale that Americans might do well to heed.

One significant growth area can be observed in the expansion of women's teams. The introduction of the feminine touch to the game is not unique to the twenty-first century, however. The first female actually played in 1991, at a time when much of the world's attention was focused on the Gulf War. Loïc Brébant (aka Charlie Halftime) of *US Foot* proclaimed, "Everywhere. They are absolutely everywhere. At home, crisp and sexy in lightweight silk negligees, or fighting Valkyries, parachuted down in the Gulf, wearing a lattice-work of green and khaki. This is evidence that girls and women today have much in common with their activist colleagues of the last century." The one area where women had not made significant gains was on the football field. Although more than twenty-two thousand Frenchwomen were licensed to play soccer, and over one thousand held rugby licenses, until recently there was only one woman who had attempted to play football.[1]

One of the first women to attempt to "poach in the restricted hunting grounds" of male football was Valerie Formaux, who was licensed to play for the Météores in 1991. Formaux acknowledged that she was made a part of the team by President Alain Lebon only to "piss off the Fédération." A nurse by profession, she had practiced a variety of sports, including judo, karate, and handball before she saw her first football game in June 1990. When she saw a game between the beginner teams of the Dogues (Mastiffs) and the Météores played live for the first time, "it was the trigger" that made her want to play herself.[2]

It was not easy to get onto the field though. Her inclusion on the team began as a joke, and she spent most of her time at practice "waxing the grass with her ass." Finally, she "got mad" and told Lebon, "I want to play!" He eventually acceded to her demand. She then had to prove to her male teammates that she would not quit the first time she was knocked down. That accomplished, she went on to practice Monday through Friday with the Dogues and Wednesday through Sunday with the Météores.[3]

Standing five feet eleven and weighing 209 pounds, Formaux, who played the difficult position of center, admitted that she did not really belong playing for an Elite Division team—yet. She did, however, accomplish a minor miracle that none of her male colleagues had yet managed to achieve: garner an interview with *L'Équipe* magazine. As miraculous as that may have been, the article began with condescension toward women who wanted to play football. Sandwiched between Gulf War stories, the magazine wondered if women who were gaining equality in the military would find new fields for their playground, "with a bonus; new accessories: helmets, jerseys, shoulder pads, and breast guards."[4]

Formaux admitted to Charlie Halftime that she had nearly lost her temper at the tone of the interview. "It's OK though, I've recovered. At the time, it was I who was the ass. But damn, the title: Valerie the Lineman . . . the androgynous . . . the new prototype player . . . isn't that a bit too much?" By casting Formaux as the new prototype, *L'Équipe* was further marginalizing the sport that it normally could not be bothered to cover. Even *US Foot* couldn't resist the impulse to focus on the salacious. Its last paragraph on her answered the question that many readers might have found a cause for concern: "What about the locker room? How does that work?" Formaux assured readers that she dressed in the referee's locker room but added that because she was a nurse, she had seen it all, and it would not have bothered her to share a dressing room with men.[5]

The article also mentioned Caroline Defour and Karine Reche, two other young women who were currently playing flag football for the Lyon Sixty-Niners, an otherwise male team. Their coach, Charly Magro, maintained, "I am not willing to leave them on the sidelines because they are as motivated as the boys, if not more so." Defour, a five-foot-two, and 105-pound fourteen-year-old, fortunately had parents who approved of her choice of sports. "Give it everything you've got," they reportedly encouraged her.[6]

Also mentioned in the same story, Yolande Betzel Lagache, at sixty-seven years old, was not a player but rather the mother of one of the players. She had begun by washing jerseys, then had taken over the operation of the Vikings of Washquehal, a small town on the Belgian border. A retired anesthesiologist, Lagache brought stability to her team, which had been traveling from town to town seeking a place to play. When asked if she could also motivate her troops, Lagache admitted that she could go on a rant when it was needed.[7]

Likewise, Nicole Osmont, the mother of two players from the Fighters of Croissy, an upscale suburb near Paris, acceded to her son's request that she take the team "in her hands" when financial difficulties arose that the players could not handle. She negotiated with the mayor of Croissy and helped the team achieve solvency. Through her efforts they were even able to import a Canadian coach.[8]

The article also mentioned other women involved behind the scenes in football, including Nathalie Jusselin, the secretary for Fédération president Jacques Accambray. Sophie Linole, who worked in the FFFA's Communication Department, was also profiled. Women had also served as referees, including Géraldine Le Mouellic and Michéle Hayére, who had been the secretary-general of the federation before joining the Commission on Referees.[9]

Despite the egalitarian tone of the article, the author seemingly couldn't resist adding chauvinistic touches such as a description of how Linole was "molded into her impeccable skirt." As an afterthought cheerleaders were also thrown into the mix. But despite some gains, French football still lagged far behind the 1,200 females who reportedly participated in Canadian flag football. The same situation pertained in the United States, where women's rugby was present on many college campuses. While the times were changing in France, of the 3,331 football players at the time, there were still only nine women playing.[10]

Although Accambray thought that women should have the chance to play, he was not a strong supporter of the movement to recruit even more females. Charlie Halftime put this down to the traditional sexism in society that saw women athletes as women first, then athletes. Eric Burtscher remembered that in addition to pissing off the FFFA, the Météores recruited some of the women on their team "because they thought they were hot." Burtscher also at one point had signed a woman to play for the Anges Bleus. Celine, he recalled, had been an "excellent receiver" but had played a only few games before being injured. He was able to slip her past the FFFA by just including her license application in a large pile of others. When she was finally noticed, Thierry Soler of the federation objected, but Burtscher pointed out that the rules did not specify that players must be male. Soler was not amused and kept Burtscher's coaching license for a time. The license form was then edited to include a box for applicants to specify their sex.[11]

Though women were beginning to poach on the formerly male-only preserve in the 1990s, it would be more than two decades before an all-female team would appear. Founded by Sarah Charbonneau in the summer of 2012, the Sparkles of Villeneuve-Saint-Georges was the first entry in what seems to be a rapidly expanding world of *football féminin*. Charbonneau, according to the Sparkles website, was a former top-level gymnast, and she was joined on the first women's team by Lucie Bertaud, a five-time French boxing champion who had won the 2007 European championship.[12]

The team was formed, despite the difficulties caused by the lack of infrastructure for football, even for men, in France. Charbonneau had cheered from the sidelines for her cousins, who played for the Filibusters (Buccaneers), the male team in Villeneuve. When she decided to start her own team, she turned to them for support. A crucial difficulty that had to be overcome was finding players. Knowledge of the game and its rules are not widespread, and the sport is considered a violent male game. Charbonneau started by "talking to her friends and expanding the circle."[13] Eventually she found enough to start practicing, guided by Mohamed Dahmane and other players from the men's team. With only one team in the country, the new challenge became finding an opponent.

The French were late in Europe in forming feminine football teams. By 2012 several nations had already established women's teams. Women's professional football had existed in the United States since the 1960s, though teams and leagues came and went frequently. In Germany the first game between the Berlin Adler Girls and the Cologne Crocodiles took place on September 2, 1987.[14] Australia was next, establishing the women's game when the West Australian Football League began play in 1987. Spain had enough teams to hold a championship of the Liga Catalana de Fútbol Americano in 1996.[15] The Graz Black Widows started playing touch football during a picnic in 1997, and by 2000 teams began contesting for the Ladiesbowl championship.[16] Sweden began playing in international women's football competition in 2008.[17] So by the time the Sparkles began training, many European teams had already been in existence for quite some time, building experience in friendly, and not so friendly, matches at home and abroad.

Less than one year after the team came into existence, it was con-

FIG. 24. The Sparkles of Villeneuve-Saint-Georges, taken before their game against the Spanish National Team in 2012. Photo courtesy of Rémy Issaly.

tacted by the Federación Española de Fútbol Americano, the Spanish football federation, which challenged the newcomers to a match against the Spanish National Team. At the time, the Sparkles were unsure that they had enough players to manage the match, but they were able to recruit sufficient new members to make the trip. They met the Spaniards on their home ground at Estado El Olivo in Madrid on May 27, 2012.[18]

The team realized that it faced an uphill battle, playing against women who had considerably more experience, and the Spanish had a total of thirty-five players from nine teams to oppose the new French team.[19] The result, a 33–6 win for Spain, reflected the inexperience of the Villeneuvians but did not discourage them. The debut of French women's football was certainly inauspicious, with the first play from scrimmage resulting in a Charbonneau fumble that was recovered by the Spaniards. There were a few bright spots though. Based on the streaming video of the game, Charbonneau never got a handle on that first handoff, and while trying to pick it up, she received a savage hit. She did not limp off of the field though but rather came off seemingly in a rage at herself for making an error. Sophie LeRois scored on end-around from the Spanish 30-yard line, but the officials called the play back and the drive stalled. The first touchdown by a French woman football player was a tight end reverse by Magali Coppry, who added the Sparkles' only score of the day from the Spanish 5-yard line.[20]

However, this groundbreaking game, the first for a women's team in France, attracted considerable press attention for the fledgling organization. Charbonneau called it "a great experience" and remembered how well their team was received by their Spanish opponents.[21] Interviews on BEIN Sport; Les Extremistes, a talk show on the MCS Extreme channel; and Destin de Sportive, which was screened on the French channel Chérie 25, gave wide exposure to the pioneers.[22] The media appearances allowed Charbonneau and Bertaud to spread the word about their team and about American football in France. One episode on BEIN Sport featured several players including Bertaud and Vincent Parisi, a martial arts instructor who helped train some of the women. The report featured players running through tires and practicing combat sports moves. It also included a segment with Thomas Villechaize, one of the presenters, learning about basic football plays from the players, who were mostly in full gear. Also taking part were men and women wearing Flash equipment. The segment gave both men's and women's football some positive press, which is relatively rare.[23]

A little less than a year after the Sparkles' defeat by Spain, the team's hard work at practice finally paid off in victory. By this time the Centaures of Grenoble in southeastern France had become the second women's team. Leading up to the game, the Sparkles' players felt some pressure; they had not expected to defeat the more experienced Spanish team, but now they were concerned that they might lose to another French team. "Losing to Grenoble would be a humiliation," was the feeling expressed in the game story on the team website. They were so nervous that many were unable to sleep the night before the game, and they organized an impromptu run-through session in their hotel's parking lot. What any guests who observed the strange sight thought about a group of women practicing football in the middle of the night was not specified but can be imagined. The pregame nerves were unnecessary, as the "Alpha" team rolled to an easy victory by a score of 62–0. Speaking of the victory, Charbonneau demonstrated a potential talent for coaching when she said of the vanquished foe, "They [the Centaures] never gave up. They were aggressive and in the game. I think this team will go far."[24]

Charbonneau also was invited to take part in a panel at the Etats Généraux du sport collectif féminin, a conference on the status of women in team sports, which was held in Bourges on March 16 and 17, 2013. Along with Charbonneau panelists included Minister of Sports Valérie Fourneyron, former athlete and current reporter Maryse Ewanjé-Epée, editorial director of *L'Équipe* Fabrice Jouhaud, Sonia Bombastor from soccer's Team France, and director of Ryder Cup 2018 for the French Golf Association Brigitte Deydier. This was significant exposure for the new feminine part of the sport and for football in general.

Sharing the stage with, among others, Marc Angelo Soumah of the FFFA, the president of the Sparkles was asked what brought her to the hypermasculine sport. After critiquing the whole idea of the Fédération Française de Football Américain ("it can't be French and also American"), the presenter asked Charbonneau why she was playing such a masculine sport and one that was so obscure in France. Charbonneau repeated the story of watching her cousins and also briefly explained the basic rules for the audience. In response to a question of why she didn't settle for playing rugby, she held that her sport, which she "adored," was preferable to rugby in that it offered a combination of rules, technique, and contact that made it superior. She argued that it was "like chess" with contact. The female presenter obviously knew little about the sport and seemed a bit surprised that women would want to play.[25] Charbonneau handled herself well and defended the sport with vigor, singing the praises of football with the fire of a true believer.

The presenter also questioned Soumah about his federation, and he mentioned the growing numbers in contact, flag football, and cheerleading. Soumah seemingly ran into some difficulty when he mentioned that the federation sponsored cheerleading. The presenter questioned him closely on this, and Soumah specified that cheerleaders had their own competitions that combined gymnastics, dance, and athleticism. In response to the presenter's query if flag was the equivalent to women in the United States playing softball rather than baseball, he agreed that was an apt comparison. Soumah also declared that while some were suggesting that the French should create a team to play lingerie football, the federation would not support it, which drew some applause from the audience. Charbonneau, on the other hand, indicated that women who decided to participate in the sexualized venture were nevertheless football players.[26]

Football féminin may receive a boost or it may be damaged by that recent development. On October 12, 2013, the Legends Football League (LFL), formerly known as the Lingerie Football League, held tryouts in Villeneuve-Saint-Georges. Reportedly, some thirty women came to attempt to make the first French entry in the LFL. Mitchell Mortoza, the president of the LFL, attended the practice session and brought in three coaches from the French National Team to help run the prospective players through their drills.[27]

The LFL is controversial in that the athletes wear very little while playing football, and the attraction for fans is not necessarily the game. Addressing that controversy, the director of the Sparkles maintained, "For my part I am not against this concept, and I find it almost even more impressive than the 11 vs. 11 football because they have no protection and are all the same playing tackle. To me they are true warriors who have been able to be heard!"[28]

The positive press that Charbonneau and the Sparkles have been able to garner has likely raised the general visibility of football in France. Any national press is a definite improvement for the sport in a country that is barley aware that football exists.[29] Being invited to represent football at the Etats Généraux at a time when there were only a few women's teams playing in France was a significant coup, even if the interest seemed somewhat bemused at times. Charbonneau and the Sparkles seem to have the ability to attract favorable publicity, and they have expanded their visibility by selling calendars, T-shirts, bracelets, and other gear.[30]

Whether the introduction of the LFL will help or hurt their image-making efforts remains to be seen. Using the somewhat specious but commonly held theory that any publicity is good publicity, the presence of lightly clad female football players might possibly turn out to be a positive for the sport. At least many Frenchmen and women would become aware of the sport in their country. Charbonneau has also parlayed her knowledge of the game and her media appearances into a contract with the MCS Extreme cable channel to do commentary on the LFL.[31]

At the 2013 Casque de Diamant game, women football players appeared on the field prior to the match as an implicit endorsement from the federation that it approved of the expansion of the game. The small French football press, composed largely of *4th&Goal*, has also promoted the sport for females. Each of *4th&Goal*'s first six issues contained a story about a female player or women's team. In its first available issue, published in June 2012, the magazine profiled Charbonneau, Bertaud, and Elsa Michanol, the Sparkles' quarterback, and added to the narrative the information that Charbonneau had met her fiancé through football.

In subsequent issues readers learned that there were already nine women's teams, including the Sparkles, playing football. The article was written by Michanol, who also contributed other articles to the magazine. Some of the teams did not have many players, but the possibility of nine-on-nine games would help them be able to play.[32] The next issue introduced Elisa De Santis Bonneteau for the Women's French National Flag Football Team.[33] At the Etats Généraux Soumah earned another round of applause by telling the delegates that Bonnateau's team had finished third in the world championships.[34] Readers also met Anne Sophie Papeil, a Swiss woman of French descent who played contact football for the Knights of Neuchâtel in Switzerland.[35] The next issue previewed the upcoming match between the Sparkles and the Centaures that would take place the next month.[36] By June 2013 the magazine reported that seven women's teams were playing in the Île de France, and they were joined by thirteen more playing in the provinces.[37]

Women's football is demonstrably gaining ground in France. Less than three years since Charbonneau created the Sparkles, there are now twenty teams practicing football, and the National Flag Team is competitive internationally. It remains to be seen if the possibility of French entry into the LFL will prove a benefit to that process or a distraction. Regardless, however, of what uniforms the women wear, if the women's game continues its rapid growth, positive consequences may follow. One possible outcome of this spread may be the realization of the dream that some French football officials have had to see football included in the Olympic Games. Inclusion in the games generally requires that new games be played by both men and women.[38]

Along with women's football another area where the French are progressing is in the success of their players on the international scene. Increasing numbers of Frenchmen are playing at North American universities, and some have made fairly impressive marks in the NFL and the NFLE.

Without question the brightest star in the French football constellation has been Richard Tardits. The story of how he came to play football for the University of Georgia and later with the Cardinals and the Patriots of the NFL has attained something of the legendary status that Laurent Plegelatte's trip to Colorado enjoys. A native of Biarritz in southwestern France, Tardits played rugby for the French Junior National team. In 1984, in order to improve his English, Tardits visited Dr. Edouard Servy, a family friend, who lived in Augusta, Georgia. Servy explained the American higher education system to the young man and mentioned that athletic prowess could help young people earn a scholarship that would pay for their education. Despite some familial resistance and the long odds stacked against such a plan succeeding, Tardits met with Georgia Bulldogs head coach Vince Dooley. The Georgia coach likely had reservations but agreed to allow him to be a "walk-on" candidate for the team.[39]

The experiment did not begin well. At the first practice Tardits lined up at tight end and was told to "block the defensive end." Not knowing how to block, he tackled the man around the legs, and Dooley reportedly thought to himself, "Ain't no way this kid's going to learn to play football." However, when the young man, who stood six feet two and weighed two hundred pounds, ran the 40-yard dash in 4.5 seconds, Dooley suggested special teams. Tardits asked, "Is it foot-bul [sic]?"

When Dooley replied that it was, Tardits told the coach, "Then I'd like that. Thank you very much!"[40]

From there the young Frenchman was fortunate that an injury opened a position at defensive end. He stepped into the breach, and by the time his career with the Bulldogs was over, he had earned his nickname "Le Sack." He accomplished this by becoming the all-time leader in that category with twenty-nine. Tardits's record stood for sixteen years until Davey Pollack, who would later be a first-round draft choice of the Cincinnati Bengals, surpassed it.[41]

After his stellar career at Georgia, where he not only starred on the field but was also a top student, Tardits was drafted in the fifth round by the Phoenix Cardinals in 1989. He was subsequently traded to the New England Patriots and played in parts of three seasons until he was injured and finally cut in 1992. The end came when new Patriots coach Bill Parcells told Tardits that his injury would not heal before training camp, and therefore he would be cut. The Frenchman told his coach that it was against the rules to cut an injured player, but Parcells only replied: "Sue me."[42] He attempted to come back from his injury with the Denver Broncos in 1994 but failed to make the team, and his NFL career came to an end.[43] While it lasted, though, he played in twenty-seven games, started one, and had one fumble recovery. Hardly outstanding statistics, but they are far and above what any other French player has accomplished.

In a 2012 telephone conversation, Tardits reflected on his football career and professed no regrets. Football paid for his education in the United. States, including an MBA that he earned while playing for the Patriots. He mentioned that, as a boy, he "never concentrated on [his] studies." Had he stayed in France, with its more rigidly tracked educational system, he likely would not have had the same educational opportunities that he had in the United States. He also remembered the "fantastic feeling" of playing before ninety thousand Georgia fans who "wanted to be [his] mother and father." Some went so far as to suggest that he marry their daughter. He remembered that all were interested in "helping the French boy."[44]

Tardits was unusual for more than merely his accent and his path to football. Because of his drive to earn a degree, he did not have much interaction with his teammates off the field. He regularly took more than twenty credit hours per quarter and was viewed as a "weird kid" by the other players, particularly because of the amount of time he spent learning the COBOL programming language. During his final season at Georgia, Tardits had already begun his master's program and would have carried an even heavier course load had NCAA rules not limited student athletes to only twenty-two credit hours per term.[45]

Despite his success Tardits struggled to learn the finer points of the game. He only began dropping back into pass coverage occasionally during his senior year. He emphasized that "four years was not enough to learn the game—one must start at eight years old." While it was "OK in college to be one-dimensional," when he arrived in the NFL, this was a serious handicap. Still, he is philosophical about his failure to have a long career in professional football. "The sports system in the U.S. is a pyramid, and it becomes harder at the top of that pyramid. It is also more ruthless at the top, but that is just the way it is, and you have to deal with it, like in business."[46]

Tardits emphasized that the football culture in the United States was so different from that in France, that it "was not much of a culture shock" to play in Georgia. Echoing the *L'Équipe* article on the 1976 tour, for him it was not merely a new culture but was "so different that it was a new world." "In the American system, only the strong survive." While it was ruthless at the top, Tardits "really liked it." In French football there is "no connection to American culture." There, following the philosophy that Plegelatte infused into the game, "Anyone can play. There is not the same mentality—you know that you will be around tomorrow whether you are good or not."[47] As we have seen, when the Anges Bleus made tentative steps toward adopting the American mind-set, they were slapped down by the federation.

Though he was the most accomplished French player of the period, Tardits played only briefly with French teams. One such occasion was a stint with the Castors when they played in the Eurobowl, and he played another time with the French National Team against Italy.[48] With his American education and perhaps some of the win-at-all-costs ethos absorbed playing football in the United States, he went on to wider fields. He is now a successful entrepreneur in Biarritz. He has worked as a commentator for the French broadcast of the Super Bowl and has been asked if that game could increase interest for football in France. His reply is instructive: "Not really. The market is limited. Those who watch the game probably already know football, and I do not think the majority of students will be watching. To develop the sport in France, it would have to be taught in the elementary schools as is basketball. We could then develop a small audience and new football players. Without it, we cannot anchor this sport in our culture."[49]

Tardits has had the most success playing the sport in the United States, but others including the aforementioned Philippe Gardent and Marc-Angelo Soumah have also had significant international careers. Gardent played linebacker for the Berlin Thunder (2003–4) and the Cologne Centurions of the NFLE (2005–7). He played at a high enough level that he was the first non-American named the Co-Defensive Most Valuable Player for that league in 2006. His play with the NFLE earned him an invitation to training camp with the Washington Redskins in 2006 and the Carolina Panthers in 2007.

As previously mentioned Soumah played wide receiver for the Hamburg Blue Devils of the Bundesliga. He then played for the Frankfurt Galaxy of the NFLE from 2001 to 2004. He did well enough there to attract NFL interest and was invited by the Cleveland Browns to their training camp in 2003.[50]

In addition to those two men, there have been other French players who have had considerable success, including:

Sébastien Sejean, who played defensive back for Laval University in Canada from 2004 to 2007 and was invited to join the practice squad of the St. Louis Rams in 2008.

Samyr Hamoudi, who played defensive back for the Barcelona Dragons of the NFLE from 1999 to 2003.

Gregory Malo, who played defensive back for Western Washington University in the NAIA from 1992 to 1996. He then played with the Portland Forrest Dragons of the Arena Football League in 1997. He also played for the Barcelona Dragons from 1997 to 1999.

Cédric Cotar, who played linebacker for the Barcelona Dragons from 2001 to 2003 and for the Cologne Centurions, also of the NFLE, in 2004.

Francesco "Pepe" Esposito, who attended training camp as a line-backer for the British Columbia Lions in 1998 and for the Toronto Argonauts of the Canadian Football League in 1999 and 2000.

Yoan Schnee, who played tight end for the Amsterdam Admirals of the NFLE from 2003 to 2007.

Patrice Kancel, who played running back for the Berlin Thunder of the NFLE from 2001 to 2004.

Laurent Marceline, who played running back for the Barcelona Dragons in 2003 and for the Düsseldorf Rhein Fire of the NFLE from 2004 to 2006.

Sandino Octobre, who played running back for the Amsterdam Admirals of the NFLE from 2003 to 2006.

Foad Adjir, who played defensive back for the Berlin Thunder in 2002 and 2003, then for the Scottish Claymores, also of the NFLE, in 2004.

Nicolas Prévost, who played linebacker for the Berlin Thunder in 2005.

Thibault Giroud, the first Frenchman signed by the NFLE, who played running back for the Barcelona Dragons from 1996 to 1997.[51]

The NFLE provided a good opportunity for French players to be noticed by the parent NFL and gave players such as Gardent, Soumah, and Sejean the chance to attend training camps for American profes-sional teams. There they had the opportunity to become part of an NFL team. That they were unable to earn a position on the various teams they tried for might well be blamed on the lack that Tardits saw in himself. He was aware that his preparation for the game was deficient in that he had not played since his early years. The French players, no matter how athletic, have so far lagged behind American players who had been training since a very young age.

When the NFLE ceased operations in 2007, a window of opportu-nity for French players closed. Some, like Sejean, have moved on to other, more competitive leagues. Sejean returned to France to help the Amiens Spartiates win the Casque de Diamant in 2012 but then sought a new challenge. He signed with the Dresden Monarchs of the German Football League in 2013. The Germans have been playing football since 1977, and the game has caught on better there than in France. Sejean reported that football was the number one sport in the city of sixty thousand, and that the Monarchs had played a televised game against a Japanese team from their X-League in 2012. Regular-season games there draw an average of five thousand fans, which eclipses the four thousand who saw the 2013 Casque de Diamant game, and are broadcast on television. The regular season is fourteen games, compared to the ten that French teams play, which will give Sejean the extra repetitions and added exposure that might earn him another chance at playing in North America.[52]

Other players, including the young Flash players taking part in the Projet High School discussed in chapter 8, are going to the United States to improve and show off their skills. An increasing number of French players are attending American colleges and universities to study, and play. Gustave Guillox, an offensive tackle who stands six feet six and weighs 310 pounds, studied as an exchange student at Ouachita Christian School in Louisiana. While there he had the opportunity to play in the Super Dome when his team won the state championship. After playing for the National Junior Team in the World Championship in Austin, Guillox decided to come back to the United States to play for Seton Hill University in western Pennsylvania. Texas Christian University also expressed interest in him, but his late entry into the recruiting pool, the difficulty that international students have negotiating NCAA rules, and family pressure convinced him to accept the offer from the smaller Catholic school.[53]

The TCU Horned Frogs, which demonstrated interest in Guillox, is a French-friendly team. Kyle Skierski, a graduate assistant for the offensive team, played for the Flash after he finished his career at the University of California–Davis. Baptiste Mullot, a quarterback who played for the Besançon Bisons, spent a semester in Fort Worth and tried out for the walk-on team, where he met Skierski. Mullot decided after trying out for the position that the amount of work he would have to do for football would make it impossible for him to complete his studies, and he therefore dropped out of the competition for the role on the TCU practice squad.[54]

In 2014 another French player with the football bug secured a spot on an American college team. Enzo Rosani had played in the Parisian suburb of Gagny and was another player who made the National Junior Team that played in Austin. When he wanted to try the next level, he asked his coach for help. Steve Guersent, who had coached at the University of Wisconsin–Stout and now coaches the Spartiates of Amiens, was glad to aid the young player. Rosani is a freshman for the Blue Devils of UWS, where he is playing cornerback. He hasn't seen much playing time yet but has three more years to fulfill his goal of becoming a starter.[55]

These are small steps that will take a long time to make an impact, if they ever do. However, should Guillox, Rosani, or some future French player manage to succeed in the NFL, the sport in France would benefit greatly. Much as has been the case with the popularity of the NBA in China when Yao Ming began to play, should a French athlete become a star in the NFL, it would raise the public's consciousness of football there. The deck is stacked against that happening, of course, but the possibility does exist. Basketball is played worldwide and is relatively simple to understand, not to mention inexpensive to play. That is not the case with football.

Even though more and more countries are playing the game (sixty-four countries have federations, according to the International Federation of American Football), it remains a complicated, expensive, and dangerous game.[56] When French readers of *Le Monde* or other national newspapers read about football, it is often stories that focus on that danger with provocative titles such as "Football américain, un siècle de dégâts [a century of damage]?" These stories nearly write themselves, particularly in the wake of the concussion controversy of 2014.[57]

Despite the difficulty of having a national press that is typically oblivious, the French are still playing. Even though French readers are treated with occasional hyperbolic stories that deliver the implicit message that to play football is to court almost certain death, the French are still mildly interested. The game that Laurent Plegelatte brought back from Colorado is slowly expanding in popularity and visibility.

If there is a Valhalla for old football players, coaches, and promoters, then some of them are looking down with pleasure. The sailors who first brought the game to the country, the doughboys and GIs who played on French fields, the airmen and soldiers of the NATO era, and the promoters who tried to convince the descendants of the Gauls that football was the wave of the future must be feeling some pride. Curt Riess, Bob Kap, Marcel Leclerc, and Bill Dodds are likely slapping themselves on the back and telling anyone who will listen, "I told you so!" They would be wrong, however. The credit for the creation of French football and its surrounding subculture rests squarely on the shoulders of Laurent Plegelatte, with a little help from others, including Silvio Berlusconi, who was part owner of La Cinq, the first private, free channel in France from 1984 to 1992.[58]

World War I, along with the Inter-Allied Games, came and went without causing much of a ripple in the French sporting world. The sporadic military bowl games and leagues of World War II were even more ephemeral, and the thousands of games played by NATO bases barely touched the French consciousness. For all their pleading and bombast, promoters such as Riess, Crowley, Tardy, Leclerc, Dodds, Kap, and Foster failed to convince many that they should begin playing the American transplant. Their seeds fell on rocky soil and were blown away by the winds of war and indifference. Those clumsy attempts at cultural imperialism failed to find the prerequisite for such efforts to succeed: consumers willing to buy what the imperialists were selling.

Perhaps if Adolf Hitler had not plunged the world into war in 1939, Jean Galia might have filled the place that Plegelatte eventually occupied. Maybe if Charles de Gaulle had not promoted the spirit of "Yankee Go Home" and had not withdrawn his nation from NATO, then USAFE and USAREUR football might have eventually found a French audience. They did so more successfully in Germany and Britain. Possibly if Bob Kap had been a billionaire, he might have had the resources that matched his ambition, and events might have turned out differently. Perchance had the NFLE located a team in Paris, football would be more accepted than it is now.

Perhaps. Maybe. Possibly. Perchance. There were so many conceivable chances for the French to accept what was, in the minds of its

boosters, the One True Sport and so little accomplishment to show
for them. Dreams die hard, but the dreams that work have concrete
reasons for their success. Only after Plegelatte had created a base for
football did a little bit of effective cultural imperialism finally render aid to the project. Even then that was not something undertaken
by American cultural imperialists, but rather a 1985 decision made
by programmers of La Cinq, a television channel owned in part by
future Italian prime minister Silvio Berlusconi, to include the NFL
among their offerings.[59]

The spread of football to France is a demonstration that in the global
marketplace of culture, some products succeed, and some fail. Some,
football américain, for instance, take longer to find a market niche.
The key is not pressure from the seller but acceptance by the buyer.
Only when a Trotskyite saw the possibilities of football as a collective sport that could toughen his personal Red Guard did the sport
begin to find a small but interested consumer base.

Football has successfully become a part of French sport, and while
it may be difficult to find there, for its devotees it is a crucial part of
that world. From one team in 1980 to more than two hundred teams
in 2013, the sport has demonstrated steady growth. Given the con-
straints, both internal and external, under which it operates, this
is impressive. External factors such as the lack of media coverage,
along with the difficulty of watching NFL games, have definitely limited the expansion potential for the sport. These are the factors that
cause the denizens of the demimonde of football to grind their teeth
in frustration.

However, just as efforts to force football on the French failed until
the French themselves found a reason to play, the internal factors at
work there have arguably limited the spread of the game. When the
FFFA sanctioned the Anges Bleus for their professionalized brand of
football that was designed to provide a spectacle for the masses, they
may very well have consigned football to the fringes of French sports.
Football grew in the United States, ironically aided by the role that
France played in both world wars, by providing a superior spectacle
that caught the attention of the masses. Football supplanted baseball
in American popularity because those in charge of the former contin-

ually tinkered with the rules to provide a more exciting game, while the national pastime only slowly embraced change.

Once again French football might very well render further aid to the American version of the game. Football, as it exists in France, is very similar to what many reformers would like to see on American college campuses: a game played for the enjoyment of the athletes, not a spectacle for the masses. Football for the masses, as it is now played, brings with it all the chances for corruption that goes along with "overemphasis."

It is no more likely that big-time college football will be deemphasized here than it is that French football will become a major sport followed by a large percentage of the population there. However, football américain might be useful as an example of what could happen should reformers ever mount a serious challenge to the current system. With the 2014 decision that football players can unionize, might we one day see an American version of the Spartacus players' sit-in at a championship game? Might the new NCAA playoff attract the same interest as the Harvard versus Yale match?

Perhaps we should pay more attention to football as it is played in France.

Afterword

The State of Play in the Twenty-First Century

Somewhere else in France, June 22, 2013

Jean-Marc and I, with our wives, stopped for lunch across the street from Stade Charlety in the Thirteenth Arrondissement in southeastern Paris. Standing at the bar was a man wearing a Tom Brady NFL jersey, and passing by the window we saw several others wearing the colors of a variety of French football teams. Not a typical day in Paris. Lunch finished, Jean-Marc and I waived as Sophie and Agnes went off to shop, which they preferred to football.

Crossing the street, we saw a few banners advertising the 2013 Casque de Diamant game hanging from the fence around the stadium. Passing through the gates free of charge, I noticed a large inflatable football helmet inside where young boys were running around and occasionally throwing footballs. Inside the stadium there were a few booths set up to promote various football-related projects. One table advertised the upcoming game between Augustana College of Illinois and the French Junior Team, which would take place later that summer in Lille. Another table contained back issues of the new football magazine *4th&Goal*, and yet another sought recruits for the Diables Rouge (Red Devils), a new women's football team.

A half hour or so before kickoff the crowd was still relatively light. Only one side of the stadium was open to seating in order to make it seem as if the Flash and the Black Panthers were playing before a packed stadium for the streaming video broadcast of the game. The official estimate of the crowd later came in at between four thousand and six thousand fans, which is around the average for the championship game.[1] This was not a World Cup match or anything that would draw large masses, but those arriving were enthusiastic.

I didn't see any celebrities of the sort who infest big games in the United States, although there was a central section of the stadium closed off for VIPs. The non-VIP celebrities in this case were the players from the various teams in France. Jackets proclaimed membership on teams such as the Red Star, the Loups Blancs (White Wolves), the Asgards, and the Phoenix. Another fan seated near me was wearing a replica jersey with the name of the Giants' defensive end Justin Tuck on the back. There was even one older fan who could still fit into his Spartacus sweatshirt. Much in evidence were females wearing jerseys from the Sparkles, the Red Star, and the Diables Rouges, all teams that were attempting to field their own entries in the growing world of *football féminin*.

The supporters of the Flash and the Black Panthers had their own sections on either side of the 50-yard line near the field. At French soccer games jamming a crowd into a confined area with supporters of the two contending teams separated only by an aisle might have ended in violence, but the atmosphere at the stadium was family-like, with everyone "ready for some football!"

The contrast between football and soccer is one that football aficionados like to make, repeatedly. When "La Marseillaise" rang out over the loud speakers, the crowd respectfully rose to its collective feat, and many sang along. Several people mentioned to me that soccer hooligans typically jeered during the national anthem and basically carried on like the ruffians they were. Not so with football. The consensus of those I talked with was that this game, and football in general, was a safe place to bring one's family.

We arrived just in time to see the introduction of a group of women who had begun to play on the teams mentioned above. Perhaps thirty players were lined up on the sideline in full pads, much to the delight of the crowd. For the most part the cheers seemed to be welcoming these young women into the family, rather than the amused applause of those who were viewing some sort of oddity. After the introductions some of the young women circulated in the concourse seeking to sign up new players. One booth, set up by the Furies of La Queue-en-Brie, had the best recruiting poster that I saw that day. It featured a football shoe complete with high-heel spikes, along with a stylized image of a woman holding a gladiator's shield and spear. The message was that women did not have to give up their femininity to play football.

As the pregame festivities continued, a small group began dancing and performing gymnastics on the field. Cheerleaders were supplied by the Templiers of Saint-Quentin-en-Yvelines, and they made their first appearance, much to the delight of the fans. Also part of the show was a group of mascots, including one from Subway, which is one of the corporate sponsors of the federation. Television (Internet) announcers made reports from the sideline, and then the teams were introduced.

The game itself was rather dull. The Black Panthers of Thonon-les-Bains defeated the Flash de La Courneuve by a score of 14–0. As sometimes happens in the Super Bowl, both head coaches were seemingly averse to taking any chances and stuck to a vanilla attack. They mostly kept it safe, running the ball between the tackles. Karim El Kolli, a former Anges Bleus and later coach of the Red Star, was disgusted after the game. He complained that both teams used maybe three or four simple plays for most of the game, with no wrinkles or trick plays.[2]

Fortunately, the federation had apparently learned from American sporting events, and there was always something going on during the game. Though there was no hot dog launcher, lucky fans had the chance to catch prizes thrown into the stands. The cheerleaders circulated through the crowd with additional souvenirs to give away, and they managed to keep up a party atmosphere.

Despite the lack of action on the field, the game served as a reunion for as much of the French football community as could make it to Paris. Old friends and rivals caught up on the latest news and remembered ancient battles. With the exception of the fans directly concerned with the outcome, the game was only an excuse for the others to dress up in their "war paint," as in the 1989 Arena Ball match, and celebrate the grand day of their subculture.

The Junior Championship between the Flash and the Canonniers of Toulon was more enjoyable from a football perspective. The outcome of the game was in question late in the final period. Aymeric Dethelot, the Flash quarterback, riddled the Toulon defense with accurate short passes throughout much of the game. However, in the third quarter either the coaches or Dethelot got greedy and went long. The Canonniers intercepted the ball and looked as if they might take the lead in the game, which saw the Flash leading 16–10 at the time. The La Courneuve defense stiffened, though, and after a few lackluster series that featured mostly running plays, Dethelot came back throwing with confidence. That was perhaps the most impressive part of the game for me, watching Dethelot put his past errors behind him and return to the form he had demonstrated earlier. He led his team to another score that made the final 23–10 Flash. Perhaps Dethelot, who must now move up to the Elite team, will continue to improve and set the model for future French quarterbacks.[3]

An even larger crowd of seven thousand (*Quad City Times*) to eight thousand (*Voix du Nord*) turned out on July 27, 2013, to watch the French National Team, coached by former Argonaut head man Larry Legualt, play against the Augustana Vikings.[4] The site for the game was the same Stade Lille Métropole that was the site of the second match between the Newton Nite Hawks and the Chicago Lions in 1977. For once Pierre-Gérard Lespinasse, a French reporter, demonstrated a sense of history when he wrote, "For the first time in 36 years, the Stade Lille Métropole hosted a football game."[5]

Sam Frasco, the Viking's quarterback, scored three touchdowns, including a 59-yard run for the score, but the French team refused to give up. The final score of the game was 20–13, but the French were encouraged that they were competitive. Significantly, both French touchdowns came on pass plays. The first came in the third quarter when Stephen Yepmo caught a scoring pass that capped a 70-yard drive, and Marcais Brice caught another with five minutes remaining. Since the quarterback position is one where the French often depend on Americans, the passing success of the junior team might indicate that the French are catching up in this area.[6]

Perez Mattison, the quarterback for the French team, identified a particular problem that French teams face when competing against Americans: the speed at which the Americans play.[7] Not in individual player speed; there are many French players who can run as fast as any American. The problem lies in individual and team reaction speed. On RADIOSSA I theorized that this was a function of the differential opportunities that French and American players have to become acculturated into the game. By the time an American athlete plays college football, he has spent countless hours practicing the sport. This acculturation begins with youth football and continues through middle school and high school. Add to that the further countless hours of film study (i.e., watching football on television), and the American advantage is significant. The player no longer needs to think about what he is doing on the field. Those players who have benefited by more practice repetitions and intense study generally do not think but merely act or react. Even top French players often must hesitate slightly and then act.

Richard Tardits contention that "four years was not enough to learn the game" acknowledged the deficit under which French players labor. He readily admitted that his success was due to his athletic ability, not to his understanding of the game. He played in the NFL and was certain that he was a better athlete than some of those he competed against for playing time. He acknowledged, however, that those lesser athletes beat him out through their superior knowledge of the game.[8]

Mattison explained, "After the break, we were able to control the speed of our opponents. Our beginning was a bit difficult, but once we adapted to the rhythm of the game, we finally found our balance." The French team had players that were as good as, or superior to the Augie Vikings, who finished with a record of only 5–5 in 2012. Yet another difficulty they had was insufficient time to practice together as a team, which allowed the Americans to hold on for the victory.[9] This team cohesion was likely a deciding factor that allowed the Anges Bleus to defeat the Sixth Fleet team in the 1980s. It would be interesting to see how top French teams such as the Black Panthers or the Flash, using their American imports, would fare against American college teams. The team from Thonon-les-Bains has already proven that it can win on the European stage and might well be able to defeat some college teams.

That might, however, come perilously close to promoting elite teams at the expense of giving athletes from several teams a shot at international glory. This could be seen as a violation of the collective and amateur ethos that the federation has worked so hard to protect.

Structural disadvantages aside, the FFFA and French football seem to be in good shape. As of December 2014, the federation boasted 208 teams with 21,085 players.[10] The federation also has announced that for the first time it will sponsor Le Challenge Féminin, a regular season and playoff for women's teams. Seven teams, including the Sparkles, will play in two divisions. Most teams will play three games, and the best team from Conférence Nord and Conférence Sud will meet for the championship.[11]

Despite that healthy outlook, other recent developments in France and Europe do raise questions about the state of football leadership in the Hexagone and on the Continent. On December 13, 2014, President Marc Angelo Soumah and the Executive Committee of the federation resigned after their plans for the next year were rejected by the General Assembly. Michel Daum replaced Soumah on an interim basis.[12] What particular issues led to the current crisis are unclear, and the effect of weakness at the top might even turn out to be a boon for French football in the long run, but that remains to be seen.[13]

At the same time, the International Federation of American Football announced that the 2015 IFAF World Championships had been canceled. The games were set to be held in Stockholm Sweden, but financial problems threatened to doom the games. IFAF president Tommy Viking reportedly had taken a leave of absence. In an article on the website of American Football International Review, Roger Kelly reported that in addition to his duties with the IFAF, Viking was also the head of the Swedish American Football Federation (SAFF), and a company called AMFAM, which had $350,000 invested in it by the SAFF. The money set aside for the championships had not been located, so the SAFF canceled.[14] Canton, Ohio, stepped into the breach and agreed to host the championship. Seven teams, including France, traveled to Ohio to play in the games. France started off well, winning its first two games against Brazil and Australia. The team's hopes for continued success were crushed by Team USA, which destroyed the French 88–0. That crushing defeat seemingly affected the French team's performance in the consolation final, when it lost to the Mexican team 20–7 to finish in fourth place.[15]

Despite the near-total indifference of the popular media discussed in chapter 10, the Internet has provided a platform for teams to publicize themselves and their sport. The talent level of French teams is rising, as evidenced by the Black Panther's 2013 Eurobowl victory and the success that the National Junior Team has had in international competition recently. French players are increasingly being exposed to football as it is played in the United States, and there are many French players who might possibly even help a Division I program.

There are some signs of disquiet though. For the 2014 season the federation proposed limiting the number of games teams would play. According to Eric Burtscher, this was done to reduce the possibility for injury.[16] Axel Duez, another Red Star player, opined, "There are fewer games this year to promote the European championship which takes place in Austria!"[17]

Conventional wisdom holds that the most likely time to be injured is when one is trying not to be injured, so concerns for the safety of players are fine, to a certain point. When the promotion of safety and avoidance of injuries become an overriding preoccupation, however, the game can suffer. The controlled danger of the sport is a motivating factor that attracts athletes to the game, and anything that takes that away might drive players to find some other way to risk life and limb. The French mainstream media already does a fine job of publicizing the dangers of the game, so for the federation to further that narrative through scheduling cannot be good for the sport in France.

The threat that fear poses to football in France is more of a concern there than it is in the United States, but there is some evidence that fear has begun to lessen the appeal of football to young men here.[18] Also, many NFL players, including Drew Breeze and James Harrison, have criticized NFL commissioner Roger Goodell's attempts to lessen on-field violence and his argument that they constitute a danger to the game.[19]

The FFFA plan to limit the number of games met stiff opposition and was dropped. The Red Star played ten games in 2013–14, and the team managed to win enough to remain in the Third Division for a second year. Its record was not what the team had hoped for, but there are signs that its fortunes might pick up in the future. In 2013 the Red Star formed a junior team, and on December 14, 2014, the junior Red Stars defeated the Paris Dragons by a score of 48–0.[20]

While French football is in good overall shape, the opportunities for explosive growth seem to belong only to the women's section of the football world. Globally, this is a perilous moment for football, with the headlines dominated by stories obsessing over the dangers of the sport. This is nothing new in the United States, and football will undoubtedly weather the current storm and remain the top spectator sport for the foreseeable future. In countries such as France, however, where the football culture is less firmly entrenched, and where the Ministry of Sports takes an active role in its operation, concern over safety might have a more profound impact. Moneyed interests are hard to oppose, and even governments largely dance to the tune of those who pay the piper. But in France the piper is paid not by football but by those who prefer to invest in helping people "sit and watch men run up and down in short pants kicking a ball to make one point."[21] Perhaps a new millionaire with money to burn and a desire to take a team to the top à la Maurice Tardy, Marcel Leclerc, Bertrand Lecuyer, or Bernard Bonnet will appear to give the sport an infusion of cash and a vision for a different future. In France, however, those entrepreneurs have so far been few and far between.

Still, football in France has found a niche. A small, noisy niche filled with enthusiasts who cannot understand why everyone does not share their passion for the game they have taken into their heart. At least the story that began with the game between the Red Star and the Kiowas in the introduction had a happy ending. My adopted team, the Red Star, kept winning. It even had the chance to play on a nice field (a rugby pitch) and contend for the championship of the Regional Division. And the team won! The Red Star defeated the Cougars de Saint Ouen by a score of 6–3. Not a smashing victory, but it propelled the team into Third Division for the next year.

Small successes aside, unless some dramatic event acts on the inertia that exists today, the current state of affairs will continue. Football will continue as a relatively obscure sport in France for the foresee-

FIG. 25. Red Star of Noisy-le-Sec after winning the championship of the Regional Division of the Fédération Française de Football Américain in 2012. The team defeated the Cougars de Saint-Ouen-L'Aumône 6–3. Photo courtesy of Jean-Marc Burtscher.

able future. French teams will occasionally have international success, a few thousand will gather to cheer on the contenders for the Casque de Diamant, and smaller numbers will watch the championship games for the lower divisions. Increasing numbers of women will find enjoyment through contact sport. Incrementally larger numbers might join their American cousins-by-enthusiasm to miss sleep as they adopt the Super Bowl weekend as an unofficial holiday. One day the International Olympic Committee might even decide to include football as a part of the games.

If nothing more than this happens, the French will go on as before, celebrating and occasionally rioting over the success or failure of the Blues in the World Cup. But a few among them will continue to experience a quickening of the pulse when their mother drops them off at the field or when they finish their last pregame cigarette and head for the locker room. Because they will know that it is time to put their pride, and their bodies, on the line. *Tout pour l'amour du jeu!*

NOTES

Preface

1. Hereafter, I will refer to American football only as football. If I mention the European brand, I will call it soccer.

2. "Kiowas: Club de Football Américain," http://www.kiowas.fr/prod/index.php /club/presentation, accessed October 23, 2012.

3. "Noisy-le-Sec Red Star Football Américain," http://redstar-footus.fr/, accessed October 23, 2012.

4. Jean-Marc Burtscher, interview by the author, Clichy-sous-Bois, France, October 24, 2012.

5. Cory Bennett, "Part II: The Fifth Down Game," *Cornell Daily Sun*, November 8, 2007, http://cornellsun.com/node/26006, accessed October 25, 2012.

6. Barry Petchesky, "Photos: French Soccer Fans Brawl With Riot Police," 2013, http://deadspin.com/photos-french-soccer-fans-brawl-with-riot-police-1471140368, accessed April 21, 2014.

7. "Histoire de la FFFA," *Fédération Française de Football Américain*, http://www .fffa.org/fr/fffa/presentation/histoire-de-la-fffa.html, accessed on April 21, 2014.

8. Crawford, *Use of Sport*.

Introduction

1. See Gems, *Athletic Crusade*, and Guttmann, *Games and Empires*. There are others, but these are two important works in the field of sport.

2. Olivier Moret, directeur technique nationale adjoint of the FFFA, interview by the author, Nanterre, France, June 7, 2012.

3. Quentin Dagbert, *Le football americain a l'heure française*, http://quentindagbert .wix.com/footusfrance#!oupratiquer/clz79, accessed November 29, 2015.

4. Holt, *Sport and Society*, 134.

5. Henning Eichberg, in Nauright and Parrish, *Sports around the World*, 363.

6. Nauright and Parrish, *Sports around the World*, 62.

7. Dine, *French Rugby Football*, 22.

8. Eugen Weber, "Gymnastics and Sports in Fin-de-siècle France," *Olympic Review*, nos. 53–54 (February–March 1972): 107.

9. Dine, *French Rugby Football*, 23.

10. Holt, *Sport and Society*, 70.

11. Naismith, *Basketball*, 151.

12. Guttmann, *Games and Empires*, 105–6.

13. Lamster, *Spalding's World Tour*, 211.

14. Zeilier, *Ambassadors in Pinstripes*, 2.

15. Zeilier, *Ambassadors in Pinstripes*, 26.

16. Chetwynd, *Baseball in Europe*, 158.

17. Chetwynd, *Baseball in Europe*, 159.

18. Chetwynd, *Baseball in Europe*, 160–61.

19. Olivier Rival, phone interview by the author, Thorigny-sur-Marne, May 14, 2012. Olivier is a French blogger who writes the *Elitefoot* blog on American football. He told me that baseball interest in southern France was stimulated by fleeing *pied noires* who had learned the game during the war. Christian Mercadier, my father-in-law, recalls being taken to a baseball game by his father as a child in Algeria during the war. He remembers that the umpire was an Algerian restaurant owner who played his role with panache.

1. Football over There

1. Wakefield, *Playing to Win*, 6.

2. Sladen, Koehler, and Matthews, *Manual of Physical Training*, 5.

3. Sladen, Koehler, and Matthews, *Manual of Physical Training*, 3.

4. Pope, "Army of Athletes," 441; "Pershing Picks Type for National Army," *New York Times*, August 8, 1917, 2; Wakefield, *Playing to Win*, 16; "Our Men in France Often Feel Homesick," *New York Times*, June 9, 1918, 40; Pope, *Army of Athletes*, 442.

5. Jean-Cristophe Tiné, "Une saison exraordinaire," Histoire oublie´d'un sport méconnu: Chronique de baseball en France sous la IIIème République, http://thenextbaseballcountrywillbefrance.blogspot.com /2013/02/une-saison-extraordinaire .html, accessed June 13, 2014); John Fass Morton, *Mustin: A Naval Family of the Twentieth Century* (Annapolis MD: Naval Institute Press), 64.

6. Morton, *Mustin*, 64.

7. *La Vie Au Grand Air*, photo located in the offices of the Fédération Française de Football Américain

8. "How the French Invented American Football," The Sports Academic, September 18, 2008, http://www.thesportsacademic.com/2008/09/how-french-invented -american-football.html, accessed November 27, 2014.

9. "How the French Invented American Football."

10. "Famous Football Formation of Late Nineties Inspired by Bonaparte," *Harvard Crimson*, October 25, 1926, http://www.thecrimson.com/article/1926/10/25/famous-football-formation-of-late-nineties/, accessed November 27, 2014.

11. "How the French Invented American Football."

12. Coubertin, *Universités transatlantiques*, 99.

13. Pierre-Jean Vazel, "Football américain, un siècle de dégâts?," *Le Monde*, August 30, 2013, http://vazel.blog.lemonde.fr/2013/08/30/football-americain-un-siecle-de-degats/, accessed April 19, 2014.

14. "Pershing Picks Type for National Army," 2.

15. "Harvard Eleven Rallies in Mass to Call of USA," *New York Tribune*, June 12, 1917, 15.

16. "Fordham Athletes Enlist," *New York Times*, January 20, 1918, 25.

17. "Army and Navy Notes," *New York Times*, January 27, 1918, 23.

18. "Yale Launches Movement to Recruit College Letter Men to Aid Army," *New York Times*, March 27, 1918, 14.

19. "Football Coaches Bound for France," *New York Times*, April 23, 1918, 14.

20. *War Department Commission*.

21. International Committee of the Young Men's Christian Athletic Association, *Service with Fighting Men*, 321.

22. See Ingrassia, *Rise of Gridiron University*.

23. Ingrassia, *Rise of Gridiron University*, 25.

24. "Footballs Sent to France," *Chicago Eagle*, February 16, 1918, 7.

25. "Football Suits for Soldiers Now in France," *New York Tribune*, October 2, 1918, 13.

26. "Football Games in France," *Chicago Eagle*, October 19, 1918, 7.

27. "The History of the YMCA in World War I," Doughboy Center: The Story of the American Expeditionary Forces, http://www.worldwar1.com/dbc/ymca.htm, accessed December 18, 2012.

28. Knights of Columbus Committee on War Activities, *Knights of Columbus War Work*.

29. Clubine, "'Better Than They Were Before,'" 83.

30. Wakefield, *Playing to Win*, 24.

31. "Football in France Keeps Liberty Lads Fit to Buck the German Line," *Tucumcari (NM) News*, May 16, 1918, 8.

32. Wakefield, *Playing to Win*, 23.

33. International Committee of the Young Men's Christian Athletic Association, *Service with Fighting Men*, plate 9.

34. Ray Schmidt, "Changing Tides."

35. Associated Press, "Cooks Prepare Feast for Pershing's Men: Thanksgiving Dinner Expected to Be the Best Ever Served to Army on Foreign Soil," *New York Times*, November 29, 1917, 3.

36. Wakefield, *Playing to Win*, 16.

37. "Big Football Game Played in France by U.S. Troops," *El Paso Herald*, November 30, 1917, 11.

38. Associated Press, "French Children See Santa in Airplane: Soldiers of Our Expeditionary Force Provide Christmas Entertainment for Youngsters," *New York Times*, December 27, 1917, 5.

39. "Sports Diversion of War: American Soldiers Utilize All Leisure Time in Athletics," *New York Times*, September 22, 1918, 31.

40. Wakefield, *Playing to Win*, 28.

41. Warren Rouse, *Grandpa's World War I Diary*, http://e.wa.home.mindspring .com/wwidiary/, accessed May 19, 2012.

42. *The Diary of a Doughboy: The Wartime Diary of Allen C. Huber*, transcribed by Robert Huskey, accessed December 19, 2012 at usgennet.org.

43. Lonnie J. White, *Panthers to Arrowheads: The 36th Division in World War I*, 189, http://www.texasmilitaryforcesmuseum.org/36division/archives/wwi/white /chap7.htm, accessed December 21, 2012, and November 24, 2014.

44. Wakefield, *Playing to Win*, 46.

45. Maj. George Wythe, *Inter-Allied Games*, 36.

46. "Big War Athletics Bill," *New York Times*, November 9, 1919, E8.

47. This seems high and may be a typo; in other places the number is put at 75,000, still a large number. Wythe, *Inter-Allied Games*, 35–36.

48. Pope, *Patriotic Games*, 152.

49. Young Men's Christian Athletic Association War Work Council, *Summary of the World War Work*, 143.

50. Young Men's Christian Athletic Association War Work Council, *Summary of the World War Work*, 143.

51. Wythe, *Inter-Allied Games*, 37–38.

52. Author unknown, *Battery A 101st Field Artillery: Being the Narrative of Battery A of the 101st Field Artillery (Formerly Battery A of Boston)* (Cambridge: Battle Press, 1919), 211.

53. Pope, *Patriotic Games*, 152.

54. This refers to Sir William Davenant, an English poet who mentioned the game of football; his game was not related to the modern game, except in the author's fertile imagination.

55. "War Football," *New York Times*, November 23, 1919, xi.

56. "War Football," xi.

57. Wythe, *Inter-Allied Games*, 38.

58. Harold Evans, "College Football in Kansas," *Kansas Historical Quarterly*, August 1940, 301.

59. Benjamin Edgar Cruzan, "A Soldier's Diary: The Diary of a Bugler," *Kansas Collection Articles*, http://www.kancoll.org/articles/cruzan/c_diary2.htm, accessed December 19, 2012.

60. Harry L. Smith, MD, "Memoirs of an Ambulance Company Officer," http://net.lib.byu.edu/estu/wwi/memoir/Ambco/officerTC.html, accessed December 19, 2012.

61. H. L. Smith, "Memoirs."

62. H. L. Smith, "Memoirs."

63. H. L. Smith, "Memoirs."

64. University of Illinois Alumni Association, "Athletics," *Alumni Quarterly and Fortnightly Notes*, May 1, 1919, 300.

65. Maj. C. J. Masseck, *Brief History of the 89th Division U.S.A. 1917–1918–1919* (Kansas City MO: War Society of the 89th Division, 1919), 2.

66. Doran L. Cart, "Kansas Football 'Over There,'" *Kansas History: A Journal of the Central Plains* (Autumn 2006): 197–98.

67. Wythe, *Inter-Allied Games*, 37.

68. White, *Panthers to Arrowheads*, 187.

69. Bernard A. Gill, former USAFE Head Coach of the SHAPE Indians, telephone interview by the author, Ada OH, March 9, 2012.

70. "89th Division Wins Football Palm," *Washington Herald*, March 31, 1919, 1; "Dr. Paul O. Withington Records by Year," *College Football Data Warehouse*, http://www.cfbdatawarehouse.com/data/coaching/alltime_coach_year_by_year.php?coachid=2551, accessed December 21, 2012.

71. Masseck, *Brief History of the 89th Division*, 44.

72. White, *Panthers to Arrowheads*, 3.

73. Chastain, *Story of the 36th*, 260.

74. White, *Panthers to Arrowheads*, 189.

75. White, *Panthers to Arrowheads*, 190.

76. Cart, "Kansas Football 'Over There,'" 196.

77. Cart, "Kansas Football 'Over There,'" 196.

78. Harold Ray and Peter Norcross, "From Lion Tamer to Bulls and Bears: The Story of George (Potsy) Clark, *LA Foundation*, 26–27, http://library.la84.org/SportsLibrary/NASSH_Proceedings/NP1980/NP1980U.pdf, accessed December 21, 2012.

79. Cart, "Kansas Football 'Over There,'" 197.

80. "89th Division Wins Football Palm," 1.

81. "89th Division Wins Football Palm," 1.

82. Wythe, *Inter-Allied Games*, 38.

83. Mennell, "Service Football Program," 248.

84. Louis A. Dougher, "War against the Hun May Make Football as Popular as Baseball for Us All," *Washington Times*, October 30, 1917, 13.

85. "Camp Predicts Big Year for Football," *New York Times*, September 30, 1917, 22.

86. "War Football," xl.

87. Mennell, "Service Football Program," 259–60. See also Lewis, "World War I"; Watterson, *College Football*; Velasquez, "America and the Garrisons Stadium."

88. Rader, *American Sports*, 233–34.

89. Paul Munsey and Cory Suppes, "Ohio Stadium: The Horseshoe," http://football .ballparks.com/NCAA/Big10/OhioState/, accessed December 22, 2012.

90. Grantland Rice, "Football Destined to Have Its Best Season in History," *Philadelphia Evening Public Ledger*, August 23, 1919, 14.

2. 1938 Riess and Crowley Tour

1. "La Vie Sportive," *Le Figaro*, March 29, 1919, 4; "Le Sports," *Le Petit Journal*, March 29, 1919, 2.

2. "Les Sports," *Le Petit Journal*, March 30, 1919, 2.

3. "The Great War: WWI Casualty and Death Tables," *Public Broadcasting Service*, http://www.pbs.org/greatwar/resources/casdeath_pop.html, accessed July 6, 2014.

4. "History," *American Football in Japan*, http://www.american-football-japan.com /footballjapan-history-eng.htm, accessed January 30, 2014.

5. Russ Crawford, "The Nationalist Pastime: The Use of Baseball to Promote Nationalism Abroad," in Briley, *Politics of Baseball*, 125.

6. R. A. Smith, *Sports and Freedom*, 13.

7. R. A. Smith, *Pay for Play*, 28.

8. Wolfgang Saxon, "Curt Riess, Author and Journalist, 90; Expert on the Nazi Era," *New York Times*, May 21, 1993, B8.

9. Robert F. Kelley, "Crowley Will Sail with Team Tonight," *New York Times*, November 30, 1938, 28.

10. Robert F. Kelley, "Crowley and Squad of 24 Players Sail for Football Tour of France," *New York Times*, December 1, 1938, 30.

11. Curt Riess, "Sports and Defense," *Nation*, March 1, 1941, http://www.thenation .com/article/161963/sports-and-defense, accessed February 12, 2013.

12. Riess, "Sports and Defense."

13. Kelley, "Crowley and Squad of 24."

14. "Fordham, Still under Consideration, Hopes for Invitation to New Orleans Contest," *New York Times*, November 29, 1938, 29.

15. Maurice Prax, "Pour et contre," *Le Petit Parisien*, December 5, 1938, 1.

16. Associated Press, "American Football Players Reach France; Sell-Out Looms for First Game Saturday, *New York Times*, December 8, 1938, 37.

17. Associated Press, "American Football Players Reach France," 37.

18. Associated Press, "American Football Players Reach France,"37.

19. Ancel, or his copy editor, misidentified Coach Stevens as Martin, but his name was actually Marvin.

20. G. L. Ancel, "25 'Frankenstein' d'une souplesse et d'une precision ettonantes," *Le Petit Parisien*, December 1, 1938, 6.

21. Ancel, "25 'Frankenstein,'" 6.

22. Ancel, "25 'Frankenstein,'" 6.

23. G. L. Ancel, "Le football américain est le sport plus violent qui existe," *Le Petit Parisien*, December 2, 1938, 6; Bureau of Labor Statistics CPI Inflation Calculator, http://www.bls.gov/data/inflation_calculator.htm, accessed November 28, 2014.

24. Joosten and Crawford, "When Football Made a 'Tour de France.'"

25. George Villetan, "Voici les rugbymen américains," *Paris Soir*, December 9, 1938, 6A.

26. "Cet Après-midi au Parc des Princes" *L'Humanité*, December 10, 1938, 1.

27. "Le rugby américain," *L'Humanité*, December 10, 1938, 4.

28. "Les 'All Stars' de New~York vont donner une exhibition de rugby américain," *Le Figaro*, December 10, 1938, 10.

29. "Les 'All Stars' de New~York," 10.

30. Jean Roux, "Les ALL STARS et NEW-YORK SELECTION aux prises cet après-midi au Parc des Princes," *Le Petit Journal*, December 10, 1938, 4.

31. Jean Monest, "Les 'américain footballers' s'entraînent: Mais ils on d'autres desires," *Le Petit Parisien*, December 9, 1938, 6.

32. Monest, "Les 'américain footballers' s'entraînent," 6.

33. Monest, "Les 'américain footballers' s'entraînent," 6

34. Michael MacCambridge, in *America's Game*, argues that the tipping point in football's rise to popularity took place during the 1958 season and in particular points to the NFL Championship Game between the New York Giants and the Baltimore Colts as one of the catalysts.

35. Jean Monest, "C'est un jeu terrible athlétique spectaculaiere: Ce premier match conquerra-t-il les sportifs?," *Le Petit Parisien*, December 10, 1938, 6.

36. Joosten and Crawford, "When Football Made a 'Tour de France,'" 15.

37. "Les 'All Stars' ont battu New-York par 25 p. à 14," *Le Figaro*, December 11, 1938, 11.

38. Jean Monest, "Le nouveau jeu: 'Very exciting!' Mais s'implantera-t-il en France?," *Le Petit Parisien*, December 11, 1938, 6.

39. Roger Malher, "Nous nous sommes bien amusés," *Le Petit Parisien*, December 11, 1938, 6.

40. See Oriard, *King Football*.

41. Herman Gregoire, "Le rugby américain? Un jeu barbare!," *Le Petit Parisien*, December 11, 1938, 6.

42. Gaston Bénac, "Des épisodes de bataille," *Paris Soir*, December 11, 1938, 1.

43. Jean Roux, "Par 25 à 14 les All Stars ont défait New-York, *Le Petit Journal*, December, 11, 1938.

44. Kelley, "Crowley and Squad of 24."

45. "Les 'All Stars' ont battu New-York par 25 p. à 14."

46. Associated Press, "Parisians Liken U.S. Football to Rugby in a Bullfight Ring," *New York Times*, December 11, 1938, 95.

47. "Les 'All Stars' de New~York."

48. Robert F. Kelley, "Crowley, Back from Trip, Reports French Liked American Football," *New York Times*, January 18, 1939, 27.

49. Associated Press, "Razzle Dazzle at Lyon," *New York Times*, December 12, 1938, 23.

50. P. Martin, "A Lyon, devant 10.000 spectateurs, New-York a pris sa revanche," *Paris Soir*, December 12, 1938, 11E.

51. "Football américain a Lyon," *Le Petit Journal*, December 12, 1938, 6.

52. Curt Riess, "Après les success de Paris et de Lyon: Une ligue de rugby américain va voir le jour en France," *Paris Soir*, December 13, 6A.

53. Riess, "Après les success," 6A.

54. Raymond Vanker, "Verrons-nous des equips françaises de football américain?," *Le Petit Journal*, December 13, 1938, 8.

55. Raymond Vanker, "Le basket-ball est un sport complet: Tout le monde peut practiquer, mais il faut être doué pour devenir champion," *Le Petit Journal*, December 14, 1938, 8.

56. Georges Briquet, The Radio Reporter's Corner, *Le Petit Parisien*, December 13, 1938, 6.

57. Jean Monest, "C'est fait: Jean Galia est 'debarque' de la Ligue," *Le Petite Parisien*, December 13, 1938, 6.

58. Monest, "C'est fait," 6.

59. M.C. "Quand le bateau sombre," *Le Figaro*, December 13, 1938, 8.

60. "New-York Selection bat All Stars, 34 pts à 33, *Le Petit Journal*, December 18, 1938, 8.

61. Associated Press, "15,000 in France See Crowley's Stars Win," *New York Times*, December 19, 1938, 27.

62. Joosten and Crawford, "When Football Made a 'Tour de France," 17.

63. Kelley, "Crowley, Back from Trip."

64. Raymond Vanker, "Verrons-nous des equips françaises de football américain?," *Le Petit Journal*, December 13, 1938, 8.

65. "New-York bat les All Stars," *Paris Soir*, December 19, 1938, 11E.

66. Associated Press, "5,000 See U.S. Elevens," *New York Times*, December 25, 1938, 60.

67. Associated Press, "Football Exhibitions End," *New York Times*, December 26, 1938, 31.

68. J.M., "L'Italie voudrait voir le football américain," *Le Petit Parisien*, December 20, 1938, 6.

69. Kelley, "Crowley, Back from Trip."

70. Kelley, "Crowley, Back from Trip," 27.

71. Wakefield, *Playing to Win*, 89.

3. *Football and the Crusade in Europe*

1. Wakefield, *Playing to Win*, 87.

2. *FM 28–105*, 6.

3. Ambrose, *Band of Brothers*, 234.

4. Jones, *Football! Navy! War!*, 107.

5. Jack O'Sullivan, "The Service Teams," *Football Illustrated Annual*, 1944, 52.

6. John Hibner, "The First Arab Bowl," College Football Historical Society, August 1992, 10, http://library.la84.org/SportsLibrary/CFHSN/CFHSNv05/CFHSNv05n4a.pdf, accessed August 24, 2014.

7. Paul Horowitz, "9th AF Eleven Wins Paris Tilt," *Stars and Stripes*, November 20, 1944, 6.

8. The Question Box, *Stars and Stripes*, November 6, 1944, 17.

9. "Navy Medics Tip Ramblers," *Stars and Stripes*, October 27, 1944, 3.

10. Paul Horowitz, "16 GI Football Squads Bid for Normandy Honors," *Stars and Stripes*, November 15, 1944, 6.

11. Jim Harrigan, "Army Tops Navy, 13–6, Behind Wayne's Passes," *Stars and Stripes*, November 24, 1944, 3.

12. "Grid Winners to Clash in Paris Tomorrow," *Stars and Stripes*, November 25, 1944, 23.

13. "Port Officers Rip Navy Gridders," 31–0, *Stars and Stripes*, December 4, 1944, 17.

14. "Thunderbolts Win 4th, 13–2," *Stars and Stripes*, December 11, 1944, 17; "9th AF Hqs. Wins," *Stars and Stripes*, December 11, 1944, 17.

15. "Unbeaten Elevens in Xmas Day Games," *Stars and Stripes*, December 25, 1944, 7.

16. "Port Teams Meet This Afternoon at City Stadium," *Stars and Stripes*, December 25, 1944, 7.

17. Paul Horowitz, "Crowley to 'Sell' New Pro Grid Loop," *Stars and Stripes*, December 25, 1944, 7.

18. "Changes in Paris Game," *Stars and Stripes*, December 31, 1944, 7.

19. "400,000 Expected at Bowl Contests," *Stars and Stripes*, January 1, 1945, 6.

20. Jim Harrigan, "30,000 Fans Expected at Riviera Bowl Game," *Stars and Stripes*, January 1, 1945, 1.

21. "Riviera Bowl Result," *Stars and Stripes*, January 2, 1945, 14.

22. "Twin Bill at Dijon," *Stars and Stripes*, January 2, 1945, 14.

23. "'Cloggers Win Mud Bowl, 7–6," *Stars and Stripes*, January 6, 1945, 6.

24. "Stevedores Win Football Game in Cherbourg, 2–0," *Stars and Stripes*, January 6, 1945, 6.

25. "Negro Ace Leads 5th Army to 'Italy Bowl' Win," *Daily Worker*, January 2, 1945, 10.

26. "Undefeated GI Teams to Play," *Stars and Stripes*, January 6, 1945, 6.

27. "GI Game Called Off," *Stars and Stripes*, January 8, 1945, 6.

28. "SHAEF Invaders Edge 'Cloggers, 2–0," *Stars and Stripes*, January 15, 1945, 6.

29. "Paris Elevens Will Try Again," *Stars and Stripes*, January 20, 1945, 6.

30. "Fifth Quarter Tally Decides for 2nd AADA," *Stars and Stripes*, January 22, 1945, 6.

31. "ETO Sports Program Released; GI Olympics to Mark Competition," *Stars and Stripes*, May 11, 1945, 3.

32. "Progress Report," Theater Service Forces European Theater, November 1945, 140, http://www.fold3.com/document/289092225/, accessed May 26, 2014.

33. "Oise Elevens Open Season Tomorrow," *Stars and Stripes*, October 5, 1945, 6.

34. "Four Grid Games on Seine Schedule," *Stars and Stripes*, October 10, 1945, 7; Robert W. Rydell and Rob Kroes, *Buffalo Bill in Bologna: The Americanization of the World, 1869–1922*, http://press.uchicago.edu/Misc/Chicago/732428.html, accessed September 1, 2014.

35. "Villacoublay Bows to Seine Section Ordnance," *Stars and Stripes*, October 1, 1945, 6.

36. "Joe Diehl, Seine Clowns, Delta Tangle Here in Loop Tilt Tomorrow," *Stars and Stripes*, October 20, 1945, 6.

37. "Turkey Day for GI Gobblers," *Stars and Stripes*, November 22, 1945, 1.

38. "Mules Trounce 89th in Final Quarter," *Stars and Stripes*, October 1, 1945, 6.

39. "101st Airborne Beats 89th Div., 7–0," *Stars and Stripes*, October 8, 1945, 12.

40. "516th Port Bn. Defeats Le Havre Eleven, 13–6," *Stars and Stripes*, November 23, 1945, 6.

41. "Red Devils Steamroller Camp Washington, 36–9," *Stars and Stripes*, November 24, 1945, 14.

42. Bill Howard, "Atomites Beaten by FA Rally," *Stars and Stripes*, December 16, 1945, 6.

43. Bill Howard, "Today's Victor Goes to Rome Bowl Contest," *Stars and Stripes*, December 15, 1945, 6.

44. Jim Eathorne, "Seine, Delta, Chanor Rule All-TSFET Eleven," *Stars and Stripes*, November 24, 1945, 6.

45. "DeGaulle Tells Yanks Goodbye," *Stars and Stripes*, November 13, 1945, 3.

46. "Reaction Mixed in Washington to GI Protests," *Stars and Stripes*, January 11, 1946, 8.

47. "Seine and Oise Sections Merge," *Stars and Stripes*, January 11, 1946, 8.

48. Dave Reznek, "ET Kickoff," *Stars and Stripes*, September 8, 1946, v.

49. "ET Grid Conference Disbanded by USFET," *Stars and Stripes*, September 20, 1946, 9.

50. Gene Levin, "508th Troopers Wallop WBS," *Stars and Stripes*, September 30, 1946, 11.

51. Bill Boni, "Slant on Sports," *Stars and Stripes*, September 21, 1946, 10.

52. Gene Levin, "Close Rivalry to Be on Tap in WBS Loop," *Stars and Stripes*, September 20, 1946, 10; "WBS League Set to Open Grid Season," *Stars and Stripes*, September 21, 1946, 11.

53. "Rheims Rams Win WBS Grid Title, Keep Slate Clean," *Stars and Stripes*, November 11, 1946, 9.

54. The United States observed Armistice Day until 1947, when the name was changed to Veterans Day.

55. William Barry Furlong, "How the War in France Changed Football Forever," *Smithsonian*, February 1986, 125–37.

56. Furlong, "How the War in France Changed Football Forever."

4. Football in the Cold

1. Jones, *Football, Navy, War!*, 63.

2. McAuliffe, *U.S. Air Force in France*, 11.

3. Barney Gill, Chuck Bristol, Russ Mericle, Dave Madril, and others, phone interviews by the author, Ada OH, 2011 and 2012.

4. David Newhouse, phone interview by the author, Ada OH, July 27, 2012.

5. "Conference Standings," *Stars and Stripes*, November 1, 1956, 20.

6. "Final Conference Standings," *Stars and Stripes*, December 2, 1954, 20.

7. "Captieux Ammunition Depot," *U.S. Army in Germany*, http://www.usarmygermany .com/Sont.htm?http&&&www.usarmygermany.com/Units/ArmyDepots/USAREUR _Ordnance%20depots.htm, accessed November 29, 2014.

8. "USAEUR, USAFE, Prep Standings," *Stars and Stripes*, October, 6, 1961, 21.

9. Bernard A. Gill, telephone interview by the author, Ada OH , November 10, 2011.

10. "1955 Conference Standings Report," *Stars and Stripes*, November 12, 1955, 20.

11. *Le Troyen Yearbook*, 1967, 43, http://www.orleansamericanhighschool .com/1967%20YEARBOOK.htm, accessed December 29, 2013.

12. Airman 2nd Class Earl Sweatt, "Senior Girls Dump Juniors in Puff Game," Châteauroux American High School, http://www.chateaurouxamericanhighschool .com/Sports/Football/Powder%20puff%20-%20adamek.jpg, accessed November 29, 2014.

13. Greg Apkarian, "Memories of Dreux," Dreux American High School, Dreux, France, http://www.dreuxalumni.org/Memories%20of%20dreux.htm, accessed August 7, 2013.

14. Dick Mullins, telephone interview by the author, Ada OH, March 9, 2012; Bureau of Labor Statistics CPI Inflation Calculator, http://www.bls.gov/data/inflation _calculator.htm, accessed August 7, 2013.

15. "USA Today Sports' College Athletics Finances," *USA Today*, http://www.usatoday .com/sports/college/schools/finances/, accessed August 7, 2013.

16. "Historical Inflation Rates: 1914–2013," U.S. Inflation Calendar, http://www .usinflationcalculator.com/inflation/historical-inflation-rates/, accessed August 14, 2013.

17. McAuliffe, *U.S. Air Force in France*, 16.

18. McAuliffe, *U.S. Air Force in France*, 1.

19. "Mules Annex USAFE Title," *Stars and Stripes*, December 4, 1950, 10.

20. Bullets Clash with Toul in USAFE Grid," *Stars and Stripes*, November 27, 1952, 10.

21. "1952 USAFE Football Record," *Stars and Stripes*, November 30, 1952, 11; "Burtonwood Blanks Toul, Gains USAFE Finals," *Stars and Stripes*, December 1, 1952, 10.

22. Barnaby Feder, "NFL Is a Hit with British," *New York Times*, August 7, 1983, S1.

23. "NFL London," *American Football at Wembley Stadium*, http://www.nfllondon.net /history.html, accessed August 13, 2013.

24. United Press International, "Grid Deaths Show Sharp Drop in 1st Half of Season," *Stars and Stripes*, November 8, 1955, 20.

25. Sterling Slappey, "'Jolly Good' Say British of Yank Football," *Stars and Stripes*, December 15, 1952, 9.

26. eggs67, "25/5/86–BAFL Anglo Week 4–Luton Flyers at Medway Mustangs," *Luton Flyers Archive*, May 30, 2013, http://lutonflyersarchive.wordpress.com /2013/05/30/25586-bafl-anglo-week-4-luton-flyers-at-medway-mustangs/, accessed August 13, 2013.

27. "Démonstration de football américain," Institut national de l'audiovisuel, http://www.ina.fr/video/AFE85004870, accessed April 22, 2014.

28. Gill interview.

29. Jerry Curtright, "The General's Yellow Flag," *Laon Ranger*, furnished by Jerry Buranski, editor, via email, January 6, 2012.

30. "Wilkinson to Head EC Grid Clinic Staff," *Stars and Stripes*, May 8, 1952, 10.

31. Mariana Gosnell, "When Airplanes Had Beds," *Air and Space*, January 2013, http://www.airspacemag.com/history-of-flight/when-airplanes-had-beds -125048102/?no-ist, accessed August 13, 2013.

32. "Charles B. 'Bud' Wilkinson," Nixon Presidential Library & Museum, http:// www.nixonlibrary.gov/forresearchers/find/textual/central/smof/wilkinson.php, accessed August 13, 2013.

33. Bureau of Labor Statistics CPI Inflation Calculator, http://www.bls.gov/data /inflation_calculator.htm, accessed August 13, 2013.

34. "Nick Saban Speaker Profile," *Sports Speakers 360*, http://www.sportsspeakers360 .com/speaker/nick-saban.php, accessed August 13, 2013.

35. BLS Inflation Calculator.

36. Vince Mullaby, "Solem Advocates 'Driving-Type' Coaching," *Stars and Stripes*, July 17, 2013, 11; BLS Inflation Calculator.

37. "EUCOM Grid Clinic Gets Underway Today," *Stars and Stripes*, July 14, 1952, 10.

38. Earlier I posited perhaps $190 million to run the league for seventeen years, so this number is one-third of the total, since French teams made up approximately one-third of the teams.

39. United Press International, "Senators Block Funds for Bases Pending Review," *Stars and Stripes*, December 30, 1952, 1.

40. "The General," Eisenhower Foundation, http://www.eisenhowerfoundation.net /general.html, accessed October 5, 2013.

41. "Forces Sportscasts Score with Senator," *Stars and Stripes*, June 18, 1954, 1.

42. Douglas Jennings, "Multimillion-Dollar USFA Project to Develop Support Comd at Leghorn Nears Completion," *Stars and Stripes*, May 29, 1954, 9.

43. "Isolated Captieux Boasts Top Facilities," *Stars and Stripes*, April 4, 1956, 10.

44. Ken Thrash, phone interview by the author, Ada OH, July 23, 2012.

45. "Daugherty to Teach USAFE Grid Clinic," *Stars and Stripes*, May 3, 1958, 31; Steve Lakos, "Coaches Devaney, Galloway Have Lot in Common—Especially Good Records," *Stars and Stripes*, July 19, 1962.

46. "Pro Football Standouts Arrive for USAFE Clinic," *Stars and Stripes*, June 19, 1964, 21.

47. "5 Skins' Gridders to Bulwark Staff for USAFE Clinic," *Stars and Stripes*, June 17, 1965, 21.

48. George Eberl, "Cooperman: A Man with a Message," *Stars and Stripes*, June 22, 1965, 21.

49. Larry Kaufman, "Raiders Clinch Trip to London," *Stars and Stripes*, November 22, 1953, 12; "Year by Year Leaders," *Mizzou Tigers Athletics*, http://www.mutigers .com/auto_pdf/p_hotos/s_chools/miss/sports/m-footbl/auto_pdf/yby-stat -leaders, accessed August 14, 2013.

50. Don Walter, "Verdun Crushes Rams, 46–18 for Com Z Title," *Stars and Stripes*, November 9, 1953, 12.

51. "Les Premiers pas du foot us, en France," *Elitefoot*, http://www.elitefoot.com /france/archives/60th/histoire.htm, accessed August 16, 2013.

52. Facebook post that has since disappeared.

53. Author's name illegible, *Stars and Stripes*, November 13, 1953, 13.

54. Don Walter, "Frenchmen Happy, Puzzled over 'Le Football Américain,'" *Stars and Stripes*, November 13, 1953, 13.

55. "La Rochelle Wins; Poitiers Triumphs," *Stars and Stripes*, September 23, 1953, 14.

56. "French Carry Ball for Com Z Grid Display," *Stars and Stripes*, December 18, 1953, 9.

57. Seymour Freidin and William Richardson, "Le Football Américain as She Is Played by the Daring Combatants of Paris," *Toledo Blade*, November 24, 1953, 16.

58. "Troops Blast Cards, 52–13, to Gain Quarterfinal Win," *Stars and Stripes*, November 15, 1953, 12.

59. Gill interview.

60. Gill interview.

61. "Donald Hemphill Obituary," *Topeka Capital-Journal*, October 2012, http://www.legacy.com/obituaries/cjonline/obituary.aspx?pid=160538674, accessed August 16, 2013.

62. Larry Kolber, "Red Birds Hold Com Z's Hopes," *Stars and Stripes*, November 13, 1953, 13.

63. Greg Kleven, "Shorty Cochran Taught Life Lessons," *Minnesota Sun Current*, August 13, 2013 http://current.mnsun.com/2013/08/kleven-column-shorty-cochran-taught-life-lessons/, accessed August 16, 2013.

64. "Three League Titles at Stake in USAFE Grid Games Today," *Stars and Stripes*, November 6, 1954, 21.

65. Jack Blood, "Chaumont, London Clash for USAFE Grid Title Today," *Stars and Stripes*, November 27, 1954, 18.

66. "Versatile Backs Use Speed, Power, in Dynamic Attack," *Stars and Stripes*, November 18, 1954, 20.

67. "Parelli Leads Rabat to Touch Crown," *Stars and Stripes*, November 11, 1955, 21.

68. "USAFE Grid Championship Tilt at Chaumont," *Stars and Stripes*, November 30, 1954, 20.

69. Don Walter, "Jordan, Retzlaff TDs Lead Vans to 12–0 Victory over Croix-Chapeau," *Stars and Stripes*, November 15, 1954, 20.

70. Bill Duren, "London Rockets Blast Evreux in USAFE Semis," *Stars and Stripes*, November 21, 1955, 21.

71. "Flyers Smash Normans, 31–6," *Stars and Stripes*, November 26, 1955, 21.

72. "'55 Ghibli Bowl Tilt Set Today in Tripoli," *Stars and Stripes*, November 24, 1955, 21.

73. Victoria Giraud, "American Football Libyan Style—in the Sand," *Words on My Mind*, http://www.victoria4edit.com/blog/?p=587, December 7, 2011, http://www.victoria4edit.com/blog/?p=587, accessed September 2, 2013.

74. Bill Pilkenton, "Passer Spears Runs Wild as Redlegs Erase Meuse," *Stars and Stripes*, November 15, 1955, 21.

75. "Croix-Chapeau Wins Basec Touch Tourney," *Stars and Stripes*, November 11, 1955, 20.

76. "NACom to Meet HACom in Benefit Grid Tilt Sunday," *Stars and Stripes*, September 16, 1955, 20.

77. Chuck Quernan, "Monnet Paces Pioneers to 20–7 Northern Triumph, NACom Clips HACom, 13–0, on Chmarra's 2 TD Passes," *Stars and Stripes*, September 19, 1955, 20.

78. Leo Levine, "High Scoring Toul Tigers Eye USAFE Tilt," *Stars and Stripes*, November 21, 1956, 20.

79. "Shrimp Bowl Bound Jets Top AF Grid 11 This Year," *Galveston Daily News*, December 10, 1959, 20.

80. "Special Regular and Postseason Games," *National Collegiate Athletic Association*, http://fs.ncaa.org/Docs/stats/football_records/d2/2010/SpecialGames.pdf, accessed August 31, 2013.

81. "Quantico Great Maj. King Dixon Returns as Head Football Coach," *Fredericksburg (VA) Free Lance-Star*, April 3 1968, 20.

82. Doug Moore, "Phantoms, R-M Vie for USAFE Title," *Stars and Stripes*, November 23, 1969, 25; Ben Abrams, "USAFE Sports Program Loses One of Its Big Guns, *Stars and Stripes*, May 27, 1970, 25.

83. Doug Moore, "Bettez Says Entertainment Should Be the Goal in Sports," *Stars and Stripes*, October 11, 1969, 25.

84. George Eberl, "Gil Bettez Not Ready to Fade Away," *Stars and Stripes*, February 3, 1981, 25.

85. "Sports History 101: 1958 NFL Championship By The Numbers," Press Box, http://www.pressboxonline.com/story/1537/sports-history-101-1958-nfl-championship-by-the-numbers, accessed September 1, 2013.

86. Jack Ellis, "Toul Nips Flyers for USAFE Title, 20–19, *Stars and Stripes*, November 17, 1957, 21.

87. Gabe Buonauro, "Tigers Trip SHAPE, 16–14," *Stars and Stripes*, November 18, 1957, 20.

88. Stan Swift, "Sembach at Work," *Sembach Veterans*, http://www.sembachveterans.org/workers31.htm, accessed September 1, 2013.

89. Jack Ellis, "Flaks Top Orleans, 20–7; Enter Finals," *Stars and Stripes*, November 18, 1957, 21.

90. Gary Smith, "Blindsided by History," *Sports Illustrated*, April 9, 2007, http://www.si.com/vault/2007/04/09/8404477/blindsided-by-history, accessed September 1, 2013.

91. Morris J. MacGregor, Jr., *Integration of the Armed Forces, 1940–1965*, (Washington DC: Center of Military History United States Army, 1985), 291; Associated Press, "Military Strength to Remain at 3,600,000," *Stars and Stripes*, December 16, 1952, 2.

92. Chuck Bristol, phone interview by the author, Ada OH , December 29, 2011.

93. Thrash interview.

94. Swift, "Sembach at Work."

95. "Conference Football Standings," *Stars and Stripes*, November 20, 1958, 20.

96. Jack Ellis, "Rams Top Laon, 30–8, for USAFE Crown," *Stars and Stripes*, November 23, 1958, 20.

97. Swift, "Sembach at Work."

98. Ellis, "Rams Top Laon."

99. Swift, "Sembach at Work."

100. "USAFE Football Staff Due to Arrive Sunday," *Stars and Stripes*, July 4, 1958, 20.

101. Thrash interview; Swift, "Sembach at Work."

102. "Flaks, Broncos Open USAREUR Playoffs," *Stars and Stripes*, November 23, 1958, 22.

103. Jack Ellis, "Flaks Beat Broncos, 22–13, to Gain Semis," *Stars and Stripes*, November 24, 1958, 21.

104. Jack Ellis, "Wiesbaden Tops Laon, 17–0," *Stars and Stripes*, November 22, 1959, 20.

105. Mike Lucas, "Braves Scalp Orioles 33–14, Gain USAREUR Finals," *Stars and Stripes*, November 23, 1959, 20.

106. "Braves' Sorta Small Seven Ready for Orleans in Semis," *Stars and Stripes*, November 20, 1959, 21.

107. Lucas, "Braves Scalp Orioles 33–14," 21.

5. Rise and Fall of French Teams

1. Gary Ruegsegger, "Yesterday's Still Here for Class of 1948," *Virginia Pilot*, July 1, 2008, http://hamptonroads.com/2008/06/yesterdays-still-here-class-1948, accessed March 3, 2013.

2. Gary Ruegsegger, "When Racial Barriers Fell in 1947," *Downtowner*, September 2010, 7, http://www.downtowneronline.com/archives/DT092010.pdf, accessed March 3, 2013.

3. Bernard A. Gill, telephone interview by the author, Ada OH, 10 November 10, 2011.

4. "Camp Polk Wins Title," *Stilwell (OK) Democrat*, December 21, 1950, 1.

5. Bob Wicker, "Coaching Staffs Play Vital Role in Freedom Bowl," *Stars and Stripes*, December 7, 1961, 21.

6. Gill interview.

7. Joseph Sheehan, "Army Eleven Launches Space Man," *New York Times*, October 1, 1958, 47.

8. Tony Germanotta, "Whatever Happened to . . . MacArthur's Football Watching Pal?," *Virginian-Pilot*, October 9, 2006, http://hamptonroads.com/node/165161, accessed February 5, 2013.

9. Gill interview.

10. Gill Interview.

11. Bob Wicker, "France Loop Title Hinges on Indians-Ranger Skirmish," *Stars and Stripes*, October 28, 1960, 20.

12. Bob Wicker, "Indians Shape Up USAFE Grid Playoff War Party," *Stars and Stripes*, November 9, 1960, 21.

13. Russ Mericle, telephone interview by the author, Ada OH, January 9, 2011.

14. Gill interview.

15. Mike Lucas, "USAFE Football Finalists Lauded by SHAPE Scout," *Stars and Stripes*, November 19, 1959, 21.

16. Mike Lucas, "Titan Coach Brigman Sees Tribe Romp against Flyers," *Stars and Stripes*, November 13, 1960, 20.

17. "SHAPE Aides Get Only Rare Look at Indians in Action," *Stars and Stripes*, November 9, 1960, 21.

18. Lucas, "Titan Coach Brigman."

19. "SHAPE Aides Get Only Rare Look."

20. Wicker, "France Loop Title."

21. Bob Wicker, "SHAPE Rips Laon for France Loop Title," *Stars and Stripes*, November 1, 1960, 20; Bob Wicker, "Wiesbaden, SHAPE Reach USAFE Finals," *Stars and Stripes*, November 13, 1960, 20.

22. Jack Ellis, "Wiesbaden Tops Laon, 17–0," *Stars and Stripes*, November 22, 1959, 20.

23. Bob Wicker, " Tribe on Warpath Keeps Romano Awake 2 Weeks," *Stars and Stripes*, November 19, 1960, 20.

24. "AFN to Air 3 Playoffs," *Stars and Stripes*, November 15, 1960, 21.

25. Jack Ellis, "Indians Beat Flyers, 11–0, for USAFE Title," *Stars and Stripes*, November 20, 1960, 20.

26. "Romano Takes Blame for 'Decision,'" *Stars and Stripes*, November 20, 1960, 20.

27. Ellis, "Indians Beat Flyers."

28. Associated Press, "284,000 U.S. Dependents Ordered to Return Home," *Stars and Stripes*, November 17, 1960, 1.

29. Jack Ellis, "Mainz Routs Ulm, 34–0, for USAREUR Title," *Stars and Stripes*, November 27, 1960, 20.

30. "Freedom Bowl Gate Slated for Relief Fund," *Stars and Stripes*, November 16, 1960, 22.

31. United Press International, "Rusk Calls Berlin Wall a Symbol of Red Failure," *Stars and Stripes*, November 19, 1961, 1.

32. "USAREUR–USAFE Grid Playoff Set Dec. 4," *Stars and Stripes*, October 20, 1960, 24.

33. "USAREUR–USAFE Grid Playoff Set Dec. 4."

34. Robert Hoyer, "Troopers Taking Target Practice," *Stars and Stripes*, November 24, 1960, 21.

35. Gill interview. (For confirmation of Gill's assertions, see Bob Wicker, "Ex-Jumper Gill Respects Mainz Game Pits Blaik Students, Too," *Stars and Stripes*, December 2, 1960, 20.)

36. Bob Wicker, "Troopers Call Off Contact Work France Fans Rally to Back Indians," *Stars and Stripes*, December 1, 1960, 20.

37. Mike Lucas, "USAFE Football Finalists Lauded by SHAPE Scout," *Stars and Stripes*, November 19, 1959, 21.

38. Gill interview.

39. "Freedom Bowl Proceeds Given to German Relief," *Stars and Stripes*, January 7, 1961, 2.

40. Jack Ellis, "Mainz Tips Indians, 10–0, in Freedom Bowl . . . Runs Win String to 21 on 2nd Half Surge," *Stars and Stripes*, December 5, 1960, 20–21.

41. United Press International, "New Orleans Police Block Hecklers at Frantz School," *Stars and Stripes*, December 9, 1960, 2

42. Josh Gerstein, "Norman Rockwell Painting Sends Rare White House Message on Race," *Politico*, August 24, 2011, http://www.politico.com/news/stories/0811/61677 .html, accessed October 14, 2013.

43. Based on photo accompanying "Troopers Battle Indians in First Freedom Bowl Today," *Stars and Stripes*, December 4, 1960, 20.

44. See Crawford, *Use of Sport*, 213–33, for discussion of similar press reaction to Jackie Robinson's entry into MLB.

45. Bob Wicker, "Orleans Optimistic over USAREUR Title Chances," *Stars and Stripes*, November 16, 1960, 20.

46. "Gregg Says Conditioning Important Football Factor," *Stars and Stripes*, November 11, 1960, 20.

47. Bob Wicker, "Hawks Subdue Knights, 21–6, Reach USAREUR Finals," *Stars and Stripes*, November 21, 1960, 21.

48. "9 Knights Boast Experience with Collegiate Grid Teams," *Stars and Stripes*, November 11, 1960, 20.

49. "Châteauroux Preps Rip Torrejón," *Stars and Stripes*, November 12, 1960, 22.

50. Keith, *Forty-Seven Straight*, 317.

51. "Oklahoma 19, Florida State 36," *SoonerStats*, http://www.soonerstats .com/football/games/recap.cfm?GameID=616#.VGjiHJRdV14, accessed October 15, 2013.

52. Gill interview.

53. "Final Conference Standings," *Stars and Stripes*, November 11, 1961, 20.

54. Bob Wicker, "Rocket-Indian 'Grudge' Tilt Resolves European Conference Championship," *Stars and Stripes*, November 10, 1961, 20.

55. "SHAPE Forfeits to Rhine-Main, Ramstein to Wiesbaden," *Stars and Stripes*, October 7, 1961, 20.

56. Wicker, "Rocket-Indian 'Grudge' Tilt Resolves European Conference Championship," 20.

57. "SHAPE, Berlin Clash in Paris Exhibition," *Stars and Stripes*, November 3, 1961, 20.

58. Bob Wicker, "SHAPE Toys with Berlin, 42–6," *Stars and Stripes*, November 6, 1961, 21.

59. Bob Wicker, "SHAPE Beats Rhine-Main, 13–3," *Stars and Stripes*, November 12, 1961, 21.

60. Bob Wicker, "Laon Beats Spang, 11–0, for Continental Title," *Stars and Stripes*, November 5, 1961, 21.

61. Mike Lucas, "Falconbury Nips Loan in Overtime USAFE Final, *Stars and Stripes*, November 19, 1961, 21.

62. Jerry Curtright, "The General's Yellow Flag," *Laon Ranger*, furnished by Jerry Buranski, editor, via email on January 6, 2012.

63. Spencer Baxter, "SHAPE Takes 39–12 Toll on Alconbury," *Stars and Stripes*, November 26, 1961, 21.

64. Bob Wicker and Leo Levine, "Coaching Staffs Play a Vital Role in Freedom Bowl," *Stars and Stripes*, December 7, 1961, 21; Bob Wicker, "Freedom Bowl Teams Hone Down to 35-Player Limit for Big Game," *Stars and Stripes*, December 8, 1961, 20; "Freedom Bowl Stars Mix in Charity Game Today," *Stars and Stripes*, December 9, 1961, 21.

65. See also McAuliffe, *U.S. Air Force in France*, 77.

66. "1961 Freedom Bowl Program," printed by the *Heidelberg Post*, December 9, 1961, 3.

67. "1961 Freedom Bowl Program," 3.

68. Crawford, *Use of Sport*, 198.

69. Wicker and Levine, "Coaching Staffs."

70. "Freedom Bowl Stars."

71. "Individual Statistics," *Stars and Stripes*, December 10, 1961, 21.

72. Bob Wicker, "Gill Looking Forward to 'Seeing Flint Rotate,'" *Stars and Stripes*, December 10, 1961, 21.

73. "World of Sports," *Stars and Stripes*, December 17, 1961, 7.

74. "Tickets on Sale at Gates," *Stars and Stripes*, December 7, 1961, 21.

75. "Troop Facilities Get Top Priority," *Stars and Stripes*, December 13, 1961, 1.

76. "SHAPE Five Whips French 79–66, to Capture Tournament," *Stars and Stripes*, December 20, 1961, 20.

77. "SHAPE Cagers Whip France in Christmas Tourney, 73–65," *Stars and Stripes*, December 16, 1961, 20; "French Army Five Stuns SHAPE to Prolong Tourney'" *Stars and Stripes*, December 18, 1961, 20.

78. "SHAPE Five Whips French 79–66."

79. "32nd Regiment Marksmanship School Makes Trained Snipers," *Stars and Stripes*, June 18, 1952, 18; Rod Powers, "Army Sniper School," US Military About.com, http://www.usmilitary.about.com, accessed December 27, 2013.

80. United Press International, "3 Americans Sneak by Rebel Lines in Congo, Tell of Government Gains," *Stars and Stripes*, September 26, 1964, 3.

81. Mericle interview.

82. "Indians Win, Tie for USAREUR Grid Title," *Stars and Stripes*, November 11, 1962, 21.

83. "Cards Trim Rangers for 15th in Row," *Stars and Stripes*, December 12, 1962, 20.

84. Jack Ellis, "Indians, Lions Will Clash for Title Sunday," *Stars and Stripes*, November 27, 1962, 21.

85. "2 Key Halfbacks Ailing for Playoff Contest," *Stars and Stripes*, November 28, 1962, 21; "Lions, Indians Clash Today in USAREUR Playoff," *Stars and Stripes*, December 2, 1962, 21.

86. "Shilling, Gill Vary on Showdown Tilt," *Stars and Stripes*, November 28, 1962, 21.

87. Jack Ellis, "Lions Rip Tribe, 34–12, for USAREUR Title," *Stars and Stripes*, December 3, 1962, 20.

88. Bob Wicker, "South Opens Ulm Camp, Shilling Maps Strategy," *Stars and Stripes*, December 8, 1962, 21.

89. Jack Ellis, "North, South All-Star 11s Clash in Scholarship Bowl," *Stars and Stripes*, December 8, 1962, 20.

90. "South All-Star Roster," *Stars and Stripes*, December 8, 1962, 21.

91. "European High School Football Roundup," *Stars and Stripes*, October 10, 1962, 21.

92. "Dreux Blanks Orleans," *Le Troyen Yearbook*, http://glitzandglitterboutique.com/1964leTroyenYearbook/page98.html, accessed December 29, 2013.

93. Klint Johnson, "Corps Crucial Highlights USAREUR Season Windup," *Stars and Stripes*, November 14, 1964, 20.

94. "Final 1964 USAFE Football Records," *Stars and Stripes*, November 28, 1964, 21.

95. Coach Nyholm, "Football on the Way," *Le Troyen Yearbook*, 1966, 74, http://www.orleansamericanhighschool.com/1966%20YEARBOOK.htm, accessed December 29, 2013.

96. *Le Troyen Yearbook*, 1967, 43, http://www.orleansamericanhighschool.com/1967%20YEARBOOK.htm, accessed December 29, 2013.

6. *Postwar Tours, 1961–1976*

1. Rose, *The Dispossessed*, 139.

2. Eichberg, Nauright, and Parrish, *Sports around the World*, 421.

3. T. G. Smith, *Showdown*.

4. See MacCambridge, *America's Game*.

5. Bernard A. Gill, telephone interview by the author, Ada OH, November 10, 2011.

6. Christian Montaignac, " Le grand coup d'essai du football américain," *L'Équipe*, June 15, 1976, 2.

7. Marcel Hansenne, "A la glorie du rugby," *Martigues Rugby*, http://martigues.rugby13.free.fr/RUGBYCHAMPAGNE.txt, accessed December 13, 2014.

8. Associated Press, "Le football américain tente sa chance," *L'Équipe*, December 13, 1961, 5.

9. Jean Lacour, "Le football américain: Toulouse et Perpignan vont tenter d'y comprendre quelque chose," *L'Équipe*, December 15, 1961, 12.

10. "Lacour, "Le football américain, 12."

11. "The Pause That Arouses," *Time*, March 13, 1950, http://content.time.com/time /magazine/article/0,9171,812138–1,00.html, accessed December 6, 2014.

12. Gill Interview.

13. Jerry Curtright, telephone interview by the author, Ada OH, January 9, 2011.

14. David Madril, telephone interview by the author, Ada OH, January 6, 2012.

15. Madril interview.

16. Madril interview.

17. Madril interview.

18. Madril interview.

19. Madril interview.

20. "Toulouse et Perpignan à l'heure du rugby américain," *La Depeche du Midi*, December 12, 1961, 10.

21. "SHAPE Indians et Rangers s'entraîneront aujourd'hui aux Minimes," *La Depeche du Midi*, December 15, 1961, 10.

22. "SHAPE Indians et Rangers," 10.

23. "Le rugby américain c'est la guerre," *La Depeche du Midi*, December 14, 1961, 11.

24. Elizabeth A. Smith and Ruth F. Malone, "'Everywhere the Soldier Will Be': Wartime Tobacco Promotion in the U.S. Military," *American Journal of Public Health*, September 2009, 1595–1602, http://www.ncbi.nlm.nih.gov/pmc/articles/ PMC2724442/, accessed March 31, 2013.

25. *SHAPE Indians Sports Program*, electronic image attachment of program in possession of Chuck Bristol, received March 12, 2012.

26. "L'équipe des 'Indians-Shape' a battu les 'Rangers,'" *La Depeche du Midi*, December 17, 1961, 15; "CPI Inflation Calculator," Bureau of Labor Statistics, http://data.bls.gov /cgi-bin/cpicalc.pl?cost1=14747.75&year1 =2014&year2=1961, accessed December 6, 2014.

27. Andre Passamar, "Le rugby américain n'a pas convaincu les toulousains," *L'Équipe*, December 18, 1961, 5.

28. My wife, Sophie, helped explain this to me.

29. Robert Daley, "Football? Merci, Non," *New York Times*, December 26, 1961, 29.

30. Daley, "Football? Merci, Non," 29.

31. Email from Robert Daley in response to a letter sent to Random House publisher, March 5, 2012.

32. Daley, "Football? Merci, Non," 29.

33. Paul Izern, "Le football américain fit bailer d'ennui le pueple catalan," *L'Équipe*, December 19, 1961, 9.

34. Izern, "Le football américain," 9.

35. Daley, "Football? Merci, Non," 29.

36. Chuck Bristol, telephone interview by the author, Ada OH , December 29, 2011.

37. Madril interview.

38. Izern, "Le football américain," 9.

39. Izern, "Le football américain," 9.

40. "U.S., French Teams Involved in Brawl," *New York Times*, March 5, 1962, 30.

41. Walt Trott, "Tickets Available for Sport Week at Sites in Paris," *Stars and Stripes*, May 19, 1972, 25.

42. Trott, "Tickets Available," 25.

43. Nancy L. Ross, "NFL Stars Fumble Ball Introducing No. 1 Sport," *Sandusky (OH) Register*, June 13, 1972, 22.

44. Trott, "Parisians Turn Out for U.S. Football," *Stars and Stripes*, May 30, 1972, 26D.

45. Trott, "Parisians Turn Out for U.S. Football," 26D.

46. Perhaps Jackson knew that he would be traded to Cleveland for the 1972 season and had some anger to work out during the game.

47. Michael Katz, "French Confounded as NFL Players Make Their Debut," *New York Times*, May 28, 1972, 81.

48. Katz, "French Confounded," 81.

49. Kelley, "Crowley Back from Trip, Reports French Liked American Football," 27; Daley, "Football? Merci, Non," 29.

50. Katz, "French Confounded," 81.

51. Walt Trott, "Frenchmen Hail U.S. Sportsfest," *Stars and Stripes*, June 2, 1972, 3.

52. John Vincour, "French Rip NFL Show," Associated Press, published in the *Montana Standard*, May 30, 1972.

53. Ron Martz, "Football Fumbles in France," *Fort Pierce (FL) News Tribune*, May 31, 1972, 15.

54. Martz, "Football Fumbles in France," 15.

55. Trott, "Parisians Turn Out for U.S. Football," 26D.

56. Trott, "Parisians Turn Out for U.S. Football," 26D.

57. Katz, "French Confounded," 81.

58. Trott, "Parisians Turn Out for U.S. Football," 26D.

59. Mark L. Ford and Massimo Foglio, "The First NFL Europe," *Coffin Corner* 27, no. 6 (2005): 3–9.

60. "NAIA Football Championship History," http://www.naia.org/fls/27900/1NAIA /SportsInfo/Championships/FB_Championship.pdf?SPSID=640523, accessed April 2, 2013.

61. "Introduce American Sport," *NAIA Newsletter & Alerts*, Fall 1976, 4.

62. George Packard, "Demi-tough," *Texas Monthly*, December 1976, 134.

63. Montaignac, " Le grand coup d'essai du football américain."

64. Gill and Mericle interviews.

65. "A and I Drops Reddies, 17–8, in Europe Opener," *Arkadelphia (AR) Siftings Herald*, June 3, 1976, 4.

66. "European Tour Itinerary for Henderson Announced," *(AR) Arkadelphia Siftings Herald*, May 25, 1976; Baker, *When Lightning Struck the Outhouse*, 212.

67. "Homecoming Rekindles Memories of 1976 European Tour," press release by Texas A&M Kingsville-Javelinas, website currently inactive, accessed April 4, 2013.

68. Baker, *When Lightning Struck the Outhouse*, 204.

69. "Jav Gridders Embark on European Tour," *Harlingen (TX) Valley Morning Star*, May 29, 1976, B4.

70. "Associated Press Reports Games between State Teams," *Arkadelphia (AR) Siftings Herald*, June 7, 1976.

71. Baker, *When Lightning Struck the Outhouse*, 205.

72. Baker, *When Lightning Struck the Outhouse*, 210.

73. "Introduce American Sport," 4.

74. Dan Synovec, "Intercontinental Football League to Fill Slate with Six Teams in 1977," *Stars and Stripes*, June 11, 1976, 30.

75. Synovec, "Intercontinental Football League," 30.

76. Packard, "Demi-tough," 134.

77. Synovec, "Intercontinental Football League," 30.

78. Montaignac, "Le grand coup d'essai du football américain."

79. Auclair, *Cantona*.

80. Montaignac, "Le grand coup d'essai du football américain."

81. Dan Synovec, "Busing Foul-Up: 2 College Grid Teams Stuck in Nürnberg Say Sponsor Failed to Pay for the Trip to Paris," *Stars and Stripes*, June 16, 1976, 2.

82. Packard, "Demi-tough," 134.

83. Packard, "Demi-tough," 136.

84. Baker, *When Lightning Struck the Outhouse*, 206.

85. Baker, *When Lightning Struck the Outhouse*, 215–16.

86. Packard, "Demi-tough," 134.

87. Baker, *When Lightning Struck the Outhouse*, 216.

88. Baker, *When Lightning Struck the Outhouse*, 138.

89. Baker, *When Lightning Struck the Outhouse*, 138.

90. "Javs Impressed with Trip," *Brownsville (TX) Herald*, June 24, 1976, 3B.

91. Bill Sutley, "Globetrotting 'Sporty' Glad to Be Home," *Arkadelphia (AR) Siftings Herald*, June 23, 1976, 4.

92. *United Press International*, "Javs Wind Up Series Sweep With Paris," *Brownsville (TX) Herald*, June 18, 1976, 2B.

93. Baker, *When Lightning Struck the Outhouse*, 214.

94. "Javs Impressed with Trip," 3B.

95. Baker, *When Lightning Struck the Outhouse*, 110.

96. Dan Synovec, "Brother Bob Plays Key Role at Henderson St.," *Stars and Stripes*, June 16, 1976, 25; Baker, *When Lightning Struck the Outhouse*, 215.

97. Baker, *When Lightning Struck the Outhouse*, 82.

98. Baker, *When Lightning Struck the Outhouse*, 82.

99. Baker, *When Lightning Struck the Outhouse*, 216.

100. Bill Hart, "Football in Europe," *Abilene (TX) Reporter-News*, June 26, 1976.

101. "NAIA Football Tour of Europe," 5.

102. Associated Press, "NFL Beware; IFL Is Here," *Midland (TX) Reporter-Telegram*, July 1, 1976, 3B.

103. Montaignac, " Le grand coup d'essai du football américain."

104. Henri Garcia, "Football du Nouveau Monde/Football d'un autre monde," *L'Équipe*, June 21, 1976, 9.

105. Packard, "Demi-tough," 134–35.

106. Packard, "Demi-tough," 138.

7. Postwar Tours, 1977–1989

1. Associated Press, "New Idea: Vive Le Football," *Stars and Stripes* (Pacific), July 7, 1976.

2. Gerry Fraley, "Bob Kap, Innovator in Kicking Approach Who Helped Bring Soccer Style to NFL, Dies," *Dallas Morning News*, March 14, 2010, http://www.dallasnews.com/sports/dallas-cowboys/headlines/20100302-Bob-Kap-innovator-in-kicking-4584.ece, accessed April 6, 2013.

3. Bill Sutley, "Globetrotting 'Sporty' Glad to Be Home," *Arkadelphia (AR) Siftings Herald*, June 23, 1976, 4.

4. United Press International, "Pro Grid Coaches Still Convinced Europe Fertile," *Sarasota Herald-Tribune*, June 24, 1977, 3C.

5. Wayne Grett, "Newton Nite Hawks to Play in Europe," *Des Moines Register*, April 21, 1977, 3S.

6. Dave Cowan, "Football in June," *Stars and Stripes*, May 29, 1977, 22.

7. Grett, "Newton Nite Hawks," 3S.

8. "Newton Nite Hawks Are Europe Bound in May," https://www.facebook.com/pages/Newton-Nite-Hawks/367646818160, accessed May 17, 2013.

9. United Press International, "Pro Football Ready for European Debut," *Wilmington (NC) Morning Star*, May 27, 1977.

10. "Newton Nite Hawks Are Europe Bound in May."

11. Nails Florio, "Nailing 'Em Down," *Chicago News Journal*, May 5, 1977, 20.

12. Florio, "Nailing 'Em Down," 20.

13. Hal Bock (AP), "Newton Semi-Pro Club to Make European Tour," *Cedar Rapids (IA) Gazette*, April 21, 1977, 21A.

14. Grett, "Newton Nite Hawks," 3S.

15. "Football—Midwestern Style, *Nevada State Journal*, May 27, 1977, 19.

16. John Parshall, "North Munich Forty: Semi-pro Nobodies to Get Identity in Europe," *Oak Park (IL) Oak Leaves*, May 25, 1977, 66; Associated Press, "Football Teams to Tour Europe," *Yuma (AZ) Daily Sun*, April 22, 1977, 83.

17. Grett, "Newton Nite Hawks," 3S.

18. "Nite Hawks Begin European Odyssey Monday May 30," *Newton (IA) Daily News*, May 27, 1977, 1.

19. "The European Tour '77," https://www.facebook.com/pages/Newton-Nite-Hawks /367646818160, accessed May 17, 2013.

20. Parshall, "North Munich Forty," 66.

21. Associated Press, "Those Grid Stars Just Keep Hoping," *Jacksonville (IL) Courier*, May 5 1977, 17.

22. "Texas Football Comes to France," *Brazosport Facts*, June 17, 1976, 2A.

23. "Newton Nite Hawks Are Europe Bound in May."

24. "Europe Bound Hawks Planning Press Workout," *Newton (IA) Daily News*, May 20, 1977, 1.

25. Florio, "Nailing 'Em Down," 20.

26. "Europe Bound Hawks Planning Press Workout," 1.

27. Jose Nogueras, presentation to Baseball in American Culture class, spring 2013. Nogueras told students that in the seventies, press sheets were either non-existent or extremely brief.

28. Associated Press, "Nite Hawks Set for Trip to Europe," *Des Moines Register*, May 26, 1977, 3S.

29. Cowan, "Football in June," 22.

30. Associated Press, "NFL Stars Are Big Hit in Vietnam," *Des Moines Sunday Register*, January 30, 1966, 2S.

31. Bernard A. Gill, telephone interview by the author, Ada OH , November 10, 2011.

32. Cowan, "Football in June," 22.

33. Cowan, "Football in June," 22.

34. Tim Kane, "Global U.S. Troop Deployment, 1950–2003," Heritage Foundation, http://www.heritage.org/research/reports/2004/10/global-us-troop-deployment -1950–2003, accessed May 18, 2013.

35. United Press International, "Nite Hawks Win Opening Game at Versailles, 26–6," *Newton (IA) Daily News*, June 3, 1977, 1.

36. "103-Yard Run Lifts Newton to Grid Win in France," *Stars and Stripes*, June 4, 1977, 26.

37. Stan Allspach, Newton Nite Hawks," Facebook.

38. United Press International, "Nite Hawks Win Opening Game," 1.

39. Jim Foster, telephone interview by the author, Ada OH, September 15, 2012.

40. Cowan, "Football in June," 22.

41. "Smith Boots 3 FGs to Spark Newton to 15–13 Triumph in France," *Stars and Stripes*, June 9, 1977, 26.

42. Newton Nite Hawks and Chicago Lions rosters, https://www.facebook.com/pages /Newton-Nite-Hawks/367646818160, accessed May 18, 2013.

43. "Smith Boots 3 FGs," 26.

44. "Smith boots 3 FGs," 26; "Nite Hawks Defeat Lions in Games in France and Germany This Week," *Newton (IA) Daily News*, June 10, 1977, 1.

45. "Football américain, mardi 20h, au Stadium Nord de Villeneuve-d'Ascq," *La Voix du Nord*, June 5, 1977, 6.

46. J.C. "Football U.S.A. (de choc) ce soir, au Stadium Nord," *La Voix du Nord*, July 7, 1977, 10.

47. Jean Chantry, "20,000 spectateurs au Stadium Nord pour découvrir le football américain," *La Voix du Nord*, June 8, 1977, 6.

48. Boo Odem, "Iowa Gridders Win Landstuhl Game," *Stars and Stripes*, June 11, 1977, 26.

49. Ron Maly, "Nite Hawks a 'Hit' in Europe," *Des Moines Register*, June 16, 1977, 3S.

50. Odem, "Iowa Gridders Win Landstuhl Game."

51. Gill interview.

52. United Press International, "Pro Football's Venture Into Europe Turns Sour," *Galveston (TX) Daily News*, June 24, 1977, 4B.

53. United Press International, "Football a Bust in First European Tour," *Redlands (CA) Daily Facts*, June 23, 1977, B2.

54. Stan Allspach, interview by the author, Newton IA, January 9, 2013.

55. "A Historic First for the Game of Professional Football," https://www.facebook .com/pages/Newton-Nite-Hawks/367646818160, accessed May 20, 2013.

56. Allspach interview.

57. Allspach interview.

58. Bobby Braddock, "We're Not the Jet Set," perf. George Jones and Tammy Wynette, *We're Gonna Hold On*, Epic Records, 1973.

59. Stan Allspach, Facebook message in response to author's query, May 20, 2013.

60. United Press International, "Pro Football's European Venture Fails," *Ogden (UT) Standard Examiner*, June 26, 1977, 3B.

61. Maly, "Nite Hawks a 'Hit' in Europe," 3S.

62. Associated Press, "Contact the Best Part of Football to Europeans," *Waterloo (IA) Courier*, June 29, 1977, 25.

63. Ford and Foglio, "First NFL Europe," 7.

64. Fraley, "Bob Kap."

65. Tim Sullivan, "34 Years Ago, Kap Put the 'Fut' in Pro Football," *San Diego*

Union-Tribune, August 17, 2005, http://www.utsandiego.com/uniontrib/20050817 /news_1s17sullivan.html, accessed May 20, 2013.

66. Steve Tappa, "QC Stallions Ready to Gallop on Gridiron," *Quad-Cities Online*, May 6, 2009, http://m.qconline.com/sports/professional/qc-stallions-ready-to-gallop -on-gridiron/article_6f47dfa9-dd4a-53d3-a677–5ff21299535f.html?mode=jqm, accessed May 22, 2013.

67. "U.S. Grid Clubs Play Today in Ludwigshafen, *Stars and Stripes*, July 4, 1979, 26.

68. "U.S. Pro Gridders Meet Frankfurt Lions Saturday," *Stars and Stripes*, July 6, 1979, 26.

69. Lars Dzikus, "American Football in West Germany: Cultural Transforma-tion, Adaptation, and Resistance," in *Turnen and Sport: Transatlantic Transfers*, ed. Annette Hoffmann (New York: Waxmann, 2004), 225.

70. "History," ArenaFootball.com, http://www.arenafootball.com/history/key -dates.html, accessed May 22, 2013.

71. Larry Siddons, "Arena Football Plans to Test European Market," *Stars and Stripes*, October 26, 1989, 19.

72. "History," ArenaFootball.com.

73. Foster interview.

74. Siddons, "Arena Football," 19.

75. "Arena Football: Mercredi 15 Novembre, 1989," *US Foot*, December 1989, 8.

76. Jean-Marc Burtscher, interview by the author, Clichy-sous-Bois, May 14, 2012.

8. Lafayette, le football est voilà!

1. Luc Bouchard, "Dix ans, et toutes ses dents," *US Foot*, special ed., no. 2, June 1991, 13.

2. Bouchard, "Dix ans, et toutes ses dents," 12.

3. Jerome Laval, "Farewell to the 'Artist,'" *Amerfoot Mag*, no. 1, December 2011, http://www.amerfoot.com/magazine/1#/3, accessed January 3, 2014.

4. Jerome Laval, "Spartacus de Paris," *Amerfoot Mag*, no. 1, December 2011 http://www.amerfoot.com/magazine/1#/4, accessed January 3, 2014.

5. Stephane Sardano, Julien Lenau, and Eric Burtscher, interviews by the author, around Paris, June 2012–July 2013.

6. Directeur technique nationale adjoint of the FFFA Olivier Moret, interview by the author, Nanterre, France, June 7, 2012.

7. Bouchard, "Dix ans, et toutes ses dents," 13.

8. "Laurent Plegelatte," *Quarterback Magazine*, 1987, elitefoot.com/france/article /Plegelatte/Laurent.htm, accessed January 4, 2014.

9. Bouchard, "Dix ans, et toutes ses dents," 13.

10. "Laurent Plegelatte," *Quarterback Magazine*.

11. Plegelatte, *Le football américain*, 14–19.

12. Stephane Sardano, interview by the author, Bussy-Saint-Georges, France, June 5, 2012.

13. "Archives françaises: Saison 1981–1982," *Elitefoot*, Elitefoot.com/france/resultats /1982.htm, accessed January 3, 2014.

14. "Laurent Plegelatte," *Quarterback Magazine*.

15. "Histoire de la FFFA," *Fédération Française de Football Américain*, http://www .fffa.org/fr/fffa/presentation/histoire-de-la-fffa.html, accessed January 5, 2014.

16. Johann Boulé, *Le Parisien*, December 7, 2000, http://www.leparisien.fr /val-de-marne/les-meteores-prennent-leur-temps-07–12–2000–2001810379.php, accessed January 4, 2014.

17. "Archives françaises: Saison 1981–1982," *Elitefoot*.

18. FFFA directeur technique nationale Thierry Soler, interview by the author, Nanterre, France, June 7, 2012.

19. Sardano interview.

20. "Histoire de la FFFA."

21. Le Cadet, "Vous souvenez de la Coupe de France?" *Sideline*, http://www.sideline .fr/tag/coupe-de-france-de-football-americain/, accessed January 16, 2014.

22. Laval, "Farewell to the 'Artist,'" 3.

23. Bouchard, "Dix ans, et toutes ses dents," 14.

24. Bouchard, "Dix ans, et toutes ses dents," 14.

25. Doug Farrar, "NFL Admits That Chargers Got Away with an Uncalled Penalty on Chiefs' Missed Field Goal," *Sports Illustrated Audibles*, December 30, 2013, http:// nfl.si.com/2013/12/29/san-diego-chargers-uncalled-penalty-kansas-city-chiefs -missed-field-goal/, accessed January 5, 2014.

26. Bouchard, "Dix ans, et toutes ses dents," 14.

27. Laval, "Farewell to the 'Artist,'" 3.

28. Eric Burtscher, interview by the author, Clichy-sous-Bois, France, June 1, 2012.

29. "Anges Bleus," *US Foot*, April 1989, 20.

30. Eric Burtscher interview, June 1, 2012.

31. "Les Anges Bleus: Le fabuleuse histoire," *Amerfoot Mag*, February 2012, 6, http://www.amerfoot.com/magazine/3#/6, accessed January 7, 2014.

32. Jean-Marc Burtscher, interview by the author, Clichy-sous-Bois, France, January 8, 2014.

33. Eric Burtscher, interview by the author, Clichy-sous-Bois, France, June 20, 2012.

34. Julien Luneau, Skype interview by the author, Ada OH, August 8, 2013.

35. Greg di Belette, "Archives françaises: 1984–1986 : Les années terribles du foot français," *Elitefoot*, http://www.elitefoot.com/france/archives/angesbleus/angesbleus .htm, accessed January 8, 2014.

36. Sardano interview.

37. Jean-Marc Burtscher, interview by the author, Clichy-sous-Bois, France, June 3, 2012.

38. Yves Perelli, Facebook Chat interview by the author, through Jean-Marc Burtscher, , Ada OH, January 8, 2014.

39. Perelli interview.

40. Sardano interview.

41. Sardano interview.

42. Sardano interview.

43. Jean-Marc Burtscher interview, June 3, 2012.

44. Sardano interview.

45. Ron Selesky, telephone interview by the author, Ada OH, October 4, 2012.

46. Jean-Marc Burtscher interview, January 1, 2014.

47. Braxton Shaver, telephone interview by the author, Ada OH, September 25, 2012.

48. Rader, *Baseball*, 21.

49. Jean-Marc Burtscher interview, June 3, 2012.

50. Belette, "Archives françaises."

51. "Histoire de la FFFA."

52. Sardano interview.

53. "Anges Bleus," 20.

54. Rader, *Baseball*, 17.

55. Sardano interview.

56. "Anges Bleus," 20.

57. Associated Press, "Heart of America All-Stars Defeat French Club, 29–13," *Lawrence (KS) Journal-World*, July 30, 1985, 4B.

58. Belette, "Archives françaises."

59. Philippe Kries, "Ooooohhhhh les blues!!!!," Facebook post on *Anges Bleus* page, July 24, 2013, https://www.facebook.com/groups/27808761377/, accessed January 10, 2014.

60. "Jetlag No Problem for Quick-Starting Lutes," *Tacoma (WA) News Tribune*, July 19, 1985. Article provided by the archivist at Pacific Lutheran University via email, January 6, 2014.

61. Jack Sareault, "Home Smiling," *Tacoma (WA) News Tribune*, July 31, 1985. Article provided by the archivist at Pacific Lutheran University via email, January 6, 2014.

62. Belette, "Archives françaises."

63. Belette, "Archives françaises."

64. R. A. Smith, *Pay for Play*, 106.

65. Belette, "Archives françaises."

66. Interview with Jean-Marc Burtscher, confirmed by Sophie Crawford, Christian Mercadier, and others.

67. Observed at Casque de Diamante game June 22, 2013.

68. Discussion on RADIOSSA (French Internet radio program dedicated to football), June 17, 2013.

69. "Nicolas Robert: Once a Beaver, Always Will Be!," *Amerfoot Mag*, May 15, 2012, 7, http://www.amerfoot.com/magazine/4#/7, accessed January 16, 2014.

70. "Anges Bleus," 21.

71. "Archives françaises: Saison 1985–1986," *Elitefoot*, http://www.elitefoot.com /france/archives/resultats/1986.htm, accessed January 14, 2014.

72. "Anges Bleus," 21.

73. "Archives françaises: Saison 1986–1987," *Elitefoot*, http://www.elitefoot.com /france/archives/resultats/1987.htm, accessed January 14, 2014.

74. "Archives françaises: Saison 1987–1988," *Elitefoot*, http://www.elitefoot.com /france/archives/resultats/1988.htm, accessed January 14, 2014; "Archives françaises: Saison 1988–1989," *Elitefoot*, http://www.elitefoot.com/france/archives /resultats/1989.htm, accessed January 14, 2014.

75. "Archives françaises: Saison 1989–1990," *Elitefoot*, http://www.elitefoot.com /france/archives/resultats/1990.htm, accessed 14 January 2014; "Archives françaises: Saison 1991–1992," *Elitefoot*, http://www.elitefoot.com/france/archives /resultats/1992.htm, accessed January 14, 2014.

76. "Les Molosses d'Asnières, le club aux ascendances prestigieuses!," *Elitefoot*, http://bybelette.blogspot.fr/2013/03/les-molosses-dasnieres-le-club-aux.html, accessed January 14, 2014.

77. Franck Richaud, "Les Anges voient rouges," *US Foot*, May 1989, 63; F.M., "Le jeu à la française," *Elitefoot*, http://www.elitefoot.com/france/article/french_flair /france.htm, accessed January 16, 2014.

78. "Anges Bleus," 21.

79. "Anges Bleus," 21.

80. Le Cadet, "Vous souvenez de la Coupe de France?"

81. Personal experience attending the 2013 Casque de Diamante game June 22, 2013.

82. "Archives françaises: Saison 1985–1986."

83. "Archives françaises: Les finales, *Elitefoot*, http://www.elitefoot.com/france /archives/finales/finales.htm, accessed January 16, 2014.

84. "Once upon a Time: The Jets of Saint Cloud Paris (1983–1992)," *Amerfoot Mag*, September 10, 2012, 10.

85. "Liste des joueurs étrangers ayant joué dans le championnat Elite (1985–2005)," *Elitefoot*, http://www.elitefoot.com/france/article/etrangers/joueursetrangers.pdf, accessed January 20, 2014.

86. Bouchard, "Dix ans, et toutes ses dents," 15.

87. "Once upon a Time: The Jets," 10.

88. "Archives françaises: Finalistes de D1 disparus," *Elitefoot*, http://www.elitefoot .com/france/archives/disparus/club.htm, accessed January 20, 2014.

89. Bouchard, "Dix ans, et toutes ses dents," 15.

90. "Once upon a Time: The Beavers," *Amerfoot Mag*, March 2, 2013, 6.

91. "Nicolas Robert," 7.

92. "Archives françaises: Les Finals," *Elitefoot*, http://www.elitefoot.com/france /archives/finales/finales.htm, accessed January 20, 2014.

93. "Matt Stashin," *Amerfoot Mag*, March 2, 2013, 6.

94. "Culte: This Mickey Is Not a Mouse," *Amerfoot Mag*, February 23, 2012, 11, http://www.amerfoot.com/magazine/3#/1, accessed January 16, 2014.

95. "Matt Stashin," 6.

96. "La Force tranquille Tom Bass," *Amerfoot Mag*, May 15, 2012, 18, http:// www.amerfoot.com/magazine/pdf_20120824192608_04.pdf, accessed January 20, 2014.

97. "La Force tranquille Tom Bass," 18.

98. Luc Bouchard, "Casque d'Or," *US Foot*, June 1990, 29.

99. "Nicolas Robert," 13.

100. "Anges Bleus," 21.

101. "Castors EIP Paris—Give Me the C," *Bide&Musique*, http://www.bide-et-musique .com/song/14875.html, accessed January 21, 2014.

102. "Nicolas Robert," 14; Pacific Residential Mortgage website, http://www .pacresmortgage.com/team/matt-stashin/, accessed January 21, 2014.

103. "Eddie Diop," *Amerfoot Mag*, May 15, 2012, 16, http://www.amerfoot.com/ magazine/pdf_20120824192608_04.pdf, accessed January 21, 2014.

104. "Bienvenue à sciences po," *Sideline*, http://www.sideline.fr/tag/castors/, accessed January 21, 2014.

105. "Archives françaises: Les Finals."

106. "Flash La Courneuve: Équipes," *Flash Football*, http://www.flashfootball. org/, accessed January 21, 2014.

107. "Flash encadrement," *Flash Football*, http://www.flashfootball.org/pagesMENU /equipes/CADRES.htm, accessed January 21, 2014.

108. "Historique Flash," *Flash Football*, http://www.flashfootball.org/pagesMENU /presentation/historique.htm, accessed January 21, 2014.

109. Luneau interview; Weasel, "Flash de La Courneuve: La success story d'un club de banlieue," *Elitefoot*, October 2004, http://www.elitefoot.com/france/archives /flashstory/club.htm, accessed January 23, 2014.

110. Jean-Marc Burtscher interview, June 3, 2012.

111. Luneau interview.

112. Luneau interview.

113. Rémi Dupré, "Julien Luneau, du casque au terrain social," *Le Monde*, February 18, 2011, http://www.lemonde.fr/week-end/article/2011/02/18/julien -luneau-du-casque-au-terrain-social_1480829_1477893.html, accessed January 21, 2014.

114. Luneau interview.
115. "Historique Flash."
116. Luc Bouchard, "Un week-end a la Plage: Stade Géo André," *US Foot*, Summer 1990, 24.
117. Personal observation, June 23, 2012.
118. Thomas Deligny, "Flash de La Courneuve: Les individus au service du collectif," *4th&Goal*, November 2012, 20.
119. Dupré, "Julien Luneau, du casque au terrain social."
120. Deligny, "Flash de La Courneuve," 20.
121. Greg di Belette, "Flash de La Courneuve: Le Success Story d'un club de banlieu," Elitefoot, http://www.elitefoot.com/france/archives/flashstory/club.htm, accessed February 4, 2014.
122. David Wright, "Away Running: A Look at a Different Paris," *Callaloo*, Winter 2009, 47.
123. "Liste des joueurs étrangers."
124. "Flash encadrement."
125. "Historique Flash."
126. Marcello Rodi, "La storia dei Gladiatori," *End Zone*, March 12, 2008, http://www.endzone.it/2008/03/12/la_storia_dei_gladiatori_roma/, accessed January 23, 2014.
127. Belette, "Flash de La Courneuve."
128. Wright, "Away Running," 47.
129. Jean-Marc Burtscher interview, June 3, 2012.
130. Dupré, "Julien Luneau, du casque au terrain social."
131. *Zulu*, dir. Cy Endfield, Diamond Films, 1964.
132. Personal observation at the Junior Championship game on June 16, 2013.
133. Dupré, "Julien Luneau, du casque au terrain social."
134. Shaver interview; "Teaching Assistant Program in France," French Embassy in the United States, http://highereducation.frencheducation.org/teach-in-france/prospective-applicants/faq, accessed January 25, 2014.
135. Dupré, "Julien Luneau, du casque au terrain social."
136. "Archives françaises: Saison 1988–1989."
137. "Histoire de la FFFA."
138. "Les Finales."

9. *Football Américain Goes National*

1. "Histoire de la FFFA," *Fédération Française de Football Américain*, http://www.fffa.org/fr/fffa/presentation/histoire-de-la-fffa.html, accessed February 12, 2014.
2. "Football Américain: Inventaire de tous les clubs français," *Elitefoot*, http://www.elitefoot.com/france/article/clubs_disparus/fffa.htm, accessed February 13, 2014.

3. Responses to my question on Facebook: "How did you begin playing football?" January 2, 2014, conversation thread can be found at https://www.facebook.com/groups/179726752066770/; directeur technique nationale adjoint of the FFFA Olivier Moret, interview by the author, Nanterre, France, June 7, 2012; Rémi Dupré, "Julien Luneau, du casque au terrain social," *Le Monde*, February 18, 2011, http://www.lemonde.fr/week-end/article/2011/02/18/julien-luneau-du-casque-au-terrain-social_1480829_1477893.html, accessed January 21, 2014.

4. Unidentified young man holding a football on the Paris Métro, interview by the author, Paris, June 20, 2013. Note: I probably scared the player, since people generally do not converse with strangers on the Métro.

5. Jean-Marc Burtscher, interview by the author, Clichy-sous-Bois, France, June 3, 2012.

6. "Touchdown dans culture clubs," *télé.nantes*, January 23, 2012, http://www.telenantes.com/Toute-l-actu/Sports/Touchdown-dans-Culture-Clubs-0251, accessed February 16, 2014.

7. Luc Arzel, "Draks d'attaque," *US Foot*, May 1989, 49.

8. "Archives françaises: Saison 1987–1988," *Elitefoot*, http://www.elitefoot.com/trance/archives/results/1988.htm, accessed February 16, 2014.

9. "Présentation," *Dockers Football*, http://dockersfootball.com/club/presentation/, accessed February 16, 2014.

10. "Présentation."

11. Denis Bourdeau, "Les Dockers lorgnent la D2," *Presse Océan*, June 19, 2013, http://dockersfootball.com/medias/presse/, accessed February 16, 2014.

12. "Interview with James Springfield This Morning at Nantes Atlantique Airport!," *Dockers Football*, http://dockersfootball.com/arrivee-de-james-a-laeroport/#more-922, accessed February 18, 2014.

13. "Recrutent," *Dockers Football*, http://dockersfootball.com/chronique-de-match/, accessed February 18, 2014.

14. Greg di Belette, "Origins: Aix prend l'acenseur," *4th&Goal*, 4, http://www.footballamericain.com/4TH_%26_GOAL-n%C2%B00.pdf, accessed February 22, 2014.

15. Belette, "Archives françaises: La légende Argonaute," *Elitefoot*, 2006, http://www.elitefoot.com/france/archives/argos/genese.htm, accessed February 22, 2014.

16. Belette, "Origins," 3.

17. Belette, "Origins," 4.

18. Belette, "Archives françaises."

19. Belette, "Origins," 4.

20. Belette, "Origins," 4.

21. "Archives françaises: Saison 1986–1987," *Elitefoot*, http://www.elitefoot.com/france/archives/resultats/1987.htm, accessed March 2, 2014.

22. Cyril Pocréaux, "La nouvelle quête des Argonautes," *Le Point.fr*, http://www

.lepoint.fr/actualites-region/2007–10–04/la-nouvelle-quete-des-argonautes /1556/0/203960, accessed March 2, 2014.

23. Belette, "Origins," 4.

24. "Archives françaises: Palmarès national," *Elitefoot*, http://www.elitefoot.com /france/archives/palmares/palmares.htm, accessed March 2, 2014.

25. Belette, "Origins," 4.

26. "Archives françaises: 2005; La FFFA a 20 ans," *Elitefoot*, http://www.elitefoot .com/france/archives/fffa/20ans.htm, accessed March 3, 2014.

27. "Philippe 'El Condor' Gardent: Portrait of a Serial Tackler," *Amerfoot Mag*, May 15, 2012, 4 http://www.amerfoot.com/magazine/4#/4, accessed March 3, 2014.

28. "Archives françaises: Les finales," *Elitefoot*, http://www.elitefoot.com/france /archives/finales/finales.htm, accessed March 3, 2014.

29. "Poule des as," *US Foot*, March 1993, 6.

30. "Archives françaises: Argonaut legend," *Elitefoot*, http://www.elitefoot.com /france/archives/argos/celebrites.htm, accessed March 3, 2014.

31. "Archives françaises: Les finales."

32. Belette, "Origins."

33. Luc Bouchard, "Bons baisers de russie," *US Foot*, June 1990, 20.

34. David Green, "Forget Soccer, Football Will Go Worldwide," *Spartanburg (SC) Herald-Journal*, July 17, 1990, 15

35. Le Cadet, "Vous souvenez de la Coupe de France?" *Sideline*, http://www.sideline .fr/tag/coupe-de-france-de-football-americain/, accessed January 16, 2014.

36. "Équipe de France Senior: Championnat d'Europe 1983," *Elitefoot*, http://www .elitefoot.com/france/edf/senior/Euro1983.htm, accessed March 4, 2014.

37. Bouchard, "Bons baisers de russie," 20.

38. Charlie Halftime, "Vendre la peau de l'Ours," *US Foot*, April 1990, 30.

39. "Archives françaises: Saison 1989–1990," *Elitefoot*, http://www.elitefoot.com /france/archives/resultats/1990.htm, accessed March 4, 2014.

40. Luc Bouchard, "Les Ours débarquent chez les Ours . . . " *US Foot*, April 1990, 32.

41. Weasel, "Football in Russia," *Elitefoot*, http://www.elitefoot.com/france/europe /pays/russie.htm, accessed March 4, 2014.

42. Halftime, "Vendre la peau de l'Ours," 30.

43. Halftime, "Vendre la peau de l'Ours," 30.

44. "Archives françaises: 2005; La FFFA a 20 ans."

45. "Archives françaises: Les finales."

46. "Peine de prison confirmée pour le préfet Bonnet," *La Dépêche du Midi*, January 16, 2003, http://www.ladepeche.fr/article/2003/01/16/142942-peine-de -prison-confirmee-pour-le-prefet-bonnet.html, accessed March 3, 2014.

47. Armelle Thoraval, "Mnef: Le Manitou Spithakis sort de prison. Malgré sa detention, il ne s'est jamais départi de son assurance," *Liberation*, April 15, 2000, http://www.liberation.fr/societe/2000/04/15/mnef-le-manitou-spithakis-sort

-de-prison-malgre-sa-detention-il-ne-s-est-jamais-departi-de-son-assur_322489, Accessed March 3, 2014.

48. Belette, "Origins."

49. Carol Matlack, "Has French Tycoon Bernard Tapie's Luck Run Out?," *Bloomberg Businessweek*, July 11, 2013, http://www.businessweek.com/articles/2013–07–11 /has-french-tycoon-bernard-tapies-luck-run-out, accessed March 3, 2014.

50. "Archives françaises: Les finales."

51. Eric Lancelle, "La Ballard Bowl: Un peu d'histoire," *FootballAmericain*, http:// www.footballamericain.com/fffa/le-ballard-bowl-un-peu-d-histoire.html, accessed March 3, 2014.

52. Belette, "Archives françaises: La légende Argonaute."

53. Belette, "Origins," 5.

54. "Archives françaises: Saison 2011–2012, *Elitefoot*, http://www.elitefoot.com /france/archives/resultats/2012.htm, accessed March 4, 2014.

55. "Archives françaises: Saison 2012–2013, *Elitefoot*, http://www.elitefoot.com /france/archives/resultats/2013.htm, accessed March 4, 2014.

56. Belette, "Origins," 5.

57. Brice Lapeyre, "Les Argonautes: La nouvelle generation garde espoir," *4th&Goal*, June 2013, 10.

58. Moret interview.

59. "Archives françaises: Les finales."

60. "Liste des joueurs étrangers ayant joué dans le championnat Elite (1985–2005)," *Elitefoot*, http://www.elitefoot.com/france/article/etrangers/joueursetrangers.pdf, accessed March 4, 2014.

61. Charles Thelliez, "Spartiates un jour, Spartiates toujours," *Le Courrier Picard*, May 30, 2012, http://www.courrier-picard.fr/courrier/Sports/Sport-en-Picardie /Spartiates-un-jour-Spartiates-toujours, accessed March 5, 2014.

62. Personal observation of the Spartiates-Flash match in Amiens, France.

63. T.D., "Les nouveaux visages des Spartiates," *FootballAmericain*, http://www .footballamericain.com/fffa/les-nouveaux-visages-des-spartiates.html, accessed March 5, 2014.

64. Florian Thiery, "Jim Criner: Les équipes ont pris conscience des talents qu'elles possedent!," *4th&Goal*, April 2013, 9; T.D., "Les nouveaux visages des Spartiates."

65. "Interview de Jim Criner des Spartiates," *Sideline*, http://www.sideline.fr /interview-de-jim-criner-des-spartiates/, accessed March 5, 2014)

66. Arranbra Belderrain, "Football américain" énorme deception des Spartiates d'Amiens relégués en D2," *France3 Picardie*, http://picardie.france3.fr/2013/06/16 /football-americain-enorme-deception-des-spartiates-d-amiens-relegues -en-d2-271319.html, accessed March 5, 2014.

67. "Joueurs imports 2014," Facebook, *Les Spartiates Amiens Picardie*, https://www .facebook.com/Spartiates.Amiens, accessed March 5, 2014.

68. "D2 Championship," *Fédération Française de Football Américain*, http://www
.fffa.org/fr/football-americain/les-championnats/classement/2.html, accessed
March 5, 2014.

69. "History," *Black Panthers de Thonon-les-bains*, http://www.les-black-panthers
.org/historique.html, accessed March 5, 2014.

70. "Archives françaises: Saison 1984–1985, *Elitefoot*, http://www.elitefoot.com
/france/archives/resultats/1985.htm, accessed March 5, 2014.

71. "Légende bretonne," *Elitefoot*, http://bybelette.blogspot.fr/2013/02/legende
-bretonne.html, accessed March 5, 2014.

72. "Les Sabres de Chàteauroux," http://www.facebook.com/Lessabresdechateauroux
/?fref=ts, accessed on September 22, 2015.

73. "Football américain: Inventaire de tous les clubs français."

74. "Football américain: Inventaire de tous les clubs français."

75. "Historique," *Nancy Tigres football américain*, http://www.sluc-tigres-nancy
.com/index.php?option=com_content&view=article&id=15&Itemid=86, accessed
March 6, 2014.

76. Gilgenback and Valton, *Kent State University Athletics*, 88.

77. Allen Moff, "Tayla Sets Record in Kent State Track and Field Season Opener,
Record Courier, March 6, 2014, http://staging.recordpub.com/sports/2013/12/09
/tayala-sets-record-in-kent-state-track-and-field-season-opener, accessed March
6, 2014.

78. Florian Thiery, "Archives françaises: Jacques Accambray, ancient président,"
Elitefoot, http://www.elitefoot.com/france/archives/accambray/itw.htm, accessed
March 6, 2014.

79. Thiery, "Archives françaises: Jacques Accambray, ancient président."

80. "Histoire de la FFFA."

81. "Équipe de France Senior," *Elitefoot*, http://www.elitefoot.com/france/edf
/senior/matchsamicaux.htm, accessed March 6, 2014.

82. Luc Bouchard, "FFFA: Trop c'est trop!," *US Foot*, December 1989, 3.

83. Bouchard, "FFFA: Trop c'est trop!," 3.

84. Jean-Marc Burtscher, email to the author, February 3, 2014.

85. Bouchard, "FFFA: Trop c'est trop!," 4.

86. Bouchard, "FFFA: Trop c'est trop!," 3.

87. Bouchard, "FFFA: Trop c'est trop!," 4.

88. Bouchard, "FFFA: Trop c'est trop!," 5.

89. Bouchard, "FFFA: Trop c'est trop!," 5.

90. Thiery, "Archives françaises: Jacques Accambray, ancient président."

91. "Archives françaises: 2005; La FFFA a 20 ans."

92. Belette, "Archives françaises: Frederick Paquet, président de la FFFA," *Elitefoot*, February 2006, http://www.elitefoot.com/france/archives/fffa/paquet06.htm,
accessed March 7, 2014.

93. "Historique."

94. Belette, "Archives françaises: Frederick Paquet, président de la FFFA."

95. Thiery, "Archives françaises: Jacques Accambray, ancient président."

96. "Archives françaises: Hall of Fame," *Elitefoot*, http://www.elitefoot.com/france /archives/celebrites/halloffame.htm, accessed March 7, 2014.

97. "Kick Off: Un mot qui compte triple," *US Foot*, Summer 1990, 2.

98. "Kick Off," 2.

99. "Kick Off," 2.

100. "Kick Off," 3; Le Cadet, "Shopping version Le Cadet," *Sideline*, http://www .sideline.fr/shopping-version-le-cadet/, accessed March 8, 2014.

101. "Kick Off," 3.

102. Belette, "Témoinages: Philippe Laville et Luc Bouchard," *Elitefoot*, June 2007, http://www.elitefoot.com/france/article/journaux/magazines.htm, accessed March 8, 2014.

103. Belette, "Témoinages."

104. Pro-Bowler, post on NFL-NCAA *Forum*, http://nfl-ncaa.forumactif.com/t226-un-nouveau-magazine-sur-le-foot-us, accessed March 9, 2014.

105. Thomas Deligny, "Masochistes? Non passioneés," *4th&Goal*, September 2012, 4.

106. "Voila, c'est fait . . . " *Amerfoot Mag*, December 2011, http://www.amerfoot .com/magazine/1#/2, accessed March 9, 2014.

107. "Archives," *Amerfoot Mag*, http://www.amerfoot.com/archive.php, accessed March 9, 2014.

108. Lionel Laské, "Good Evening . . . on RADIOSSA," *4th&Goal*, November 2012, 31.

109. Personal observations from 2011 and 2012.

110. Belette, "Témoinages."

111. "Flash TV Live," http://www.dailymotion.com/Flash_de_La_Courneuve #videoId=xoact0, accessed March 9, 2014.

112. "Panthers TV," http://www.les-black-panthers.org/pc/panthers-tv.html, accessed March 9, 2014.

113. Personal experience watching the final in 2012.

114. "Sports U.S.," *Le Monde*, http://www.lemonde.fr/football-americain/, accessed March 9, 2014.

115. Antoine Mairé, "'Foot américain' prier n'est pas jouer, sauf pour Tim Tebow," *Le Monde*, December 13, 2011, http://www.lemonde.fr/sport/article/2011/12/13 /foot-americain-prier-n-est-pas-jouer-sauf-pour-tim-tebow_1618032_3242.html, accessed March 9, 2014.

116. "Aussi," *L'Équipe*, http://www.lequipe.fr/Aussi/, accessed March 9, 2014.

117. Personal experience June 22, 2013.

118. *L'Équipe*, http://www.lequipe.fr/Football-americain/Actualites/Les-black-panthers-enfin-titres/380621, accessed March 9, 2014.

10. *Leveling the Playing Field*

1. Charlie Halftime, "Femmes et foot," *US Foot*, March 1991, 22.

2. Halftime, "Femmes et foot," 23.

3. Halftime, "Femmes et foot," 23.

4. Halftime, "Femmes et foot," 22.

5. Halftime, "Femmes et foot," 23.

6. Halftime, "Femmes et foot," 23.

7. Halftime, "Femmes et foot," 24.

8. Halftime, "Femmes et foot," 24.

9. Halftime, "Femmes et foot," 24.

10. Halftime, "Femmes et foot," 24.

11. Eric Burtscher, interview by the author, Clichy-sous-Bois, France, June 20, 2012.

12. "Qui sont les Sparkles?," Sparkles-footus.com http://www.sparkles-footus.com/pages/qui-sont-les-sparkles.html, accessed April 3, 2014; "Destin de sportive: Lucie Bertaud," Diffusé sur *Chérie25*, http://www.youtube.com/watch?v=biyUDH_9xnM, accessed April 3, 2014.

13. "Sarah Riahi la pro des touchdown," Sportfilles.com, http://sportfilles.com/portraits-8/sarah-riahi-la-pro-des-touchdown/, accessed April 10, 2014.

14. "Gründung des AFVD," *American Football Verband Deutschland*, http://www.afvd.de/text.php?Inhalt=page&ID=132&menu=18, accessed April 3, 2014.

15. "Palmares" Fútbol Americano Femenino, http://fafemenino.blogspot.com/p/palmares.html, accessed April 3, 2014.

16. "History," *Black Widows*, http://www.blackwidows.at/, accessed April 3, 2014.

17. "Sweden," *International Federation of American Football*, http://ifaf.org/countries/federation/2/203, accessed April 3, 2014.

18. "Zoom sur l'équipe féminine de football américain des Sparkles de Villeneuve-Saint-Georges," *Fédération Française de Football Américain*, http://www.fffa.org/fr/football-americain/actualites/saison-2011–2012/zoom-sur-l-equipe-feminine-de-football-americain-des-sparkles-de-villeneuve-saint-georges.html, accessed April 10, 2014.

19. "Las chicas de España ante las Sparkles francesas," NFLhispano.com, http://www.nflhispano.com/2012/05/24/las-chicas-de-espana-ante-las-sparkles-francesas/, accessed April 10, 2014.

20. "Elles osent le foot us (épisode 2)," *Les Sparkles*, https://www.youtube.com/watch?v=AlOS6ikh4vo, accessed April 10, 2014.

21. "Les Sparkles de Villeneuve St Georges Américain Féminin," Facebook post, May 28, 2012, http://www.facebook.com/LesSparkles, accessed November 26, 2015.

22. "Vidéos," Sparkles-footus.com, http://www.sparkles-footus.com/videos/, accessed April 10, 2014.

23. "Les Sparkles sur *Bein Sport*," Sparkles-footus.com, http://www.sparkles-footus.com/videos/les-sparkles-sur-bein-sport.html, accessed April 10, 2014.

24. "Les Sparkles en route vers l'avenir . . . ," Sparkles-footus.com, http://www.sparkles-footus.com/pages/actualite/page-1.html, accessed April 10, 2014.

25. "Les premiers Etats Généraux du sport collectif féminin en équipe," bourges-sportfeminin.com, http://www.bourges-sportfeminin.com/, accessed April 12, 2014.

26. "Les premiers Etats Généraux."

27. Lucy Bertaud, "La LFL dans l'antre des Sparkles!," Sparkles-footus.com, http://www.sparkles-footus.com/pages/actualite/page-7.html, accessed April 10, 2014.

28. "Sarah Riahi la pro des touchdown."

29. Julien Streiff, interview by the author, Ada OH, January 15, 2014. Streiff was an exchange student taking a course with me at ONU during the spring semester of 2014, and is from Metz, France. When I asked him about football there, he told me that the sport wasn't played in his country. He was therefore surprised when I gave him a copy of a *4th&Goal* article on the Artillieurs (Gunners) of Metz.

30. "Sarah Riahi la pro des touchdown."

31. Lucie Bertaud, "Une Sparkles consultante LFL pour une chaîne du câble," Sparkles-footus.com, http://www.sparkles-footus.com/pages/actualite/page-4.html, accessed April 12, 2014.

32. Elsa Michanol, "Football féminin: La pratique prend son envol," *4th&Goal*, September 2012, 10.

33. "Elisa De Santis Bonneteau: Passionnenment flag," *4th&Goal*, November 2012, 29.

34. "Les Premiers Etats Généraux."

35. Thomas Depaepe, "Anne Sophie Papeil: La guerriére des Knights," *4th&Goal*, January 2013, 33.

36. Elsa Michanol, "Les premiers Yards: Féminines en Ile-de France," *4th&Goal*, April 2013, 30.

37. Elsa Michanol, "Les féminines posent les premieres pierres," *4th&Goal*, June 2013, 34.

38. Philippe Hadef, "Le reve olympique: Bernard Thomas, un reveur sachant rever," *US Foot*, April 1991, 7.

39. "'Le Sack' Always Took the Right Fork in the Road," Georgiadogs.com, August 30, 2011, http://www.georgiadogs.com/sports/m-footbl/spec-rel/083011aad.html, accessed April 19, 2014.

40. Hank Hersch, "Vive Le Sack," *Sports Illustrated*, October 1988, http://cnnsi.com/vault/article/magazine/MAG1067915/index.htm, accessed April 19, 2014.

41. Loran Smith, "Le Sack," Georgiadogs.com, August 7, 2012, http://www.georgiadogs
.com/sports/m-footbl/spec-rel/080712aaa.html, accessed April 19, 2014.

42. "'Le Sack' Always Took the Right Fork."

43. "Archives françaises: Hall of Fame," *Elitefoot*, http://www.elitefoot.com/france
/archives/celebrites/halloffame.htm, accessed April 19, 2014.

44. Richard Tardits, telephone interview by the author, Ada OH, May 30, 2012.

45. "'Le Sack' Always Took the Right Fork."

46. Tardits interview.

47. Tardits interview.

48. "Archives françaises: Hall of Fame."

49. "Richard Tardits : "Au football américain, il y a toujours un point d'interrogation,"
Intern@ute.com, http://www.linternaute.com/sport/dossier/football/football
-americain/superbowl/richard-tardits.shtml, accessed April 19, 2014.

50. "Archives françaises: Hall of Fame."

51. "Archives françaises: Hall of Fame."

52. Thomas Deligny, "Sébastien Sejean: Excité de découvrir la GFL!," Football
American.com, http://www.footballamericain.com/footballamericain-com/sebastien
-sejean-excite-de-decouvrir-la-gfl.html, accessed April 19, 2014.

53. "Itw de Gustave Guilloux, joueur de NCAA," *Sideline*, April 12, 2013, http://
www.sideline.fr/itw-de-gustave-guilloux-joueur-de-ncaa/, accessed April 19, 2014.

54. Thomas Deligny, "Baptiste Mullot: QB aux Horned Frogs," *4th&Goal*, September 2012, 8–9.

55. Colin Marklowitz, "French Student Is a Football Player, and No, He Isn't
Playing Soccer," *Dunn County (WI) News*, October 19, 2014, http://chippewa.com
/dunnconnect/sports/college/french-student-is-a-football-player-and-no-he-isn
/article_18dbe05a-bb96-5314-9309-e2c9514509a0.html, accessed December
16, 2014.

56. "Federations," *International Federation of American Football*, http://ifaf.org
/countries/federation_list, accessed April 19, 2014.

57. Pierre-Jean Vazel, "Football américain, un siècle de dégâts?," *Le Monde*, August
30, 2013, http://vazel.blog.lemonde.fr/2013/08/30/football-americain-un-siecle
-de-degats/, accessed April 19, 2014.

58. Greg di Belette, "Temoinages (Philippe Laville et Luc Bouchard)," Elitefoot,
June 2007, http://www.elitefoot.com/france/article/journaux/magazines.htm,
accessed November 27, 2015.

59. Belette, "Temoinages."

Afterword

1. "Archives françaises: Les Finals," *Elitefoot*, http://www.elitefoot.com/france
/archives/finales/finales.htm, accessed April 20, 2014) (I had heard four thousand reported).

2. Karim Elkoli, interview by the author, Paris, June 22, 2013.

3. Thomas Depaepe, "Anthony Mahoungou: La soif de victoire est dans notre ADN," FootballAmericain.com, http://www.footballamericain.com/fffa/la-courneuve -flash/anthony-mahoungou-la-soif-de-victoire-est-dans-notre-adn.html, accessed April 1, 2014.

4. Steve Batterson, "Frasco Rushes for Three Scores, Augie Beats French National Team," *Quad-City Times*, July 27, 2013, http://qctimes.com/sports/college/augustana /frasco-rushes-for-three-scores-augie-beats-french-national-team/article _569b171e-c104–5152-bbbb-c43f6038ff74.html, accessed April 20, 2014.

5. Pierre-Gérard Lespinasse, "Football américain: Un court revers encourageant pour les Français en vue de l'Euro 2014," *La Voix du Nord*, July 30, 2013, http://www .lavoixdunord.fr/region/football-americain-un-court-revers-encourageant-pour -les-ia19b0n1445930, accessed April 20, 2014.

6. "Vikings Beat France 20–13 behind Three Touchdowns by Sam Frasco," Athletic. Augustana.edu, July 28, 2013, http://www.athletics.augustana.edu/news/2013/7/28 /FB_0728134455.aspx?path=football, accessed April 20, 2014.

7. Lespinasse, "Football américain."

8. Richard Tardits, telephone interview by the author, Ada OH, May 30, 2012.

9. Lespinasse, "Football américain."

10. "Histoire de la FFFA," *Fédération Française de Football Américain*, http://www .fffa.org/fr/fffa/presentation/histoire-de-la-fffa.html, accessed December 20, 2014.

11. "Calendrier challenge football américain féminin saison 2014/2015," *Les Sparkles de Villaneuve St Georges—Football américain féminin*, https://www.facebook .com/LesSparkles/photos/a.870940149600423.1073741838.207492969278481 /975002045860899/?type=1&theater, accessed December 10, 2014.

12. John McKeon, "French American Football Federation (FFFA) Replaces President, American Football International Review, http://www.americanfootballinternational .com/french-american-football-federation-fffa-replaces-president/, accessed January 11, 2015.

13. Quentin Dagbert, "Interview: Olivier Rival Talks about Troubles in Football in France," TouchdownEurope.net http://www.touchdown-europe.net/2013/05 /interview-oliver-rival-talks-about.html, accessed January 13, 2015.

14. Roger Kelly, "2015 IFAF World Championships Cancelled in Sweden," *American Football International Review*, http://www.americanfootballinternational .com/2015-ifaf-world-championships-cancelled-in-sweden/, accessed January 11, 2014.

15. Author's personal observation while attending the four games that France played.

16. Eric Burtscher, interview by the author, Clichy-sous-Bois, France, June 20, 2012.

17. Axel Duez, interview by the author, La Courneuve, June 15, 2013.

18. Anne Linsky, "Half of Americans Don't Want Their Sons Playing Football," *Bloomberg Politics*, http://www.bloomberg.com/politics/articles/2014–12–10/bloomberg -politics-poll-half-of-americans-dont-want-their-sons-playing-football, accessed December 20, 2014.

19. Christian Red, "Drew Brees' Harsh Criticism of Roger Goodell Shows That NFL Boss Is One of Pro Sport's Most Hated Commissioners," *New York Daily News*, December 13, 2012, http://www.nydailynews.com/sports/football/anti-goodell -sentiment-surges-bountygate-article-1.1219786, accessed April 20, 2014.

20. J. M. Burtscher, "Les cadets du Red Star," *Ipernity*, http://www.ipernity.com /doc/335501/album/740752, accessed December 20, 2014.

21. George Packard, "Demi-tough," *Texas Monthly*, December 1976, 138.

BIBLIOGRAPHY

Ambrose, Stephen E. *Band of Brothers: E Company 506th Regiment, 101st Airborne from Normandy to Hitler's Eagles Nest*. New York: Simon & Schuster, 2001.

Apkarian, Greg. "Memories of Dreux," Dreux American High School, Dreux, France. http://www.dreuxalumni.org/Memories%20of%20Dreux.htm.

Auclair, Philippe. *Cantona: The Rebel Who Would Be King*. London: Macmillan, 2009.

Baker, George Golman, Jr. *When Lightning Struck the Outhouse: A Tribute to a Great Coach Ralph "Sporty" Carpenter*. Fayetteville AR: Phoenix International, 2011.

Briley, Ron, ed. *The Politics of Baseball: Essays on the Pastime and Power at Home and Abroad*. Jefferson NC: McFarland, 2010.

Cart, Doran L. "Kansas Football 'Over There,'" *Kansas History: A Journal of the Central Plains* (Autumn 2006): 194–99.

Crawford, Russ. *The Use of Sport to Promote the American Way of Life during the Cold War: Cultural Propaganda, 1946–1963*. Lewisville NY: Edwin Mellen Press, 2008.

Chastain, Capt. Ben-Hur. *Story of the 36th: The Experience of the 36th Division in the World War*. Oklahoma City: Harlow, 1920.

Chetwynd, Josh. *Baseball in Europe: A Country by Country History*. Jefferson NC: McFarland, 2008.

Clubine, Douglas L. "'Better Than They Were Before': Athletics and American Military Preparedness during the Great War." Master's thesis, Michigan State University, 1994.

Coubertin, Pierre de. *Universités transatlantiques*. Paris: Librarie Hachette, 1890.

Dine, Philip. *French Rugby Football: A Cultural History*. Oxford: Berg, 2001.

Eichberg, Henning, John Nauright, and Charles Parrish, eds. *Sports around the World: History, Culture, Practice*. Santa Barbara CA: ABC-CLIO, 2012.

English, George H. *History of the 89th Division*. Kansas City MO: War Society of the 89th Division, 1920.

FM 28–105: *The Special Service Company*. Washington DC: War Department, January 5, 1944.

Foglio, Massimo, and Mark L. Ford. "The First NFL Europe," *Coffin Corner* 27, no. 6 (2005): 3–9.

Gems, Gerald. *The Athletic Crusade: Sport and American Cultural Imperialism.* Lincoln: University of Nebraska Press, 2006.

Gilgenback, Cara, and Theresa Valton, eds. *Kent State University Athletics: Images of Sports.* Charleston SC: Arcadia Press, 2008.

Guttmann, Allen. *Games and Empires: Modern Sports and Cultural Imperialism.* New York: Columbia University Press, 1994.

Hofmann, Annette R., ed. *Turnen and Sport: Transatlantic Transfers.* Münster: Waxmann, 2004.

Holt, Richard. *Sport and Society in Modern France.* London: Macmillan Press, 1981.

Ingrassia, Brian M. *The Rise of Gridiron University: Higher Education's Uneasy Alliance with Big-Time Football.* Lawrence: University Press of Kansas, 2012.

International Committee of the Young Men's Christian Association. *Service with Fighting Men: An Account of the Work of the American Young Men's Christian Associations in the World War.* New York: Association Press, 1922.

Jones, Wilbur D. *Football! Navy! War! How Lend-Lease Players Saved the College Game and Helped Win World War II.* Jefferson NC: McFarland, 2009.

Joosten, Christian, and Denis Crawford. "When Football Made a 'Tour de France.'" *Coffin Corner: The Official Magazine of the Professional Football Researchers Association,* May/June, 2011, 15–17.

Keith, Harold. *Forty-Seven Straight: The Wilkinson Era at Oklahoma.* Norman: University of Oklahoma Press, 1984.

Knights of Columbus Committee on War Activities. *Knights of Columbus War Work.* New Haven: John J. Corbett Press, 1998. http://www.kofcmuseum.org/km/en /resources/www1.pdf, accessed December 18, 2012.

Lamster, Mark. *Spalding's World Tour: The Epic Adventure That Took Baseball around the Globe—and Made It America's Game.* Cambridge MA: Public Affairs, 2006.

Lewis, Guy. "World War I and the Emergence of Sports for the Masses." *Maryland Historian* (Fall 1973): 109–22.

MacCambridge, Michael. *America's Game: The Epic Story of How Football Captured a Nation.* New York: Anchor Press, 2005.

McAuliffe, Lt. Col. Jerome. *U.S. Air Force in France, 1950–1967.* San Diego: Milspec Press, 2005.

Mennell, James "The Service Football Program of World War I: Its Impact on the Popularity of the Game." *Journal of Sport History* (Winter 1989): 248–60.

Morris J., Jr. *Integration of the Armed Forces, 1940–1965.* Washington DC: Center of Military History United States Army, 1985.

Naismith, James. *Basketball: Its Origins and Development.* Lincoln: University of Nebraska Press, 1996.

Nauright, John, and Charles Parrish. *Sports around the World: History, Culture, Practice.* Santa Barbara CA: ABC-CLIO, 2012.

Norcross, Peter, and Harold Ray. "From Lion Tamer to Bulls and Bears: The Story of George (Potsy) Clark." *NASSH Proceedings,* 1980.

Oriard, Michael. *King Football: Sport and Spectacle in the Golden Age of Radio and Newsreels, Movies and Magazines, the Weekly and Daily Press.* Chapel Hill: University of North Carolina Press, 2003.

Plegelatte, Laurent. *Le football américain.* Paris: Editions Denoël, 1988.

Pope, Steven W. "An Army of Athletes: Playing Battlefields, and the American Military Sporting Experience, 1890–1920." *Journal of Military History* (July 1995): 435–56.

———. *Patriotic Games: Sporting Traditions in the American Imagination, 1876–1926.* Oxford: Oxford University Press, 1997.

Rader, Benjamin. *American Sports: From the Age of Folk Games to the Age of Televised Sports.* Upper Saddle River NJ: Pearson Education, 1990.

———. *Baseball: A History of America's Game.* Urbana: University of Illinois Press, 1992.

Rose, Peter I. *The Dispossessed: An Anatomy of Exile.* North Hampton NH: Louise W. and Edmund J. Kahn Institute, 2005.

Sladen, Fred W., Herman J. Koehler, and Philip Matthews. *Manual of Physical Training for Use in the United States Army.* Washington DC: Government Printing Office, 1914.

Schmidt, Ray. "Changing Tides: College Football, 1919–1930." *College Football Historical Society Newsletter,* August 2000, 13–16.

Smith, Ronald A. *Pay for Play: A History of Big-Time College Athletic Reform.* Urbana: University of Illinois Press, 2011.

———. *Sports and Freedom: The Rise of Big-Time College Athletics.* Oxford: Oxford University Press, 1988.

Smith, Thomas G. *Showdown: JFK and the Integration of the Washington Redskins.* Boston: Beacon Press, 2012.

Velasquez, Joseph Paul. "America and the Garrisons Stadium: How the U.S. Armed Forces Shaped College Football." *Armed Forces and Society,* June 7, 2012, 353–58.

Wakefield, Wanda Ellen. *Playing to Win: Sports and the American Military, 1898–1945.* Albany: State University of New York Press, 1997.

War Department Commission of Training Camp Activities. Washington DC: Government Printing Office, 1917. https://archive.org/details/wardepartmentcom 00unitrich, accessed December 18, 2012.

Watterson, John Sayle. *College Football: History, Spectacle, Controversy,* Baltimore: Johns Hopkins University Press, 2000.

Wythe, George. *The Inter-Allied Games: Paris 22nd June to 6th July.* Paris: Games Committee, 1919.

Young Men's Christian Association War Work Council. *Summary of the World War Work of the American Y.M.C.A.* Springfield MA: International Committee of the Young Men's Christian Association, 1920.

Zeilier, Thomas. *Ambassadors in Pinstripes: The Spalding World Tour and the Birth of American Empire.* Lanham MD: Rowman & Littlefield, 2006.

INDEX